A CONCISE GUIDE TO

Successful Employment Practices

J.D. Thorne

Third Edition

CCH INCORPORATED
Chicago

This publication is designed to provide accurate and authoritative information in regard to the subject matter covered. It is sold with the understanding that the publisher is not engaged in rendering legal, accounting, tax or other professional service and that the author is not offering such advice in this publication. If legal advice or other expert assistance is required, the services of a competent professional person should be sought.

Editorial Staff

Senior Acquisitions Editor: Donald J. Hull

Developmental Editor: Sharon Sofinski

Cover Design: Erika E. Lenz

Interior Design and Production: Erika E. Lenz

Production Specialist: Kathryn M. Astrom

ISBN 0-8080-0508-1
© 2000, **CCH** INCORPORATED
4025 W. Peterson Ave., Chicago, IL 60646-6085
All Rights Reserved
Printed in the United States of America

TABLE OF CONTENTS

CHAPTER THREE

Compensating Correctly
Wage and Hour Law Compliance

CHAPTER FOUR

Hiring Legally and Right

CHAPTER FIVE

Proper Supervisory Methods

CHAPTER SIX

Keeping Union-Free Status

CHAPTER SEVEN

Terminating Employees

CHAPTER EIGHT

Winning Denials of Unemployment Compensation Benefit Claims

CHAPTER NINE

Handling Equal Employment Opportunity Law Challenges

CHAPTER TEN

Miscellaneous Employment Law Issues

About the Author

Attorney J.D. Thorne practices law at the Milwaukee, Wisconsin-based Employment Law Managers law firm. Since 1977 his law practice has focused on representing business management interests in issues involving labor relations, human resources, and employment law matters. He earned his undergraduate degree at the University of Wisconsin-Madison and his Juris Doctorate at DePaul University of Chicago. He is admitted to practice in the state courts in Illinois and Wisconsin, the Eastern and Western Federal District Courts of Wisconsin, and the Seventh Federal Circuit Court of Appeals in Chicago. A member of the state bars of Wisconsin and Illinois, he has served on the Board of Directors of the Labor and Employment Law Section of the State Bar of Wisconsin, the Wisconsin Chapter of the Industrial Relations Research Association, and CCH National Panel of Labor Law Experts.

Attorney Thorne's experience includes representing employers in National Labor Relations Board union representation elections and unfair labor practice litigation, union collective bargaining negotiations, and labor contract grievance arbitration. His experience in employment law matters includes representing business clients before state and federal administrative agencies in workers' compensation, equal rights, unemployment compensation, OSHA, and wage and hour law matters.

As a speaker for numerous university and industry trade association programs, his appearances include presentations on labor relations and employment law matters to attorneys, business owners, managers, and human resources and industrial relations professionals at seminar programs across the country. Such programs have included talks at the prestigious Stetson University Labor and Employment Law Conference in St. Petersburg, Florida; the Upper Midwest Employment Law Institute in Minneapolis, Minnesota; the annual conventions of the Association of Law Firm Administrators in Chicago and Jewelers of America in New York; the Annual Labor Relations Conference of the American Foundrymen's Society at Marco Island, Florida; the Management Institute of the North American Die Casting Association in Las Vegas, Nevada; the Annual Employment Law Conferences for the San Diego and the Guam Employer's Associations; the Annual Legal Seminar of the National Catholic Religious Legal Office in Danvers, Massachusetts; the Kansas City Office of the Grant Thornton Accounting Firm's "Breakfast Briefing;" and the University of Wisconsin-Milwaukee Management Institute.

Attorney Thorne is the author and narrator of an audiocassette program produced by Federal Publications, Inc., of Washington, D.C., entitled *Successful Employment Practices*. His syndicated column, "Preventive Labor Relations," appears in various industry trade publications with international circulation. Articles written by Attorney Thorne have appeared in the official publication of the United States Chamber of Commerce, *Nation's Business*; the nationally distributed Chicago weekly magazine, *Business Insurance*; and the New York–based monthly magazine, *Small Business Reports*, published by the American Management Association. The two-day seminar program developed for the National Center for Continuing Education of Tallahassee, Florida, entitled "1999 Employment Law Update," was presented by Attorney Thorne in 14 cities across the nation.

The first edition of A *Concise Guide to Successful Employment Practices* was included in the national Society for Human Resources Management of Alexandria, Virginia "Catalogue of Recommended Publications," and was recognized as a "book tip" by the magazine *Nation's Business*. The second edition was endorsed to all of the nationwide employer association groups of the National Industrial Council by the Washington, D.C.–based National Association of Manufacturers (NAM). Book reviews of the second edition appeared in *Lawyer's Weekly* of Boston and *Wisconsin Lawyer Magazine* of the State Bar of Wisconsin.

Preface

The purpose of this book is to help the reader avoid problems in managing employees on a day-to-day basis. My experience suggests that the best results are achieved in squarely facing employee relations, human resources, and employment law challenges when action taken now may prevent litigation later. My viewpoint is that of the employer.

These chapters explain the employment law issues confronting management and discuss what to do, and why and how to do it. I wrote *A Concise Guide to Successful Employment Practices* as the one book I want to reference on my office bookshelf when presented with an employment challenge.

These goals have remained unchanged for the Third Edition. The aim has been to keep the book user-friendly. This edition has been revised to make the text useful in the educational setting as well as the employment setting. To accomplish this, the text remains organized in a straightforward manner and written in a style meant to be easily understood. However, the text has been enhanced by the addition of questions and answers for each chapter to be used as a reference for understanding the principles discussed. Moreover, expanded checklists, updated sample policies, and new anecdotal examples have been added throughout to keep the book current with the ever-changing practical and legal labor relations and employment law environment.

New material addressing current case law changes has been added to several chapters to provide a broader base of authority, such as analysis of recent U.S. Supreme Court cases involving sexual harassment. The development of case law regarding the Americans with Disabilities Act in Equal Employment Opportunity Law compliance is also featured. New developments since the publication of the second edition are covered throughout, such as updated theories on "covenant-not-to-compete" and employment contract issues, tests for independent contractors, and the legal interpretations regarding liability for "leased" employees. Incorporated in this third edition are enhancements of issues previously covered, but which have emerged as major challenges since the publication of the first edition in 1990 and the second edition in 1996. These include information on conducting an investigation of a sexual harassment complaint, reasonable accommodation for Americans with disabilities, and interviewing in the hiring process to avoid improper inquiries about disabilities in violation of the Americans with Disabilities Act. Also included is information on newer tort-related litigation involving theories of "negligent hiring" and "negligent supervision."

The book provides instruction on legal issues as well as information on useful policies and procedures that have been tried and proven successful. This *Concise Guide* helps the reader recognize potential issues before they arise, when they can be most easily resolved by applying the operative principles discussed.

The scope of this book includes the employment process from hiring to firing, and from policy-making in the employee handbook to proper compliance with certain state and federal regulations. Chapters on supervisory techniques and policies to maintain union-free status are added to give a better total picture of the proper proactive personnel practices that add to the bottom line.

The *Concise Guide* features easy-to-read explanations of various employment laws, narrative replete with how-to checklists, and actual case histories culled from solving these riddles for clients. While dealing with employers, it has been my experience that no two businesses are alike in their operation and no two employees are alike in their behavior. However, there are systematic approaches that can lead to success in dealing with the often-confusing nature of labor relations and employment law.

Please keep in mind that case law is always evolving, which often requires the examination of current situations by competent legal advisors. Nevertheless, what follows is a concise guide to preventive personnel principles in labor relations and employment law management. These principles support the day-to-day decision-making necessary to effectively deal with the ever-present challenges of today's regulatory employment law environment. The material was born out of my own practice of law representing businesses and other organizations.

When faced with what seems to be a situation calling for the strength of Hercules, combined with the wisdom of Solomon, to untie a Gordian knot of epic dimensions, please reach for this book of strategies.

At age 80, just after the publication of his great *Autobiography*, Ben Franklin was reported to have quipped, "At least I will never have to think about writing a Second Edition." However, for me, the opportunity to do so has been very rewarding, and I look forward with confidence to the impact this third edition will have in helping companies and businesses successfully compete in the global marketplace while staying in compliance with our nation's labor and employment laws.

September 2000   J.D. Thorne

Acknowledgments

I have greatly benefited from the opportunity to speak at various employment law related seminars and programs. These have greatly added to my experience, some of which has been incorporated in this third edition. For this I would like to thank several people in particular. These individuals include Mr. Robert Engelardt, Vice President for Human Resource Programs of the American Foundrymen's Society, Inc.; Mr. Bill Gibson, Executive Director of the Guam Employers Council; Mr. Joseph Sczempka, Jr., of the San Diego Employers Association, Inc.; Mr. John C. Metcalf, Director of Human Resources Policy of Wisconsin Manufacturers and Commerce; Mr. George Halaska, President of Executive Agenda, Milwaukee, Wisconsin, and roundtable leader for The Executive Committee; Mr. Allen Hron of Jewelers of America; Mr. Ron Bula of the University of Wisconsin-Milwaukee Management Institute; Margaret McHale, Esq., of the national Catholic Religious Office of Baltimore, Maryland; and Mr. Joe Weil of the National Center for Continuing Education.

I would also like to thank Mr. Robert Garber of Federal Publications, Inc., of Washington, D.C., for the opportunity to prepare and narrate the six-tape audiocassette program, *Successful Employment Practices*, which was distributed by his organization nationwide. Also, my thanks are extended to Mr. James Buchanan of Madison, Wisconsin for his wonderful editing of the five-hour video series, "Successful Employment Practices, the Video," taken from a presentation to the Assistant Club Managers Association–Badger Chapter.

I would like to extend my appreciation to Dr. Michael Mercer of Mercer Systems, Inc., Barrington, Illinois, for co-authoring with me a paper entitled "Legal Rules and Bottom Line Reasons for Psychological Testing" and to Charmaine Clowney, J.D., of the University of Wisconsin-Milwaukee Office of Diversity Compliance for her assistance and expertise in developing material related to dealing with diversity in the workplace. I would also like to thank Sue Jeffers, proprietor of Stub and Herbs in Minneapolis, Minnesota, for allowing me to use her quote on the importance of hiring right and Susan Fronk, President of the Management Resources Association of Milwaukee, Wisconsin and Palatine, Illinois, for her insight into the challenges for employers in the next decade. For research assistance, I thank M. Scott Cruz, a University of Illinois law student.

Many thanks are due as well to Don Hull, CCH Senior Acquisitions Editor, for his vision and gentle guidance of the third edition project; to Sharon

Sofinski, CCH Developmental Editor, for her detailed, excellent editorial work in perfecting the third edition manuscript; and my continuing gratitude to CCH Managing Editor Larry Norris for his great work on the first and second editions.

Last and most important of all is the unending support of my wife Cindy, and my three inspiring children: Andrew, Erik, and Julia.

CHAPTER ONE

Establishing the Proper Employment Relationship

The At-Will Employment Relationship

Using Individual Employment Contracts

Independent Contractor Agreements

Test Your Knowledge

of Employment Relationship Issues

1. What is the normal legal relationship called between an employer and an employee where there is no written contract with a fixed term of employment?

2. Under what circumstances can an employee with no written contract for a fixed term of employment generally be discharged from employment?

3. What exceptions to the normal relationship are generally recognized by law to the employment relationship when there is no contract for fixed term of employment?

4. Name three things an employer can do to preserve the normal employment relationship.

5. What is a leased employee, and how does the employment relationship change from the normal relationship in such an arrangement?

6. Name three factors that should be present for an independent contractor employment relationship to exist between an employer and an individual performing work for it.

7. When an employer seeks to prohibit an employee from competing with it after the employee separates from employment with it, what kind of restrictions can it reasonably place on its employee?

8. Under what circumstances can an employer require its employees to first arbitrate or mediate statutory objections to any aspect of the employment relationship before or instead of pursuing statutory remedies?

9. What can an employer do to protect against disclosure of confidential material learned by an employee in the course of employment?

10. Is there any possible remedy for an employer to pursue when it is obvious that a former employee can use proprietary information and knowledge for a new employer in competition with it?

The answers to these questions are at the end of this chapter.

Are successful employment practices really important to an employer?

One easy answer to that question can be found in the numerous awards and settlement amounts that are reported in contested legal cases and for violations of labor relations and employment law in cases nationwide. For example, in settling race discrimination claims with a group of employees, Texaco, Inc. paid $176.1 million in 1996. To settle sexual harassment charges that had been estimated potentially as high as over $150 million for as many 500 complainants, the tidy sum of approximately $40 million was paid by the Mitsubishi Corporation. In a recent fiscal year it was reported that the U.S. Department of Labor (DOL) investigated over 36,000 employers for violation of the Fair Labor Standards Act and ordered them to pay more than $92 million in back wages to 190,000 employees. There is no question that employment practices claims can amount to *real money*. Just one such claim might scuttle a small enterprise right out of business. This is perhaps why insurance is now being successfully sold as a component to help manage these risks.

Some employment practices situations are just as mind-boggling, even though the dollar amounts involved are not as great. For example, an employer was required to defend an action alleging retaliation where the charging employee's own psychiatrist testified that she suffered from an adjustment disorder that caused her to overreact to perceived slights and attribute malicious motivations to others without justification.[1] In the August 28, 1996, *Milwaukee Journal Sentinel* it was reported that although reinstated by an arbitrator, a county sheriff would not take back a deputy fired two years earlier amid allegations he had sex with a woman in squad car. The arbitrator had ruled that either the allegations were untrue or the behavior did not affect the deputy's job performance. "He doesn't deny it. He just denies it while he's working," the sheriff said. The deputy's attorney pointed out that none of the women had filed a complaint!

What should employers do in such a legal environment?

The starting point is setting up the proper employment relationship, and confirming that relationship either through statements on the employment application and in the employee handbook or through the device of an employment contract. Accordingly, these are the primary topics of Chapter One. Later in the chapter, other kinds of relationships will be discussed, including those of "leased" employees and independent contractors.

The At-Will Employment Relationship

Establishing the proper employment relationship must be a top priority with every employer. The employment relationship fundamentally affects each phase of the organization and its operation. Of paramount importance are the legal considerations and risks that must be managed to insure the organization's well-being. This chapter provides insights on establishing the proper employment relationship, a relationship that will not only be efficient, but will help reduce liability risks faced in today's regulated workplace.

The employment relationship has been subject to increasing regulation in the United States on the municipal, state, and federal levels. A variety of laws regulate the relationship and help protect the interests of individual employees and groups. The National Labor Relations Act, Title VII of the Civil Rights Act of 1964, the Age Discrimination in Employment Act of 1967, the Fair Labor Standards Act, the Family and Medical Leave Act, and the Americans with Disabilities Act of 1990 are some of the more prominent laws that impact employers.

In addition to these laws, both state and federal legislatures and many state courts have added to these protections by allowing claims for relief based upon the concept of wrongful discharge. Cases involving this claim are among the most expensive legal liabilities facing employers. Wrongful discharge suits are applied against union and non-union employers alike. Moreover, state law negligence claims of negligent hiring, negligent supervision, and negligent retention are being allowed to proceed.

In the absence of contrary language in an employment agreement or a union contract, the general rule has been that the employment relationship is terminable at-will. In other words, an employer has the right to discharge an employee at any time for good cause, bad cause, or no cause at all, as long as the cause cannot be proven to violate any of the above-mentioned statutes. However, despite the fact that an employee may have agreed to work for a specific wage without any contractual guarantees or other form of job security, the courts and the legislatures frequently come to the aid of the employee.

In the legislative arena, employee protection is exemplified by state statutes that limit an employer's actions in the at-will employment relationship. For example, in many states, statutory law protects employees from discharge resulting from whistle-blowing or reporting illegal activity of an employer. In the courts, the at-will relationship has been modified judicially through the use of both contract and tort law analysis. Most state courts will allow an action of "wrongful discharge" for an employee's discharge from employment that would violate "public policy." Other courts have held that there may be an implied contact in some employment situations. This contract would then carry with it an implied requirement of "good faith and fair dealing." Such a covenant has been held to be breached in situations involving, for example, the discharge of a long-term employee on the eve of earning substantial benefits as a result of past services, such as a pension or profit-sharing agreement.

One of the most disconcerting developments from the standpoint of management is the use of employee handbooks or employee manuals, or oral representations made to employees at the time of hire, as a basis to create an enforceable contract obligation between the employee and the employer. For example, some employers issue a detailed personnel policy manual stating that employment would only be terminated for "just cause." When an employee is discharged for poor performance, he or she may file suit for not being terminated for just cause. Instead of the employer having the power to make the decision to discharge for any reason, the employer's "reason" was now subject to review by the court as to whether or not the reason amounted to just cause.

In other cases, courts have found that manuals that include a grievance procedure on disciplinary actions have created an implied "employment contract." If the grievance procedures are not explicitly followed by the employer, employees may be able to claim a case against the employer for wrongful discharge in some jurisdictions.

In defending claims, attorneys for management often can persuade the courts to dismiss wrongful discharge actions against employers *before* a case would ever be submitted to a jury or judge. If the employer has retained the right to discharge an employee at-will, then there is no issue of fact to be determined. However, when a plaintiff's attorney gets the case to a jury, which is more likely to be sympathetic to the "long-suffering" employee than to the "big company," large damage awards can result. Damage awards in the millions of dollars are all too common. Accordingly, it is important for employers to do what they can to protect themselves in this hostile environment by establishing an at-will employment relationship.

Exceptions to the Employment-at-Will Relationship

Legally, there are several exceptions to the employment-at-will principle. The first of these exceptions is for civil service positions in municipal, state, and federal governments. Generally speaking, such government employees can only be discharged from employment by following specific guidelines found in the various civil service regulations. They include due process procedures for the public sector employer to follow. Moreover, even in the absence of such regulations, public sector employers have a legal duty to apply due process procedures when making discipline and discharge decisions. This is not necessarily the case for the private sector employer who maintains the employment-at-will relationship with an employee.

The next exception to the employment-at-will doctrine has been called the "group contract" exception. Generally, most group contracts are union contracts. By collective bargaining between the parties—the employer through its management and the employees through the union, their exclusive representative—agreement is reached in all matters concerning wages, hours, and working conditions in an employing unit. Most union contracts state that an employee can only be discharged for just cause. *Just cause* is a term of art in the industrial relations field that has gained broader and deeper significance through years of union-management grievance arbitration. Accordingly, it is an exception to the at-will relationship agreed upon by the parties. In fact, because of rulings by the National Labor Relations Board (NLRB) pursuant to the National Labor Relations Act (NLRA), even if a contract is silent regarding the power of an employer to discipline or discharge for just cause, if there is a grievance/arbitration clause in the contract, a requirement to discipline or discharge only for just cause would be implied as being present in the contract. Therefore, no employee may be disciplined or discharged unless the employer meets the standards set out by an arbitrator as to whether or not the management action amounted to just cause.

Another exception to the at-will principle is that an individual employee and the employer may agree by individual contract to exact terms of the employment relationship. Individual contracts are becoming increasingly common, especially with highly compensated individuals, in order to establish with certainty the rights of both parties when severing the employment relationship. An example of such individual contracts includes a golden parachute agreement which states that in the event of a termination, especially one due to a merger or acquisition, the employee will be entitled to certain fringe benefits, such as lump-sum payments and severance pay arrangements. Sometimes these concessions are necessary to recruit superior talent, particularly on the executive level. In addition, employment agreements with individual employees can be extended to other employees as well.

In addition to municipal, state, and federal legislators passing laws eroding the at-will relationship, the courts have also created new exceptions.

In some cases, courts have found that an employer that has issued an employee handbook may have created an implied contract with its employees and thereby adopted different standards than the at-will employment relationship. For example, one court held that "a handbook may . . . convert the employment relationship into one that could only be terminated by adherence to contractual terms," i.e., those terms stated in the handbook.[2] The terms were held to be accepted by employees by virtue of their continuing to work after receiving a copy of the employee handbook.

Therefore, in many states, terminated employees, through the actions of their attorneys, can make it a question for a jury to decide whether an employee handbook can be considered such a contract. The jury will then also decide whether the contract was adhered to by the employer in discharging the employee.

What are the kinds of "promises" in an employee handbook that a court might deem as legal consideration so that a contract by implication forms and binds both parties? One is the issuing of an employee handbook that states that in the event of layoffs, any layoff will be based on an employee's seniority. Another example is where a company differentiates between those employees still within a probationary period and those who are not, and provides a different process for discharging employees in each group. In these instances, the company impliedly sets up an arrangement or relationship different from the employment-at-will relationship.

Another potential problem is a handbook that establishes a hierarchy of rules, the infraction of which could lead to discharge. This may be held to imply a promise that an employee would be entitled to different treatment depending upon the type of the alleged misconduct. This action on the part of the employer can lead to a finding of an implied contract. Most importantly, such relationships are often found where a non-union employer voluntarily adopts the just cause standard for employment.

In exchange for such promises on the part of the employer, the employee also makes promises that lead the courts to find a contractual relationship.

Many employers ask employees to sign forms that "acknowledge the fact that an employee handbook has been received" and indicate that they "understand the policies and rules and agree to accept them as a condition of continued employment." In addition, some employees are told that they must give a certain time period of notice before leaving employment. The courts have interpreted these kinds of obligations as directly benefiting the employer.

While it may be the opinion of many that such promises by the employee are hardly adequate consideration to support an enforceable binding contract by implication, in many states that question will be up to a jury to decide in any contested case. Most courts affirm the principle that they will not by implication alone convert an employee handbook produced by an employer for the guidance, orientation, and instruction of the employees as to its policies, rules, and regulations into an *express contract*. However, it is clear that by virtue of these decisions, all employee handbooks should be reviewed to see if they may have such effect. To avoid this unintended result, consider the following recommendations.

First, do not have employees accept or agree to abide by the terms of an employee handbook. Such wording implies that employees really have a choice in the matter and that they could work without abiding by such rules, which is nonsense. The only real purpose for the employee's signature on a receipt form is to establish that the employee actually had notice of the rules and regulations of employment. Such notice can similarly be established by having the employee's supervisor insert a note into the employee's file stating that the employee has received a copy of the employee handbook containing the rules and regulations. An example of a receipt notice follows.

Employee Handbook Receipt Form

_____, (Name of Employee) has received a copy of the XYZ Company, Inc. employee handbook this ____ day of _____, 20____.
Employee Signature:_____
Supervisor Signature:_____

In addition, some courts have held that *requiring* adequate notice from an employee prior to quitting may give rise to an implied contract because such an obligation on the part of an employee directly benefits the employer. To avoid this problem, it is more sensible instead to *ask* that an employee give notice prior to quitting. After all, it is impossible to enforce a requirement that an employee give adequate notice prior to quitting. In reality, an employer just wants time to be able to hire a replacement. To make the request to receive sufficient notice more forceful, an employer could add that failure to provide adequate notice of quitting may be reflected in any reference requested by a former employee's new employer.

Because some courts investigating the employment relationship look at the probationary period to find supporting consideration indicating a contract, employers should avoid referring to probationary period and instead let employees know that they can be fired at any time. Many employers wrongly feel that in non-union situations they have greater leeway in dismissing employees during a probationary period. However, in an at-will employment relationship, the employer's power to terminate the relationship is absolute at any time. Promising a different procedure or progressive disciplinary system after passing probation *limits* that power voluntarily. Indeed, most managers prefer the flexibility and authority inherent in policies that do not promise a more lenient response to employee misconduct after completion of a probationary period. Such policies, which can be communicated in the employee handbook or by other means in the employment process, may be worded as follows.

> We try to be very careful to hire only those people we feel reasonably sure are qualified to do their work, are conscientious in the performance of that work, and are compatible with others already working here. However, we may make mistakes. If it turns out that we have hired someone who will not or cannot do the work satisfactorily or is not compatible, it will be necessary to terminate our employment relationship in order to keep our business in a strong competitive position.

If employment is terminated consistent with the corporation's right to discharge at-will, whether or not any severance pay is given is up to the discretion of the corporation's Board of Directors. Dishonesty, absenteeism, leaving work without notice, poor quality work, insubordination, and possession or use of intoxicating beverages, unauthorized medical drugs, or controlled substances at work or in a manner affecting work are examples of behavior that could lead to discipline up to and including discharge.

If an employer must have a probationary period, then it might be better to call such a period a "trial period." Then state that upon completion of such a trial period, the employee will be entitled to additional compensation, perhaps in the form of a salary increase or entitlement to health insurance benefits.

It is also important to distinguish the employee handbook, meant to serve as a guide to the workplace, its policies, procedures, obligations, and benefits, from an *implied promise or contract* meant to statically fix conditions of employment forever. Instead state that the employee handbook *may be changed at any time as business conditions change.* This is especially applicable to professional organizations and smaller businesses that must encourage flexibility and responsibility for high performance instead of rigid rules and personnel procedures.

Moreover, to avoid claims of implied contract when issuing an employee handbook, another devise is to add a prominently displayed *disclaimer.* The disclaimer usually appears in the Introduction to the employee handbook. Some courts have held that a failure to set out a disclaimer in bold or underlined print and place it prominently in the employee handbook may invalidate the employment-at-will relationship. This is especially true when other circumstances establish that the employee may have held a good-faith belief in the employer's past practice of following only certain disciplinary steps pursuant to provisions of the work rules or the employer's oral promises alleged to be contrary to the employment-at-will relationship. Such a disclaimer need say nothing more than, "The employment relationship between the company and its employees is that of employment-at-will. Accordingly, either the employee or the employer may terminate the relationship at any time for any reason. Nothing in the employee handbook should be construed to imply any other relationship."

The employment-at-will relationship can be further protected in the hiring process. Many employment applications include the following language before the signature line of the employee:

> I certify that the facts set forth in the above employment application are true and complete to the best of my knowledge. I understand that falsified statements on this application in any detail shall be considered sufficient cause for disqualification from further consideration for hire or for dismissal.

> I authorize [the employer] to make any investigation of my personal or employment history and authorize any former employer, person, firm, corporation, or government agency to give [the employer] any information they may have regarding me. In consideration of [the employer's] review of this application, I release [the employer] and all providers of information from any liability as a result of furnishing and receiving this information.

> I further agree that, if employed, my employment can be terminated with or without cause, and with or without notice, at any time, at either [the employer's] or my option. I understand that no personnel recruiter, interviewer, or other representative of [the employer] other than [specify title] has any authority to enter into any agreement for employment for any specified period of time. I also understand that any employment manuals or handbooks that may be distributed to me during the course of my employment shall not be construed as a contract or contract by implication.

Lastly, many companies confirm the at-will relationship after hiring with a simple form to the newly hired employee using disclaimer language again so there is no mistaking the relationship. One company uses the following form.

> Your starting date is:_____.

> Your introductory period is:_____.

> Your starting wage is:_____.

> Your supervisor is:_____.

> Your normal payday is:_____.

Your break time is:_____.

Your lunch time is:_____.

Your first weekly payday is:_____.

Your insurance eligibility is:_____.

Your employment relationship with XYZ Company, Inc. can be terminated with or without cause, with or without notice by you or the company.

Employee:_____ Date _____

Human Resource Manager:_____ Date _____

All of this may sound severe, especially as businesses have to work harder to attract, train, and retain valuable and competent key employees, but for most organizations, such precautionary measures will not affect their ability to do so. In fact, these measures will attract, not deter, top performers who do not worry about their own competence and ability to succeed and appreciate the company's effort to build the most aggressive team possible in order to best compete in today's world market.

Using Individual Employment Contracts

Individual employment contracts can be used by employees, upon their recruitment, for self-preservation in the event of a termination of employment. Sometimes these are referred to as *golden parachute* employment contracts. However, the principle of using a specific individual employment contract for each employee can also be attractive to the employer, as it can confirm the at-will employment relationship. It can also confirm that there is no employment relationship at all, if that is the case. For example, business contracts can help confirm an independent contractor relationship for services to be rendered to a business by an individual.

The use of individual employment contracts may be especially attractive to smaller businesses and professional employers. Such contracts not only confirm the at-will employment relationship, but also define and preserve other employer rights as well. These rights can include prohibitions on the part of the employee from divulging to outside parties trade secrets, such as client and customer lists or special methods of production, or other information considered confidential. The agreements can also include arrangements calling for restrictions on the right of a former employee to compete in business against his former employer.

Lastly, a recent trend has been to include in employment contracts terms that will mandate the use of mediation and/or arbitration alternative dispute resolution techniques to resolve employment-related disputes. Disputes can include equal employment opportunity discrimination complaints that would otherwise end up in state or federal courts.

While each individual employment contract will be subject to judicial analysis and interpretation in any action to enforce it in a given case, there are general rules to follow in creating agreements capable of being enforced when necessary.

Are these agreements important? That depends on the nature of one's business needs. However, it is an important question for business owners and managers to consider, especially for executive, professional, or sales employees.

When making the determination of how important individual employment contracts are to one's business, consider the following story. The president of a small Midwest manufacturer and distributor thought that his vice president of sales was slipping and should be replaced. The vice president was shrewd enough to read the telltale signs of impending termination from the president's actions. Accordingly, he began to secretly copy as much important company data as possible for his own personal use. The vice president even copied the computer file that included the name of every customer, the contact person at each customer, all sales in the last three years to each customer, and the price of every item sold. With this file and other information, he went across town to the company's main competitor and asked for employment. Armed with such vital information, he was able to take away forty percent of his former employer's market share over the next two years while vehemently denying the possession of the stolen information. Since there was no employment contract and it was virtually impossible to prove the possession of such information, legal action was not practical, and it took several years for the company to recover its former position.

Restrictive Covenants in Employment Contracts
Employment contracts are commonplace in establishing the relationship between an employer and an employee. In fact, enforceable contracts can arise even if *not* in writing. Such contracts happen when an employer extends an *offer* that is *accepted* by an employee to perform services under the direction and control of an employer. Such agreements may be subject to certain restrictive terms and conditions, typically in return for monetary or other compensation from the employer.

An offer might be initiated by the employee as well as the employer. Its terms should be specific, communicated, and understood by both employer and employee. The offer can be oral or in writing. It can be given in an interview or by telephone, computer, or facsimile as long as it is given by an individual authorized to extend it. What makes it enforceable in a court of law is that under the law there has been established a *mutual assent* between the parties. In other words, both parties had a meeting of the minds, either verbal or written, where they both agreed to the same employment terms and conditions at the same time. This agreement will then be exemplified by what the parties do as a result. If the employee goes to work pursuant to the employer's direction and control, and is compensated consistent with his or her understanding of the agreement, and this relationship continues over time, an enforceable contract has been created. This is true whether or not a written document memorializes it.

Accordingly, the preventive labor relations philosophy holds that to control and manage this contractual relationship, it is best to reduce to writing the terms, conditions, limitations, or restrictions the employer desires to be sure that these can be legally enforced to protect an employer's legitimate business interests. This will serve to confirm the understanding of both parties to the employment relationship before the relationship begins instead of litigating it all after it ends.

What legitimate business interests is an employer desiring to protect in using written employment contracts? First, the loss of an employee to a competitor will waste the employer's investment in training and compensation. Moreover, employees generally develop and cultivate customer relationships that can be extremely valuable assets to a business. These relationships would never have been made without the existence of the employment relationship.

Also, information developed by an employee about customers and potential customers can be very valuable. Such information may include the identity of customer decision-makers, special customer preferences, customer contract expiration dates, volume and types of products customers order, and volume discounts customers demand. This information, and more, is only available to the employee because of his or her position with the employer and is, therefore, highly confidential.

Departing employees also may know many secrets about their employer. This confidential information may include such things as company business plans, research, vendor support, strategic planning, and even important vision commitments.

Lastly, an employer may have a legitimate business interest in simply attempting to preserve its workforce from excessive turnover of personnel. A stable workforce reduces expenses on hiring and training, and should also be more efficient and productive.

On the other side of the issue, these employer concerns are balanced by the concerns of the public at large in our laws and court systems. The public at large has an interest in preserving the right of its citizens to have mobility in the pursuit of happiness. To protect an individual's right to change jobs, employers must be conscious of the fact that restrictive covenants will be viewed closely to determine whether or not they are reasonably necessary to protect an employer's legitimate business interests.

For example, in determining the enforceability of a covenant not to compete concerning a physician at a health clinic, one state court put it this way:

> The following canons of construction of restrictive covenants have been adopted: (1) These restrictions are prima facie suspect; (2) They must withstand close scrutiny to pass legal muster as being reasonable; (3) They will not be construed to extend beyond their proper import or further than the language of the contract absolutely requires; and (4) They are to be construed in favor of the employee.[3]

Many state statutes also closely regulate the enforceability of restrictive covenants in employment agreements. For example, this same court went on to state the following:

> . . . A covenant not to compete within a specific time in a specific territory is lawful "only if the restrictions imposed are reasonably necessary for the protection of the employer." Five inquiries are made in evaluating the enforceability of a covenant not to compete. The covenant must: (1) be necessary for the protection of the employer; (2) provide a reasonable time restriction; (3) provide a reasonable territorial limit; (4) be reasonable as to the employee; and (5) be reasonable as to the general public. . . . [The Statute further] provides that any unreasonable portion of the covenant not to compete voids the entire covenant even if the remaining portions would be enforceable.

Accordingly, while enforcing such contracts can be difficult, if the contract is properly worded and not overly broad as to what it attempts to do, it can be enforced in court when necessary. It can also act as a deterrent in many situations because its mere existence may stop employees from violating the terms of the agreement.

In order to pass the test of the courts that the agreements must be reasonable as a matter of public policy, agreements should be drafted as *narrowly* as possible, with the restrictions being derived from the nature of the business interest being protected.

In one situation involving a covenant not to compete being drafted for a dental office, the proprietors were asked where the majority of their patients lived. Ninety percent came from a three-mile area around the dental office. Accordingly, the employment contract was drafted to read that any dentist employed by the clinic would be restricted from practicing within a three-mile radius of the clinic's office.

The owners of the clinic were then asked how often the patients came in to see them. Most of the patients came in once every six months. Accordingly, the duration of time of the noncompete clause was set at six months. The beauty of these arrangements was that although these restrictions were generally perceived as less than what may have been enforced in other instances in the dental industry in general by the courts, they were tied in to what was needed in reality to protect the legitimate business interests involved. The dental office could proceed with confidence that it could enforce its covenants not to compete should a dentist it employed desire to work for a competing neighboring clinic. Moreover, because they were reasonable, they were also not unduly onerous to individual dentists the clinic sought to employ. With a reasonable contract offer, the clinic had no problem in recruiting new dentists.

As an interesting aside, in a real-world situation, one clinic dentist received a higher offer from a competing clinic with offices within the three-mile area. This offer came within three months of the dentist signing his employment agreement. When the dentist left to work with the competitor, the matter was openly discussed with the owners of the competing clinic, pointing out the contract's reasonable noncompete clause. In this particular instance, to avoid a lawsuit, the competing operation asked whether the clinic would agree not to sue if the dentist were transferred to an office outside the three-mile limit. This was a satisfactory outcome to everyone because the legitimate business concern that the departing dentist would try to attract his former patients was unlikely to take place.

In another situation, in the printing industry, 75 percent of the customers of a business came from within a 250-mile radius of the business. Accordingly, this was the radius used to set the geographic limit of the noncompete clause. When setting the clause's time limit, the owner mentioned that because technology was changing so rapidly, in one year's time the state of the art would be totally different. Therefore, a one-year time limit was appropriate. After researching the cases where contracts had been enforced in the printing industry, it was decided that these restrictions would be held reasonable if the contract ever came to enforcement.

Relative to sales employees, many courts have held that a restriction can be effective no longer than is necessary for the special relationship or identification of the salesperson with the organization to fade from the minds of the customers. Some courts have approved a period of as long as two years' duration, but it is clear that any greater period will require a very strong relationship to the legitimate business interests being protected by the employer to justify its enforcement. In general, a company should seek a period no longer than what it is likely to take to effectively introduce existing customers to new sales personnel. In addition, consider how long information relative to price and other customer-related details will be important in making sales. How soon will the information gained by salespersons in the performance of their job be obsolete in being useful in taking sales away from the employer?

It is also important to keep the focus of the covenant on restricting competitive activities by an individual rather than competitive employment. For example, precluding a sales individual from work as a secretary for a competitor might be considered overreaching, nullifying the entire agreement in some jurisdictions. However, if the focus is on specific selling activities, where the confidential information and customer relationship will be useful to the employee against the employer, the agreement is more likely to be held as one protecting legitimate business interests.

Lastly, the scope of the restriction must not be overbroad as well. Banning solicitation of all company customers and potential customers whether known or unknown to the employee might be considered too broad in scope and nullify an otherwise enforceable restrictive covenant not to compete. In an effort to increase the likelihood of enforcement capabilities, a company might restrict sales personnel from calling on customers they actually served in their territory as opposed to all company customers and potential customers at the time of the termination of employment.

Protecting Trade Secrets and Confidential Information in Employment Contracts

The majority of states have adopted the Uniform Trade Secrets Act. It defines a "trade secret" as:

> . . . Information, including a formula, pattern, compilation, program, device, method, technique, or process that: (i) derives

independent economic value, actual or potential, from not being generally known to, and not being readily ascertainable by proper means by, other persons who can obtain economic value from its disclosure or use, and (ii) is the subject of efforts that are reasonable under the circumstances to maintain its secrecy.

While a trade secret may, therefore, be almost any type of information, generally the courts will analyze its entitlement to protection by several methods.

First of all, the information must have value. In most jurisdictions this value can be potential (such as something still in the development stages) as well as actual. However, this is seldom a problem because parties generally do not litigate over information that is useless.

A second test involves whether or not the information is or can be readily known or learned. For example, information that may be common knowledge within an industry is generally not protected.

Thirdly, information sought to be protected must be maintained in secret. While it is clear that information will not have much value unless it somehow can be utilized in some way to employees, potential customers, or others, it should be *identified* as being confidential and secret when used in this context.

Accordingly, in drafting such agreements it is important that the employees know what information the company views as confidential or secret. Therefore, employers should strive for clarity in the descriptions of what is to be kept confidential and what is considered secret. In addition, the contract can make it clear that the company welcomes questions relative to whether or not particular information may be confidential. Requiring employees to maintain such information in confidentially marked company notebooks and materials will help.

To protect access to confidential information, such as customer lists, trade secrets, or other proprietary information for a reasonable period after employment, it is important that both parties in the contract acknowledge what information is considered protected.

For example, a recitation along the lines of the following would be important to document in the employment contract. First, describe the nature of the employer's business. Then state that the employee acknowledges the following: (1) the employer's products are highly specialized items, (2) the identity and particular needs of the employer's customers are not generally known in this type of business, (3) the employer has a proprietary interest in the identity of its customers and customer lists, and (4) the documents and information regarding the employer's methods of production, sales, pricing, costs, and specialized requirements of the employer's customers are highly confidential and are, therefore, considered trade secrets.

In one contract, the employer, after the acknowledgments, drafted the language this way:

> Trade Secrets and Confidential Information. During the term of this agreement, Employee will have access to and become familiar with various employer trade secrets and confidential information. Employee acknowledges that this confidential information and trade secrets are owned and shall be continued to be owned solely by Employer. During the term of employment and for a time period of one year after the termination of employment, Employee agrees not to use this information for any purpose or to divulge this information to any person other than the Employer or persons to whom Employer has given its consent in writing unless this information has already become common knowledge or unless Employee is compelled to disclose it by virtue of governmental process.
>
> Under no circumstances shall Employee remove from Employer's office any books, records, documents, customer lists, or any copies of documents of Employer without Employer's written permission; nor shall Employee make any copies of these books, records, documents or customer lists for use outside of Employer's office except as specifically authorized in writing by Employer.

Contracts Mandating Arbitration of Employment Disputes

The United States Supreme Court held that a claim brought under the Age Discrimination in Employment Act (ADEA) can be subjected to compulsory mandatory arbitration by contract instead of litigation in state and federal courts. The Civil Rights Act of 1991 further supports this practice by stating a legislative preference by the U.S. Congress that employment discrimination claims should be resolved in alternative dispute forums. Since state and federal district courts and Courts of Appeal have been reaffirming that agreements to arbitrate any employment discrimination claims are enforceable if entered into in a knowing and voluntary manner, many employers seeking to reduce costs of litigation have been including clauses to this effect in their employment contracts. While the issue has not been entirely settled legally, in part because the underlying fact situation presented to the U.S. Supreme Court was somewhat unique, many courts are upholding these agreements when the language is specific enough to involve a knowing and voluntary agreement between the parties.

Further, in most courts, these agreements to arbitrate are given full force and effect. This is due to the fact that Section 2 of the Federal Arbitration Act (FAA) provides that, "a written provision in any . . . contract evidencing a transaction involving commerce to settle by arbitration a controversy thereafter arising out of such contract or transaction . . . shall be valid, irrevocable and enforceable."

Accordingly, instead of costly, time-consuming proceedings in federal or state courts to adjudicate claims of employment discrimination for alleged violations of state or federal equal employment opportunity law, wrongful discharge, or breach of employment contract claims, etc., these issues will be handled by private arbitrators more quickly and at far less expense. Receiving a decision on such claims more quickly also serves to reduce back pay and liability. In the event a lawsuit is filed by an employee, the courts will upon motion defer to the arbitration process as mandated in the employment contract, and dismiss its jurisdiction over the decision making in the case. Instead, the proceedings and the decision will be conducted by a private arbitrator, and the court's only role will be to enforce the arbitrator's decision.

If it is important for an employer to minimize its expenses in litigating claims this way, a clause such as the following could be included in the employment agreement.

Arbitration. Any dispute, claim, or controversy related to or connected with employment of employee, including but not limited to the Civil Rights Act of 1991, the Americans with Disabilities Act (ADA), the Older Worker Benefit Protection Act, the Age Discrimination in Employment Act (ADEA), Title VII of the Civil Rights Act of 1964, the Equal Pay Act, and any and all other municipal, state and federal laws regulating the employment relationship, shall be determined by final and binding arbitration according to the Voluntary Labor Arbitration Rules of the American Arbitration Association, and judgment upon any award may be entered in any court having jurisdiction. It is further agreed between the parties that in any arbitration proceeding it will be within the authority of the Arbitrator to award such remedies as may be appropriate to the decision as if such claims had been filed in administrative agency proceedings or courts of law in which claims of violations of the above referenced statutes would have been applicable. Such proceedings shall be consistent with the provisions of the Federal Arbitration Act (FAA).

Generally, state law is involved relative to the enforcement of employment contracts containing restrictive covenants, and there is a wide variation from state to state concerning what is and is not enforceable. Accordingly, such contracts are best professionally drafted for employers on a case-by-case basis. The key is to make restrictions only as required by the necessity of the business interest one is seeking to protect. However, an example of what can be done is presented in the following contract drafted for an accounting firm.

Employment Contract Example

This Agreement, entered into as of the __ day of _____, 20__, by and between _____, a Service Corporation, hereinafter called "Corporation," and _____, an accountant duly licensed to practice accounting in the State of _____, hereinafter called "Accountant,"

Witnesseth:

Whereas, Corporation is engaged in the practice of public accounting in the State of _____, and

Whereas, Accountant is desirous of practicing accounting as an employee of Corporation,

Now, Therefore, in consideration of the mutual promises and agreements herein contained:

It Is Agreed by and between the parties hereto as follows:

1. Employment. Corporation hereby employs Accountant and Accountant hereby accepts employment upon the terms and conditions hereinafter set forth in this Agreement.

2. Term. Employment hereinunder shall continue until terminated by either party, with or without cause, upon not less than ten (10) days' prior written notice. Accountant shall have no right, common-law or statutory, to continued employment with Corporation. Accountant's employment shall automatically terminate upon the death of the Accountant, disqualification to practice accounting in the State of _____, or acceptance of employment or election to a public office which restricts or limits Accountant's right to engage in the private practice of accounting in _____.

3. <u>Duties.</u> Accountant shall provide accounting and related services to Corporation's clients along the lines of services and duties usually performed by members of the accounting profession, and will, under the direction and control of the Board of Directors of Corporation, faithfully and to the best of Accountant's ability perform such duties and any such other duties as may be occasionally assigned by the Board of Directors. Accountant agrees to devote Accountant's entire time, energy, and skills to such duties while so employed by Corporation.

4. <u>Compensation.</u> Corporation shall pay to employee compensation for services rendered to Corporation such salary as shall be established by the Board of Directors or one authorized by the Board of Directors; such compensation will include group life and family or single medical policies of insurance, and such profit sharing, bonus, or additional compensation as deemed appropriate by the said Board of Directors.

5. <u>Restrictive Agreements.</u> In consideration of Corporation making this Agreement and employing Accountant, Accountant agrees that during the period of one (1) year immediately after the termination of Agreement and within the geographic area of _____, _____, _____ and _____ Counties,

a. Accountant will not, either directly or indirectly, make known or divulge the names of any of Corporation's clients;

b. Accountant will not directly or indirectly, either for Accountant or for any other person, firm, corporation, or proprietorship, call upon, solicit, divert, or take away or attempt to solicit, divert, or take away any of the clients of Corporation for whom Accountant rendered accounting, auditing, tax consulting, or business counseling services during the employment of Accountant.

c. Accountant will not perform in a professional capacity [as distinguished from private employment] any accounting, auditing, tax consulting or business counseling services for any person, firm, or corporation for whom, to the knowledge of Accountant, such services have been rendered by Corporation during the employment of Accountant.

d. Accountant will not form an association with or employ or offer to employ in professional employment [as distinguished from private employment] as a public accountant anyone who has been a member of the staff or of the organization of the Corporation.

e. Accountant will not use or disclose or cause to be used or disclosed, directly or indirectly, to any person, firm, or corporation any information, work in process, business, trade secret, or any secret, confidential, or proprietary information acquired while employed by Corporation.

f. Accountant shall provide all records necessary to carry out the intent of this Agreement and shall report immediately to Corporation when services as described above have been provided to a particular client or information disclosed or used as provided above.

g. Where Accountant performs accounting services in violation of this contract not to compete with Corporation as described in paragraph e, Accountant agrees to pay to Corporation as liquidated damages an amount equal to one hundred percent (100%) of the gross fees billed by Corporation to such client over the twelve (12) month period immediately preceding the employment termination date of Accountant and any and all reasonable attorney's fees incurred by Corporation connected with any action, legal or otherwise, necessary to enforce the Agreement.

6. Notices. Any notice hereby required or permitted to be given shall be sufficiently given if in writing and mailed by registered or certified mail, postage prepaid, to Corporation at its principal place of business and to Accountant as Accountant shall designate in writing to Corporation.

7. Entire Contract. This Agreement shall constitute the entire contract between the parties and supersedes all existing agreements between them, whether oral or written, with respect to the subject matter hereof. The failure of either party to demand, in any one or more instances, performances of any of the terms, covenants, and conditions of this Agreement shall not be construed as a waiver or a relinquishment of any right granted hereunder or of a future performance of any such term, covenant, or condition.

8. Governing Law. This Agreement shall be construed and enforced in accordance with, and the rights of the parties shall be governed by the laws of _____.

9. Severability. Should any provision of this Agreement not be enforceable in any jurisdiction, the remainder of the Agreement shall not be affected thereby.

In Witness Whereof, the parties have hereunto executed this Agreement as of the day and year first shown above.

Corporation by:_____

Accountant:_____

Executive Compensation: Avoiding Executive Employment Disputes

Although executives and other key employees are covered by general employment laws, their positions and knowledge make their situations unique, from a legal perspective, a personal threat perspective, and a public relations perspective (within the company, the industry, and/or the public at large). Several issues arise when companies deal with executives and other key employees—from hiring to firing and beyond.

In employment agreements, many companies take extensive steps to assure that they maintain an at-will employment relationship with all of their employees, top to bottom. Offer letters can preserve and confirm this at-will relationship. Employee handbooks often state that the handbook is not to be construed as an employment contract and no employee has an employment contract unless it is in writing and signed by a high-level officer (often the CEO). Further, many company bylaws expressly state that officers serve at the pleasure of the Board of Directors.

Many employment agreements with executives or other key employees require post-termination compensation of some sort. When companies terminate the employment relationship with executives or other key employees who do not have employment agreements, they generally have a great deal of flexibility and can negotiate separation packages as they see fit, depending upon the circumstances.

However, despite the good reasons to avoid employment agreements with executives and other key employees, many companies are forced to enter into such agreements, or will benefit from having them. Reasons to enter into these types of agreements include:

1. Market forces. Many executives and key employees have other employment options and are in high demand. They may not be willing to accept employment without contractual commitments.

2. Lock-in minimum commitments. Although no agreement can force an employee to stay for a minimum period, employment agreements can offer incentives for people who stay, or disincentives for those who resign before a designated period of time.

3. Incentives. Most executives and key employees are highly motivated to perform. Incentive packages in agreements can direct their energies toward such desired goals.

4. Minimize exposure, expenses, and threats. A disgruntled former executive or other key employee can create a tremendous threat to the employer, from a legal perspective, a business threat perspective, and a public relations perspective. These employees often have knowledge of trade secrets or other confidential information; have knowledge that could help or hurt the company in disputes with third parties; develop relationships with other employees (e.g., an entire sales force might want to "follow their leader"); develop relationships with customers who might also follow them; and can cause harmful discussions within the company, within the industry, among customers, and in the media. An employment agreement addresses all of these issues. It can take the guesswork and risks out of negotiations.

Possible issues to address in employment agreements include:

1. The general terms and conditions. The agreement should make it clear that the employment relationship is subject to the terms and conditions of the agreement itself. Also, it should state that the employee is subject to the same policies and terms as all other company employees, as described in employee handbooks and other pertinent policies except as otherwise specifically provided in the agreement. Even high-level employees must be aware that they are subject to general company rules and requirements (e.g., policies regarding sexual harassment, ethics, legal behavior, etc.).

2. An agreement should discuss "duties." Although it is helpful to describe the employee's initial title and duties (perhaps with a reference to a job description as an exhibit), companies should be careful about this provision. Disenchanted employees often claim breaches of agreements, claiming the employer changed the title and/or duties. Generally, this section of the agreement should:

   a. State the expectation that the employee will devote substantially all of his or her business hours and energy to the performance of the duties;

   b. State that the title and/or the duties are flexible and may be changed from time to time by the company, and state who has the authority to make changes (e.g., the CEO, the Board of Directors, etc.). Do not draft the agreement in a way that good-faith changes would constitute a breach or otherwise give a disenchanted and/or terminated employee an opportunity to claim that he or she should not be obligated to perform his/her post-termination obligations (no-compete, anti-solicitation, trade secret, etc.); and

    c.   Establish who the employee will initially report to (e.g., a particular officer, the Board of Directors, etc.) and, if appropriate, make it clear that the reporting arrangement may be changed by the company from time to time.

3.   Term of agreement should be stated clearly.

    a.   A specific period of time such as two years with no reference to what happens once it expires. Presumably, once this type of agreement expires, the relationship either is over or converts to an at-will relationship. For example, if a bonus plan continues to be enforced (as it was during the term of the agreement), does it mean that a post-termination compensation package continues to apply? Do other provisions such as no-competes, confidentiality clauses, etc., also continue to apply? The agreement should be clear as to these points.

    b.   "Initial term with anticipated renewals" is another method of describing the term of agreement. Employment agreements are often drafted to have an initial term (e.g., one year), with the expressed understanding that the agreement may continue into the future. If that is the desire of the parties, they should state whether the agreement automatically renews itself at the end of each term, absent adequate notice by one party to the other not to renew (*evergreen* agreements); or whether the parties must renegotiate a new agreement at the end of its term and, absent that, the agreement will terminate.

    c.   Some agreements have no term at all. These become at-will relationship agreements. The point of the agreement is to set forth the parties' rights and obligations, both during the course of employment and upon termination. The agreement may change the obligations, depending upon who decides to terminate the relationship and when. Consider, for example, an agreement that provides the employee with a substantial severance pay decreasing over time. This type of provision might adequately address the employee's initial concerns without creating an overly generous separation package.

4.   Agreements should spell out compensation, reimbursements, and benefits. Executives and other key employees often have unique compensation packages. In addition to base salaries and basic benefits, benefits may include intricate bonus plans, incentive compensation plans, separation or severance plans, stock options, and so on.

These may or may not be specifically included in an employment agreement. Employment agreements nevertheless should typically include coverage of at least the following:

a. Base salary. Employment agreements typically set the base salary for the first year with the understanding that the salary will be subject to annual performance review and adjustment.

b. The agreement should include bonus and other incentive packages agreed upon. Employment agreements may indicate that an annual bonus will be considered, at the discretion of the employer, or set up an objective or combined bonus plan that sets out criteria such as "percentage of sales." A common source of disagreement over bonuses and other incentive packages is whether the bonus is payable if an employee leaves before a particular bonus period (e.g., fiscal year) is over. The agreement should state whether a mid-year departure will entitle the employee to a pro rata share of the annual bonus, the entire bonus, or no bonus at all. (This may depend upon the reason for departure.)

c. The agreement should explain how the company will reimburse the employee for ordinary, necessary, and reasonable business expenses, subject to standard procedures, approvals, and paperwork.

d. The agreement should include a statement concerning employee fringe benefits. Agreements often summarize benefits available to the employee. It must be clear that references in the agreement to particular employee benefit plans established or maintained by the company do not change the terms and conditions of those plans or preclude the company from amending or terminating those plans.

5. An employment agreement should discuss termination issues. This is important because the employer may have a very different view of post-termination packages, depending upon the reason for the departure. Agreements often state that employees will or may be terminated for any of the following reasons:

a. Death of the employee.

b. Disability of the employee. This should also be set out as a ground for termination. However, care should be taken to ensure that the agreement does not violate the Americans with Disabilities Act or the Family and Medical Leave Act. Many agreements state that, subject to these laws, the employee will be presumed to have such a disability if he or she is substantially incapable of performing his or her duties for a particular period of time (twelve weeks would be the minimum under the FMLA; the ADA may dictate a longer period of time).

c. Termination by the company *for cause* can be delineated. The agreement should make it clear that the company can terminate, at any time, for cause. Such agreements must carefully and clearly define *cause*. Various types of misconduct, illegal activities, intentional breaches of the duty of loyalty, etc., are often included in the definition. Employers are well served to word the definition of *cause* to include several less heinous employee actions that would, nevertheless, justify termination. These may include such things as the employee's material breach of any of his obligations under the agreement; dishonesty; use of alcohol or drugs in a manner that affects employee performance; conviction of a felony or any crime involving misrepresentation, moral turpitude or fraud; commission of any willful or intentional act that could reasonably be expected to injure the reputation, business, or business relationships of the company, or create a legal exposure as a result of the employee's wrongdoing; the existence of any court order or settlement agreement prohibiting the employee's continued employment; or any other reason or act of misconduct that would permit the discharge of an employee under disciplinary guidelines applicable to the employee as an employee subject to the employee handbook.

d. Termination by the company without causes should be covered as well. This situation causes new employees the most concern. An employee may wonder: What if the employer decides to terminate the employment relationship due to a change in business plans, a downturn in the market, a personality dispute, or some other reason like "it's just not working out?" In this situation, fairness, and a new employee's negotiating demands, warrant post-termination separation packages.

e. Voluntary termination by the employee should be covered. No law can prevent an employee from voluntarily terminating employment. The employer might as well make it clear that the employee has this right, however, the agreement should state that if the employee voluntarily quits, separation payment obligations will not apply.

f. Cover the situation where termination is the result of a divestiture, acquisition, or merger.

6. Post-termination compensation packages should be spelled out. Employers should not agree to pay separation pay simply because an employment agreement is terminated. The reason for the termination is critical. Reasons include death of the employee, disability of the employee, termination for cause, and termination as result of divestiture, acquisition, or merger.

7. Agreements should mention policy on confidential information, trade secrets, patent developments, etc.

8. Non-competition agreements should be covered specifically. If non-competition agreements are not in the agreement, but are contained in a separate agreement, it is a good idea to make reference to that separate agreement.

9. Non-solicitation/non-disparagement clauses can be included. These also apply for a period of time after the termination of an employee.

10. Cover the situation requiring an employee to cooperate in claims. Former disgruntled employees are often relevant witnesses in claims or lawsuits. If the former employee was an executive or other key employee, he or she may have critically important information.

11. Many agreements contain provisions discussing "indemnification" issues. These include the company's obligation to indemnify and hold the employee harmless from potential liabilities incurred by the employee as a result of performing services for the company.

12. Miscellaneous "boilerplate" provisions include such things as "entire agreement" choice of law, severability of clauses, modifications of agreement, notices, assignment issues, and whether or not binding arbitration to resolve issues is a part of it.

Employers often think it is easier to simply create a one-page letter agreement to define employment terms. There is nothing wrong with a simple offer letter. However, the offer letter should assure that it is identifying only the initial job title, duties, and salaries; should mention that the employee is subject to all of the company's rules, policies, etc.; should state upfront any and all preconditions of employment (such as drug testing, physical exams, the signing of non-compete agreements, etc.); and should clearly state that the employment relationship is at-will, i.e. that either party can terminate the employment relationship at any time and for any reason. Sometimes it is easy to provide for separation pay in the form of a notice. For example, "either party may terminate the employment relationship by providing one month's notice of intent to the other party."

The Inevitable Disclosure Doctrine

As a word to the wise for employers who are tempted to try to acquire another company's work product by hiring the employee of a direct competitor, there is a remedy available for the business harmed by such a strategy. By utilizing the theory of *inevitable disclosure*, an employer may obtain a court injunction prohibiting a former employee from using knowledge he or she would inevitably disclose that is protected work product. While this may appear as an extraordinary remedy fit only for exceptional high profile situations, it is important to be cognizant of it

A cause of action can be maintained for misappropriation of trade secrets. Such action will usually be based under Section 757 of the Restatement (First) of Torts (1939) or under the Uniform Trade Secrets Act (UTSA). It is provided, for example, in Section 757 of the Restatement:

> [o]ne who discloses or uses another entity's trade secret, without a privilege to do so, is liable if (a) he discovered the secret by improper means, or (b) his disclosure or use constitutes a breach of confidence reposed in him by the other in disclosing the secret to him.

In some circumstances, the law presumes that the use or disclosure of trade secrets is inevitable. Therefore, the only way to prevent the employer's trade secrets from improperly invading a former employee's next new work environment is to judicially—by injunction—prevent the former employee from working in the same specialized area as before.

For example, in *PepsiCo, Inc. v. Redmond*,[4] there is authority for restraining a former employee from going to work for a competitor. A three-pronged test was established in the Circuit Court's analysis: (1) does the employee have knowledge of a protected trade secret, (2) would there be similarity in positions such that it would be extremely difficult for the employee to avoid relying on or using said trade secret?, and (3) is there some element of reason to distrust or rely on promises that the employee would not abide by the restrictive covenant?

In *PepsiCo*, the former employee in question had been the general manager of California operations for the employer. When he quit to become chief operating officer for a direct competitor, having knowledge of strategic marketing plans, the employer sued. It was held that the state trade secret act in question authorized the trial court to enjoin "actual or threatened" misappropriation of a trade secret. This was shown to the court's satisfaction when it was demonstrated that the defendant's new employment would inevitably lead him to rely on the plaintiff's trade secrets. The court not only enjoined the former employee from revealing his former employer's marketing plans to his new employers, but further enjoined his starting employment for six months.

This doctrine may not apply in every jurisdiction or be capable of proof as so powerfully developed in the *PepsiCo* case, but courts are more and more becoming aware of these kinds of disputes in today's competitive marketplace for employees

Managing Leased Employee Exposure

Employee leasing has become a common business practice. Many of the early employee leasing programs were set up primarily as a means to legally manipulate and reduce high workers' compensation experience modifiers. However, they also had the advantage of saving businesses from tedious government paperwork required when employing "employees," and, through the pooling of higher numbers of employees, saved smaller business enterprises expenses for health insurance and other benefits. Accordingly, employee leasing companies—which are now called Professional Employer Organizations (PEOs)—have remained popular and are gaining wider acceptance as a legitimate business tool to provide a wide range of benefits to businesses. They are particularly applicable to the franchise industry.

Many PEOs characterize their services as a contractual relationship whereby employer responsibilities are allocated between the PEO and the client company. Under such PEO/client relationships, the allocation of duties and responsibilities may simply include the contracting of employment-related services such as payroll accounting and employee benefit administration. However, most PEOs seek to provide labor to the client company in a co-employer capacity whereby both client and PEO assume employer status.

For example, a Florida appeals court in *J.M. Foster, Inc. v. N.A.S. Logan, Inc.*[5] decided that if the employee has an express or implied contract of employment with the client, if the work being done is essentially the client's, and if the client has the right to control details of the work being done, then the client is liable for workers' compensation benefits. This decision follows the *borrowed servant doctrine*, defined in *Black's Law Dictionary*, sixth edition, as follows: "If an entity to which an employee is lent is the employer of the servant at the very time negligent act occurs, it is upon the entity, as a special employer, that liability rests. However, if the entity lending the employee is the employer at the time of injury, then the entity, as general employer, incurs liability.*

In another case, the United States Tax Court in *Professional and Executive Leasing, Inc.*[6] established a test consisting of the following factors to determine whether an employment relationship exists for the client:

1. The degree of control over the work of the employee;

2. Any significant investment that the PEO has made in the workplace;

3. The realization of profit or loss by the PEO;

4. Whether the employee's activities are an integral part of the overall business operations of the client;

5. The right to hire and fire;

6. The degree of permanency and duration of the work relationship;

7. How the parties actually treat the relationship; and

8. What the parties consider that relationship to be.

Problems can crop up in certain situations. For example, liability exposures or coverage gaps for insurance purposes can arise from employee leasing when:

● The client company may be deemed the employer and be held responsible for providing workers' compensation benefits.

● If the PEO or its insurer becomes insolvent, the client may be left with the responsibility of paying claims.

● The PEO may not maintain appropriate insurance. If the client is deemed to be a co-employer, the client may end up being responsible for any claims that go unpaid.

● The PEO's insurers might attempt to subrogate against the client for injuries to leased employees.

● The PEO may choose not to or be unable to honor the contract, including any indemnification or hold-harmless obligations.

- The leased employee (when not considered an employee of the client) might attempt to sue the client as a third-party claimant. Such suits are not covered generally under the standard comprehensive general liability policies.

- There may be uncertainty regarding the client's liability for wrongful employment practices.

In light of these possible challenges, the first line of defense is to be sure a company is selecting a PEO that has adequate supply banking and credit references, that can demonstrate that payroll taxes and insurance premiums have been paid, that has client and professional references, and that meets all state licensing requirements.

In negotiating a contract, certain provisions may be appropriate:

- An indemnity agreement with wording that the PEO will defend and indemnify a company for claims that arise out of any aspect of the PEO's operations. This is opposed to the standard wording that requires indemnity for claims arising out of the PEO's negligence. Using the word *operations* makes the protection broader.

- Be careful to avoid the assumption of risk in clauses that the PEO may require the client to hold the PEO harmless for a wide range of liabilities.

- The company should ensure that the PEO's liability is not contractually limited to the value of the contract. Damages might well be much higher than the contract's amount.

- The service contract should clarify the intent of both parties regarding liability issues. For instance, the contract should stipulate whether the PEO is the sole employer of the leased worker and clarify its responsibilities for claims. Clarifying each party's intent in the contract may eliminate disputes.

- Be sure to get a certificate of insurance evidencing all relevant policies. Some companies prefer to obtain a true and exact copy of each policy from the insurance company, which will provide exact details regarding coverage.

- Either by amendment to the certificate or an endorsement to the insurance policy, the company could ensure that the PEO's insurance company will give advanced notice to the client company if coverage is changed or canceled.

- Obtain a waiver of subrogation from the PEO's workers' compensation and liability insurance. Without such waivers of subrogation, the PEO's insurer may be able to subrogate against the client company for recovery of any claim payment arising out of an injury alleged to have been caused by the client company. For example, the client company might be accused of being negligent in its duty to provide a safe working environment.

- Consider whether or not the client company should be included as a named insured under the PEO's workers' compensation policy. The same holds true for being named on the PEO's general and umbrella liability policy, and for "employment practices liability policies" that may be in place. Such liability can include employment-related claims based on discrimination, sexual harassment, wrongful discharge, wage and hour disputes, allegations of negligent hiring retention and supervision, failure to provide benefits, and alleged violations of federal and state Family and Medical Leave Act laws.

In conclusion, the importance of establishing the proper employment relationship cannot be overstated. In today's business world, with its emphasis on adversary relationships and litigious-minded individuals, the costs are simply too high and the potential liability too great to ignore this important aspect of employment law.

Confirming Independent Contractor Arrangements

In many cases, employers want to establish that there is no employment relationship in existence between an individual and the company; that is, that an individual is an independent contractor. An independent contractor relationship has several advantages. Economically, the employer has no responsibility to pay the many employment taxes that go hand-in-hand with an employment relationship, such as FICA and unemployment compensation. In addition, the employer is not liable for workers' compensation insurance. Because of the lack of these obligations, the employer may actually be able to afford to pay, a greater amount to the individual for the services rendered. Furthermore, where there is no employment relationship, the employer should not be subject to lawsuit for discrimination or wrongful discharge. Independent contractors have no right under the NLRA to even engage in protected concerted activity or create a union.

However, while it is easy to see that, at first appearance, the independent contractor relationship may be desirable, employers must be aware of the fact that this is an area of intense scrutiny by the IRS and other state and federal agencies that have a vested interest through the derivation of tax revenue in closely examining such relationships.

If any such relationship is challenged, the employer bears the burden of proof in establishing that there is an independent contractor relationship and not an employment relationship.

The most important question in this respect is if the employer has the right to direct and control the individual's performance, both as to results and as to means and details of accomplishing the results. This does not only mean actual control, but also potential exercise of that control. In determining this issue, an examination will be made of whether the employer has the right to discharge the individual. If so, it is indicative of an employment relationship; if not, the relationship is more likely an independent contractor relationship. Another factor is whether the employer furnishes the individual tools or other implements, equipment, etc., for doing the job. If so, the relationship is more likely to be regarded as an employment relationship. If the employer furnishes the individual a specific place where the individual regularly works, the relationship is also more likely to be an employment relationship. If the individual in question maintains a principal place of business other than the premises where the work is performed, the individual is more likely to be an independent contractor. In addition, if the individual generally proclaims self-employment, makes his or her services available to the public, maintains a set of books in a businesslike fashion that record income and expenses, and incurs the risk of losing money as well as the opportunity to make money, he or she is more likely to be an independent contractor.

The IRS traditionally uses a 20-factor test to determine the existence of an independent contractor relationship, and accordingly whether or not Social Security and income tax deductions must be made. The 20 factors are described as:

1. Instructions: Whether the employer has a right to instruct an individual about when, where, and how he/she is to work.

2. Training: Whether there are indications that the employer wants services performed in a certain manner.

3. Integration: Whether the continuation of business depends upon performance of those certain services.

4. Services rendered personally: Whether the worker performs the work himself/herself.

CHAPTER ONE

5. Hiring supervising and paying assistants: Whether the individual controls workers on the job.

6. Continuing relationship: Whether work is performed at frequently reoccurring intervals.

7. Set hours of work: Whether the employer sets a schedule of hours for the individual to work.

8. Full-time required: Whether the individual is free to work when and for whom he/she chooses.

9. Performing work on the employer's premises: Whether the employer has a right to compel the worker to travel a designated route, to canvass a territory within a certain time, or to work at specific places as required.

10. Order or sequence set: Whether there are established routines and schedules.

11. Oral or written reports: Whether regular reports are required.

12. Payment by hour, week, month: Whether payment is made by the job or on straight commission.

13. Payment of business and/or traveling expenses: Whether these items are covered by the employer.

14. Furnishing of tools and materials: Whether these items are provided by the worker or employer.

15. Significant investment: Whether the worker invests in facilities, e.g., rental space.

16. Realization of profit or loss: Whether the worker is subject to risk of loss due to investments, not payment for services.

17. Working for more than one firm at a time: This must be more than minimal.

18. Making service available to the general public: This should be on a regular and consistent basis.

19. Right to discharge: Whether the employer exercises control through threat of dismissal or whether the individual cannot be fired as long as he/she produces a result in accord with contract specifications.

20. Right to terminate: Whether each party has the right to terminate the relationship.

The 20 factors have been divided by the IRS into three main groups or "categories of evidence." These are (1) behavioral control facts; such as instructions by the employer on how work is to be done and the provision about training practices, methods, and procedures; (2) "financial control," or exactly who has risk/reward of profit or loss from the work activity; and (3) the relationship of the parties, such as inclusion of the worker in company-provided benefits like health insurance or tax-qualified retirement, annuity, or cafeteria plans.

The mere provision of a 1099-MISC form will not alone suffice to establish an independent contractor relationship. As stated earlier, the employer bears the burden of proof to establish an independent contractor relationship to the IRS. To do so requires meeting three elements of proof. First, the employer must establish a reasonable basis for its treatment of the relationship. Has the employer relied on a court case or administrative IRS ruling or previous audit finding of independent contractor status? Is it usual and customary in the trade to do so? Did the employer rely on the professional advice of its tax accountant or attorney? Secondly, has the employer been consistent in its treatment of individuals as independent contractors? Thirdly, has the employer been consistent in how it reports the relationship through issuing the proper forms, such as the 1099-MISC, for each independent contractor?

In one interesting situation that illustrates these principles, the status of three types of employees at a resort was questioned. The resort owners thought that all were independent contractor relationships. The first class of employees were domestic employees employed three days per week from 8:00 a.m. to 12:00 noon to clean and vacuum rooms, make beds, change towels and linens, and do what was otherwise necessary to clean the resort lodge rooms. These domestic workers also provided services to other area resorts on their unscheduled days. The resort also had a contract with an individual to maintain the grounds and mow the lawn as needed to keep it looking neat and orderly. This individual had no set hours and exercised his own judgment as to when the grass needed to be cut. However, when cutting the grass, he used the lawn mower owned by the resort owners. The third class of employees included two masons hired to build fieldstone pillars on either side of the entrance to the resort. These masons had their own truck and tools and were paid a set contract price to erect the pillars. In this case, it was found that the domestic workers were employees because of their set hours and set duties which provided evidence that the resort owners had direction and control over their work, even though the domestic employees also worked for other resort owners. The individual mowing the lawn was held to be an independent contractor because he controlled his own hours and the quality of the result of the services he rendered, even though he did use equipment furnished by the resort owners. As for the masons, it was clear that they were independent contractors because they also controlled their time, held themselves out to the public as doing this kind of work, and took the risk of profit or loss pursuant to a contract for the work to be performed.

Defining Independent Contractor Agreement by NLRB Analysis

In *Roadway Package System, Inc.* and *Dial-A-Mattress Operating Corp.*, the NLRB reached opposite conclusions in determining whether truck drivers for two different companies are employees or independent contractors. In *Roadway*, the Board adopted the analysis of the Restatement (Second of Agency § 220) which lists ten factors to consider. The Board found that all factors should be weighed in the equation and rejected its own position in *Roadway* that the "right to control" factor should predominate (unanimous decision, Gould concurring). In *Roadway*, the Board affirmed the Regional Director's conclusion that the drivers are employees because they do not operate independent businesses; they perform functions essential to the company's normal operations; they receive company training and do business under Roadway's name with its guidance; they operate under its substantial control; and they have no substantial proprietary interest beyond and investment in their trucks, with no significant entrepreneurial opportunity for gain or loss. In *Dial-A-Mattress*, the Board reached an opposite result, because the drivers have no guaranteed minimum compensation; they hire their own helpers or employees and have sole control over them; they own and have complete control over their vehicles, and can decline orders without penalties; and many have company names, hold state business certificates, own more than one vehicle, have business addresses and tax identification numbers, file corporate tax returns, and maintain workers' compensation insurance (Gould dissented in *Dial-A-Mattress*).

The factors the Board will look at to determine whether an individual is an employee or an independent contractor include the following:

- Extent of control over the details of the work.

- Whether or not the one employed is engaged in a distinct occupation or business.

- Whether the duties of the occupation are usually performed under the direction of any employer or by a specialist without supervision.

- The skills required in the profession.

- Who supplies the equipment and the place of work for the person doing the work.

- The length of time of employment.

- The method of payment—time or by the job.

- Whether work is part of the regular business of the employer.

- Whether or not the parties believe they are creating the relation of master and servant.

- Whether the principal is or is not in the business. [Restatement (second) of Agency, § 220.]

Employers wanting to limit potential exposure to challenges to independent contractor relationships should be aware of the following:

1. When advertising for independent contractors, employers should be careful not to place newspaper ads in the "Help Wanted" section. Avoid using phrases such as "wage offered" or "steady work" in the ad. Instead, look for independent contractors who place their own ads under "Situations Wanted" or "Trade Services."

2. In setting up the relationship, avoid setting a regular pattern of daily or weekly hours. Self-employed individuals presumably have the opportunity to select when and where they will work in relation to all their customers.

3. Allow contractors to supply their own tools wherever possible in the performance of the services required. This will demonstrate that there is a risk of loss as well as opportunity for profit, a hallmark test in these situations.

4. Use contractors who normally advertise their services in some manner. Keep on file any circulars or telephone directory ads. Ask for and keep business cards.

5. Allow contractors to hire their own assistants. Insist that contractors pay the assistants they hire, and account for the appropriate payroll taxes for them.

CHAPTER ONE

6. Employers should not include independent contractors under the company insurance coverage for worker's compensation, health insurance, or other benefits that are provided for employees.

7. If possible, compensate independent contractors on a job basis rather than by the hour or on a weekly salary. Professional services normally calculated by an hourly rate, such as for an attorney or accountant, may be an exception.

8. Always ask for an invoice or statement before paying for any work that has been performed. If possible, make checks payable to a company or business rather than to an individual.

9. Avoid directly reimbursing contractors for any expenses they may have, such as gas, car mileage, and meals, unless provided for by contractual agreement. Such expenses should be considered as included as part of the independent contractor's overall fee unless specifically provided for by contract.

10. Remember that in theory an independent contractor cannot be discharged from employment because he or she is not an employee. If dissatisfied with performance, look to the contract for the remedy. If there is no written agreement, simply offer no more work to sever relations.

11. Avoid restricting the ability of the independent contractor to work for others, except where appropriate for the protection of trade secrets or other proprietary information.

12. Specify time limits in the contract if possible. Have a specific termination date, or a defined period of notice for cancellation or for cause.

13. In setting up the work parameters, avoid set hours of work or other means of direction and control over an independent contractor. Do not provide an office, nameplate, business cards, or uniforms (unless necessary for security or like reasons) that are required for or provided to employees. Make sure the independent contractor has a separate business address off the employer premises if the independent contractor needs an office on site to complete a project.

14. Avoid offering independent contractors discounts or other benefits offered to employees, exclude independent contractors from em-

ployee events such as company picnics and parties, and do not include independent contractors in extensive training programs designed for employees only.

To confirm the validity and existence of an independent contractor relationship, it is best to have a contract in writing signed by both parties. Some states require a contract for this type of relationship. A sample of such a contract for a management consultant follows.

Sample Independent Contractor Agreement

THIS AGREEMENT, made and entered into this ___day of _____, 20__,

between _____, hereinafter referred to as "Corporation," and _____, hereinafter referred to as "Consultant,"

WITNESSETH:

A. Corporation desires to retain the services of Consultant pursuant to the terms, compensation requirements, and conditions set forth below;

B. Consultant is willing to be retained by Corporation pursuant to the terms, compensation requirements, and conditions set forth below;

NOW, THEREFORE, IN CONSIDERATION of the mutual covenants and agreements contained herein, the parties agree as follows:

1. The Corporation agrees to utilize services of Consultant in the capacity of _____.

2. The Consultant's relationship with Corporation shall be that of an independent contractor, and nothing in this contract shall be construed to create an employer and employee relationship for any purpose. Consultant shall be free to exercise his own independent judgment as to all aspects of the services to be performed, including, but not limited to, the manner and means of achieving the results requested of such services. In addition, Consultant is expressly free to perform services for other parties while performing services for Corporation.

3. Consultant agrees to perform all services as requested by Corporation to the best of his ability and according to the standards, rules, and regulations required by the _____ profession.

4. Consultant agrees to carry malpractice liability insurance relative to any service he may perform for Corporation.

5. This contract shall be continuous, but may be terminated by either party, for any reason, by giving five (5) days' notice in writing to the other party, delivered in person or mailed to the last known address of such party.

6. All services rendered by Consultant under this Agreement will be the property of Corporation.

7. Consultant agrees that he is responsible for the payment of all applicable Social Security, Unemployment Insurance, and any other tax payments as required by the State of _____ or the U.S. government and or any agency that is a part thereof.

8. No verbal statement heretofore or hereafter shall affect or change this Agreement; any modification thereof must be made in writing and signed by all parties.

9. This Agreement shall be governed by the laws of the State of _____.

10. Corporation agrees to compensate Consultant for services rendered pursuant to this Agreement _____.

11. During the rendering of services by Consultant for Corporation, and thereafter, Consultant will hold in strictest confidence and not use or disclose to any person, firm, or organization any information, work in process, business or trade secret, or any other secret proprietary, or confidential matter relating to Corporation or its clients which are not generally known to the public, except insofar as such disclosure or use may be required in the course of the rendering by Consultant of the services requested by Corporation.

IN WITNESS WHEREOF, the Parties have signed this Agreement in duplicate this ____ day of _____, 20__, at [city], [state].

Corporation by: _____

Consultant: _____

Endnotes

[1] *Ali v. Mount Sinai Hospital,* SDNY, 68 CCH EPD ¶44,188.

[2] *Ferraro v. Koelsch,* 124 Wis2d 154, 368 NW2d 666 (1985).

[3] *Streiff v. American Family Insurance Co.,* 118 Wis2d 602, 348 NW2d 505 (1984).

[4] F.3rd 1262 (7th Cir. 1995).

[5] 483 So. 2d 553 (1986).

[6] 89 TC 225 (1987).

[7] 326 NLRB No. 72 (1998).

[8] 326 NLRB No. 75 (1998).

Answers to Chapter One Test Your Knowledge

1. Employment-at-will relationship.

2. Any circumstance and no circumstance; any reason, no reason, or even a bad reason.

3. Implied contract, violation of public policy, and legislative exceptions of state, federal, or municipal law and administrative code such as found in equal rights, Americans with Disabilities Act (ADA), and the prohibitions against "retaliation" for filing claims or complaints contained in such statutes.

4. (1) Issue an employee handbook confirming the at-will relationship with "disclaimer language."
   (2) Put "disclaimer language" on the application of employment.
   (3) Use "disclaimer language" in an offer of employment letter.

5. A "leased employee" is an individual who is actually the employee of another company under a business establishment's direction and control through a lease agreement.

6. (1) The relationship should be in writing in a contract.
   (2) The independent contractor controls the time and place of the work being done.
   (3) The compensation for the work is tendered in response to a statement or invoice presented for work performed.

7. Within limitations appropriate to the business necessity, restrictions on the solicitation of company customers for a reasonable *time period* in a reasonable *geographic* area or other definable territory.

8. Pursuant to employment contract.

9. Restrict use of such trade secret information in an employment contract.

10. Through use of the "inevitable disclosure" doctrine, an employer might be able to convince a court to grant an injunction prohibiting a former employee from working for a competitor.

CHAPTER ONE

CHAPTER TWO

Employer Policies That Pay Off

Preparing the Employee Handbook

The Purpose of an Employee Handbook

Content of an Employee Handbook

What to Avoid in an Employee Handbook

Test Your Knowledge

of Employee Handbooks

1. True or False? A company should not issue a set of work rules in an employee handbook because if an employee violates the employer's interest by his or her conduct, and the conduct is not strictly forbidden by the rules, the employer cannot act to discharge the employee.

2. Which of the following statements are important for a company to make in the "Introduction" to an employee handbook?
    a. This handbook may be modified, updated, or changed at any time by the company.
    b. The employee may be discharged consistent with the company's right to discharge an employee at will.
    c. The company wants an employee to communicate any dissatisfactions he or she may have with the company.
    d. All of the above.

3. Which of the following are basic psychological needs of employees that can be met by an employee handbook?
    a. The feeling of security because the obligations of employment are clearly spelled out.
    b. The need for respectful and fair treatment because with published work rules there should be no favoritism of one employee over another for reasons unrelated to work.
    c. The knowledge of how to advance to higher earnings and greater responsibility.
    d. A sense of purpose in the work being done.
    e. All of the above.

4. True or False? If an employer has more than 50 employees, the federal Family and Medical Leave Act mandates that the employer publish its policy allowing such leave and the procedures for taking it in the employee handbook, if the employer publishes one.

5. True or False? Pursuant to the National Labor Relations Act, it is an unfair labor practice for a non-union employer to express its opinion in the employee handbook that it would prefer to keep its union-free status.

6. True or False? An employer can legally in its drug and alcohol policy retain the right to discharge from employment an employee who refuses to submit to blood or other tests to determine compliance with its policy.

7. True or False? An employer can legally stipulate in its workers' compensation policy that after any lost-time work accident every injured employee may be subject to blood or other tests to determine compliance with the drug and alcohol policy.

8. True or False? A non-union employer should publish in its work rules that employees will be discharged only for just cause.

9. True or False? Any list of work rules should accompanied by a statement that such list includes not all of the rules, but only some of the rules.

10. True or False? On an employee handbook receipt form, the employer should state that obeying all of the rules and policies is a term and condition of employment at the company.

The answers to these questions are at the end of this chapter.

The Purpose of an Employee Handbook

Employee handbooks serve a number of purposes: they introduce employees to the company, outline the company's expectations of its employees, meet employees' psychological needs, and serve legal purposes.

Introduce Company and Philosophy

The preventive labor relations philosophy holds that the way to manage employees and avoid labor problems is to lead by example and communicate by word, and deed the manner in which a company intends to operate to successfully serve its customers. This communication principle begins with the owner or chief executive officer and continues down the chain of command through supervisors to entry-level employees.

Communicating concise, easily understood principles delivers standards against which the pursuit of excellence can be measured. How can this be effectively communicated throughout the entire organization? For many organizations, there is no better place to start than with an employee handbook.

This chapter examines the transmitting of management's philosophy and policy decisions through its employee handbook. All employers want to receive a good day's work from each employee and to avoid labor problems. Employers publish employee handbooks to achieve these goals. However, wise employers concern themselves not only with what they want from their employees, but also with what employees want in return. In addition, there is a third party to this transaction—the most important of all—the customer. An employee handbook can be the perfect communications tool to help educate employees about how the company's business is best administered to serve the customer who pays the wages for all.

Explain Expectations: Company and Employees

It is becoming increasingly important legally to announce employment policies upfront. In this sense, the employee handbook serves as a shield to help deflect employment law challenges to company action, such as in the discharge of an employee. In areas such as equal opportunity, sexual harassment, drug and alcohol abuse, family and medical leave, and no-solicitation rules, specific policies must be conveyed to employees. In fact, if a company has at least 50 employees, making it large enough to be covered by the federal Family and Medical Leave Act (FMLA), it must publish in its employee handbook its policy and procedure relative to how an employee exercises the right to apply for such leave. Another example relates to publishing company policies prohibiting sexual harassment. Recent U.S. Supreme Court decisions allow the employer an affirmative defense. When an internal complaint procedure exists and an employee fails to use it but quits instead, the employer can defend itself. Where better to communicate the complaint procedure than in the employee handbook?

To me, the employee handbook is the perfect place to communicate these policies to employees anyway, regardless of whether required by law. The handbook becomes a record of the company's intent that can be easily introduced as evidence in any legal or other challenge to company decision-making in personnel matters. As discussed later in this chapter, one way to defend challenges to employment decisions is to establish that the employer did not condone by neglect an employee's prior improper behavior. Reducing to writing descriptions of the behavior an employer expects, and has a right to expect, from its employees will help defend against such challenges when those expectations are not met by an employee.

Some, usually smaller, employers are understandably wary of reducing their policies to writing, fearing that doing so will limit their managerial freedom. Instead, a "management by memos" approach takes hold. The problem with this approach is that ultimately memos, which may date back many years, collect in a file in a manager's office, and no one but the manager knows about or sees them until a time comes to apply one in a particular circumstance. The benefit of this approach is that it allows the manager to give the appearance of impersonal decision-making while at the same time allowing a case-by-case approach. For example, since only the manager knows of the existence of any particular memo policy, he or she can pick and choose when to pull it out of the file and apply it. In one sense this might be thought to be good practice because a manager can hide behind an apparent lack of personal responsibility when applying a memo policy. After all, the manager is just applying what was already worked out to cover the situation.

However, is this the way to lead people? What one might gain with the management by memos approach is far outweighed by the other positive benefits, both legal and managerial, of publishing such policies in an understandable and organized manner for all to see and know. Employers that fear that an employee handbook will lock the company into unalterable courses of action that may not be appropriate for every case should be aware that they can also build management discretion in the employee handbook, yet still provide the stability that published philosophy, policies, and work rules bring. It is possible to design a handbook that will be firm where it needs to be firm, such as when dealing with alcohol and drug policies, and yet also be flexible where managers want flexibility, such as in dealing with discipline and discharge decisions. In fact, this very flexibility is better established by publishing a handbook upfront for all, including governmental agencies and civil juries in contested cases, to see.

Meeting Basic Employee Needs

Before plunging ahead, it is important to note the results of industrial psychological research that indicate what employees really want from their jobs. This research shows that adequate attention to five basic wants satisfies most employees.

First in importance is security. Employees want a steady job as long as they work and behave normally. A good employee policy manual should give the employee a feeling of security by making clear the obligations of employment and the fruits of living up to those obligations.

The second desire of employees is respectful and fair treatment. Employees want no favoritism of one person over another for reasons unrelated to work. Again, knowledge of the rules and philosophies of proper behavior at a business serves to reduce the fear that employees are strictly at the mercy of the persons above them in the management chain.

The third desire of employees is the opportunity to advance to both a better job and higher earnings. Belief that such opportunities exist will increase the loyalty of employees and decrease turnover. The employee handbook can be used to communicate the ways and means of advancement and emphasize a company's philosophy of promoting from within, where possible.

The fourth consideration has been described as the feeling that employees are doing something worthwhile. Employees want to think they are making a contribution to the business and, perhaps in some small way, to the progress of mankind by becoming a part of the great mechanism by which all advance. The handbook creates a sense of belonging and purpose, which in turn bolsters employees' self-esteem and performance. The employee handbook gives employees, in writing, an understanding of the relationship of each employee's job to the product or service the company offers. In addition, it may even show the employee how the company's services help its clientele progress.

Surprisingly, the last desire on the list is money. Employees expect rates of pay that are fair for jobs in their organization and that are comparable in the community. According to industrial psychology research, wages are not a priority for employees. High wages alone do not assure the accomplishment of what a company wants in labor relations: a good day's work and the avoidance of labor problems. Extremely low wages, on the other hand, often result in employee turnover, discontent, and labor troubles somewhere down the line.

The perfect vehicle to communicate the organization's intent to serve these employee interests and its efforts toward successful labor relations is a properly prepared employee handbook. A handbook serves these important needs in both union and non-union situations.

How can the effectiveness of personnel policies be measured? No employer sets up a business just to see how many people can be employed or to see how well those employees can be treated. A company hires people because there is work to be done. Unless personnel policies and their administration clearly contribute to productivity, quality, and service, they are a waste of time and effort and should be avoided. However, a good policy handbook gives direction to the goal of preventing labor problems. Moreover, the best time to establish or change personnel policies is before situations arise, remembering always that an employee handbook is a means to an end and not the end in itself.

Legal Purposes Served

By announcing policies and rules to employees as they are hired via the handbook, a company can more easily demonstrate in any legal forum that an employee should have known of their existence. For example, a simple four-step process can establish a company's defense that it had a legitimate business reason to discharge an employee.

First, the company must establish that it has rules. If these rules are in the employee handbook, the company can simply introduce the employee handbook into testimony. Second, the company should demonstrate that the employee was aware of the rules. Introducing into evidence a copy of the receipt form showing that the employee received a copy of the handbook often defeats an employee's allegation that he or she was ignorant of any employer rule governing the conduct for which he or she was fired. The employer must then prove that the rule is reasonable. Often, this can be done in the body of the rule as it is written into the employee handbook. In general, a rule will be deemed reasonable if violation of it harms the employer's business or property. After laying this foundation, an employer can establish by witness testimony that the employee actually violated the rule.

Employee handbooks can also be invaluable in explaining company procedures. As previously mentioned, in order for a sexual harassment policy to be valid, the courts have consistently ruled that the policy must explain how to properly make a complaint. The same is true for an explanation of FMLA policies. The employee handbook can and must explain to the employee just how to apply for this leave.

Another legal purpose served in the employee handbook is informing an employee about the benefits that are available and the extent of those benefits. Not only will the company get mileage out of the good things it does for an employee in addition to paying a wage, but the employee will also have an understanding about the extent of these benefits.

Lastly, if it is the company's policy to have an at-will employment relationship with its employees, this fact can be confirmed in the employee handbook. In fact, companies have used disclaiming language in the employee handbook confirming the employment at-will status to counteract arguments from employees that oral promises were made delineating a different relationship.

Content of an Employee Handbook

An employee handbook is best divided into four separate sections. The first section introduces the employee to the company's philosophy and provides a general orientation to the company. Next comes a section that explains what the company expects of its employees. The third section gives an explanation of what employees can expect from the company, including wages and fringe benefits. The fourth section can deal with *closing matters*. The closing matters section describes what happens if an employee quits or is discharged, reviews the suggestion and complaint policies, and delivers a rousing "conclusion."

Section One: Philosophy of the Business

The first section of the employee handbook typically includes an introduction to the company, its mission and vision statement, a brief company history, a discussion of business and professional ethics, and an explanation of the company's views on unions.

Introduction

The introduction to the employee handbook is important for several reasons. The first section of any book sets the tone for the reader. Remember, the handbook should be written so that it is read and not just put on the shelf, thrown in the wastebasket, or put at the bottom of a locker, never to be seen again until called for by an attorney representing an employee just discharged from employment.

It is important to start the book with enthusiasm so that the rest of it will be recognized as being of value to the employee who reads it. Probably the first subject in the new employee orientation will be a thorough

CHAPTER
TWO

review of the employee handbook. Indeed, many employee handbooks are used as recruiting tools. This is especially important today when qualified, competent, and enthusiastic employees are difficult for a company to attract and retain.

Secondly, there are legal purposes to accomplish in the introduction. As discussed in Chapter One, it is important to establish an employment-at-will relationship with employees. Many companies use the introductory section of the handbook to underscore this relationship. A good example of an employee handbook introduction appears below.

Sample Introduction

Welcome! We are pleased to have you with us.

This is your handbook. It is meant to be an informative guide to the principles, policies, procedures, and benefits of our company. By acquainting yourself with this book, you will have a better understanding of what our customers expect from us, what we expect from you, and what you may expect from the company.

PLEASE UNDERSTAND THAT THIS EMPLOYEE HANDBOOK IS NOT INTENDED TO BE A CONTRACT OF EMPLOYMENT.

If you do not understand something in the handbook, please ask about it. You will find we are a friendly group of people and want you to feel at home quickly. You are now part of an organization that has grown and prospered through the wholehearted efforts of every person who works here.

This employee handbook will be updated and occasionally modified to keep it current with the ever-changing conditions of our business. What does not change is our belief that job security for all of us who earn our livelihood at the company is created through producing quality products delivered on time, which results in satisfied customers who place repeat orders with our company, and not with our competitors.

We try to be very careful to hire only those people we feel reasonably sure are qualified to do that work, are competent in the performance of that work, and who will be compatible with others already working here. However, we may make mistakes. If it turns out that we have hired someone who will not or cannot do the work satisfactorily, or is not compatible, it will be necessary to terminate our employment relationship in order to keep our business in a strong competitive position.

We hope that you will be happy working at our company. In our opinion, the only challenges that cannot be resolved are those we do not know about. Accordingly, we welcome your ideas, suggestions, or dissatisfactions about the operations of the company. We welcome the opportunity to air concerns and think through to resolutions of the challenges that we may occasionally face. We are certain that it is this type of teamwork that will result in the continuing development of our business as a growing, prosperous enterprise through which we all can mutually benefit.

It has been, and will continue to be, our policy to offer competitive wage rates and benefits, and to provide safe, pleasant working conditions so that we can attract and retain our valuable employees. This is because, in our opinion, our most important asset is a loyal, enthusiastic employee.

Sincerely,

Company President

This kind of an introduction does several things. It not only sets a welcoming tone, but also implies that employee performance is expected. This type of statement helps companies recruit top performers.

In addition, in informing employees that the handbook can be updated, changed, and modified, the company is also laying the foundation that the employee handbook is not a contract by implication. This is the type of language that could be taken to a jury in a contested case.

Further, it is important to publish the disclaimer affirming the at-will employment relationship to avoid any confusion, as negative and distasteful as such language may seem. It is better there is no mistaken understanding on any employee's part as to what they are signing on for when they begin work at the company. True performers expect this kind of relationship, and are not put off by it. In fact, they would prefer this type of arrangement because they expect employees, themselves included, to be let go if they do not perform. Performers also understand that such a legal relationship provides better management flexibility in maintaining a quality workforce, which gives the company and its employees the best opportunity to succeed in the competitive modern business world. Of course, in the public sector such language is not appropriate because of the intervention of civil service and other regulatory protections afforded public employees.

This subject always brings to mind an incident that took place in a class I was teaching for a university business outreach program. The class was on "The Law of the Workplace," and contained students who were both management and union representatives. After pontificating on the importance of confirming in the employee handbook the at-will employment relationship, a hand shot up from one of the students, a union organizer. She said she would never work for a company that had as one of its basic policy statements that an employee might get fired. In this golden teaching moment, I replied, "See, it works. If that is your attitude, the company probably would not want you to work for it either."

A good introduction in an employee handbook sets performance expectations and informs employees that the company wants them to be involved in the organization. It makes it clear that the company wants their questions, inquiries, input, and even their complaints and dissatisfactions. Of course, mere words on paper will never be enough, but the handbook can become the cornerstone of the employee relations program, providing the direction needed to steer a proper course through the sometimes-choppy waters of employee relations.

The introduction is so important that it should be the first thing an employee or prospective employee reads in the handbook, even before the table of contents.

Mission and Vision Statement
Industrial psychologists and students of organizational behavior and group dynamics believe that the mission statement of a group is important. In theory, a mission gives unity to the group because there is agreement on what everyone is trying to accomplish through their working efforts. Such statements can be very simple. However, they not only convey to the employee the philosophy of the company, but also provide a sense of direction. A strong mission statement lets the employee know that the company is not a social fraternity or sorority; there is work to be done and a definite purpose to the work, however simply that purpose may be expressed. This is a sample of what one company uses as its mission statement in the employee handbook:

Sample Mission Statement

1. Our company is in the business of manufacturing and selling packaging materials.

2. The prime objective of the company is to earn a profit sufficient to provide us with job security, competitive wages and benefits, and opportunity for advancement through growth.

3. This can best be accomplished by providing our customers with superior service, acceptable quality, and competitive pricing.

4. Job security can then be created by manufacturing quality products, shipped on time, so that we will have satisfied customers who will then place repeat orders in our shop and not the shop of our competitors.

In addition to a mission statement, many employers today spend a great deal of time, money, and effort to develop as part of its strategic plan a *vision statement*. Generally, a vision statement differs from the mission statement in a subtle way. It is not meant to define the purposes for the organization's existence, but rather to describe the goals it strives to achieve. What better place to communicate this vision than in the employee handbook? One nonprofit agency defined its mission and described is vision this way:

Sample Vision Statement

Our agency will be a regionally recognized progressive provider of quality innovative programs that foster the independence of persons with disabilities in cooperation with families.

A dynamic, committed team of board, professional staff, and volunteers will deliver highly personalized service in a variety of agency-based and satellite locations.

Our growth will be supported by increased funding resources, expanded and diversified territory, and community collaboration.

Brief History
To new employees, knowing the history of the company leads to not only a sense of belonging, but also a sense of security. All companies can be proud of their history, whether they have only been established for three years or have enjoyed a long, rich tradition of excellence.

Each company is unique, and, therefore, its history is unique. Its uniqueness is a positive quality that separates it from the competition. Historical statements and explanations of what the company does are important psychological components to building loyalty and a sense of belonging. All people like associating with a winner. It gives us an identity. It makes us feel good about where we work, what we do, and who we are as individual people. Consider the following.

Sample Company History

We started in the restaurant business in 1954. At that time, our restaurant had only twelve stools for inside seating and carhop service. As time went on, remodeling and additions were made to that building, and it now seats 135 people.

In 1981, we decided to build a second restaurant. It was opened in April of that year, with seating for 200 in the dining room and 68 in the cocktail lounge. Banquet facilities were also completed later that year for 240 people.

These two restaurants have built a fine reputation for quality and service in the community. This reputation has been made by serving good food in a clean atmosphere created by capable, conscientious employees. We hope you can help us maintain our reputation.

Business Ethics

Business ethics are more important today than ever before. Media coverage of unethical business operations abound, but successful businesses understand that their survival depends on establishing relationships with their customers based on trust and ethical conduct. The employee handbook is an excellent place to highlight the company's commitment to ethical business dealings and reinforce this value as part of its culture.

Each business has specific needs. For example, not only do accounting firms and legal firms depend upon meeting certain standards of ethical conduct proscribed by their profession, other enterprises such as medical clinics, banks, and insurance agencies have their own code of conduct which must be met on a day-to-day basis. One medical clinic described it this way in the employee handbook:

Sample Confidential Information and Professional Ethics Statement

The relationship between a doctor and his patient is a very personal one and is strictly confidential, both ethically and legally. An employee may acquire certain facts relative to patients in due course of employment. All such information, whether of a medical or a business nature, is to be considered strictly confidential. All employees are warned to hold such information inviolate. Under no circumstances are the business or medical affairs of our patients or of the clinic to be discussed with any outside party. Violations of this duty will subject an employee to disciplinary action up to and including immediate discharge from employment.

No medical information, or reports, may be released to patients, their spouses, or relatives, or to outside organizations, except as directed by specific instruction from the physician concerned or the manager. Persons requesting such information should be referred to one of them. If their request has been made in writing and signed by the patient, only then may this information be released.

Other organizations have different concerns. For example, one financial institution discussed the following subjects: Confidentiality, Release of Customer and Bank Information, Personal Use of Acquired Information, Interdepartmental Exchange of Information, Investments and Personal Finances, Securities, Transactions, Borrowing, Personal Benefits, Limits on Authority, Improper Payments, Compliance with Laws, Use of Official Stationery, Outside Employment, Politics, and Acting in Any Other Fiduciary Capacity Except with Corporate Approval.

What Our Customers Expect from Us

It is vital that the importance of the customer not be understated. After all, the reason for a company's existence is to serve its customers. Again, the employee handbook is the perfect place to underscore this attitude, particularly for a new employee. In addition, there may be other functions that a company would like to underscore with customers, and these can also be included in this section. Relative to the philosophical aspect of a customer's importance, one company used the following anonymous quotation:

Who Is the Boss?

Here is a question I will bet you could ask 1000 working people and never get the right answer. The question is: "Who is the boss?"

There is only one boss, and whether a person shines shoes for a living or heads up the largest corporation in the world, the boss remains the same. It is the customer. It is the customer who pays everyone's salary and who decides whether a business is going to succeed or fail. The customer does not care if a business has been around 100 years. The minute it starts treating the customer badly, the customer will put it out of business. In fact, if you look back at who the most successful companies were 75 years ago, of the top 100 companies, only a little more than 15 percent are even in existence today.

This boss, the customer, has bought and will buy everything you have or will have. He has bought all of your clothes, your home, your car, your children's education and your vacation. He pays all of your bills, and he pays them in exact proportion to the way you treat him. A man who works deep inside a big plant on an assembly line might think he is working for the company that writes his paycheck, but he is not. He is working for the person who buys the product at the end of the line, the customer. In fact, this customer can fire everyone in the company from the president on down. How does he do it? He does it by simply spending his money someplace else. This is one of the reasons why taking pride in the work we do is so important to us personally. Doing an exceptionally good job will not only bring joy and satisfaction, but will also help get more customers, keep the ones we have, and ensure that we continue to get a paycheck from our real bosses—the customer.

Some of the largest companies that had flourishing businesses a few years ago are no longer in existence. Why? They could not, or did not, satisfy the customer. They forgot who the boss really was! (Author unknown.)

Another item that can be covered in this section is how to relate to the customer. Of course, this is especially important to retail establishments or service establishments, but it can be important to manufacturing establishments as well.

Most companies emphasize that such customer comments or complaints be directed to the manager or person in charge for appropriate action. In most instances, the employee should not try to handle the situation alone. Let the employee know that the company wants those individuals with the necessary training and job responsibility to handle customer comments, complaints, or requests.

Customer relations issues may be specific to a business. One restaurant states the following:

Courtesy and Service

It is imperative to the success of any restaurant that all employees have a friendly, courteous, and helpful attitude. Customers evaluate a restaurant by the way they are treated, the way the employees act, and the impression they leave with the customer.

Hostesses and waitresses must be friendly, courteous, and helpful. This can be shown by smiling and greeting our customers. You, for the moment, represent the restaurant as far as the customer is concerned. Your actions and your attitude toward them can bring them back again and again, or can quickly turn them against you and us.

In addition, it has been our experience that a smiling face will definitely be reflected in the size of the tip.

A financial institution expressed it this way:

> Each of us represents the Bank. The way we do our jobs gives the customer and potential customers an image of our entire organization. These people judge all of us by how they are treated with every contact with any one of us. Therefore, our first priority always is to assist any customer or potential customer. To this end, our appearance, our dress, our physical fitness, the letters we write, and our manners on the telephone are a reflection not only of ourselves, but also of the professionalism of the Bank.

A medical clinic expressed its concerns this way:

What Our Patients Expect from Us

> Nothing is more important than every member of the staff being courteous, friendly, helpful, and prompt in their attention accorded to patients and their relatives. If at times their demands seem unreasonable, remember they are ill or worried and are undergoing an experience that may be most trying. What is involved may seem like a little thing to you, but to them it is of vital concern at the moment. Patients are individuals who need your help and the help of all the people on the staff. By doing your best for them, you will reflect credit on yourself and the Clinic. Cheerfulness, friendliness, politeness, and tactfulness are personality traits that are important. The effect of these qualities on the patient's morale will be remarkable. The key to high "personality ratings" is consideration, human kindness, and sympathy for the people you meet every day. Try to view yourself from the patients' side of the waiting room. This also applies to your dealings with your fellow employees. A good attitude toward your job shows itself in accomplishments.

Expressing the Company's Attitude Toward Unions

If the company is non-union and intends to remain that way, one of the most important preventive steps to take is to help employees understand its position, which can legally be done in the employee handbook. To some employers, this seems very controversial. The attitude is that the mere mention of a union may bring forward thoughts about unions among the employees. Some companies feel that by mentioning unions and unionization, they will create controversy within their own numbers and bring those employees who believe that a union would be good for the company to the forefront. However, my experience is the opposite. Letting employees know that although the decision to designate a union as their exclusive bargaining representative is strictly their own, doing so is contrary to the business interest of the employer in its opinion. If this is the case, then it is better the employees know upfront. Also, it may be best to mention the subject when there is no union organizing drive going on, because during such a drive, all company statements are subject to the organizer's rebuttal of "Why does the company fight the union if it wouldn't be good for the employees."

Lastly, by letting employees know on the first day of employment the company's attitude toward unions, one will hopefully be sensitizing the uncommitted or impartial employees who have had no experience with unions to form an opinion of whether a union would be good or even necessary at their place of employment. Accordingly, if a union organizer or co-employee at some time in the future begins circulating union authorization cards to employees, some may remember the company's opinion about unions as expressed on the first day of employment. They may be sensitive to the fact that signing a union card is something the company would not like them to do. They may be more open to the company's viewpoint as to why a union may not necessarily be beneficial to them and thus may be less likely to sign a union card.

Some companies decide that they do not want to play up the union aspect in the employee handbook. In this case, sometimes companies can merely include in the introduction a short paragraph such as the following:

> We believe our company can operate best without a union because it is our policy to have honest and open two-way communication with our people. We do not feel a need for an outside third party telling any of us what we should or should not do.

Standing alone, that may sound like a strong statement. However, included as part of the introduction, it can get the point across without overemphasizing it.

Other companies, however, wish to be more aggressive in dealing with this subject. Often, these are companies that have already successfully defended themselves against a union organizing drive. One such company states the following in its employee handbook:

The Company's Attitude Toward Unions

> It is the policy of the company to deal directly with our employees, rather than through an outside third party who may know little or nothing about our business. We believe that the best interests of our employees are served through management practices, fair treatment, and positive employee relations.

We recognize, however, that occasionally challenges may arise, but we firmly believe that in maintaining good, honest communication with our employees, we can resolve such problems in a mutually satisfactory manner. We feel that if you have an opportunity to express your problems, suggestions, and comments to us directly, which we encourage you to do, we do not need a union's help. In return, we promise to listen and to do our best to give you a responsible reply.

We accept the responsibility to resolve problems through open, honest, and frank communication and fair and honest treatment. We believe that the prompt attention to ideas and challenges is part of our responsibility as managers of the company.

Employees have the right to join and belong to a union. Employees also have the right not to belong to a union. It is our firm commitment that it is not necessary for any employee to become a member of a union or be required to pay union dues in order to receive fair and equitable treatment at our company.

Our employees receive competitive wages and benefits, and have received these without having to pay anyone union initiation fees, monthly dues, possible assessments, and possible union fines. It is our desire to continue to pay competitive wages and benefits to our employees, without their having to give anything to a union. Therefore, should a union organizer approach you to sign a union authorization card, please understand that you have the right not to sign any such card.

We recognize that no organization is free from day-to-day problems, but we believe that we have the policies and practices to help resolve problems, rather than fight one another like adversaries.

We want to keep, as much as possible, our company free from the often artificially created tensions that may be brought upon by the intervention of outsiders, such as a union. In our opinion, a union is of no advantage to any of us and could potentially hurt the business upon which we all depend for our livelihood.

There may be other situations when proclaiming the employer's opinion concerning union representation is important. For example, in a merger/acquisition situation, the new buyer has the opportunity to communicate with its employees how it feels about the employee's choice concerning unionization. This is what one acquiring company chose to say to its new employees on the subject of unionization in its employee handbook:

We accept the responsibility to resolve problems through open, honest, and frank communication and fair and honest treatment. We believe that the prompt attention to ideas and challenges is part of our responsibility as managers of the company.

Employees have the right to join and belong to a union. Employees also have the right not to belong to a union. It is our firm belief that it is not necessary for any employee to become a union member or remain a union member in order to receive fair and equitable treatment.

It is our desire to pay competitive wages and benefits in order to attract and retain our most valuable asset—a loyal and enthusiastic employee.

If you choose to be a union member, we respect your right to do so. If you choose not to be a union member, we respect your right to do that too.

Because the union that existed at the predecessor of this Company had a contract with it requiring all members to be union members after thirty (30) days of employment, and because labor relations law presumes that all union members wish to remain union members of this union, the Company is required by law to recognize the former union as the exclusive representative of production and maintenance employees for the purposes of collective bargaining.

However, because this former contract is no longer in effect and is not being adopted by the Company, the former contract no longer applies. Because the former contract no longer applies, neither does the former contract clause requiring every employee to become and remain a union member after 30 days of employment in order to hold their job at the Company.

Unless this changes by the negotiation and agreement between the Company and union in a future collective bargaining agreement, ALL PRODUCTION AND MAINTENANCE EMPLOYEES WILL HAVE A CHOICE TO EITHER BE A UNION MEMBER OR NOT BE A UNION MEMBER.

Section Two: What the Company Expects from Employees

The second section of the employee handbook should cover the company's policies on equal employment opportunity, the trial and training (probationary) period, physical exams, attendance and punctuality, drug and alcohol abuse, work rules, safety, and other general employees policies. All of these topics are discussed in detail below.

Equal Employment Opportunity Policy

It is important to establish to employees, and as an affirmative defense where necessary, that the company's commitment to equal employment opportunity in its hiring, firing, promoting, and all other employment-related decision-making is a function of company policy and not mere rhetoric. As with all other important policies, the perfect place to communicate this is in the employee handbook. It can be listed in the second section as "What the Company Expects of Its Employees."

While it is important to state company EEO policy in the employee handbook, given the changing nature of employment laws and court rulings concerning them, it is a mistake to become too detailed in the wording of such a clause. For example, many states list a far greater number of protected classes of employees than are covered under federal law. In addition, many municipalities exceed the regulations and laws promulgated by individual states. For example, in its Municipal Code, the city of Madison, Wisconsin embraces 17 different protected classes under its equal employment opportunity regulations. Accordingly, in reviewing and auditing employee handbooks, an almost universal mistake is that any comprehensive listing of all the protected classes is invariably wrong because it either states one that is not protected or, more likely, leaves a protected class out. The response to this is to be very simple in the wording of the equal employment opportunity clause. One such company worded its clause as follows.

Sample Equal Employment Opportunity Policy

XYZ Co., Inc., is an Equal Employment Opportunity employer. It is our policy to provide equal employment opportunity to all qualified persons, consistent with federal, state, and municipal equal employment opportunity law.

This policy shall apply to all phases of the employment relationship, including the hiring, upgrading, promoting, transferring, laying off, terminating, compensating, and recruiting of personnel.

Moreover, the Company supports the equal right of all employees to work in an environment free from harassment because of an employee's membership in any class protected by Equal Employment Opportunity law. In particular, unwelcome sexual advances, requests for sexual favors, and other verbal or physical conduct of a sexual nature are serious violations of our policy and will not be condoned or permitted.

> Any employee found to have acted in violation of the foregoing policy shall be subject to appropriate corrective disciplinary action, up to and including discharge from employment.
>
> All complaints of discrimination or harassment in violation of our equal employment opportunity policy should be directed to any member of management. Management has the full responsibility to receive and investigate complaints involving violations of this policy as confidentially as practicable.

Included in this equal employment opportunity policy is a prohibition against *harassment* based upon membership in any protected class and, in particular, sexual harassment.

This concept became important when the U.S. Supreme Court held that the creation of a hostile sexual atmosphere or the allowing of same to exist after complaints is the equivalent of sex discrimination in violation of Title VII of the Civil Rights Law. In recent decisions, this concept has been expanded to include harassment because of membership in any class protected by the Civil Rights Law, such as race, religion, national origin, etc.

Complaints of such harassment may be investigated and prosecuted by both state and federal equal rights agencies. Employers can be held responsible for the acts of their agents and supervisor employees with respect to this kind of harassment regardless of whether the specific acts complained about were authorized or even forbidden by the employer, and regardless of whether the employer knew or should have known of their occurrence.

With respect to conduct between fellow employees, employers can be held responsible for acts of harassment in the workplace where the employer, or its agents or supervisory employees, knew or should have known of the conduct, unless it can be shown that the employer took immediate and corrective action to stop it once it became aware of such conduct.

A further troubling aspect to employers is the concept that such claims can be filed by a *class* of employees, in addition to just a single employee.

Defining harassment or the creation of a hostile environment is difficult. However, relative to sexual harassment, about which there has been more litigation to help define it, it is clear that unwelcome sexual advances, requests for sexual favors, and other verbal or physical conduct of a sexual nature may be considered harassment when:

- Submission to such conduct is made either explicitly or implicitly a term or condition of the individual's employment;

- Submission to or rejection of such conduct by an individual is used as a basis for employment decisions affecting such individual; or

- Such conduct has the purpose or effect of unreasonably interfering with an individual's work performance or creating an intimidating, hostile, or offensive working environment.

It is important to remember that an employer's potential liability is not limited to harassing actions committed solely by a management employee. Employers can also be subject to claims if one employee sexually harasses another, or even in certain situations if the harassment is done by a third party, such as a customer. The same is true for harassment due to an employee's membership in any other protected class. It is important to have a procedure in place to deal with these situations; merely having a general policy may not be enough to satisfy the courts. In one case, for example, an employer had an established grievance procedure, but the plaintiff testified that she was afraid she would lose her job if she used it. Therefore, the court found that the policy was ineffective. The fatal flaw identified by the court was the fact that the plaintiff would have had to take her complaint to the manager who was harassing her pursuant to the chain of command listed in the complaint procedure. Moreover, several courts have commented that the lack of a harassment policy and complaint procedure may in and of itself be evidence of employer liability. See Chapter Nine for a more complete analysis.

Trial and Training Period Policy

Many employers think that it is important to have a probationary period for new employees. Probationary periods are a longstanding method used to evaluate new employees and are used most often in a union environment. In the union environment, passing probation carries with it special status; the employee will be eligible to become a member of the union and, therefore, less easily discharged by an employer who must show a just cause reason for any discharge. The idea is that employees are more easily discharged during their probationary period than after they have passed it. However, this consideration need not be present in the non-union environment.

By making a probationary category applicable to the review and evaluation of employees in the non-union environment, it will be easier to discharge an employee who does not pass scrutiny for the first month or few months of employment. Many courts have looked at this, as discussed in Chapter One, and have concluded that in the non-union situation a probationary period can be used against employers to show that the employee has a greater expectation of continued employment after passing a probationary period. It can be an example of where the employer has, on its own, promised expectations to the employee of other than at-will status upon the successful passing of probation. In light of that interpretation, the establishment of a probationary period in a non-union environment can actually reduce the employer's rights to discharge an employee. Accordingly, many commentators suggest that a probationary period be deleted in its entirety because it unnecessarily restricts the employer's ability to discharge an employee once that probationary period is passed. Moreover, such a convention does nothing to enhance the employer's power, but actually reduces it.

However, for many non-union employers, the purpose of this "get-acquainted period" or "training period" is to afford both the company and the employee a period of time to evaluate the other. Not every job is going to be good for every particular employee. Accordingly, the relationship should be severed by either party if it does not meet needs relative to the job to be done or the compensation and other benefits the employee hopes to receive. Severing the relationship is best accomplished early in employment rather than later. One company used the following in its employee handbook to establish such a policy.

Sample Trial and Training Period Policy

All new employees enter a trial and training period of 90 days upon employment. This period is intended to allow you and your supervisor to learn how well you are suited for employment at our company. During this period, every effort is made to give you an opportunity to succeed. If any questions arise, please talk to your supervisor. Reviews will be scheduled with your supervisor to discuss your progress during this 90-day period. It should be understood, however, that it is your responsibility as an employee to establish good attendance, satisfactory work performance, and complete compliance with all policies. At the conclusion of this period, which may be extended if warranted, you will be eligible for company health insurance and will receive an increase in the hourly wage consistent with your supervisor's recommendation.

It is wrong to assume that including a probationary period will give the company more of a free hand in discharging employees during the period than after it. While this may be true in the union environment, in the non-union environment with an at-will employee, promising some other standard for discharge upon completion of the probationary period may result in a determination that the company's power to discharge an employee is limited by its own policies after the successful completion of such a period by the employee. To avoid this result, do not promise regular employee status or any other special status upon successful completion of the probationary period. Promise instead to increase the employee's wages or begin eligibility for fringe benefits. Remember, employers want to make certain that its policies do not limit its power to terminate employees for any reason. In fact, an all too common experience is the reverse: the employee stays on his best behavior to successfully complete probation, and then performance slides after attainment of a more secure status. Another problem occurs when an employee's once-steady performance changes because of other factors. When this happens, the wise employer should not voluntarily restrict its power to discipline or discharge the offending employee.

Physical Examinations

There are some who believe that it is appropriate to put in the employee handbook certain pre-employment matters. The requirement of physical exams, however, also extends to the scope of time after an employee is hired. It is an area worth mentioning not only to explain to the employee that the company retains the right to require physical examinations at management's discretion in determining compliance with alcohol and drug abuse policies, but also because such exams may be necessary to determine an employee's fitness to work. Of course, in a union environment, such policies would require negotiation with the employee's representative.

There are many who advocate that all offers of employment should be conditional upon the successful passing of a physical exam, whose primary purpose is to establish a baseline for preventing workers' compensation claims of work-related aggravation of an existing or pre-existing condition. Just as an insurance company will routinely require a physical exam, including blood testing, of any applicant for life insurance policies, an employer should do the same or at least retain the discretion to do so within its managerial rights. Of course, in the union situation, such post-employment rights are a subject of mandatory bargaining where any new policy may be a change from past practice.

When drafting such policies, it must be kept in mind that relative to employment discrimination, physical fitness standards must be applied only as reasonably necessary for the specific work to be performed. Also, relative to federal contract compliance for federal contractors, affirmative action regulations require that government contractors under both the Vietnam Veterans' and Rehabilitation Acts do not discriminate in regard to physical exams. The requirements are that all physical and mental requirements shall be reviewed and be limited to the specific job, and the result of any medical examination shall be kept confidential except as is necessary to inform supervisors regarding work restrictions or safety and health personnel regarding possible emergency treatment.

Disability discrimination issues are complex. Employers should avoid asking applicants general questions about the existence of any disabilities or health conditions. The same is true for existing employees. Questions that are too broad could lead to later charges of discrimination violating the Americans with Disabilities Act.

However, many employers find it advantageous to remind employees that they may be asked to take a physical examination. This is particularly important after a workers' compensation injury that requires time off from work to recover. On many occasions, the employer may require its own physical examination to help it defend against allegations that an injury was really a workers' compensation injury or that the injury aggravated a pre-existing condition. Many employers also will require a blood or alcohol test immediately following any lost-time accident. It is advisable to mention this requirement upfront in the employee handbook.

One company stated the following as its policy.

Sample Physical Examinations and Testing Policy

As a part of the employment process, you may be required, at the company's expense, to successfully complete a physical examination. This is for your protection as well as the company's protection.

After you are hired, you may also be asked to take a physical exam, conducted by a company-appointed physician, if a question regarding your health arises. Truck drivers will be required to take a driver physical every two (2) years as required by the Department of Transportation. Occasionally, job-related tests are given to help determine suitability for a particular job or promotion. Management also retains the right at its discretion to test for compliance with our drug and alcohol policy.

Attendance and Punctuality Policy

An attendance and punctuality policy emphasizes the importance of attendance and prompt reporting for work. Most employers tell their employees that they are expected to be at their workstations, ready to work, at the beginning of their work shift. If employees are unable to report for work because of illness or other reasons, or if they will be tardy, they should be aware that it is their obligation to inform the employer before the start of the work shift so appropriate scheduling arrangements can be made.

One company used the following language to emphasize its policy and the importance of attendance.

Sample Attendance Policy

The operation of a manufacturing plant such as ours requires employees to be on duty regularly to perform the work assigned. When employees are absent, jobs have to be reshuffled, machines may be left idled, and our customers may have to suffer for it. This can result in the loss of orders, the loss of customers, and eventually the loss of jobs. Excessive absenteeism will subject an employee to corrective disciplinary action up to and including discharge. When absence is due to illness, employees may be asked to present proof in the form of a Physician's Certificate or statement of treatment. Being absent without leave is considered a serious offense. Any employee who has remained absent for a period of sixteen (16) working hours or more without notifying the company will be subject to immediate discharge.

To emphasize the importance of punctuality, one company used the following language.

Sample Punctuality Policy

All employees are expected to be at their place of work and ready to work at their scheduled starting times and are expected to work until their scheduled quitting times. Excessive tardiness is not acceptable and may result in loss of pay and corrective action up to and including discharge.

There are, it seems, as many different policies as there are different business operations. What is required by one type of business may not be needed by another. Where attendance and tardiness on the part of the employees are not a constant challenge to the supervisor, in fact, no formal policy may be needed. However, if employers do not have a minimum 90 to 95 percent average employee attendance, an attendance policy may be a good strategy.

In order to control absenteeism and monitor attendance in the workplace, companies may use a dual approach to positively modify the undesirable attendance behavior of their employees. To encourage the employee's commitment to be present and on time on a regular basis, companies can reward good attendance through bonus systems and use corrective progressive discipline pursuant to a tightly constructed policy. For employers with attendance problems who are looking for policies to use in their employee handbooks, the sample attendance bonus program and attendance policy that follows may be adaptable for use in such situations.

Sample Attendance Bonus Policy

CHAPTER TWO

Good attendance is an absolute must for a company to produce a quality product efficiently, sell it at a competitive price, and meet the customers' requested delivery dates. Every employee is an integral element in meeting the requirements of our customers. By not keeping our customers satisfied, we jeopardize XYZ Company's future and our jobs. The key ingredient of any successful company is the people who work there. For these people who consistently put forward that extra effort to get to work on time and maintain a good attendance record, XYZ Company will reward them through a unique type of bonus program.

The particulars of the program are as follows:

Each bonus period will consist of four (4) three- (3-) month periods per year: January, February, March; April, May, June; July, August, September; October, November, December.

Bonuses for perfect attendance will be paid at the end of each month, and the reward will be larger for qualifying in consecutive months ($10 for the first month, $20 for the second month, $40 for the third month).

Examples:

1. Sam qualifies for each of the three months in the first quarter. He would receive $10 for January, $20 for February, and $40 for March.

2. Audrey qualifies for the first and third months of the second period. She would receive $10 for April, $0 for May, and $10 for June.

3. George qualifies for the second and third months of the third quarter. He would receive $0 for July, $10 for August, and $20 for September.

These rules for qualifying are simple and easy to understand:

You will be allowed one point per calendar month.

Each workday will be divided into two (2) half-days (from beginning of shift to lunchtime, and from beginning of work after lunch to quitting time).

One point will be assessed for missing any part of a half-day (from being one minute late to missing the whole half-day).

> There will be no exceptions (you are either present or absent, late or on time) with the exclusion of scheduled vacations or for the treatment of an industrial accident (at the time of injury only).

> You must be scheduled to work for the entire month to be eligible for the attendance bonus.

Some companies prefer to be more specific than others with their attendance policies. This may be particularly important to union operations, which must be able to justify attendance-based discharges as just cause for discharge to arbitrators. It is good practice to leave as much discretion in the hands of the immediate supervisor as possible. A good supervisor should know in his or her "gut" when an employee's attendance is abusive to the company and his or her coworkers. In such instances, exercising the right to ask the employee for a medical excuse sends the employee a strong message that the supervisor is *on* to him or her. In the case of attendance abuse, following a standard set of corrective disciplinary responses such as a word of casual advice, a first warning, a "job in jeopardy" warning, and then a discharge will be sufficient. The employer must be sure that supervisors are adequately trained in order to be generally consistent with one another in the application of their discretionary corrective discipline. However, most arbitrators will give sufficient leeway if the disparity between one supervisor's generosity and another's is not so great that the employee would not be appropriately *on notice* when attendance was putting his or her job in jeopardy.

Some companies, however, prefer a more structured attendance policy. In some cases this is because their own supervisors are afraid of having discretion. Such supervisors would rather merely apply company standards, and not get involved individually with problem workers. In these situations, some companies employ a no-fault attendance policy. This means that the company will not take into consideration the reason for an employee's absence; it will instead merely allow what it considers an appropriate amount of absences, and then terminate employees no matter what the reason if their absences exceed this amount.

Companies, particularly unionized companies, should understand that there is a potential downside to no-fault policies. It is more difficult to have attendance discharges upheld by arbitrators or found by unemployment compensation administrative law judges as misconduct connected with employment such that the employee would be ineligible for benefits. However, these objections notwithstanding, attendance policies are fairly easy to administer. If a policy is cut and dried, companies are less exposed to allegations of favoritism or abuse of discretion. Unfortunately, by not accounting for the excuse given by an employee, they may also

CHAPTER TWO

lose otherwise good employees because of the strictness with which no-fault policies are administered.

An example of a more structured policy follows.

Sample No-Fault Attendance Disciplining Policy

It is expected that people will be at work on time. Individuals not reporting to work on time must telephone and report the absence or tardiness before the start of their shift.

Employees who leave work during the day must notify a supervisor of their reason for leaving. Employees who punch out for lunch and do not return to work must call in and state their reason for not coming back to work.

Failure to notify XYZ Company of absence or tardiness before the start of the shift will result in corrective progressive discipline as follows:

1. First time in a twelve (12) month period—counseling meeting (first warning).

2. Second time in a twelve (12) month period—written warning and counseling.

3. Third time in a twelve (12) month period—termination.

Absences of three (3) consecutive workdays without contact from an employee will result in automatic termination of the employee.

To return to work from a medical (including industrial) leave of absence, the employee must bring in a medical release from the doctor to XYZ Company on the day prior to the return date for approval.

The doctor's explanation must cover all days that the employee was absent from work and state that the employee was unable to work during the time absent from work.

Failure to comply with these requirements may result in the employee being sent back to the doctor for proper release and time charged as per the attendance policy described below.

Tardiness is defined as not being at the scheduled place ready to work at the scheduled time. Tardiness can occur when reporting to work after the start of the shift or for being late returning to work from break or lunch. Pay may be deducted for tardiness.

Counseling and warning notices will be considered in progressive discipline for one (1) year from the date of the occurrence of the failure to call in, tardiness, or absence.

Absences which total more than seventy-two (72) hours of time off in any one-year period will result in termination.

Eight (8) incidences of tardiness in any one (1) year will result in termination.

Time off for the following will not be included in the consideration of corrective discipline as defined above:

1. Authorized leave of absence (personal or medical);

2. Jury duty;

3. Vacation and holidays;

4. Bereavement leave;

5. Authorized union business;

6. Industrial injuries;

7. Layoff for lack of work or disciplinary suspension from work; or

8. Medical leaves of absence granted pursuant to the company's Family and Medical Leave Act Policy or of at least five (5) working days, unless the person is admitted to the health care provider for procedures such as outpatient surgery and pre-admission testing.

Administration of the absence/tardiness policy will be as follows:

1. Consultation meeting between the supervisor and the employee after twenty-four (24) hours of absence, and/or three (3) tardies.

2. Written warning to the employee when total time off equals forty-eight (48) hours and/or four (4) tardies.

3. A two (2) day suspension from work when the total time off equals sixty-four (64) hours and/or six (6) tardies.

4. Termination of the employee when total time off equals or exceeds seventy-two (72) hours of absence and/or eight (8) tardies.

Doctor and dentist appointments will be included in the seventy-two (72) hours of absence time pursuant to the above, unless such absence is for authorized medical leave.

If a person agrees to work voluntary overtime, or is assigned mandatory overtime, the same absence/tardy policy applies.

Tardiness occurrences and absence hours will be charged against the employee in the following manner:

1. Not being prepared to work at the scheduled starting time or arriving up to one (1) hour late for the scheduled work day will be charged as one (1) tardiness occurrence. An individual arriving more than one (1) hour late will be charged for a tardiness occurrence for the first hour, with time over one (1) hour late being charged as absence time.

2. Leaving work after punching in prior to normal quitting time or arriving one (1) or more hours after the scheduled starting time will be charged against absence time, as stated above. Missing the entire day or days not defined as excused in Item G will be charged as absence time for the number of hours the individual was scheduled to work that day.

Remember, there are as many different ways to approach absenteeism as there are management attorneys and management consultants. Some believe that the best method is to merely state that attendance at work is important and to leave the enforcement of that policy to the discretion of the supervisor.

Drug and Alcohol Abuse Policy

Within their work rules, some companies list one similar to the following:

Possession or use of intoxicating beverages, unauthorized medical drugs, and controlled substances on company property or use of such substances in a manner which affects work will subject an employee to corrective discipline up to and including discharge.

Note that the rule is broadly written. It precludes not only mere possession on company property of such substances, but also possession or use in a manner which affects work such that abuse of substances away from the workplace still can be actionable by the company against the employee.

Although employers generally are not trying to police their employees, it is important to notify employees that the company may, at its discretion, rigidly enforce such policies. If this represents a change in corporate policy or such new attention to an existing policy represents a change, then this should be communicated to the employees in written form and through company meetings. Sometimes, a plant "safety committee" is the perfect vehicle through which to communicate with employees.

Moreover, some companies like to add specific policies to the employee handbook for emphasis. What follows is a sample of what one company chose to write.

Sample Alcohol and Drug Policy

Pursuant to our work rules, every employee should know that any employee possessing or using intoxicating beverages or illegal drugs at work or in a manner which affects work will be subject to discipline, up to and including discharge. This includes any such substances found in lockers or in employees' automobiles on company premises. Given the nature of our work, which requires safety at all times, there are no exceptions to these policies.

If you have an alcohol or drug abuse problem, you must understand that the company does not discriminate against such individuals. In fact, the company will help employees who admit to such a problem by referring them to the appropriate clinics and giving them leaves of absence to attend these clinics.

Because the safety of our employees is of utmost concern at XYZ Company, we cannot tolerate any employee conduct that may harm our ability to work safely and sanely. If you have a personal problem and need help in addressing it, see the management at once, and we will confidentially help you resolve it.

Please be advised that XYZ Company retains the right, at its discretion, to ask employees to take blood or other tests to determine compliance with our alcohol and drug policy. In addition, the company may inspect employee lockers and automobiles located on company premises to determine compliance with our alcohol and drug policy. Failure to submit to such tests or inspections may be considered insubordination and lead to corrective discipline, up to and including discharge.

Some companies believe that they first must have "probable cause," similar to a police officer enforcing criminal violations, before asking an employee to submit to tests or inspections. This is not so; such constitutional rights do not apply to private companies, but only to public law enforcement activities and governmental employers in the public sector. However, be advised that if an employee refuses to submit to the same, a private citizen cannot force an employee through bodily persuasion to submit to such requests. An employer may punish the refusal to submit to such tests by discipline up to and including discharge for insubordination.

Work Rules

The employer has the right to establish reasonable work rules in both union and non-union situations. Although, in a union setting, any change in existing work rules would be a change in wages, hours, and working conditions. Therefore, absent a waiver from the union, such new work rules might have to be negotiated with the union pursuant to an employer's duty to bargain under the National Labor Relations Act. In the non-union environment, establishing reasonable work rules also is imperative in establishing legitimate business reasons for discharge so that the employer will be able to defend such decision-making if and when necessary.

In establishing disciplinary rules, it is very important to avoid making such rules inflexible. When rigid rules are set, if one step in the disciplinary progression is missed, problems can ensue. It can be argued that the employee has been, by implication, promised to be given multiple progressive disciplinary steps before discharge, such as a first warning, second warning, and traditional suspension from work prior to discharge. This implied promise may impose a limit on the employer's power if the employee's behavior becomes so serious that the employer wants to skip steps in the discharge process. Employers must determine how general rules need to be to avoid being limited to certain areas of misconduct in order to discharge. At the same time, they must determine how specific rules need to be so that it can be argued that the employee knew or should have known that the behavior jeopardized or would jeopardize the employer's business or operation.

Most employee discharge situations involve either a continuing disregard for the employer's rules and regulations, which culminates in an incident that cannot be ignored, or a single serious harmful or potentially harmful incident. The single serious incident should be so obvious to the employee that any reasonable person would know that such behavior is contrary to the employer's rightful interests. Given the conflicting management philosophies regarding work rules, a happy medium would allow the employer to communicate to its employees the kind of behavior it expects without limiting its power to discharge for behavior that would be impossible to foresee at the time of the writing of a handbook.

Employer policies are also affected by the nature of the business enterprise in which the employee handbook is going to be used. For example, there is a marked difference between a handbook appropriate for an accounting firm consisting mostly of white-collar exempt professionals and one for a manufacturer of light electronic components employing mostly hourly production employees. Policies found in these handbooks may be different than those found in a handbook for a semiskilled nursing health care facility employing both an hourly workforce and professional employees. In most cases, the more "professional" the operation, the less specific the rules need to be.

While no two businesses are alike, all employers may be judged in courts of law as to whether their handbooks are a "contract by implication" in any discharge action and whether in any such discharge action the company complied with its own internal policies. In addition, when drafting such policies, it is important to understand that generally, when one makes a list, one is legally deemed to have specifically excluded everything not on the list.

Remember that the purpose of work rules is to be used as a means to an end, not the end in itself. Employers want to get a good day's work from each employee and to avoid labor problems. It is to achieve these aims that an employer implements work rules in an employee handbook. Indeed, industrial psychological research is clear that employees expect fairness in the determination of whether they will be progressing to better jobs and higher earnings or will be terminated from employment. No employer sets up a business just to see how many one can hire or how well one can treat those hired. Unless work rules and their administration clearly contribute to productivity, quality, and service, they are a waste of time and should be avoided.

In a recent situation, with a small manufacturing firm, I recommended that because the workforce was so small in number that a short recitation of examples of the kinds of behavior that might cause discharge from employment might be better than the previous long list of rules. This generally gives the employer more discretion in the decision to discharge. However, the owner reminded me that although the theory being suggested might indeed provide the company with more flexibility, the unemployment insurance adjudicators still preferred seeing a list of work rules in the objection to a claim for benefits that the claimant had violated as opposed to analyzing whether or not the employee's behavior that led to the discharge violated the employer's legitimate business interest. It is a question of balance that the business owner must decide. However, it is not necessarily required that there *must* be a written rule specific to every employee violation for misconduct to win a denial of unemployment insurance claims or be a defense in general to any other employment law claim. The real test is an objective test: Would a reasonable employee know that his or her behavior was likely to cause harm to the employer's business or property?

Sample Work Rules (Long Form)

There are certain standards of behavior that all employees are expected to observe, which we refer to as work rules. These are intended for the protection and welfare of each and every employee and are also necessary for the company to conduct its daily business in a consistent and orderly manner.

A partial listing of these rules has been outlined below. Each of these has been carefully considered and will be uniformly and fairly enforced.

Violation of these standards may, at the company's discretion, subject an employee to progressive disciplinary action or immediate discharge from employment consistent with the company's right to discharge at will.

There are two general classifications of violations of these work rules: major and minor. A major violation will result in serious disciplinary action up to and including termination.

The following rules fall in the major classification:

1. Stealing, including tampering with or using slugs in vending machines;

2. Disobedience or insubordination, refusal to perform an assigned job;

3. Willful destruction or defacing of company property or tampering with equipment for which you are not authorized (including restrooms);

4. Absence of two consecutive days without notifying the company;

5. Verbal threatening or inflicting of bodily injury to another person;

6. Alteration of time cards, including punching another employee's time card;

7. Possession or use of intoxicating beverages or illegal drugs on company property, or use of such substances in a manner which affects work;

8. Possession of weapons in the plant;

9. Illicit and immoral acts that interfere with company operations;

10. Falsifying records, including application for employment;

11. Leaving the company premises during working hours without permission;

12. Willful or reckless negligence that can result in a safety hazard;

13. Violation of the no-solicitation rule;

14. Gambling on company premises; and

15. Restricting output or encouraging others to do so.

The second classification is minor violations. Any work rule violation in this category may result in the following disciplinary action:

A. First offense: Verbal warning and counseling.

B. Second offense: Written warning and counseling.

C. Third offense: One (1) day suspension without pay.

D. Fourth offense: Subject to termination.

Rules falling in this classification are the following:

1. Shirking work or leaving assigned work areas to avoid work;

2. Washing up or leaving work station before allowed time at end of shift;

3. Doing work for personal benefit on company time or equipment without permission;

4. Repeated negligence resulting in excessive scrap, inferior work, the breaking of tools, or wasting of supplies;

5. False statements about other employees;

6. Use of abusive language toward another employee or visitor;

7. Contributing to unsanitary or unsafe conditions;

8. Violation of published safety rules or engaging repeatedly in unsafe acts on company property;

9. Horseplay, such as wrestling or playing practical jokes;

10. Violation of policy pertaining to absenteeism;

11. Failure to notify the company during the first day of absence;

12. Displaying an uncooperative attitude;

13. Permitting visitors in the plant, at any time, without the permission of the management;

14. Smoking in restrooms; or

15. The playing of personal radios in the manufacturing area (including headsets).

In the health care setting, a long-term care nursing facility used the following long list of work rules:

1. Patient or resident abuse; behaving in an abusive manner toward patients and residents. Patient or resident abuse may include physical and verbal abuse, as well as any action that causes fear or intimidation of a patient or resident.

2. Withholding information from Administration that involves knowledge or observation of patient or resident abuse.

3. Insubordination; willful failure to carry out the orders of a supervisor.

4. Abandoning assignment during working hours.

5. Disorderly conduct; disrupting or contributing to the disruption of the workforce.

6. Inflicting harm on any person or damage to the facility property.

7. Theft of property belonging to a resident, visitor, another employee, or the facility.

8. Appearing for work or being at work in a condition not conducive to performing the assigned work activities.

9. Substance abuse or intoxication while on facility premises.

10. Unauthorized possession or distribution of intoxicants or drugs at any time. This may include but is not limited to alcohol; narcotics; hypnotics; barbiturates; amphetamines; legal, illegal, or controlled substances.

11. Threatening a resident, visitor, or another employee.

12. Fighting or like inappropriate behavior.

13. Possession of a weapon on the facility premises.

14. Sleeping or giving the appearance of sleeping during work hours.

15. Engaging in an immoral, indecent, or illegal activity on the facility premises.

16. Requesting sexual favors or other verbal or physical conduct of a sexual nature, or making unwelcome sexual advances towards coworkers or visitors.

17. Falsifying records or giving false information to any facility representative.

18. Misuse of confidential information.

19. Obtaining employment, promotion, or benefits under false pretenses.

20. Punching of another employee's time badge or altering your own or another's timecard.

21. Punching in earlier than scheduled or punching out later than scheduled.

22. Receiving visitors (families or friends) on the facility's property during scheduled work hours.

23. Eating or drinking in unauthorized areas, except where special permission has been given by the supervisor.

24. Being in the facility in unauthorized areas when not on duty without authorization of the supervisor.

25. Leaving your regularly assigned work location without notifying your immediate supervisor.

26. Failure to comply with the facility dress code.

27. Unauthorized use of a resident's or the facility's telephones. Use of the facility phone for personal incoming or outgoing calls.

28. Failure to clean up the area where snack or lunch foods were eaten.

29. Use of profane or abusive language in resident areas.

30. Leaving the facility's premises during a paid break period without following proper procedures.

31. Failure to work as scheduled after a layoff, vacation, or holiday.

32. Drinking or eating any resident food at any time.

33. Circulating false or malicious rumors.

34. Failure to attend mandatory, in-service, or staff meetings without prior approval of your supervisor.

35. Careless or inefficient performance of duties, including failure, inability, or lack of effort to maintain proper standards of performance.

36. Failure to report an accident or injury immediately to a supervisor; falsifying information regarding a work-related injury.

37. Failure to comply with safety and/or sanitary regulations, rules, and conditions.

38. Smoking in unauthorized areas.

39. Failure to follow care plans which results in injury or illness to an employee or resident.

40. Soliciting or distributing written material in patient care areas.

41. Failure to return to work after a disciplinary action.

42. Failure to comply with established written facility policy and procedures.

43. Posting literature on bulletin boards or elsewhere without approval.

44. Defacing bulletin boards or approved posted notices.

45. Failure to adhere to instructed procedures for lifting, transferring, and/or moving residents.

46. Negligence which results in or could result in harm to a resident or employee.

47. Violation of facility computer policies.

48. Any conduct, behavior, or action deemed by management as detrimental to the facility, its residents, or staff.

The facility's corrective action program is designed to encourage individuals to become satisfactory employees rather than punish them. Corrective action may take the form of an oral warning, a written warning, and/or termination. Management reserves all rights to immediately terminate an employee based upon an employee's unacceptable conduct.

The facility also reserves the right to add to, modify, amend, or eliminate any rule in the discretion of management at any time with or without notice.

The facility has the option of applying any level of discipline to the conduct engaged in by an employee as it deems appropriate. The facility in its discretion may decide to give a verbal warning, written warning, or suspension with or without pay prior to discharge, or go directly to discharge.

In the more professional setting, or for smaller employers, a shorter version of the work rules is often best; the longer the list of rules, the less meaningful each individual rule becomes. Also, given the sometimes unpredictable nature of people, there still may be behavior violations that do not exactly fit any of the rules, no matter how comprehensive the employer tries to be in drafting them.

Listed below is a sample of work rules used by an accounting firm. In this example, management makes no attempt to delineate every possible kind of improper behavior. That is part of its effectiveness. This way the individual act speaks for itself more loudly than the rule prohibiting it. However, administrative agencies seem to prefer a specified list, even though there is no actual legal requirement for establishing a specific rule being violated if the conduct in violation of the standards of behavior an employer has a right to expect should have been obvious to the employee. For example, the Ten Commandments do not have to be specifically recited in the employee handbook for there to be a finding of misconduct for violations of them that are connected with employment. Nonetheless, this short list of basic work rules covers a lot of ground. These basic work rules should put the employee on notice of the standards the employer expects, and has a right to expect.

Sample Work Rules (Short Form)

We try to be very careful to hire only those people we feel reasonably sure are qualified to do their work, are conscientious in the performance of that work, and who will be compatible with others already working here. However, we may make mistakes. If it turns out that we have hired someone who will not or cannot work satisfactorily or is not compatible, it may be necessary to terminate our employment relationship in order to keep our firm in a strong competitive position.

If your employment is terminated consistent with the corporation's right to discharge at will, whether any severance pay is given is at the discretion of the Board of Directors. Dishonesty, absenteeism, leaving work without notice, poor quality work, insubordination, and possession or use of intoxicating beverages, unauthorized medical drugs, or controlled substances at work or in a manner affecting work are examples of behavior that could lead to discipline up to and including discharge.

Safety Rules

Maintaining a safe and clean environment for work is a mandate for all businesses, but is especially imperative in light of the recent emphasis on safety by the federal government in environmental legislation, workers' compensation guarantees, and occupational safety and health mandates. Indeed, one must be very careful in drafting a safety rule, bearing in mind that it is a two-edged sword.

By having rules, employers admit that there are certain standards, in addition to federal standards, by which it expects its employees to operate. Sometimes this may make an employer hesitant to establish too many safety rules because of the myriad of unforeseeable situations that may arise when employees and supervisors, sometimes unknowingly, disregard safety regulations to get a job done. Employers, in defense of litigation regarding this subject, must have policies to show that their own rules were disregarded independently by the employee. The issue will then be if the employee was adequately informed as to the safety rules and regulations and if those same regulations were administered and enforced by the employer where necessary. In this regard, remember that not enforcing safety rules is worse than not having them at all.

Under the General Duty clause of the Occupational Safety and Health Act (OSHA), all employers must maintain a safe work environment. In addition, many states have safety provisions and penalties for violations of the employer's duty to furnish a safe environment. For example, one state statute reads as follows:

Wisconsin Safe Place Statute

101.11 Employer's duty to furnish safe employment and place. (1) Every employer shall furnish employment which shall be safe for the employees therein and for frequenters thereof and shall furnish and use safety devices and safeguards, and shall adopt and use methods and processes reasonably adequate to render such employment and places of employment safe, and shall do every other thing reasonably necessary to protect the life, health, safety and welfare of such employees and frequenters. Every employer and every owner of a place of employment or a public building now or hereafter constructed shall so construct, repair, or maintain such place of employment or public building as to render the same safe.

The statute goes on, but the idea is not difficult to understand. The employee handbook is the perfect place to express the employer's concern for safety. In fact, once the employee has been so informed and the employer has enforced its safety policies, the employer will have evidence that the employee was, or should have been, aware of the safety rules. In fact, in some states, the employer or its insurance carrier can avail itself of decreased penalties if any industrial, compensable workers' compensation injury can be shown to have been the fault of the employee. Although all safety rules are purely a function of each unique work environment, what follows is an example of what one company uses in its employee handbook to express its safety policy and basic safety rules. The key element in these policies is enforcement. These policies must be enforced, if violated, by corrective progressive discipline pursuant to the employer's discipline policies.

Sample Safety Policy TWO CHAPTER

XYZ Company is making every effort to provide you and your fellow workers with a safe and sanitary working environment. Your cooperation and participation is essential to our mutual accomplishment of a fully safe and accident-free job site. Safe working conditions and safe workers depend upon safety awareness and action by all employees at all times.

In addition, we maintain a Safety Committee, comprised of management and employee members who meet at regular intervals. Occasionally, you may be asked to serve on this Committee.

Failure to follow safety rules will subject an employee to corrective discipline according to the work rules.

Basic Safety Rules

A. General

1. Advise your supervisor of any potential safety hazards you may observe, no matter how minor.

2. All accidents and injuries, however slight, should be reported to your immediate supervisor.

3. No-smoking rules shall be strictly observed in all posted areas and in any area where common sense indicates there is a danger to employees, equipment, material, or building. (Smoking is allowed in the lunchroom and restrooms only.)

4. Food, soft drinks, coffee, etc., are permitted only in the lunchroom area.

5. Any employees taking prescribed medication must inform their supervisor prior to the start of their work shift.

6. Common sense health and sanitation rules must be observed for the welfare and consideration of all who earn their livelihood at the XYZ Company.

7. All work areas must be maintained in a safe, orderly, clean, and presentable condition at all times.

8. Conduct which would endanger you or another employee will not be tolerated.

B. Personal Items

    1. Proper work attire is required. Clothing that is loose flowing or contains loose sleeves, belts, ties, scarves, chains, or jewelry shall not be worn around operating machinery.

    2. Hair which is longer than collar length, or which if combed forward covers the eyes, must be secured to the head by means of a hairpin, hairnet, cap, or other device.

    3. Shoes that offer adequate protection are required to be worn by employees. All material handling employees must wear steel-toed safety shoes. No gym shoes or penny loafer shoes will be allowed.

    4. Ear protection must be worn in all noisy areas where required by OSHA regulation.

    5. Safety eyeglasses must be worn at all times in working areas of the plant.

    6. Gloves must be used when working with cleaning fluids or other caustic solutions.

    7. Any protective equipment suggested by any supervisor must be worn.

C. Running Machinery

    1. All machine guards must be used during production operation.

    2. Machines must be shut off before any attempt is made to clear up production problems.

    3. Always use the two (2) button concept, if available, on your machines; never defeat machine interlocks.

D. Material Handling

    1. Only one (1) person is allowed out on a forklift at a time.

CHAPTER TWO

2. Employees will not ride or pedal manual pallet lift trucks or hand trucks at any time.

3. To lift properly, use your legs and not your back. The back should be straight and almost vertical. Be sure to get help with heavy loads.

General Employee Policies

The following are several areas of general information about which employees should be informed.

Change of Status

Employees have an obligation to keep the company informed of any change in their personal situation, such as their current home address, marital status for purposes of benefit calculation, new dependents, etc. This can be important information if the need arises to communicate directly with employees by mail.

This is one policy statement that was used in an employee handbook in order to inform the employee of his obligation.

Sample Notice of Status Change Policy

Please keep the company informed of any change in marital or family status, such as marriage, divorce, separation, birth, death, etc. These changes could affect withholding, hospitalization, insurance, etc., and for your protection, we must keep company records up to date. It is important that we have your correct address and phone number in case of emergency. The company will not be held responsible for not having a correct current address and phone number for an employee.

Time Recording

The next subject of general information important to the employee is the method of time reporting. Where there is a time clock, it is important that employees know that they are required to use it and how it works. Where there is no time clock, employees should be instructed on the method of recording time, whatever it happens to be. Emphasis should also be made that honesty is of the utmost importance in reporting time. One company that had a time clock used this language:

Sample Time Clock Policy

Your time card is the only record of the hours you have worked. The pay you receive is figured from it. You must punch your time card at the beginning and end of your shift. If you forget to punch in or out, take your card to your supervisor so that your time may be recorded and authorized. You must punch out anytime you leave the premises unless you are on company-authorized business. You may not punch another employee's card, nor may you have another employee punch your card. Violations of company policy relative to the time clock may lead to discipline in accordance with the company's disciplinary procedure as outlined in the work rules.

For professional organizations, time recording is just as important as it is for manufacturing. Employers are responsible for keeping records of all hours worked for the purpose of wage and hour record-keeping for exempt employees as well as nonexempt employees in certain circumstances. A professional accounting firm used the following language:

Sample Time Recording Procedures

All employees are provided with a folder that includes transaction codes, categories, and client numbers. These documents and policies provide a complete array of recording methods. All weekdays, including holidays, vacations, and absences of any kind must be recorded on your time sheet. Time sheets shall be submitted on a daily basis no later than 10:00 a.m. the following business day. Consult your manager if you find the list incomplete.

Personal Telephone Use Policy

It is important for many companies to regulate personal telephone calls. Accordingly, this is a fit subject for the general information portion of what a company expects of its employees. In giving seminars across the country, I often do an informal poll of the attendees, asking how many companies have problems with the personal use of the telephone by their employees. Invariably, 60 percent or more of the seminar attendees raise their hands.

Telephone use policy is particularly important for service companies who rely heavily on telephones for their customer contact. One financial institution used the following language.

Sample Telephone Policy

Telephone courtesy is paramount at the Bank because a high percentage of our customer contact is via the telephone. A high level of professionalism should be maintained in all telephone conversations. Relaying clear and accurate information and messages is essential to the successful operation of the Bank.

CHAPTER TWO

Our service image to our customers and our spirit of cooperative team-work demands that we make use of our telephone system to its maximum advantage. Instituting or receiving a number of personal telephone calls limits access via telephone by our customers or each member of our staff who may need your assistance.

Therefore, please keep in mind the following guidelines when receiving or making necessary personal telephone calls:

Indicate to the party who has placed the call, or the person to whom you are calling, that the conversation is of a personal nature.

Indicate to the party you are speaking with that you must be brief in your conversation so that your telephone may be freed for company use. As a general rule, these personal telephone conversations should not exceed two minutes in length.

While each of us would like the opportunity to handle our personal conversations during our workday as often as possible, the Bank feels that we should identify the normal criteria as to when these calls are acceptable:

Notification to responsible parties of the need to work overtime or provide alternative transportation arrangement.

Conversations with relatives or personal friends when an emergency situation arises.

Brief conversations to make luncheon or dinner arrangements.

Personal calls considered unacceptable are those made strictly for conversational purposes or calls that exceed the time limit established for personal business. Strictly prohibited is the use of company telephone for participation in radio contests or other similar activities.

In the manufacturing setting, one company explained its telephone policies as follows.

Sample Telephone Policy for a Manufacturer

A telephone for personal calls is located in the plant. This telephone is to be used only before or after working hours, during a lunch period or break period, or at other times only with your supervisor's prior permission.

During working hours, employees will be allowed to answer emergency calls only. Other personal calls will be accepted as a message and given to the employees by their supervisor. Employees may use the company-provided phone located in the lunch area to return calls during lunch or break periods or after work.

Lastly on this subject, in most jurisdictions it is legal to monitor employee telephone usage. However, if this is being done, the best advice is to let the employees know that the company may, from time to time, monitor telephone use in the same way it monitors computer usage. If this is important to the company, it may also be appropriate to advise employees that violations of the company telephone policy may result in corrective discipline up to and including discharge from employment.

Computer and E-Mail Policy
In this modern age it is difficult to imagine how work ever got done without the computer technology available to employers today. However, technological advances have spawned the need for new policy as well. For example, employers have filed class action claims alleging race and sex discrimination by circulated e-mail containing racial and sexual jokes, thereby creating a hostile work environment. It is imperative, therefore, that written policies clearly defining the limitations on employee use of company computer equipment be developed and published to employees. Employees should be trained concerning the policy, and the employer from time to time should exercise its rights pursuant to the policy to monitor compliance with it.

While such policies must be tailored to fit the particular needs of each employer situation, policies normally cover the following points:

1. Computer equipment and messages via disk, e-mail, or other method are allowed for business purposes only.

2. All messages are company property.

3. No solicitation is allowed using the company computer system.

4. No messages are allowed that may be deemed offensive, discriminatory, or intended to frighten, intimidate, abuse, or harass another employee, a customer, or an outside party.

5. No messages are to reveal trade secrets, proprietary information, or confidential financial information, or infringe upon copyrighted materials.

6. The company may monitor, review, and disclose any e-mail, disk, or other computer information. Employees must have no expectation of privacy. Employees must understand that deleting a message will not protect the privacy of any information.

7. All passwords must be revealed to the company.

8. Discipline up to and including discharge from employment may result from violations of the company computer policy.

One small company uses the following.

Computer/Communication Policy

The e-mail, computer, Internet, telephone, mail, and voice mail systems are company property. These systems are in place to facilitate your ability to do your job efficiently and productively. These systems are solely for business purposes, and any unauthorized use is prohibited. The I.S. (Information Systems) Department must authorize, schedule, and determine how software will be installed on any computer. Requests for new or updated software must be submitted to I.S. in writing. I.S. will authorize, schedule, and determine software installation.

Violations of these rules will be noted, and I.S. may remove unauthorized software at its discretion. The Company may intercept, monitor, copy, review, and download any communications or files you create or maintain on these systems. When using these systems do not send or reveal materials of a sensitive nature or that constitute "confidential information" unless the information is properly coded to prevent interception by third parties.

Your communications and use of our e-mail, computer, internet, and voice mail systems will be held to the same standard as all other business communications, including compliance with our anti-harassment and anti-discrimination policies. We expect you to exercise good judgment in your use of our company's system. Management should be notified of unsolicited, offensive, or otherwise inappropriate materials received by any employee on any of these systems.

Failure to abide by these rules, even a single incident, is grounds for discipline up to and including termination from employment.

No-Solicitation Policy

It is important, particularly for non-union employers, to ban solicitation by employees. Many companies do not wish to condone the practice of union employees organizing and soliciting other employees for union membership while on the employer's premises and working for the employer.

It is legal to ban such solicitation. However, it must be carefully written to avoid being what the National Labor Relations Board would define as *overbroad*. It also must be consistently enforced to ban all solicitations, not just union solicitations, to avoid being discriminatory in violation of labor laws.

Employers are best advised to check with management labor relations counsel when updating a policy or originating one. National Labor Relations Board policy has changed dramatically over the years in this area. One NLRB officer has unofficially said that he has never seen a no-solicitation policy that was legal. Accordingly, if a policy in this area is to be written, it must be carefully written and periodically reviewed to maintain compliance with current legal interpretation.

Many employers do not like work time being used for solicitation of any kind. Sometimes employee teamwork can be jeopardized if the "soft" moral equation on each purchase of Girl Scout cookies and Kiwanis candy rolls is not carefully and equitably made between employees. Some employees just do not like to be asked for charitable contributions while at work, and they will appreciate the policy and enforcement of such a policy. This approach will also provide a consistent message for supervisors who must explain to employees that work time is for work and break time is for everything else.

One employer, mindful of both objectives, created a policy as follows.

Sample No-Solicitation Policy

> Solicitations and distribution of literature by employees to other employees are not permitted for any purpose during working time in working areas of the company.

Again, this is a very technical area of management labor relations law. There are specific rules for no-solicitation policies for industries like health care institutions and retail establishments, and in certain situations a stronger rule may be adopted. Literature of a political nature that is highly inflammatory and likely to disrupt plant discipline may be banned, even if it contains union propaganda interpreted as being protected speech pursuant to the National Labor Relations Board interpretations of the National

Labor Relations Act. In addition, there may be situations where even the simple policy above is presumptively invalid. Seek specific labor relations advice from competent counsel before implementing a no-solicitation rule.

Parking

Parking is one of those subjects that could be placed in either the benefit section (what the employees can expect from the company) or in the policy section of the employee handbook. It is important enough to be addressed, wherever it is placed. If, for security reasons, the company expects all employees to use the company parking lot, then such information should be given to the employee in the employee handbook. Sometimes, for safety purposes, employees should be told not to park on certain public areas to ease the ingress and egress of vehicles such as delivery trucks. One company used the following language in describing its parking situation.

Sample Parking Lot Policy

Parking in the company lot is provided for your convenience. Your cooperation in parking in an orderly manner will allow for maximum use of the lot. The company is not liable for any damage to cars or their contents in the parking lot. Parking in neighboring companies' lots is not permitted. Also, parking in the street and on driveways is not permitted in order to allow free access to all trucks in our receiving docks. If you park in the company lot during non-business hours, please allow security personnel to escort you to and from your vehicle.

Lockers

The next general subject is often an explanation of the company's policy concerning lockers. At many companies lockers are unnecessary, but at others, having a locker is essential due to the nature of the work.

The most important point to stress in such a policy is that lockers are company property and, as such, may be subject to search at the company's discretion. However, this must be balanced against the employees' reasonable expectation of privacy of their personal property. The closer one gets to a search on an employee's person, the more the issue of privacy comes into play. If companies might in the future want to search cars, lunch buckets, briefcases, purses, etc., employees should know in advance that such personal property on the employer's premises is subject to search and that such search is necessary as a term and condition of employment. Of course, this type of policy is easily justifiable in retail establishments such as department stores, grocery stores, and the like, but it can also be important to help protect trade secrets, processes, or patents. In these cases, there should be a waiver not only in the handbook, but also on the employment application form, where the employee's signature implies an understanding of the terms and conditions of the job.

Employers should know that many states have their own statutes on unlawful invasions of privacy. These include intrusions upon the privacy of another which are highly offensive to a reasonable person, and such statutes command that any such searches should take place in an area where reasonable persons would consider it private or in a manner that is not actionable for trespass.

One company's locker policy is as follows.

Sample Lockers Policy

All plant employees will be assigned a locker for their use. The locker may be locked; however, the company retains ownership of the locker and may occasionally investigate the inside of the locker and note all contents, providing a copy to the employee. Any such inspection is at the employer's sole discretion. In addition, it is the employee's responsibility to keep his or her locker neat and clean. Food must not be left in lockers from day to day. The company is not responsible for lost or stolen personal articles that may have been placed in the locker.

Smoking

This is a topic that years ago was generally considered insignificant, but times have changed. In developing a policy on smoking, several items must be considered. While in the past no one considered secondhand smoke a health issue, smoking is now considered inappropriate unless expressly allowed or permitted by a company in authorized areas.

In many companies, smoking takes on a broader significance. Wherever the preparation of food is involved, concerns about the food itself, as well as the health and hygiene of the food production worker, demand a smoke-free environment. This may also be true in health-related occupations on the premises of health care providers.

Moreover, this subject is increasingly affected by governmental regulation. As of this writing, there are no federal prohibitions on smoking. However, in many states and municipalities, there are many restrictions on the areas where an individual is allowed to smoke. The general rule now is that smoking is prohibited unless expressly permitted. If this is the case for an employer, this policy should be specific and communicated to the employee in the employee handbook. For example, one company states that its policy is to "allow smoking on company property, but only outside the main building."

In other companies, smoking may be allowed in private offices, but not in general areas where employees may congregate, such as reception areas, meeting rooms, and general office areas, as well as in manufacturing areas. Remember, it may be important to those employees who do not smoke that smokers do not infringe upon the right to breathe smoke-free air. Indeed, protection against inhalation of secondhand smoke may even develop into a legal right, actionable against the employer. This is discussed more fully in Chapter Ten.

Here is a sample of the smoking policy a health care facility published in its employee handbook.

Sample Smoking Policy

As a health care facility, we discourage smoking by our residents and employees. If you must smoke, adhere to the following standards:

1. Smoking in any resident area, staff work area, or non-designated smoking area is prohibited. Smoking is not allowed in the employee break room either because this room is designated for use by employees during meal times.

2. Smoking is allowed in designated employee smoking areas only.

3. Smoking in the designated resident smoking lounge by employees is prohibited.

Please clean ashtrays carefully when through. Never leave butts of cigarettes and matches around at random.

Housekeeping

Employers should emphasize the importance of housekeeping in the corporate culture. Emphasizing its importance in a company's philosophy may help a supervisor correct the bad habit of an otherwise capable employee. Something simple often works best, such as the following.

Sample Housekeeping Policy

It is the policy of our company to provide a clean and safe work environment for its employees. This policy requires all employees to keep their assigned work area clean and neat and to do their share in maintaining a safe and accident-free workplace. This policy includes the lunch room and locker area.

Hygiene

This, again, is an area that each employer should consider addressing in the employee handbook to notify employees in advance as to what the company expects. In some states, state statute also provides that an employee must be notified at the time of hiring about hygiene requirements. Some might refer to this as a "dress code," but it really goes beyond such a concept. While it is true that a manufacturing operation is likely to have lesser standards for the style of clothes necessary for the performance of the work than service or retail operations, hygiene requirements are equally important in both contexts. This is an example of what one food processing business used in its handbook:

Sample Hygiene Policy

Each employee is expected to maintain good personal hygiene to include, but not be limited to, the following:

a.   Notify plant management of open cuts and sores;

b.   Wear clean, light-colored clothing;

c.   Wash hands thoroughly after eating, going to the lavatory, picking up non-sanitary objects, or leaving the production area for any reason;

d.   Do not wear jewelry to work areas;

e.   Always wear hair and/or beard nets while in production area;

f.   Do not chew gum, chew tobacco, or play radios on company property; and

g.   Employees who have been assigned white uniforms are expected to wear and maintain those uniforms in good condition at all times.

Security

This issue delves into the limits of an employer's power in regard to the privacy of its own employees. This subject is discussed in greater detail in Chapter Ten.

Many companies are surprised to learn the extent to which they can protect their business interests if they suspect employee theft or other security risks. Generally, the employer has the right to do what is reasonably necessary to protect itself. Unlike public employment, where employers may be subject to United States constitutional prohibitions on search and seizure matters, private sector employer action is not as limited. While no employer may plan to search desks, lockers, or the person of its employees, sometimes that need may arise. Thus, it should be mentioned that the employer has that right and may exercise it at its discretion if it is deemed necessary. This should not be treated as threatening employees, but rather as informing them of what they may expect in certain circumstances.

Again, this is a concern that applies to both the office and the shop. Where sometimes shop employees have been known to see "scrap" as not having any value to the company, such scrap may indeed be valuable. If this is the case, employees should be told beforehand if and when such material may be taken home. Moreover, in retail or office situations, employees should know that the company will protect its property. For example, one retail establishment specifically mentioned security in its handbook as follows.

Sample Security Policy

Security is important to the company given the nature of our business. The company may, at its discretion, occasionally hire and place outside investigators to observe policy compliance by employees within the company.

The company also reserves the right to randomly check personal belongings that are on the employer's premises, such as bags, purses, shopping bags, etc. Objection to this policy may be considered insubordination, which may subject the employee to discipline up to and including discharge.

Dress Code

The law in some state jurisdictions is that if a company requires a dress code, employees must be informed about it when they start work. However, as a general rule, this is an important subject to touch on in the employee handbook, even if not explicitly required by law. Most management consultants recommend that such a clause not be too specific, but instead state that the judgment as to whether work attire is appropriate is one for management to make on a case-by-case basis. Additionally, some feel that it is important for the company to also state that in the event of attire not meeting the standards the company rightfully expects, the company, at its discretion, may send the employee home without pay to dress appropriately. One company worded its policy as follows:

Sample Personal Appearance Policy

Personal grooming is important. All employees are to be neat and clean when at work. Clothing should be appropriate to the job. Management, in its discretion, may determine the appropriateness of attire and may impose discipline for inappropriate dress.

Bulletin Boards

The subject of bulletin boards is more complex than one might think. The key, however, is to make sure the company policy requires prior management approval before an item can be posted on the company bulletin board. Remember that the company bulletin board is an important communication space. If neglected, it can become a real problem area. For example, although most managers would agree that the employee bulletin board is not the place management would want to see notices about a union meeting, in removing such notices the company may be violating the National Labor Relations Act, unless it had beforehand established through past practice a policy of removing unapproved bulletins of any nature.

One company's policy reads simply as follows.

Sample Bulletin Board Policy

The company expects each employee to have read and understood the messages posted on the bulletin board. Employee notices may only be posted after management approval.

Section Three: What the Employee Can Expect from the Company

Wage Policies

It is important for a company to announce upfront what its wage policies are so that the employee knows what to expect. It is important to go over some of this information with the employee, especially during an employee orientation session. Publishing what a company does in compensating its employees both reassures new employees and reminds current employees about the benefits of working at the company. In addition, laying out the policies will make their administration much easier. The more specific a company can be here, the better. Remember that employee handbooks can be used as a recruiting tool to attract employees who will make a positive contribution to the enterprise.

Working Hours

For federal and state law wage and hour purposes, it is important to identify and define a company's workweek. For many businesses, it is also important to describe the general working day. Is it one shift or three shifts? When are the break periods, if any? How much time is allowed for lunch? One company describes it this way:

Sample Working Hours Policy

For Wage and Hour purposes, our workweek begins at 12:01 a.m. Monday and ends at 12:00 Midnight Sunday. The regular office hours are 8:00 a.m. until 5:00 p.m. As a general rule, these should be adhered to by every employee. The practice of arriving early to leave early or arriving late and leaving late is prohibited. Our clients have come to rely on our presence during these hours and irregularities can be disturbing to them.

Our hours provide for a one-hour lunch period. However, if you are away for more than an hour, please make up the time.

This may sound like an unusual policy, but it was used in a professional accounting firm, and seemed to work well. Another example of an unusual workweek is the following.

Sample Workweek Policy

The workweek begins on Sunday and ends on Friday. It is our desire that no work be performed by company personnel from sundown Friday until sundown Saturday night.

Payday

Paydays vary from company to company, so it is important to let employees to know what they can expect. Examples range from a weekly payday (which is typical of the construction industry) to bi-weekly, semi-monthly, and monthly paydays. One company has as its policy a payday of the 5th and 20th day of each month. Keep in mind that the only real legal limitation is that some states require by statute or administrative code provision that a pay period be no longer than one month. Many service industries typically pay on the 15th and last day of every month. If these days fall on a weekend or holiday, then the last business day preceding the regular payday will be used.

Also, it is not uncommon for paychecks to be directly deposited to bank accounts. If this is an option, it should be explained in the employee handbook.

Some employers will use this policy as the place to inform employees that salary advances will be discouraged.

Sample Payday Policy

For every week of work, payday will be the following Friday at the end of the workday. Night shift employees will receive their pay at the end of their shift on Thursdays.

In the event you are unable to receive your paycheck, it will be mailed to you at your address of record with the company, unless other prior arrangements are made with the payroll department for special handling of your check.

If you would like to register for direct deposit of your payroll check with your bank, please inform the payroll department.

Deductions for Social Security and federal and state income tax will automatically be made from your paycheck as required by law. Such amounts will be shown on each paycheck. No other deductions shall be made from your paycheck without express authorization from each employee.

Please be advised that salary advances are not permitted. The company expects all employees to exhibit proper care of their financial situation.

Overtime

It is usually important to mention the company overtime policy in the handbook. Employees who fall into the categories of executive, administrative, professional, and outside sales as defined by the Fair Labor Standards Act and who are paid on a salary basis within the criteria established by the FLSA are considered "exempt" from the payment of overtime. However, for nonexempt employees, several facts about company policy are important. First, employees will want to know at what rate the company will compensate for overtime hours. By law, companies are only obligated to pay overtime at time and one-half the regular rate of pay for all hours worked over 40 hours in any given workweek. Sometimes, employees have the misconception that they are entitled to receive overtime for all hours worked over eight in a day. This is not the general rule, although it may be the case where there is a union contract that stipulates it, unless the employer voluntarily decides to pay it, or under certain conditions in federal or state contract work pursuant to the Davis-Bacon law and state laws like it.

Additionally, many companies want employees to know that they are not to work overtime hours unless specifically authorized by their supervisors. Too many overtime hours can quickly run up the labor costs associated with any business. On the other side of the coin, many companies also want employees to know ahead of time that if they are asked to work overtime hours, they *must*. If there is some system in place to equalize overtime hours, this too should be explained.

Usually problems with overtime come in two forms: First, employees who work it all the time complain about too much overtime; and second, employees who feel they are not getting their fair share of overtime complain that they can't make as much money as they would like. Having a policy in place ahead of time can help eliminate these problems.

Sample Overtime Policy

Although we will attempt to schedule all employees to work forty (40) hours per week, there are certain occasions when overtime work may become necessary. Overtime pay will be at the rate of one and one-half (1-1/2) times the employee's hourly rate of pay for all time worked in excess of forty (40) hours in any workweek. If Holiday or Sunday work is performed, it will be paid at the rate of two (2) times the hourly rate.

Overtime work is sometimes difficult to plan for as we respond to customer needs. Every employee may work occasional overtime on a regular basis. If overtime is necessary, the company will attempt to give as much advance notice as possible. However, it may occur that an employee may be expected to work overtime with very little notice. All overtime work must be approved in advance by the employee's supervisor. All requests to work overtime will be considered mandatory unless excused by the employee's supervisor.

All paid time off from work, such as for vacations, sick/personal days, and holidays, is not actual working hours and, therefore, will not be included in the determination of hours worked in excess of forty (40) hours in any workweek.

Wage Reviews

Many companies rue the day they instituted an annual wage review policy when they discover their supervisors are simply too busy to perform reviews at or near the employees' anniversary dates. Negative reviews are also a problem; most supervisors are loath to give negative employee reviews because of their fear of confrontation. Most supervisors feel that the employee's morale would be destroyed by such a review, and, for these reasons, they hesitate and put off this task at every opportunity. Nevertheless, proper performance appraisals are considered absolutely necessary by most management experts.

If the company policy is to provide employees with such a review, it is best to let the employee know about it in the employee handbook. This may provide the opportunity of letting employees know about behaviors the company values in its employees. One company described its salary review policy in the following manner.

Sample Salary Review Policy

The company will endeavor to provide employees with a salary review at the completion of the trial and training period and at or about the anniversary date of employment on an annual basis.

Wage and salary levels are based in part on market studies of similar organizations within our industry and within our geographic location for similar position levels and areas of responsibility.

Job performance is the primary factor in your wage or salary level. Your job performance evaluation will be based on factors including, but not limited to, the following:

1. Quality—workmanship of the highest standard;

2. Quantity—consistent production of a good day's work;

3. Safety—ability to perform the job safely;

4. Attendance—always on the job (reliable and dependable);

5. Need for supervision—never idle when there is work to be done (i.e., a self-starter);

6. Cooperative—Always open to suggestions and willing to help out in emergencies;

7. Relationship with fellow employees—helpful, friendly, courteous to all; and

8. Being a team player.

Paid Time Off Work

Paid time off work includes holidays, vacations, sick leave benefits, temporary paid leaves of absence, funeral pay, and jury duty pay.

Holidays

Whatever paid holidays the employer observes, it is important that the employees be informed of them. Typically many companies will also demand that for a holiday to be paid, the employee must be in attendance both the day before the holiday and the day after it. For some operations, in addition to the basic six holidays of New Year's Day, Memorial Day, Fourth of July, Labor Day, Thanksgiving Day, and Christmas

Day, other days may be established as holidays. Alternatively, such extra days may be staffed by only a skeleton crew. It all depends on the nature of the business enterprise.

Typically, if a holiday falls on a Saturday, the preceding Friday would be celebrated as the holiday and if it falls on a Sunday, the following Monday would be observed as a paid holiday. It is important to note, however, that for purposes of wage and hour law, paid time off work for observance of a holiday is not considered as *time worked* for the determination of overtime pay, unless the company has a policy of doing so. In this case, it then becomes part of the implied "contract of employment" with the employee and such holiday hours must be counted. Accordingly, it is important to avoid ambiguities wherever possible. One company used the following wage policy concerning holidays.

Sample Holiday Policy

The company will provide holidays for each full-time employee who has worked a scheduled day before and after the following holidays, with pay equal to eight hours at the regular straight-time rate. These holidays are New Year's Day, Memorial Day, Independence Day, Labor Day, Thanksgiving Day, and Christmas Day.

Some companies add to this in various ways. For example, one company used the following as an addition to its holiday policy:

Other holidays may be declared by the Board of Directors and from time to time employees may be granted floating holidays; this is when a holiday is declared, but the office is still open. Individuals may like to work on the holiday and take a floating holiday at some later time. Traditionally, the three floating holidays have been: President's Day, Columbus Day, and Veterans Day. The company is responsible in accommodating the needs of employees for time off to observe religious holidays if these days occur on a day when the company is open for business. When time off is requested by an employee for religious purposes, he or she may be granted the necessary time off, but without pay. An employee who chooses to take a vacation day in order to observe the religious practice will be eligible for vacation pay that day.

Any employee who is terminated or quits prior to earning the floating holidays will not be compensated for them.

Lastly, for some employers, operating a skeleton crew over certain days may make more sense than either scheduling a complete workday or scheduling a half-day holiday. Examples include the Friday before Easter, the day after Thanksgiving, Christmas Eve, and New Year's Eve. During the traditional holiday season, one professional office puts up a posting in October asking for volunteers to work on a skeleton crew for the day after Thanksgiving, Christmas Eve until noon, and New Year's Eve until noon. Each employee is asked to sign up for one of the three days.

There is nothing in state or federal law requiring an employer to give time off with pay to observe a holiday. However, failure to do so may make recruiting much more difficult.

Vacation Policy

Again, there is nothing in state or federal law that mandates employers to grant paid vacation time. However, failure to do so again would make recruiting of personnel difficult. However, how much vacation time should be granted is clearly the prerogative of the employer.

Common vacation issues include whether or not unused vacation time may be carried over from one year to the next, whether unused vacation will be paid out at time of employment termination, whether accruing vacation will be paid out to a terminating employee, and how a new employee will earn vacation rights.

Typically, most vacation policies operate on the calculation of either an anniversary or calendar year. In either case, an employee earns vacation in one year, and if employed at the end of the year (December 31 or the last day of an anniversary year), the employee is vested with those vacation rights to take in the following year. During the next year the employee is accruing vacation rights which if employed at the end of the year will vest to be taken in the following year.

Understanding how this works is important, especially in determining rights to vacation pay for employees terminating from employment. Wage and hour law interpretations state that if an employee has vested vacation time coming when he or she terminates employment, that vacation pay must be paid.

A sample vacation pay policy is below.

Sample Vacation Pay Policy

Paid vacation time is earned each calendar year to be used in the following calendar year. Accordingly, from a new full-time employee's start date through December 31 of that year, there is no vacation allotment with the company.

During the next calendar year of employment with the company, a new employee shall be entitled to receive one (1) day of paid vacation for each full month worked during the prior year, up to a maximum of ten (10) working days.

During the next seven (7) years with the company, each employee who was with the firm on December 31 shall be entitled to a two (2) week paid vacation which may be taken any time during the following year.

Thereafter, each full-time employee who shall have been with the company for eight (8) or more years on any December 31 shall be entitled to a three (3) week paid vacation that may be taken any time during the following year.

Unused vacation time may not be carried over into the next calendar year. An employee whose employment is terminated for any reason at any time during the calendar year shall not be entitled to any vacation pay for that year. However, if the employee has not taken vacation time due for the previous year, the employee shall be paid vacation pay for such previous year.

The length and time of vacations are subject to the approval of each employee's supervisor and should be scheduled as far in advance as possible. For scheduling purposes, a vacation schedule is posted on the company bulletin board. Single days of vacation may be taken if scheduled in advance of the day requested with the supervisor's permission.

Some companies also run into the problem of the workaholic employee who wants to both work and receive vacation pay in order to make more money. Because a company's vacation pay policy is totally at its discretion, if this is a problem for the employer, it is possible to mandate that vacations must be taken or lost.

Additional vacation considerations may also be covered in the vacation policy. One company handled these additional matters as follows.

Regular part-time employees will be granted paid vacation time on a pro-rata basis. If an employee leaves employment through resignation, after having given at least two weeks' notice, accrued vacation will be paid according to the vacation schedule on a pro-rata basis.

In general, a minimum of two weeks' notice is required for all vacation requests. The company will make every effort to meet an employee's request. However, it is important to understand that all departments must be staffed with a sufficient number of employees so as to meet the needs of our customers. Where there is more than one request for the same period of time in the same department, the most senior employee will receive first preference.

Extra pay will not be given in lieu of vacation. In the event a holiday falls within a scheduled vacation period, employees would be entitled to another vacation day off in the current calendar year.

Sick Leave Benefits

Many companies have developed a policy of paying for sick leave and setting the number of days that the employee may be paid when taking such leave. Of course, with paid sick leave there is always a temptation for the employee to take time off for such things as a mental health day. Irrespective of the possibility of abuse, most employers recognize that it is preferable to have employees stay home when they are sick instead of attempting to work and infecting everyone else at the workplace. One employer's sick leave policy is below.

Sample Sick Leave Policy

With respect to sick leave, each full-time employee will be entitled to five (5) days off work with pay per calendar year in the event of the *actual* illness of the employee or a member of the employee's immediate family.

There will be no carryover of unused sick days from one calendar year into the next calendar year.

New, full-time employees, during the partial calendar year and subsequent calendar year, will earn sick leave days at the rate of one (1) sick day for every two (2) months of employment, up to a maximum of five (5) sick days in any one calendar year.

In the event it is necessary to take a sick leave day, the company must be notified prior to the start of the employee's work shift.

Partial sick leave days may be used in one-half day increments when needed.

At its discretion, the company may require certification of the illness requiring sick leave from a licensed physician. The company also reserves the right to have any employee examined by its own physician.

CHAPTER TWO

Recently there have been some imaginative new twists on the subject of paid sick leave. Some are aimed at reducing absenteeism and others are attempts to streamline administration. If an employer is willing to experiment with something truly different, one approach eliminates all paid time off, increasing each employee's pay by the amount equivalent to the paid time off formerly provided for vacation, sick leave, personal time off, etc. The idea is to allow employees the ability to schedule time off, but at their own expense. In other words, if the employee wants to take a day off, he or she may, but it will be an unpaid day. Of course, the regular rules apply that such time off must be scheduled in advance and taken only with the approval of the supervisor. Many employees prefer the advantage of pocketing the extra cash. For those who prefer time off instead, that is available too. Other advantages are that such a system makes the administration of the Family Medical Leave policies much easier because there would be no substitution of paid time off for unpaid leave under such policy.

Another trend is to combine sick days and vacation days together. Under this policy, while the number of potential days off may increase, employees who do not take sick days will increase their vacation time or perhaps be paid out in a bonus at the end of the year for unused paid time off. This system, too, should be easier to administer and allows each employee the flexibility to choose what is more important to him, time or money. This is a disadvantage, however, for the workaholic who needs to take a break from time to time, although proper supervision should be able to handle this potential challenge.

Any approach to paid time off has its own set of circumstances, benefits, and drawbacks. Sometimes the mere change of such a policy is unsettling to employees used to something else. However, if the company does a good job of selling the policy, employees may be interested in making a switch from a traditional system to a new one.

Temporary Paid Leaves of Absence
Companies recognize that emergencies occur that require occasional days off, whether they are an employee's personal emergency or emergencies in the world at large. Other reasons for time off include funerals, emergency weather conditions, medical appointments, or other similar difficulties. Some companies simply have a policy of allowing paid *personal* days off of work without requiring an employee to supply a reason. Whatever the policy, the employee should be made aware of what the company permits. One company used the following policy successfully.

Sample Temporary Paid Leaves of Absence Policy

Full-time employees are permitted occasional absences for short periods of time for compelling personal reasons such as medical or dental appointments, attendance at funerals, problems with children at school, etc., without having such absences charged against sick leave, vacation time, or regular work time. The approval of the employee's supervisor must be obtained in advance with notice provided to the personnel department. This notice must be in writing indicating the length of time to be taken and the reason for it. The company asks that doctor and dental appointments be scheduled in such a manner as to minimize time away from the company. For example, please try to schedule doctor and dentist appointments as the first appointment of the day or the last appointment of the day whenever possible. While we understand this is not always possible, we appreciate efforts that can be made.

Funeral Pay

For some employers, it is easier to specifically address the issue of funeral pay directly in the employee handbook. Management decision-making is necessary to determine how long such funeral pay will last and to what personal relationships it will extend. One company has the following policy.

Sample Funeral Leave Policy

The company maintains a funeral leave policy for employees to provide compensation during absences from work due to the death of an immediate family member. Employees may receive up to two (2) days off with pay for the death of an immediate family member when the funeral does not require overnight lodging. Employees may receive up to three (3) days off with pay when the funeral is out of town and requires overnight lodging. For the purposes of funeral leave, immediate family is defined as spouse, children, grandparents, parents, brothers, sisters, mothers-in-law, fathers-in-law, brothers-in-law, and sisters-in-law.

Of course, this area is left up to the total discretion of the company. At some companies, no policy is appropriate, because the companies may award time off for such circumstances according to a *personal leave* or *temporary paid leave of absence* type of policy. However, for others it may be important to spell out the exact stipulations of this benefit so that it is not abused. While this policy does not address the question of the domestic partner, the company can, upon recommendation of the supervisor or manager, decide to award pay in such circumstances even though it may not exactly fit the definition in the employee handbook. Such a determination can be left to a case-by-case analysis by the manager closest to the scene.

Jury Duty Pay

Employers who do not provide a leave of absence for employees to perform jury duty expose themselves to legal liability. The federal Jury System Improvement Act of 1978 prohibits employers from discharging "permanent employees who perform jury duty in federal court." Most states also have legislation making it unlawful to discipline employees called for jury service. Remember, a jury summons is an order of the court and must be responded to in the same manner as a subpoena, unless the employee is released by the court from serving such duty.

In practice, employees are called for jury duty so infrequently that it is seldom a problem for the employer. However, it is good to announce relevant company policy beforehand so that employees will know what to do if the matter ever arises. Additionally, the question is often asked whether such time away from work will be compensated by the employer so that the employee will not lose any wages because of community service. Most employers will make up the difference between the statutory court-ordered jury pay compensation and what the employee normally would receive had they been able to work. Generally, because such call to service happens so infrequently and is generally of only a few days' duration, this does not impose an enormous financial burden on the company. Failure to make up the difference is detrimental to the employee as well as discouraging to the kind of employer-employee relationship most companies desire.

However, there should be limits to a company's generosity. Indeed, what would happen if a company's policy guaranteed that an individual's compensation would not be lessened by jury service, and then the employee is chosen for a long jury trial? Usually, if an employee explains to the judge in whose court they have been called to serve as a juror that employer compensation will only be given for the first two weeks of a trial, most judges will not insist upon forcing such jurors to sit at their extreme economic disadvantage where the trial is likely to be long. One company uses the following for its jury duty policy.

Sample Jury Duty Pay Policy

The company supports our employees' civic responsibilities and, accordingly, employees are encouraged to accept jury duty if at all possible.

If an employee's absence for jury duty will cause undue hardship on the department's work performance, the company may request and assist the employee to be excused from such jury duty.

Employees summoned for jury duty will be given a leave of absence to do so and the company will pay the difference between jury duty pay and the employee's regular daily wage for up to ten (10) working days in any twelve (12) month period.

Employees will be required to furnish proof of jury service and payment for it in a written statement from the court. Employees are expected to be at work while not performing jury duty. If an employee reports for jury duty and is excused, he or she must report for work as promptly as possible.

Unpaid Leave of Absence Policies

In the normal course of business it may become necessary for an employee to take a leave of absence. Leaves of absence may be for a specific reason for a short duration, may be personal in nature for no apparent reason, or may be required leaves subject to detailed procedures for long periods of time, such as military leave. Unpaid leave of absences may be required for medical purposes, due to either injury on the job or away from work.

In addition, all companies covered by the FMLA (employers of 50 or more employees) are mandated by statute to address this issue in the employee handbook. Also mandated is information that informs the employee how to apply for such a leave and how the leave will be administered.

Military Leave

In 1994, President Clinton added to existing law by signing the Uniform Services Employment & Re-employment Rights Act of 1994. Pursuant to United States Code, for more than 50 years the national policy has been to assure citizen soldiers that they can return to the civilian job they held before entering military service and can return to that job without any loss of seniority. In addition, an extensive body of case law has evolved that is consistent with the new legislation, and it too remains in full force and effect.

Specifically, some of the rights provided to veterans under the Uniform Services and Re-employment Rights Act of 1994 are: (1) a service member is free to perform military service of limited duration, either in active military service or in the reserve, without fear of reprisal or other adverse action by his or her employer; (2) this service member will be required to provide notice of impending military service whenever possible and, if requested by the employer, to document honorable service upon returning to civilian employment; (3) a service member who leaves a civilian job would continue to be deemed on furlough or leave of absence and would be entitled to other rights and benefits that are available to other employees on leave of absence; (4) this Act qualifies the service member's right to continue employer-sponsored health insurance; (5) a veteran's right to pension benefits that would have accrued during military service is guaranteed under the Act, but a pension plan would not have to pay earnings or forfeitures on made-up contributions; and (6) a service member returning to federal employment is assured that employer-provided and contributory pension benefits will be restored with little if any loss of benefits.

In general, federal law requires employers to give re-employment rights to people who leave their jobs to serve in the armed forces, if these people satisfactorily complete the period of active duty and have a certificate to that effect. These employees generally are eligible for re-employment rights if they serve not more than four years of active duty, or five years if duty is extended at government request. In addition, employers are prohibited from discriminating against members of the military reserves or the National Guard. In addition, the Military Selective Service Act requires that employers in both public and private sectors grant leaves of absence to reservists and members of the National or Air National Guard for weekly, weekend, or summer camp training. The Act also addresses emergencies, such as the Persian Gulf War, where members of these military units are called to active duty.

Some companies handle this subject in the employee handbook as follows.

Sample Military Leave Policy

A regular full-time permanent employee who leaves the service of the Company to join the military forces of the United States during time of war or other national emergency or who is drafted into the military service at any time shall be granted a military leave without pay. Such leave will extend through a date 90 days after he or she is released from such service. Proof must be filed with the Executive Director. Such employee shall be restored to the position vacated or to a comparable position with full rights and without loss of seniority or benefits accrued and not taken while serving in the position occupied at the time the leave was granted, provided that the employee make application to the Executive Director within 90 days after release, and is physically and mentally capable of performing the work of the former position. Failure of an employee to notify the Company within this time period of intent to return to work shall be considered as a termination of employment.

Personal Leave

Personal leaves are generally leaves of absence taken without pay for reasons unrelated to work. Employers often fear that someone may take a personal leave and then not return from it, meaning the company will have wasted time in delaying hiring a replacement. Indeed, some people do take a personal leave of absence only to use the time to find another job.

An important feature in any personal leave clause is that it is to be granted solely at the discretion of management. In addition, most managers feel it is wise to limit the length of the leave to no longer than six months. This is what one company used to describe its policies:

Sample Unpaid Personal Leave Policy

All employees are eligible to request personal leaves of absence due to unusual circumstances. Such requests are granted at the sole discretion of the company. The company's policy is to use a reasonable, consistent, and fair approach toward granting time off. Criteria it may consider includes the reason for the request, the length of the leave, the effect of the work load on others, the frequency of such requests, the employee's attendance and performance record, and the needs of the company at the time of the request. If granted, such leaves will be made for no longer than six (6) months.

Remember that one of the main challenges for business is keeping the services of key, competent employees. Being flexible in granting unpaid personal leave may just be the solution in a crisis, or even a burnout situation.

Medical Leave

The key criterion in developing a medical leave policy is that all employees are treated equally. This means the nature of the employee's medical condition that is the reason for the leave should not matter. If a physician certifies that the employee is medically unable to work, whether the medical condition is work-related or not, then the employee must apply for medical leave pursuant to the provisions of the company policy. In particular, there should be no separate maternity leave policy outside the medical leave of absence policy. By law, pregnancies and maternity leave must be treated the same way as any other medical disability.

A good medical leave policy should do several things for the employer. First of all, it should limit the period of time an employee will be carried on the company's payroll records. While such period can be extended, many companies carry an employee only for up to six months of medical leave. Of course, employees may reapply for employment if their medical condition requires a longer time away from work. If companies seek to retain the services of valuable employees, once they are medically ready to return to work, employees with a good track record would be just the kind of employees companies would want to re-employ. However, if companies suspect the employee to be a *workers' compensation malingerer*, the reverse may be true. Putting a time limit on the length of medical leave provides the company with a legitimate, nondiscriminatory reason to separate an employee from its payroll, as long as the policy is consistently applied across the board for all employees. Indeed, this issue has been litigated in numerous workers' compensation cases where employees have filed a claim for unreasonable refusal to rehire an employee after workers' compensation injury. Decisions in these cases have affirmed the principle of the employer's right to limit medical leaves of absence to a specific period of time. The only limitation is that an employer may not count leaves of absence taken under the company's FMLA policy. In addition, any return to work may be subject to reasonable accommodation of an employee's disability, if such medical disability exists.

While such time is totally within the discretion of the company as it sets its policies, many companies will carry an employee for up to six months of medical leave. After this time, the employee may apply for employment, but will do so as a new employee.

Another feature of many policies is requiring the employee to maintain current medical verification of inability to work on file at the company. This, too, will help eliminate the occasional malingerer. It is not uncommon to see physicians certifying a temporary medical condition without placing time limits on the healing process. However, once a notice is given to the employee that he or she may be removed from the payroll in one or more months, it is amazing to many to see how fast healing accelerates.

Another feature of the medical leave of absence policy is reserving the right to ask for a second medical opinion. Again, in cases where a company may suspect a problem, this is the only way to address it. For example, in one recent case, when the company called the home of the employee out on medical leave, the person answering the phone said, "Oh, Sally is not here today. She is water-skiing at the lake." The value of reserving the right to require a second medical opinion paid for by the company cannot be understated in managing such cases.

One company states its medical leave policy the following way.

Sample Medical Leave of Absence Policy

Medical leave of absence without pay will be granted to employees because of illness or injury, including maternity, for a period of not more than six (6) months, provided that the request is accompanied by a physician's written statement that the leave of absence is recommended by the physician and should include the estimated time of physical incapacity.

An employee may return to work any time during the next six months and maintain all benefits and seniority as long as the following requirements are met:

a.   The employee presents a release from his physician; and

b.   An opening for work exists at XYZ Corporation (not necessarily at the same position or labor grade as when leave was granted). A bumping of an employee of lesser seniority will not be permitted.

If after six months the employee is still unable to return to work, employment will be terminated and the employee will lose all seniority and benefits; any rehire would be considered as a new employee and seniority would begin anew.

Two or more periods of medical leave due to the same or unrelated causes will be considered one period of medical leave unless they are separated by a return to full-time work for a continuous period of at least 30 calendar days.

While on medical leave, it will be the employee's responsibility to supply to XYZ Corporation, between the 1st and 10th of each month, proof from a physician of continued inability to return to full-time employment. Failure to supply this proof will result in immediate termination of employment.

The effect on employee benefits for employees on medical leave will be:

a.   Seniority will continue as though working.

b.   Any unused vacation must be used prior to granting a medical leave of absence.

c.   Vacation accrued for the next year will be in accordance with the vacation policy.

d.   Medical insurance will remain in force and cost shared in accordance with existing split (including dependent coverage) for two months immediately following the month in which the leave of absence began. After this, the employee's medical coverage is terminated; however, if the individual remains eligible under the law, the employee will have the option of continuing medical insurance (at his or her expense through the company) at the group rate, for an additional period as required by law.

e. Holiday pay will not be granted to an employee on medical leave of absence.

Family and Medical Leave

Much has been written on the Family and Medical Leave Act (FMLA). The purpose of the Act is to balance the demands of the workplace with the needs of families by entitling employees to take reasonable leave for medical reasons, for childbirth and adoption, and for the care of a seriously ill child, spouse, or parent.

Employers of 50 or more employees are required to have a family and medical leave policy. If the company has an employee handbook, the FMLA mandates that the employer's policy and instructions for applying for such leave *must* be in the employee handbook.

The FMLA establishes certain minimum federal standards, and where these standards conflict with state laws that require more or less generous provisions, the employer must follow whatever policy grants the employee the most possible benefit.

A family and medical leave policy should cover the following items:

● how an employee should request leave;

● whether medical certification, including second and third opinions, are required;

● company policy regarding the substitution of paid leave for unpaid family and medical leave;

● whether an employee who fails to return to work after a leave will be required to reimburse the employer for health insurance premiums covering the leave period; and

● whether an employee on leave is entitled to earn employment benefits.

In general, employees are eligible by law to take family and medical leave if they have been working for an employer covered by the Act and have worked for the employer for at least 1,250 hours over a 12-month period.

While family and medical leave does not cover every event within family life, in general, an employee has the right to ask for an unpaid leave of absence when the following events take place:

- a son or daughter is born to the employee;

- a son or daughter is placed with the employee for adoption or foster care;

- the employee needs to care for a seriously ill spouse, son, daughter or parent; or

- the employee himself or herself has a serious health condition.

It is important to note that it is not unlawful sex discrimination for an employer to deny male employees paternity leave when it grants female employees maternity leave on the basis of their having a medical disability. However, the granting or refusal to grant extended maternity leave in the employer's discretion would be discriminatory if it refused to grant paternity leave on an extended basis or applied different terms and conditions to such leave. It is even possible that an employer provides *extended maternity leave* beyond the 12 weeks required by the FMLA, but does not provide additional paternity leave. In this situation, the employer might be guilty of unlawful sex discrimination although its action did not violate the FMLA.

Additionally, the FMLA allows an employer to require medical certification from an employee seeking leave because of a serious health condition and allows an employer to place an employee in an available alternative position when the employee wishes to take leave intermittently or on a reduced leave schedule for planned medical treatments.

Employees who take FMLA leave because of their own serious health condition need not, in each instance, be so physically and mentally incapacitated as to be generally unable to work. For example, an employee who must be physically absent from work from time to time in order to receive medical treatments is eligible for leave for the time necessary to receive such treatment.

FMLA leave entitlements for medical reasons are predicated upon the existence of a serious health condition, either that of a family member or the employee's own condition. A serious health condition is defined as an illness, injury, impairment, or physical or mental condition that involves:

- inpatient care in a hospital, hospice, or residential medical care facility; or

- continuing treatment by a health care provider.

Generally, the condition will be considered a *serious health condition* if it or its treatment causes an employee to be absent from work on a recurring basis for more than three days.

Eligible employees are entitled to 12 workweeks of leave during any 12-month period. FMLA leave may be taken intermittently or on a reduced leave schedule when medically necessary. Taking leaves in this way reduces an employee's usual number of hours either on a daily or weekly basis, but it does not reduce the total leave entitlement beyond the amount of leave actually taken.

Under these circumstances an employer can require that the employee take a temporary transfer to an available alternative position. The employee must be qualified for such position and must receive equivalent pay and benefits. The transfer itself must make sense in that it should be better suited to accommodating recurring periods of leave than the employee's regular position. Transferring an employee to another position as a punitive measure is not allowed under the FMLA.

There are limits to when *parental* leave may be taken. Although employees need not take parental leave at the actual time of the child's birth or placement, the right to take parental leave expires 12 months after the child's birth or placement. In addition, an employer may insist that parental leave not be taken intermittently or on a reduced schedule.

Employees who request leave for prime medical treatment must make a reasonable effort to schedule such treatment so as not to unduly disrupt the employers' operations. This, of course, is subject to the health care providers' approval as well.

Under the FMLA, employees must notify employers of their intent to take leave for foreseeable events, typically within 30 days whenever possible. In addition, an employer may require that an employee on leave report periodically on his or her medical status and intention to return to work. The employer may also require certification of a serious health condition. Certification may also be required when an employee is returning to work or when an employee is unable to return to work after using all available family and medical leave. This certification should be issued by a health care provider and provided to the employer in a timely manner. The employer has a right to require a second health care opinion, but it cannot come from a health care provider that is employed on a regular basis by the employer. If the two opinions differ, a third opinion from a health care provider who is selected jointly by the employer and the employee may be sought. This third opinion would be final and binding on both parties.

Information in the medical certification should at least include a statement of the date the condition began, its probable duration, appropriate medical facts as necessary, and the necessity of the reason for the leave request.

While this type of leave is typically unpaid, depending on the reason for the leave, earned paid leave may be substituted for any part of an employee's 12-week leave entitlement. This "substitution" is at the option of either an employee or the employer.

While employees also retain their earned employment benefits while on leave, they are not entitled to continue to accrue additional seniority or benefits. Included in the term "employment benefits that are retained" are: (1) group life insurance; (2) health insurance; (3) disability insurance; (4) sick leave; (5) annual leave; (6) educational benefits; and (7) pensions.

Either the employer or the employee can decide that vacation or personal leave be substituted for unpaid leave. However, such substitution of paid leave is limited so that an employee would not be able to substitute accumulated paid sick or disability leave to offset unpaid leave taken to care for an infant or for a child that is placed with the employee for adoption or foster care. This is because the employee is not sick.

On the other hand, accumulated paid vacation or personal leave can be substituted for whatever reason the leave is taken because of any of the triggering events.

Note that the employer is not required to provide paid sick or medical leave in any situation in which the employer would not normally provide it. However, an employer may not trade shorter periods of paid leave for longer periods of unpaid leave.

Employees on leave are not entitled to any right, benefit, or position of employment other than those they would have received if they had not been on leave. For example, if an employee on leave would have been laid off, the employee, even though he or she is on leave, may still be laid off from work.

Employers must maintain coverage under any group health plan for the duration of an employee's FMLA leave. However, if employers are not providing health insurance benefits, they do not have to provide them merely because someone is taking an FMLA leave. Such coverage for health insurance must remain at the same level and the conditions for which it would have been provided must remain the same as if the employee had continued in employment continuously during the duration of the leave.

Employers have the right to be reimbursed by an employee for the premium that they pay to maintain health insurance coverage during the leave if the employee does not return to work after taking the leave. This is true unless the reason the employee did not return to work was due to the continuation, recurrence, or onset of a serious health condition that would have entitled the employee to leave, or because of other circumstances beyond the employee's control.

Most employees returning from leave must be returned to the job positions they held when they went on the leave or to equivalent positions. The term *equivalent* means substantially similar in benefits, pay, and other terms and conditions of employment.

Employers are prohibited from engaging in any act that interferes with employees' exercise of their right to take FMLA leave, discharging or discriminating against employees for opposing any practice that is unlawful under the FMLA, and discharging or discriminating against employees who participate in a proceeding or inquiry related to the FMLA. Employees are likewise protected if they file a charge, give information, or testify in connection with any inquiry or proceeding relative to the FMLA.

Relief for employers' violations of the Act is available to employees for both money damages and equitable relief such as employment, reinstatement, or promotion. The amount of money is based on lost compensation or monetary losses, such as the cost of providing care up to the equivalent of 12 weeks' pay. An additional equal amount, known as liquidated damages, is also recoverable unless the employer shows that it had reasonable grounds to believe its actions were not unlawful. The attorney fees for the employee may also be recovered where the employee is forced to sue to protect his or her rights and prevails.

The Department of Labor has reported that in 91 percent of the cases where a violation was found, the complaints were successfully resolved within 30 days and the remedy involved either a restoration of the job, wages, and benefits or the granting of FMLA leave. In only nine percent of the cases was the matter under review for potential litigation.

A sample employer FMLA policy follows.

Sample Family and Medical Leave Act Policy

1.0 Purpose

The company recognizes the occasional need for time away from work to participate in early childhood rearing and care of family members who have serious health conditions.

This policy allows eligible employees to take reasonable leaves of absence for the birth, adoption, or placement of a child; for the care of a spouse, son, daughter, or parent who has a serious health condition; or because the employee is unable to perform the functions of his/her position due to serious health conditions.

The provisions of this policy are in compliance with state and federal law. Wherever state and federal laws conflict, the law allowing the greater benefits on any particular issue is to be followed.

2.0 Eligibility

All non-key employees are eligible for a family leave of absence if they have been employed by the company for at least twelve (12) months, and have worked an average of 20 hours per week in the past 12 months consecutively.

Employees applying for and granted a family leave of absence are required to meet notification and documentation requirements as outlined further in this policy. Failure to meet these requirements may result in the denial or revocation of a family leave.

3.0 Basis and outline of Leave of Absence

3.1 Eligible employees are entitled to up to 12 workweeks of leave during a twelve (12) month period as defined in section 6.4 for one or more of the following reasons.

   a.   Birth of an employee's son/daughter;

   b.   Placement of a son/daughter for adoption/foster care;

   c.   Employee's spouse, son, daughter or parent has a serious health condition, and the employee is needed to attend the family member's basic needs, both during periods of inpatient care and during periods of home care;

   d.   An employee is unable to perform the functions of his/her position due to a serious health condition.

3.2 The entitlement to leave under paragraphs a. and b. above expire at the end of the 12-month period beginning on the date of such birth or placement.

3.3 If both an employee and his/her spouse are employed by the company, their combined time off may not exceed 12 workweeks during any 12-month period for the birth, adoption, or foster care, or to care for a parent with a serious health condition. Each spouse is, however, eligible for the full 12 weeks within a 12-month period to care for a son, daughter, or spouse with a serious health condition.

3.4 The company may require an employee on an intermittent leave to transfer temporarily to an available alternative position for which the employee is qualified where it better accommodates recurring periods of leave than the employee's regular position.

3.5 Intermittent leave cannot be taken for birth, adoption, or foster care purposes, unless the employee and the company agree otherwise. If approved, this leave must be taken during the year of the birth or placement.

3.6 The company may require that the employee obtain subsequent recertification of medical necessity on reasonable basis.

3.7 The employee on a leave must notify Personnel periodically (at least twice a month) of his/her status and intention to return to work. Personnel will then notify their immediate supervisor of this information.

4.0 Return to work—restoration

4.1 When an employee returns to work following a leave, he or she will be:

    a.   Restored to the position held by the employee when the leave began or at the company's discretion;

    b.   Restored to a substantially equivalent position with substantially equivalent benefits, pay, and other terms and conditions of employment.

4.2 For an employee who would be laid off if he or she had not been on family leave, any right to reinstatement would be the same as if he/she had been working when the layoff occurred.

5.0 Vested Benefits

5.1 Taking a family leave will not result in the loss of any employee benefit vested prior to the date on which the leave began.

5.2 Continuation of Employee Benefits. An employee on a family leave may remain a participant in the company's employee benefit plans throughout the duration of the leave, as if actively at work. You will be required to pay the same cost of coverage as if you were working.

5.3 If the employee fails to return to work at the conclusion of the leave, the company may require the employee to reimburse the company for the full cost of health care coverage during any period of the leave.

6.0 Application for Family Leave of Absence.

6.1 It is the responsibility of the employee to complete the necessary written request form available in the personnel office.

6.2 The Personnel Department must be notified in writing of any changes in physicians treating self or a family member, and any address or forwarding information applicable to the employee on leave of absence, so accurate records can be maintained.

6.3 A copy of this form concerning the leave will be in the medical file located in the Personnel Department.

6.4 Leave provisions are determined by certain Federal and State Guidelines. Time frames are determined to be:

Federal leave is calculated on a 12-month rolling calendar based on the date of application of the leave of absence.

State leave is calculated on the calendar year.

7.0 Communication

7.1 This policy will be communicated to all company employees through the appropriate Personnel Department. The communication vehicles used should ensure employees understand the benefits and responsibilities under this plan. Examples of communication to you include a copy of this policy personally delivered to you, the employee handbook, and employee rules posted in a timely manner on the employee bulletin board.

8.0 Review and Revision

8.1 It is the responsibility of the Personnel Department to upgrade, update, amend, or revise this policy as necessary after review by our corporate counsel and distribute to all employees in a timely manner.

9.0 Definitions:

1. Employee Benefit—all benefits made available to employees by the company, including group health, life, short and long-term disability insurance; vacation; educational benefits; and 401(k)—regardless of whether these benefits are provided by a practice or written policy. Overtime is not an employee benefit as defined under the family and medical leave laws.

2. Parent—the biological parent of an employee, an individual who stood in place of the parent to that employee when the employee was a son or daughter.

3. Son/Daughter—a son or daughter must be under 18 years old or 18 years or older but incapable of self-care because of physical or mental disability. He or she must be either a biological child, adopted child, foster child or step child, a legal ward or child of a person standing in place of a parent.

4. Spouse—the husband or wife of the employee. This definition does not apply to unmarried domestic partners.

5. Key Employee—Highly compensated salaried employee or those in upper 10% of highest paid employees. May be exempt from federal Family and Medical Leave, if absence puts an undue hardship on the future of the company. Non-key Employee—Eligible for family leave, not highly compensated employee.

6. Certification—Medical provider's statement regarding necessity for the leave; should include the date the serious health condition commenced, its probable duration, and medical facts regarding it. It should also state the name of the person who is unable to work because of it. Must be submitted within fifteen (15) calendar days from request of leave.

7. Intermittent—Brief periods of absence.

8. Reduced Schedule Leave—Reduces the usual number of hours per day or week of an employee.

9. Serious Health Condition—An illness, injury, impairment, or mental or physical condition that involves:

   a. Any period of incapacity or treatment in connection with or consequent to inpatient care (i.e., overnight stay) in a hospital, hospice, or residential medical care facility;

   b. Any period of incapacity requiring absence from work, school, or other regular daily activities, of more than three (3) calendar days that also involves continuing treatment by (or under the supervision of) a health care provider; or

   c. Continuing treatment by (or under supervision of) a health care provider for the chronic long-term health condition that is incurable or so serious that if not treated would likely result in a period of incapacity of more than three calendar days and for prenatal care.

   d. Voluntary cosmetic treatments (such as most treatments for orthodontia or acne), which are normally not medical by necessity under Serious Health Conditions if inpatient hospital care is required.

e. Restorative dental surgery after an accident, or removal of cancerous growth are serious health conditions provided all the other conditions of this regulation are met.

f. Treatments for allergies, for stress, or for substance abuse are serious health conditions if all the conditions of the regulation are met. Prenatal care is included as a serious health condition. Routine physical exams are excluded.

10. Physical or Mental Disability—impairment that substantially limits one or more of the major life activities of an individual.

Additional Benefits

Additional benefits that should be covered in the employee handbook include employee assistance programs, educational assistance, personal growth and advancement, fringe benefits, workers' compensation, and unemployment compensation insurance.

Employee Assistance Programs

Employee assistance programs (EAPs) are programs set up by employers to help their employees deal with personal problems such as marital troubles, problems with children, mental health problems, and drug and alcohol problems. While these are programs designed to help employees with what are really "off-the-job" kinds of problems, they are important because such problems affect the workplace by leading to workplace tension, diminished safety, lower productivity, and employee turnover. Indeed, many believe such programs pay for themselves, if only in the reduction of health care costs since employees may be more likely to seek treatment if it can be arranged confidentially and without out-of-pocket costs. Because of their effectiveness, EAPs have become increasingly common in American business in the last decade and are projected to be even more prevalent in the future.

A company, depending upon its size, may run an EAP by hiring a trained employee or counselor. Such assistance is also rendered on a contract basis by consulting firms that provide services for a fee. Many health care institutions now offer such programs. In fact, many employer associations utilize the service through participation in group health insurance policies. The number of insurance companies offering employer's group coverage for outpatient rehabilitation through an EAP is continuing to rise. Some statistics show that of every 100 employees in a company, approximately 10 to 12 have some type of personal problem affecting their work. Moreover, because of the Drug-Free Workplace Act, all companies with federal contracts must have policies and procedures in place to deal with drug use and must offer employees education and referrals for treatment.

A well-designed EAP includes key components. First, the program must gain the trust of employees if it is going to be successful. For example, if there is a union at the company, the union should be involved in establishing the program. Cooperative labor-management programs may have a higher success rate than voluntary, unilateral programs.

Second, employers should give employees a written description of the program, usually in the employee handbook. The description should express a desire and commitment to help employees, provide incentives for employees to use the EAP to deal with personal problems, explain the details of how to do so, and give assurance of confidentiality if an employee uses the program.

Employers are advised to take an active role by encouraging self-referral, in which the employee comes to the EAP voluntarily.

Legally, employee assistance programs also help the employer establish that it is making a "reasonable accommodation" to employees who may be considered handicapped because of their alcohol or drug abuse problems. Indeed, most agencies dealing with discrimination complaints on the state or federal level recognize that where an EAP has been offered by the company, an individual discharged because of continued substance abuse after completion of the program is not being discriminated against in violation of the handicapped discrimination statutes. This is also true under the Americans with Disabilities Act (ADA).

This is what a sample clause might look like in an employee handbook:

Sample Employee Assistance Program Policy

As part of the company's employee benefits package, the company has contracted to have an Employee Assistance Program (EAP). We understand that in anyone's life, there can be times where there is a need of special help for personal problems. It is the intention of the company to help its employees receive this assistance when it is needed. Please contact your supervisor, the Personnel Department, or any member of management to help you confidentially seek any assistance you may need in dealing with personal problems that may affect your ability both at work and at home to accomplish your goals. We recognize that crises occur in people's lives. We are not perfect and we do occasionally have problems. At XYZ Company, we believe that it is all right to come forward and admit to needing help.

Educational Assistance

Many companies provide employees a stipend to pursue outside education and training. While wage and hour law dictates that such training must be outside the employee's regular job duties if such training is not to be compensated, employers often want to encourage such training even though it will not be paid time. The company's educational assistance policy should be outlined in the employee handbook. It is a benefit to both the company and the employee and might be underutilized unless made known to the employee. There are many ways to set up such programs. One company phrased its policies as follows.

Sample Educational Assistance Policy

Our company supports the continuing education of our employees. Our company's Educational Assistance Program can be used for the purpose of maintaining or improving current job description requirements or to provide support for the attainment of undergraduate and graduate degrees.

All full-time and regular part-time employees are eligible after one year of employment. Full-time employees are eligible for $800 and regular part-time employees for $500 for courses taken in a calendar year. One-half of the money is paid before the start of the course and one-half after successful completion of the course.

To apply for such assistance, please contact your department head or the Human Resources Department for pre-approval of reimbursement for continuing education.

Personal Growth and Advancement

Employers need to attract and retain valuable, competent key people. Employees want jobs from which they can advance to higher wages and better working conditions. For a stable workforce, it is best for employers to promote from within wherever possible. Indeed, many places of employment are attractive to job applicants as much for the experience they will obtain in their careers as for the wages and fringe benefits they will receive. Promoting from within encourages people to stay, and the opportunity that others observe and take advantage of may set an individual company's culture apart, giving it a competitive edge. Accordingly, advising employees that personal growth and advancement is an intrinsic part of employment at the company should be highlighted in the employee handbook. Companies should also be sure to post all positions available internally.

A company should document its promotion policies and commitment to promoting from within. One accounting firm states its policy as follows:

Sample Personal Growth and Enhancement Policy

Staff Development

Our firm believes in a policy of recruiting topflight professionals to our firm, rewarding their talents with commensurate salary and benefits, and providing numerous opportunities for continuing education and personal growth.

Wherever possible, we will promote from within based upon a candidate's professionalism, track record of career growth, and personal commitment to practice development.

In manufacturing operations, it is important to advise the employees of the method of promotion as well. In unionized operations, this is often a subject of collective bargaining under either "job posting" procedures or a detailed "seniority" clause. The main issue generally is the balancing of the relative weight of a candidate's seniority within the company with the relative weight of a candidate's skill and ability. In addition, in unionized operations, such clauses may force agreement on the company's right to hire from outside the company ranks if there are no qualified applicants already working. The definition of what makes an individual qualified can be an important issue in determining management's power to select its workforce. However, for the company operating in a union-free environment, announcing promotion policies beforehand is an important part of an overall strategy to remain union-free. This may also be especially true where a union has been decertified by the employees and company management is formulating its policies unilaterally for the first time.

In a manufacturing setting, one such company described its policy in the employee handbook as below.

Sample Personal Growth and Advancement Policy

Advancement

A. In the event of a job opening, the company will post a notice for three (3) working days.

B. The notice will show the title, rate of pay, and description of the duties required for the job. Any employee may apply in writing for the job within the three (3) days that the job is posted. All jobs will be posted on Mondays, and people will be transferred to the posted jobs on the following Monday or after any applicable job reviews have been completed.

C. The company will fill posted positions with employees it considers to possess the most superior qualifications, ability, and experience to do the job. When two or more applicants, in the company's opinion, have approximately equal qualifications, abilities, experience, etc., as outlined in the seniority section, the more senior applicant will be selected. It is the policy of XYZ Company to promote from within when possible; however, the selected employee will be required to meet minimum job standards. If the employee proves unsatisfactory on the job after a reasonable trial period, the employee will be returned to his or her previous job, and the vacancy may be filled with a new employee.

D. If, in the company's opinion, none of the applicants meet the minimum job qualifications or all applicants prove unsatisfactory, or if no one applies for a posted job, the company will fill the position through other means.

E. Any new employee hired or any current employee selected for a posted job cannot bid on another posted job for a period of six (6) months from the date of placement.

Fringe Benefits

Fringe benefits are a major part of what employees expect as compensation. Often, employee benefits are standard for all employees in the firm. In the employee handbook, employers usually mention the kinds of benefits that are available, but leave the specifics to the individual policies themselves. This is because benefits may change from time to time and can also be quite complicated to administer. The employee handbook can inform employees of the kinds of benefits that are available and then refer them to the human resources department or operations manager for detailed information. Benefits include:

● health insurance,

● life insurance,

● sickness and accident insurance,

- accidental death and dismemberment insurance,

- retirement plans,

- 401(k) plans, and

- profit-sharing plans.

In today's employment market, the strategy is often to retain key employees with the "golden handcuffs" of the fringe benefit package. If an employer adopts this strategy, where better to communicate it to employees or future candidates for employment than in the employee handbook itself?

Many innovative ideas are developing that combine better benefits for employees at a significantly lower cost to the employer. For example, MedSmart Healthcare Network, Inc., of Dallas, Texas (www.powerx.net) and National Health and Safety Corporation of Horsham, Pennsylvania (www.nhlt.com) offer employers a medical discount card ("POWERX") which enables employees to access single or family medical benefits including pharmaceuticals, medical equipment, dental services, and even long-term nursing home care for parents and family members at substantial (up to 50 percent) point-of-purchase discounts. This includes savings on medical care provided by chiropractors, physicians, and hospitals within its huge PPO provider network of over 70 percent of the doctors and hospitals in the United States.

The discount card can be used as a supplement to traditional health insurance or can be combined with catastrophic insurance coverage to provide a medical benefits program at a small fraction of the cost of traditional health insurance. Moreover, the discount card program allows employees to receive coverage for procedures such as cosmetic surgery and experimental treatments that are not normally covered under traditional health insurance plans. Sometimes an insurance carrier's or HMO's control over medical providers results in cost-cutting demands that may reduce the quality of care. A discount-oriented program will eliminate this concern.

This kind of program may be especially invaluable to employers who self-insure their employees. This is because the discounts go straight to their bottom line whenever the employee uses the medical discount card. Accordingly, employers who use such innovative programs should explain the benefit to their employees in the employee handbook. In today's competitive market for employees, such a program may positively affect an employer's ability to find, recruit, and retain its employees.

Workers' Compensation

Despite the fact that companies are required by law to carry workers' compensation, it is still important to discuss this benefit in the employee handbook. It is important to let employees know that in order to claim such benefits, it is best to report accidents *immediately*. Employees should also be informed about the company's disability management program, if one exists. This is becoming more and more important as workers' compensation costs continue to rise. According to a recent study, the average cost of disability per employee, which includes workers' compensation payments and disability insurance, typically accounts for five percent of total payroll, or an average of $3,372 per injured employee. One company's policy follows.

Sample Workers' Compensation Insurance Policy

All employees are covered under a workers' compensation insurance policy at the company's expense for job-related accidents. The company should be notified immediately of accidents of any nature, whether or not a claim will be made under this policy. Please know that failure to do so may result in a denial of your claim for workers' compensation benefits.

While you have the right to select a health care provider of your own choosing, please be advised that, in its discretion, the insurance carrier may also request a medical opinion of the cause, extent, and nature of an injury. Failure to submit to such medical exam may result in a denial of coverage.

For assistance regarding the submission of claims to the company's insurance carrier, please contact the company administrator or human resources department. If you have questions regarding the claim, the company will be happy to direct your questions to the insurance carrier so that they can be answered for you.

All injuries, regardless of how minor, must be reported. All first aid treatments must be recorded in the first-aid room by the group leader or supervisor.

A standard drug screen and alcohol profile will be conducted on any employee who reports a work-related injury that requires medical attention.

Unemployment Compensation Insurance

Again, this is a benefit to employees that the law requires companies to pay. Although it is administered separately by each state, the federal government plays an important part in its general requirements. Here, it is important to let employees know that this benefit is available if they are qualified to receive it and that, in the appropriate circumstance, the company may object to eligibility. However, in this context, it is important to mention the fact that while the company may object to benefits being paid, it is the state agency that decides eligibility. This is what one company used to inform its employees on this subject:

Sample Unemployment Compensation Insurance Policy

The purpose of unemployment compensation is to replace part of your income if you are laid off or terminated through no fault of your own. The company pays the full cost of unemployment compensation, but it does not decide who is eligible for benefit payments or how much such payments should be. In its discretion, eligibility for benefits may be challenged by the company because its tax contribution may increase for all employees according to its account with the state Unemployment Compensation Division. However, final eligibility determination is decided by the state Job Service in accordance with state law.

Section Four: Closing Matters
Employee Separation
Employee separation should be discussed in the employee handbook in the section on closing matters. Employee separation issues are twofold: (1) when an employee quits, or (2) when the employee has been fired.

If an Employee Quits
With regard to resignation, employers should make it clear in the employee handbook that an employee should provide the company with advance notice to allow for an orderly transition of personnel. However, because some courts have looked at this issue relative to the determination of employment-at-will status, the company must not demand that it receive advance written notice of a voluntary quit, but instead ask for it. Some courts have interpreted language such as, "The employee *shall* . . . " or "You *must* inform the company if you intend to quit . . . " as a commitment on the part of the employee which inures solely to the benefit of the employer and as an obligation on the part of the employee which smacks of a contractual relationship.

The legal and practical alternative is to ask employees to give the company advance written notice of voluntary termination of employment. The actual *quid pro quo* is that employees can then anticipate receiving a better recommendation for their next employment. One company words its policy as follows:

Sample Voluntary Termination of Employment Policy

If you plan to quit employment, we ask that you inform your supervisor in writing at least two weeks in advance with a copy to the personnel office. This is to help the company in its planning for an orderly transition and to give the company time to find someone to take your place.

Failure to do so may be reflected on future references for employment you may ask the company to provide for you.

If an Employee Is Discharged

The closing matters section of the handbook is an excellent place to renew the company's commitment to excellence and to underscore the fact that no job is permanent. Although some companies prefer to reaffirm the at-will relationship in the handbook's Introduction or work rules section, the closing matters section can also be used for that purpose. One company uses the short form of work rules here instead of listing them when discussing its termination from employment policies.

Sample Termination of Employment Policy

We try to be very careful to hire only those people we feel reasonably sure are qualified to do their work, are conscientious in the performance of that work, and will be compatible with others already working here. However, we may make mistakes. If it turns out that we have hired someone who will not or cannot work satisfactorily or is not compatible, it will be necessary to terminate our employment relationship in order to keep our business in a strong competitive position.

If your employment is terminated consistent with the corporation's right to discharge at will, whether any severance pay is given is at the discretion of the Board of Directors. Dishonesty, absenteeism, leaving work without notice, poor quality work, insubordination, possession or use of intoxicating beverages, unauthorized drugs, or controlled substances at work or in a manner affecting work and any conduct deemed to be otherwise detrimental to business operations are examples of behavior that could lead to discipline up to and including discharge from employment.

Exit Interview

Many employers find it beneficial to have an exit interview with every separating employee. While sometimes this may be impossible, it is a good idea to let the employee know that exit interviews are company policy. This policy should be stated in the employee handbook. One company uses the following language.

Sample Exit Interview Policy

As soon as the company becomes aware of a resignation or termination from employment, an exit interview is scheduled. The purpose is to discuss with the employee the reasons for the separation and to give the employee with an opportunity to provide the company with information concerning his or her experience while employed at the company.

Arrangements for the following will also be made at this time:

- The returning of keys;

- The returning of company and security identification;

- The returning of any and all other company property such as company manuals or other records;

- The computing of vacation pay that is due;

- The leaving of a forwarding address, if applicable;

- Providing closure on insurance plans and health insurance continuation options;

- Making arrangements to return other company property such as tools or uniforms;

- Discussing employee pension plans;

- Returning any company credit cards or telephone calling cards.

Retirement

Many companies urge their employees to coordinate retirement plans with them. The employee handbook may be the place to reinforce this procedure. A sample retirement policy follows.

Sample Retirement Policy

The opportunity to retire and realize retirement dreams is afforded through proper retirement planning. The company supports its employees with several programs to help enhance and achieve the financial goals needed to enjoy retirement. The company's human resources staff will provide referrals to outside agencies that conduct retirement programs dealing with every issue of retirement . . . financial, recreational, and psychological adjustments.

Planning for retirement is an important transition process for each employee. A very important part of that transition is the opportunity to transfer the knowledge and experience learned to another employee. Everyone would like to leave with the thought that everything will be in good order after they retire. Therefore, depending upon the position level of the retiring employee, it is encouraged that notice be given several months in advance to allow for smooth transition of duties to someone else. The retiring employee's manager should be brought into the entire planning process as soon as possible to help with this transition.

The company's retirement programs include the Pension Plan, the 401(k) Savings & Investment Plan, and the opportunity to extend health insurance benefits as needed.

Financial services such as direct deposit to an IRA account and other automatic savings programs are also available to employees.

The company is very interested in its retirees and actively encourages involvement with them. This extended family of retirees is an important asset to our company's success.

Complaint/Suggestion Policy

Now that the employee handbook has presented the employer's no-nonsense approach on employee separation matters, it is important to focus on the positive. Many companies like to include in the concluding section another statement emphasizing their desire for good communications. Sometimes this is embodied in what is called the "complaint/suggestion policy." Here is an example of one such policy:

Sample Complaint/Suggestion Policy

It is our desire to work with well-informed employees. Employees can only be well-informed if we have good communications. Good communications must be two-way. If something needs clarification or if you have a question, suggestion, or complaint, we want you to discuss it with your supervisor. If you are not satisfied at this point, we want you then to go to the next supervisor in line for satisfaction. If necessary, you may speak with any member of the management team. We want to answer any concern and listen to any suggestion you may have.

This policy is to assure good employer/employee relations through communication and understanding. We respect the rights, privacy, and dignity of each one of our employees and will investigate your matter as confidentially as possible and get you an answer as soon as possible.

However, we can only do this if you come to us. In our opinion, the only problems we cannot resolve are those we do not know about. We give you our commitment that if you talk to us, we will listen and respond.

Conclusion

In concluding the employee handbook, this is what one company chooses to say:

Sample Conclusion

We hope you find this book informative concerning the policies, work rules, and benefits at our company. Accordingly, we welcome your ideas, comments, suggestions, or dissatisfactions concerning the operations of our company. We welcome the opportunity to air concerns and think through to solutions to the challenges that we may occasionally face. It is only through maintaining and improving upon our competitive position in our industry that we can create real job security for all of us who earn our livelihood at our company. We must, at all times, think of our customers as our employers and always provide them with quality products that will keep them coming back.

We are certain that it is this type of teamwork and pride that will result in the continuing development of our company so that we can all benefit.

What to Avoid in an Employee Handbook

One threshold question often asked in developing an employee handbook is, "Should we have an employee handbook at all?" Typically, this question is raised out of the fear that having an employee handbook is going to limit a manager's ability to take action because of its terms and conditions. In particular, the fear is that it will limit the range of management authority in discipline and discharge matters. In other words, a manager won't be able to fire an employee because of what is written in the employee handbook.

However, the benefits of having an employee handbook far outweigh any fears that it will tie a manager's hands. In fact, having a handbook that states that management retains its discretion to discipline up to and including discharge for even a single incident will aid in retaining management's power to act.

For example, in a recent case, the lack of an employee handbook reserving management's right to act and confirming the employment-at-will status allowed an employee to claim that he received oral representations by an employer to the contrary. In this regard, the court in *Labus v. Navistar International Transportation Corporation*, D.C. N.J., 119 LC (p56,634), stated:

> Oral representations by an employer to an employee may have given rise to an implied contract of employment. The employee did not receive a policy manual to contradict oral assurances of employment. Nor did the employee have a written employment contract to define the terms of his employment. Therefore, the uncontradicted statements of company policy could have had the appearance of corporate legitimacy, and the employee's claim, therefore, survives the employer's motion for summary judgment to dismiss the case.

In this case, the employee's complaint had to be settled by a judge or jury. In other words, because there was no employee handbook, the company has to litigate the issue.

However, this does not mean that an employer should not be careful about what it says in its employee handbook. The idea is to reserve the employer's rights by confirming them in the employee handbook and avoid making statements of company intent that limit the employer's rights.

In order to avoid an employee handbook becoming a contract of employment, there are certain things to keep in mind.

First, do not promise in the employee handbook that employees will be discharged only for just cause. *Just cause* is a term of art that has been developed over years of management labor relations in a union environment. If the company is a non-union employer, there is no need to voluntarily adopt such a standard. While it may be argued by some that adopting a just cause standard will aid a company in remaining a non-union entity, in my opinion such a statement in the employee handbook will not discourage union organizing efforts.

Secondly, it is a mistake to refer to someone as a *permanent* employee. This term can be used to denote something different than the employment-at-will status most companies wish to retain. Again, this is a carryover perhaps from labor management relations in a union setting. The better, and more appropriate, term would be *regular* employee. In actuality, there are really only four recognized classes of employees. These are regular full-time, regular part-time, temporary, and casual employees. Unless a company's intention is otherwise, there should be no reference to someone having permanent employee status.

The next area to avoid may come as somewhat of a shock to many readers. It is my recommendation that there be no such thing as a *probationary period*. Again, this is a historical term from labor management union relationships. In many union operations, a new hire is put on a probationary status, usually for the first 30 days of employment. After 30 days, if, according to the supervisor, the employee passes this period successfully, the employee becomes a union member, starts paying union dues, and is covered by the union contract. In this situation, it makes sense to have a probationary period because management must take a close look at employees who will become union members.

However, the courts have interpreted the presence of a probationary period to be an element in the employment relationship indicative of a situation where an employee handbook becomes a contract by implication. This is something non-union companies that wish to have an employee handbook should avoid. In addition, in non-union settings, a probationary period does not serve the purpose for which it was originally intended in the union setting. That is, as soon as an individual becomes an employee, he or she becomes covered by all the various employment laws and equal rights laws even though he or she may be on such probationary status.

One manager questioned why his discharge of an employee during a probationary period was being questioned as sex discrimination. He was surprised at my response that even though the employee was discharged during a probationary period, she still had rights to file a complaint pursuant to the Equal Employment Opportunity and complementary state or municipal statutes and codes. In fact, according to some courts, having a probationary period actually may serve to give an employee more rights if the employee successfully completes it. This is not the intent of an employer who wishes to maintain an at-will employment relationship with its employees. The better practice is to refrain from using a probationary period. If a company feels it must have such a period, then even though it may be only a semantic difference, it is better to call this time a "get acquainted" or "trial and training" period instead.

Another common mistake is making a list of work rules without a disclaimer that the list is not intended to be a compilation of *all* of the rules. There is a legal principle which states that whenever anyone makes a list, an intention is being shown to include all of the things on the list to the exclusion of all things not on the list. When this principle is applied to work rules, it is a recipe for disaster because it is impossible to codify or pigeonhole human behavior. No one expects it.

The true test is whether or not a reasonable person in like circumstances would understand that his or her behavior is harming the employer's legitimate business interests. Moses came down from the mountain with ten rules that seem to have stood the test of time. They do not have to be reiterated in every employee handbook either. The better practice is to say that either the following list includes *some* of the company rules, or the list items are *examples* of the kinds of behavior that may lead to discipline up to and including discharge.

Several courts have written that compelling an employee to give two weeks' notice before quitting constitutes a promise on the part of the employee which serves as consideration to the employer to create a contract by implication in an employee handbook. Of course, this demand is impossible for an employer to enforce. It is best to *ask* that an employee give two weeks' notice, not demand it.

Lastly, avoid using a receipt form which states the employee agrees to abide by the rules and regulations listed in the employee handbook as a condition of employment. This too smacks of a contractual relationship, and the courts have pointed to it as an indicia of a contract by implication. Legally, all that is necessary in proving a legitimate business reason for discharge or winning a denial of an unemployment compensation claim is the establishment that the employee *should have known* of the kind of behavior that would put one's job in jeopardy. Introducing into evidence a simple employee receipt form is enough to meet that burden of proof. An example of what to avoid is the following:

I, _____ , do hereby certify that I have read and do understand all the provisions set forth in this work guide. I also certify that I understand and will abide by all the production standards, work rules, attendance rules, and safety rules set forth and can also expect to receive all the benefits and incentives due as such requirements are met.

Date: _____   _____
                            Employee signature

Instead, the following simple receipt form is legally preferable and sufficient.

I, _____, have received a copy of the XYZ Company employee handbook.

Date: _____   _____
                            Employee

Date: _____   _____
                            Supervisor

Implementing a New or Revised Employee Handbook

Once a draft of an employee handbook has been created, it is best to have it critiqued by as many people as possible. A company's supervisors should review the manual and assess whether it meets their needs. Remember, it is the supervisors who will be using the manual to enforce the policies in it. In addition, while the handbook occasionally will be updated, changed, and modified to keep it consistent with ever-changing business conditions, the goal should be to create a manual that will need as little amending as possible.

Once there is a management consensus on the handbook, it is best to implement it with employee input. Depending upon the size of the organization, small group meetings should be held between management and employees to discuss various issues. In the small group setting, the new or revised employee handbook can be distributed and discussed.

Sufficient time should be allowed to explain the handbook's contents to employees in detail and to answer any questions. Instruct employees to take the book home and share it with their families to make sure that there are no misunderstandings. Inform them that in about a week's time, another meeting will be held to discuss additional questions. Emphasize that the company understands that the employees are closest to their jobs and that their input into a handbook that will be fair and understandable to all is important.

At the next meeting, there may be few questions concerning the content from employees if the management draft has been carefully prepared. If there are questions, management is frequently surprised at the good points employees raise if small group meetings are held with the proper atmosphere of cooperation and discussion. Quite often, the handbook can be implemented as is at the second meeting. Have employees then sign receipt forms stating that they have received the book. By proceeding in this fashion, the handbook is understood to be an important document by the employees, and supervisors can more easily administer its rules and policies as situations arise. Additionally, such an approach fosters harmony and goodwill because of the employer's good faith and effort in involving employees in what is surely an important aspect of their employment.

In introducing revisions to an employee handbook, again there is no substitute for the personal touch. Depending upon how many changes are introduced at once, the best method is for the supervisor to explain the changes in small group meetings. Employees should be informed that a new "replacement" page should be inserted in place of the appropriate page in the existing manual. Any employee questions should be answered. There is nothing improper about changing policies; the company may change past practice at any time by providing notice of such changes to employees. There is no better way to memorialize and underscore the importance of the changes than in the employee handbook itself.

Generally, there needs to be no "consideration" for any changes given to an employee. This is especially so when the company has confirmed its right to change its policies at its discretion by so stating in the introduction to the employee handbook. To memorialize the action of a change in policy, the employer should keep memos to employees concerning the change. Often companies use the method of putting the date that the policy became effective in the margin on the bottom of each page. This indicates when the policy was changed and that the employee was given notice of the change on the particular date.

An employee handbook is one of the most important company documents. When it is done right, it is well worth the time, trouble, and expense. It may even improve morale and foster teamwork among current employees and become an excellent recruiting tool for attracting new ones.

Answers to Chapter Two Test Your Knowledge

1. f, 2. d, 3. e, 4. True, 5. False, 6. True, 7. True, 8. False, 9. True, 10. False

CHAPTER THREE

Compensating Correctly

Wage and Hour Law Compliance

Fair Labor Standards Act

Overtime Requirements

Wage-Hour Exemptions

Child Labor Laws

Test Your Knowledge

of Wage and Hour Law

1. True or False? After eight hours in a day an employer must begin to pay overtime wages, according to federal law.

2. True or False? After forty hours in a workweek an employer must begin to pay overtime wages at time and one-half the regular rate of pay.

3. What are the requirements under federal law for a lunch period to be an unpaid period?

4. In determining whether an employee must be paid for time spent at meetings, lectures, and training classes, which of the following four factors must be true for such time to be unpaid time?
    a. Attendance is outside the employee's regular working hours.
    b. Attendance is, in fact, voluntary.
    c. The course, lecture, or meeting is not directly related to the employee's job.
    d. The employee does not perform any productive work during such attendance.
    e. All of the above.

5. True or False? In determining whether time spent "on call" must be paid, the most important factor to consider is whether or not the employee can use the time effectively for his or her own purposes. Therefore, requiring an employee to carry a beeper device for contact if needed does not unduly restrict an employee even if the employee must physically remain within the range of the device.

6. True or False? To qualify as exempt from the overtime requirements, an employee must be paid on a salaried basis as well as meet other requirements.

7. True or False? The paying of compensatory time is permissible in the private sector. In other words, it is permissible to "bank" hours worked without pay in one week and have the employees take an equivalent amount of time off in another week in order to avoid paying overtime.

8. What is meant when an employee is "suffered or permitted" to work, and how does it affect the determination of the number of hours worked for the computation of compliance with federal wage and hour law?

9. Certain duties of an executive are managerial in nature while others may be nonexempt in nature. Which of the following kinds of duties are managerial in nature such that the employee is exempt?
   a. Interviewing, selecting, and training employees.
   b. Performing the same kind of work as employees under one's supervision.
   c. Keeping production records of subordinates.
   d. Setting and adjusting pay rates and work schedules.
   e. Making sales, replenishing stocks, and returning stock to shelves.
   f. Checking and inspecting goods in a production operation.
   g. Keeping records for employees not under one's supervision.
   h. Preparing payrolls.
   i. Evaluating employees' efficiency and productivity.
   j. Disciplining employees.

10. True or False? If a complaint triggers an audit of an employer, the wage and hour department limits its investigation to the circumstances concerning the complaining employee.

The answers to these questions are at the end of this chapter.

Wage and hour law is a vital area of employment law that applies to almost every employer. Miscalculations, naive managerial orders, misunderstandings, false beliefs, and previously unaudited and, therefore, undetected incorrect methods of doing business can all prove costly and embarrassing if they amount to violation of state and federal regulations, however innocent the intent or fair the purpose. Violation reports, issued by both state and federal investigators, can cover every employee and former employee going back two or even three years in certain circumstances. How common are such mistakes? The U.S. Department of Labor announced that in a compliance survey in the nursing home industry, 30 percent of the facilities were in violation of the minimum wage, overtime, or child labor provisons.[1]

This chapter covers the standards for minimum rates of pay, overtime pay, definitions for working hours, child labor, discrimination in rates of pay because of sex (the Equal Pay Act), and other miscellaneous statutory and administrative law provisions.

Most of the discussion will center on the statutory provisions of the Fair Labor Standards Act of 1938 (FLSA). However, on certain details, state legislation is often more stringent and may be controlling in a given situation. In fact, Section 18 of the FLSA expressly provides that nothing shall excuse noncompliance with any federal or state law that establishes higher standards.

A disarming feature of wage and hour law is that all too often following common sense is not enough. Consider the following true scenario.

During small group meetings with the employer, several employees mentioned that they would prefer to limit their lunch hour to 15 minutes instead of the normal 30-minute lunch break in order to leave work 15 minutes earlier in the day. Since the company was going to receive the same amount of actual labor from the employees, it okayed this new arrangement.

However, the end result of this seemingly innocuous change in policy turned out to be quite substantial. In general, in order for a lunch or other break to be unpaid time, it should be a minimum of 30 minutes long. Under federal law this is a guideline, even though under many state laws it is required by specific administrative code provisions. Accordingly, even though the actual amount of working time did not change, all employees had effectually added 15 minutes of paid time per day to what would be considered *their* normal working time. The additional working time was not recognized by the employer.

Assuming a five-day, eight-hour normal working time, each week was now converted to a five-day, 41-1/4 hour working week. Since in most work-weeks the employees were working an additional one and one-quarter hours past 40 hours, the additional hours worked would have to be paid at time and one-half instead of at the regular rate for the hours over 40 in a regular workweek.

After three years of operating in this manner, a complaint was filed with the Wage and Hour Department by a disgruntled ex-employee for the allegedly due back wages and overtime. The liability was broken down as follows. Assuming a $10-per-hour regular rate, and assuming each employee took a two-week vacation every year, the overall calculation was similar to the following:

$10 x 1.5 = $15

$15 x 1.25 per week = $18.75 additional pay
due each employee per week.

$18.75 x 50 weeks per year = $937.50 per employee per year.

Multiply this number by three years, the maximum statutory liability for a willful violation. This equals $2,812.50 per employee. Multiply this number by the number of employees involved. In this case, 150 employees followed this schedule in the company plant operations. The resulting liability was $421,875.00. Recall the fact that if an employee exercised his or her right to file a private lawsuit in federal court to enforce the demand, the court would have the right to add what it would call liquidated damages of a like amount to insure that the employer would not profit by withholding proper wage payments from its employees. Accordingly, this doubles the damages, bringing the total to $843,750.00. Add responsibility to pay the plaintiffs' attorneys' fees and costs for bringing the action, and an employer's own attorneys' fees and costs to defend against the action, and the possible total expense to the employer for making this wage and hour error is close to $1 million! While the case was ultimately settled, the potential exposure was staggering for a seemingly simple decision to do what the employees themselves wanted. In other words, it pays to pay attention to wage and hour law compliance.

Fair Labor Standards Act Background

The FLSA establishes minimum wage, overtime pay, record-keeping, and child labor standards for covered employment unless a specific exemption from coverage is applicable.

The law applies equally to men and to women. It applies to the private sector and in most respects to the public sector. It applies to workers at home, to those telecommuting, as well to those in industry, service, non-profits, and construction. It applies regardless of the number of employees or whether the employment is full- or part-time. However, there are certain things, surprisingly enough, that are not covered by the law.

- The FLSA does not require extra pay for Saturdays, Sundays, holidays, or even after eight hours in a day.

- It does not require pay for vacation, holiday, or severance. It does not even require an employer to give employees the day off on holidays or to give them vacations.

- Whether time off is granted or premium rates are paid after eight hours of work in a day depends upon the policy of the employer and not the "public policy" of the federal wage-hour statutes.

The original FLSA was adopted during the Great Depression. At that time, unemployment was widespread, pay was low, and many people were in whole or in part dependent upon public relief. The purposes of the wage-hour laws were said to be:

- to curb deflationary forces, increase purchasing power, and improve the standard of living by establishing a minimum hourly wage;

- to spread employment by making it more expensive for the employer to work a few employees longer hours by mandating overtime compensation;

- to spread employment by eliminating competition from child labor, whose working conditions were too often unsafe and deplorable; and

- to eliminate unfair competition by employers using "substandard" labor rates to reduce costs.

In interpreting the FLSA, the courts long ago made clear their point of view: "The manifest declared purpose of the statute was to eradicate from interstate commerce the evils attendant upon low wages and long hours of service in industry . . . The statute is remedial, with a humanitarian end in view. It is, therefore, entitled to a liberal construction."[2]

The original FLSA in 1938 provided that the statutory minimum wage be $0.25 an hour and an overtime rate of one and one-half times the employer's hourly rate be applied for hours worked in excess of a certain maximum number, presently 40 per week. As of this writing, the applicable minimum wage is $5.15 per hour. This is not dependent upon whether the employee's pay is calculated by the hour, piecework, commission, or salary. However, the overtime rate has remained constant at time and one-half for all hours worked in excess of 40 hours per week.

The federal Wage-Hour Division of the Department of Labor (DOL) is responsible for administering the FLSA. In addition, most states have their own departments administering their own statutes. Voluntary compliance is a key to the enforcement of the FLSA. However, violations can be enforced directly in four ways:

1. civil actions by employees through private attorneys;

2. civil action by the Secretary of Labor on behalf of employees to collect back wages;

3. civil injunction suits by the Secretary of Labor to restrain violations from continuing; and

4. criminal proceedings by the Attorney General to punish flagrant, willful violations.

Being charged with the responsibility of securing compliance with the FLSA, authorized representatives of the Wage-Hour Division may investigate and gather data regarding the wages, hours, and other conditions and practices of employment. Accordingly, they may enter business establishments and inspect the premises and records, transcribe records, and interview employees. Employers are required to observe record-keeping regulations and permit inspection of the records of all employees, whether exempt or nonexempt, complaining or not complaining. Further, no one shall be excused from producing evidence (pursuant to subpoena) on the ground that he or she might be incriminated or subject to penalty or forfeiture.

Finally, no employer can assume that its operations will never be subjected to an inspection. Such investigations and inspections fall into four basic categories:

1. inspections pursuant to complaints received from employees or business competitors;

2. reinspection of firms previously found in violation;

3. routine investigations of employers; and

4. continuing spot-checks of industries.

Overtime Requirements

Employees entitled to overtime pay must be paid for each hour of work in excess of 40 hours in a workweek, at a rate of not less than one and one-half times their regular rate, unless specifically exempted.

The term *regular rate* means an hourly rate, and the determination of the regular rate is the key to understanding and meeting the overtime requirements of the Act. Generally, the regular rate is determined by dividing the total compensation for a workweek by the total hours actually worked in that workweek, excluding any payments properly credited as overtime premiums.

The regular rate may be more, but never less, than the statutory minimum rate. Remember, however, that there is no limitation in the Act on the number of hours an employee may work in any workweek. In addition, the FLSA does not require overtime pay for hours in excess of eight per day or for work on Saturdays, Sundays, holidays, or regular days of rest as such.

The workweek is determined as follows. Each workweek stands alone. The FLSA takes a single workweek as its standard and does not permit averaging of hours over two or more weeks, except for certain health care provider employees. For example, if an employee works 30 hours in one week and 50 hours in the next, the employee must receive overtime pay for the hours worked beyond 40 in the second week, even though the average number of hours worked in the two weeks is 40. This standard is true regardless of whether the employee works on a standard or swing shift schedule and regardless of whether the employee is paid on a daily, weekly, biweekly, monthly, or other basis. The rules also apply to employees paid on a piecework basis or on commission. Only exempt employees are not required to be paid overtime after 40 hours in a week.

An employee's workweek is a fixed and regularly recurring period of 168 hours, or seven consecutive 24-hour periods. It need not coincide with the calendar week but may begin on any day and at any hour of any day.

The most common mistake in this area, which can result in large back-pay awards in some circumstances, is paying employees who would otherwise be exempt on an hourly basis, without paying time-and-one-half for hours worked over 40 in a workweek. If certain employees can be considered exempt, they should be salaried and given an appropriate year-end bonus if the hours worked turn out to be more than estimated.

However, the most frequent reason for inspection seems to be as a result of a complaint filed by a current or former disgruntled employee.

Wage-Hour Exemptions

Exemptions from coverage are generally considered to be the most complicated area of the law. Some exemptions suspend minimum wage, equal pay, and overtime requirements. Others apply only to minimum wage and overtime provisions. The courts have held that all exemptions must be strictly construed. Exemptions do not excuse the employer from the record-keeping provisions.

If an employer meets the requirements set forth in any of the specific exemption provisions of the FLSA, it is relieved from complying with either or both the minimum wage and overtime provisions. The determination of whether a specific exemption is applicable to the work of a given employee is an issue entirely independent of whether the employee is covered by the FLSA. These are distinct questions. The exemptions and exceptions take a wide variety of forms. Express exemption from one requirement may not carry with it exemptions from all others. In addition, when an employee engages in both exempt and nonexempt activities during the same workweek, the exemption is generally defeated for the entire workweek.

The first basic rule to be followed in exemptions is that bona fide executive, administrative, and professional employees (including academic administrative personnel or teachers) and outside salespersons are exempt from the minimum wage and overtime requirements if they meet the tests for each category. Because this is where most employers make mistakes, these tests will be carefully examined.

The exemptions from the FLSA are really more important than the law itself. Also, because they allow exemptions from the standard rules, the courts have uniformly maintained that the requirements for exemptions will be strictly construed. "An employer who claims an exemption under the Act has the burden of showing that it applies," stated the U.S. Supreme Court.[3] Meeting the conditions specified in the language of the FLSA are "explicit prerequisites to exemption."[4] Accordingly, unless the precise conditions and requirements of an exemption are met, the exemption will not be recognized. However, there is some comfort in this area of the law in that the law is relatively certain and, therefore, predictable.

The law focuses on an analysis of the employee's duties and responsibilities and the salary that is paid (except in the case of doctors, lawyers, teachers, and outside salespersons). In reviewing the tests described below, remember that the salary levels are not minimum wage requirements. No employer is required to pay an employee the salary specified in the regulations unless the employer desires to claim the exemption. Also remember that a job title does not make an employee exempt; nor is that employee exempt simply because the pay is *based* on salary rather than an hourly wage. However, paying an exempt employee on an hourly basis will always defeat the claim of exempt status, with the exception of bona fide computer programmers and computer analysts, who are paid 6.5 times the applicable minimum wage.

Under recent interpretations by the DOL of federal court decisions on the question, it is important to note that the exemption from having to pay overtime can be lost if a company docks otherwise salaried exempt employees for absences from work of less than a full day of absence. In other words, failure to pay the full daily regular rate because an employee is absent from work for half a day or one-fourth of a day or some other increment less than a full day has been interpreted to cause the loss of the exemption from overtime pay. In fact, not only does a particular employee in question lose the exemption, but all other similarly situated employees do as well, even if such other employees may not have had deductions from their salary made for less than a full day of absence.

In some jurisdictions, even deductions for less than a full day from leave of absence banks, such as for personal, sick, or vacation days, in increments of less than one day may cause this class of employees to lose the exemption. This is because pursuant to the regulations, it is stipulated that an employee is not considered to be paid on a salary basis if the compensation is subject to reductions "because of variations in the quality or quantity of the work performed."

Accordingly, employers should not make a reduction in pay for absences of less than a full day. Until either the interpretation of the law and the regulations is modified by the United States Supreme Court, or changed by Congress or the DOL, an employer is better off disciplining employees for such absences, up to and including discharge from employment for excessive absences from work over and above that permitted by the Family and Medical Leave Act.

Executive Employees
In order for an employee to be exempt as a bona fide executive, he or she must meet all of the following tests:

- The primary duties of the employee must be in management of the enterprise or of a customarily recognized department or subdivision of such enterprise.

- The employee must customarily and regularly direct the work of at least two or more other employees.

- The employee must have the authority to hire and fire, or recommend hiring and firing; or be a person whose recommendation on these or other actions affecting employees is given particular weight by those making the decision to hire and fire.

- The employee must customarily and regularly exercise discretionary powers that require judgment rather than simply following direct orders clearly given.

- The employee must devote no more than twenty percent (20%) of his or her hours of work to activities not directly and closely related to the managerial duties. In the case of a retail or service establishment, no more than forty percent (40%) of the hours of work can be devoted to activities not directly related to management duties.

- The executive employee must be paid on a salary basis at the rate of at least $155.00 a week.

The percentage test for nonexempt work would not apply to an employee who is in sole charge of an independent establishment or a physically separated branch establishment, or who owns at least an interest in the enterprise in which he or she works.

There is also a special proviso for executives paid at least $250.00 a week on a salary basis. If such "highly" paid executives regularly direct the work of at least two or more other employees and the primary duty is management of the enterprise or a recognized department or subdivision of an enterprise, then such managers qualify as exempt executives. This is known as the "short test."

The executive exemption does not include employees training to become executives, but not actually performing the duties of an executive. It also does not include highly paid skilled workers who have no "executive" functions, such as mechanics, linotype operators, carpenters, and other craftsmen.

An executive's function is managerial in nature. Duties include:

- interviewing, selecting, and training employees;

- setting and adjusting pay rates and work schedules;

- keeping production records of subordinates for use in supervision;

- evaluating employees' efficiency and productivity;

- disciplining employees;

- deciding on types of merchandise, materials, supplies, machinery, or tools; and

- providing for safety of employees and property.

The following are examples of nonexempt duties:

- performing the same kind of work as employees under supervision;

- performing any production work, even though unlike that performed by employees, which is not part of the supervisory function;

- making sales, replenishing stocks, or returning stock to shelves, except for supervisory training or demonstration purposes;

- performing routine clerical duties, such as bookkeeping, billing, filing, or operating business machines;

- checking and inspecting goods as a production operation, rather than as a supervisory function;

- keeping records for employees not under his or her supervision;

- preparing payrolls;

- performing maintenance work; and

- repairing machines, as distinguished from occasional adjustment.

For example, it is not uncommon for small retail franchise operations to employ a manager, an assistant manager, and perhaps one other employee. However, although the assistant manager has a title and is paid on a salaried basis, such assistant manager must be paid overtime for all hours worked after 40 hours in any given workweek because the assistant manager is not supervising two or more employees.

Administrative Employees

In order for an employee to be exempt as an administrative employee, the primary duty of the employee must be either being responsible for performing non-manual work directly related to the management policies or general business operations of an employer, or being responsible for work that is directly related to academic instruction or training carried on in the administration of a school system or educational establishment. In the course of this work, the administrative employee must customarily and regularly exercise discretion and independent judgment, as distinguished from using skills and following procedures. This includes having the authority to make important decisions. The administrative employee also must:

- regularly assist a proprietor or a bona fide executive administrative employee;

- perform work under only general supervision along specialized or technical lines requiring special training, experience, or knowledge; or

- execute special assignments only under general supervision.

The administrative employee must not spend more than 20 percent of his or her time in the workweek on nonexempt work, i.e., work not directly and closely related to the administrative duties. In a retail or service establishment, the rule would be not more than 40 percent of the work time in nonexempt work. Lastly, the administrative employee must be paid on a salary or fee basis at a rate of not less than $155.00 a week.

Here, a key sticking point is often determining the duties that call for the exercise of independent judgment. For example, a "price checker" for a grocery store who merely copies the prices of items on a competitor's grocery shelf is not exercising discretion or judgment. However, the individual who uses such information to establish a store's prices is using independent judgment and discretion, and is, therefore, exempt if the other pertinent conditions of employment are present.

As in the case of executive exemptions, there is a special proviso for high-salaried administrative employees. The percentage limitations on nonexempt work do not apply to an administrative employee who is paid on a salary or fee basis of at least $250.00 a week if the primary duties of the position call for responsible office or non-manual work directly related to management policies or general business operations, and such primary work duty includes work requiring the exercise of discretion and independent judgment.

Types of administrative employees include, but are not limited to:

- executive or administrative assistants, such as executive secretaries, assistants to the general manager, confidential assistants, and assistant buyers in a retail trade;

- staff employees who are advisory specialists for management such as tax, insurance, or sales research experts; personnel directors; purchasing agents; safety directors; credit managers; etc.;

- those who perform special assignments, often away from the employer's place of business, such as management consultants, lease buyers, etc.; and

- academic administrative personnel performing work directly in the field of education, such as superintendents of school systems and the assistants whose duties are primarily concerned with the administration of such matters as curriculum, quality and methods of instructing, etc.

Professional Employees

This exemption includes the learned, artistic, and teaching professions. Several tests are involved to determine this status. The primary duty of a professional employee must be work requiring knowledge of an advanced type in the field of science or learning, such as medicine, law, or teaching, customarily obtained by a prolonged course of specialized instruction and study. The work that is done must be original and creative in character and depend primarily upon the person's invention, imagination, or talent. Work as a certified teacher or a position recognized as such in a school system also qualifies. In any of the above, the work must consistently require the exercise of discretion and judgment and be predominantly intellectual and varied, as distinguished from routine or mechanical. Lastly, to be exempt, such employee must not spend more than 20 percent of the time in the workweek on activities not essentially a part of, and necessarily incident to, such professional duties. The salary must be at a rate of not less than $170.00 a week. If the salary or fee is paid at a rate of more than $250.00 a week, then the 20 percent test for nonexempt work does not apply.

However, please note that the salary requirement does not apply to practicing lawyers, doctors, or teachers and is different from the $155.00 salary required for executive and administrative employee exemptions.

Outside Salespersons

An outside salesperson's exemption depends upon where the person works and whether he or she is employed to sell. An outside salesperson is exempt if customarily and regularly working away from the employer's place of business selling tangible or intangible items or obtaining orders or contracts for services. The hours of work of an outside salesperson in activities other than these must not exceed 20 percent of the hours worked in the workweek by normal nonexempt employees of the employer. There is no salary test for outside salespersons.

Section 6 of the FLSA requires payment of a minimum hourly wage to all covered employees who are not exempt or not qualified for subminimum rates of pay. The minimum wage (and overtime) provisions impose an absolute obligation upon the employer to pay the statutory minimum wage free and clear. In other words, deductions from the minimum wage are permitted only for the reasonable costs of board, lodging, and other facilities. The FLSA is not limited to employees who are paid by the hour; its requirements are also applicable to employees who are paid on a piecework, salary, fee, or any other basis. In essence, the minimum wage requirement is met if, in each workweek, the straight-time wages paid to an employee equal the sum of the number of hours worked multiplied by · the statutory minimum rate.

Accordingly, an employee hired solely on an hourly-rate basis must be paid at least the statutory minimum rate. Furthermore, an employee performing two separate tasks at different hourly rates must be paid at least a minimum rate for each hour worked. In other words, hourly rates for one job or for two or more different jobs cannot be averaged over the workweek to meet the minimum wage requirements; each rate paid must be equal to or higher than the statutory minimum.

If an employee is paid on a fixed weekly wage (salary), this wage, when divided by the number of hours worked during the workweek, must equal or exceed the statutory minimum hourly rate. The same is true for fixed monthly or semimonthly wages.

A worker employed on a piece-rate basis also must be paid in compliance with the minimum wage requirements. While an employee under a piece-rate and incentive plan need not actually earn the statutory minimum rate for each hour worked, the hours and earnings for the total weekly period must be sufficient to bring the average hourly rate for the workweek up to the applicable statutory minimum rate.

Tips received by an employee who qualifies as a "tipped" employee may be credited toward the employee's minimum wage up to 40 percent of the minimum rate. If a lesser amount is received in tips, only the amount actually received can be credited. If more than 40 percent is received in tips, the employer nevertheless has to pay 60 percent of the applicable minimum wage rate. A "tipped" employee is an employee engaged in an occupation in which he or she customarily and regularly receives more than $30 a month in tips.

Hours Counted as Working Time

The time for which an employee is entitled to compensation under the FLSA is an interesting and often surprising concept. Working time for which an employee must be compensated includes:

- all time during which an employee is required to be on duty; and

- all time during which an employee may be "suffered or permitted" to work.

Accordingly, under certain conditions, time spent in idleness or nonwork-related activity may still have to be paid for by the employer. The determination depends upon the facts of the individual case as interpreted by the U.S. Department of Labor.

On the following pages, the considerations that are used to determine compensable work time will be explained. These include the definitions of:

- when an employee is *suffered or permitted* to work;

- *waiting time*;

- *on-call time*; and

- when *rest and meal periods* must be paid and other miscellaneous matters.

Suffered or Permitted to Work

Under the wage and hour statutes as they are interpreted by the enforcing agencies, work not requested but *suffered or permitted* is determined to be work time and, consequently, employers must pay employees for these times.

Employees, especially conscientious employees, may voluntarily come in early before the work shift begins and/or may continue working after the work shift is over. The reason is immaterial. If the employer knows or has reason to believe that the employees are continuing to work, the time is working time and it must be paid for. However, an employer need not pay at an overtime rate after eight hours in a day unless bound to do so by its own policy or a collective bargaining agreement.

As an example of this principle, imagine that a lifeguard has scheduled hours to watch swimmers until 8:00 p.m. However, being a conscientious employee, he practices being a business-getting, ingratiating guardian and allows the swimmers to swim until sundown, even though sundown isn't until 9:00 p.m. in the heart of the summer. The owner should be aware of this because of the additional revenue at the candy counter, through its time-and-billing computer cash register. So, the owner of the beach and employer of the lifeguard, even though not physically present at the beach each night and not, in fact, even aware that this practice goes on, may still be investigated and charged for these hours by the Wage-Hour Department. In fact, it is a "willful violation," according to the federal courts.

If the employer knows or has reason to believe or if it can be shown that it should have known or should have had reason to believe that work was being performed, such time must be counted as hours worked.

In all such cases, it is the duty of management to exercise its control over the workplace. Management cannot sit back and accept the benefits without compensating for them. The mere promulgation of a rule against such work is not enough. Management must exercise the power of enforcing the rules and the schedules of its place of business.

Waiting Time

What is *waiting time*? Whether waiting time is time worked under the FLSA depends upon the particular circumstances of a given case. The determination involves "scrutiny and construction of the agreements between particular parties, appraisal of their practical construction of the working agreement by conduct, consideration of the nature of the service, in its relation to the waiting time, and all of the circumstances. Facts may show that the employee was engaged to wait or they may show that he waited to be engaged," said one court.[5]

Consider the following example of a frozen custard stand, where sometimes it is so busy at 5:00 p.m. that the customer lines at the order counter get very long. At other times, no one is there. Accordingly, the night shift is scheduled to begin at 5:00 p.m. to accommodate the long lines. But when 5:00 comes and no one is there, the manager gives the employees each a soda and asks them to punch in at 6:00 p.m. instead of their regular starting time. However, he tells them to punch in if it gets busy. Is there liability? Yes.

The U.S. Supreme Court, in interpreting the Fair Labor Standards Act, has ruled as follows:

> An employer, if he chooses, may hire a man to do nothing, or to do nothing but wait for something to happen. Refraining from other activity often is a factor of instant readiness to serve, and idleness plays a part in all employments in a standby capacity. Readiness to serve may be hired, quite as much as service itself . . . [6]

These principles are applicable even though there may be a custom, contract, or agreement not to pay for the time spent waiting. No private understanding can negate the federal or state law.

On-Call Time

On -call time, when employees are required to remain on the employer's premises or so close to it that they cannot use the time effectively for their own purpose, is working time, according to wage and hour law. For example, in one case involving a health care institution, the employer violated the overtime provisions of the FLSA by failing to pay employees in its radiology department at one and one-half times the regular rate for on-call hours the employees worked in excess of their 40-hour workweek. In this particular case, on-call time required that the employee hold himself ready to be present if the workload exceeded the level that could be handled by the personnel on duty at that time.

However, this is distinguished from the situation where employees are not required to remain on the employer's premises, but are merely required to leave word at their homes or with company officials about where they may be reached. This is not working while on call.

Rest and Meal Periods and Other Considerations

Relative to rest and meal periods, rest periods of short duration, running from five minutes to about 20 minutes, are not uncommon. However, these must be counted as hours worked. In addition, these periods of rest may not be counted to offset other working time, such as compensable waiting time or on-call time as discussed above. This is one area where some state laws are more stringent than the federal law. In some states, in order for such time to be uncompensated, the employee must be completely relieved from duty and be free to leave the place of business for at least 30 minutes.

Concerning lectures, meetings, training programs, and similar activities, generally, attendance may not be counted as working time only if all four of the following criteria are met:

1. Attendance is outside the employee's regular working hours;

2. Attendance is, in fact, voluntary;

3. The course, lecture, or meeting is not directly related to the employee's job; and

4. The employee does not perform any productive work during such attendance.

In regard to voluntary or involuntary attendance, the time is not truly voluntary if the employee is given to understand or led to believe that the present working conditions or the continuance of the worker's employment would be adversely affected by *non*-attendance.

The Equal Pay Act

The Equal Pay Act of 1963 prohibits wage discrimination on the basis of sex, and applies to all employees covered by the minimum wage provisions of the Fair Labor Standards Act. In addition, the investigation, administration, enforcement, and exemptions of the FLSA are similar to those of the Equal Pay Act.

Equal pay law is to be distinguished from the doctrine of *comparable worth*. The Equal Pay Act prohibits an employer from paying wages to employees of one sex at rates lower than those accorded employees of the opposite sex for "equal work on jobs," described by the statute in terms of equality of the "skill, effort, and responsibility" required for performance under similar working conditions in the establishment where they are employed. The key terms of the Equal Pay Act are *equal skill, equal effort*, and *equal responsibility*. The terms constitute three separate tests, each of which must be met for the equal pay standards to apply. The term *equal* has been construed by the courts to mean *substantially equal* rather than identical.

Comparable worth is a different concept. The proponents of comparable worth believe that women, as a group, are underpaid for their work because women are concentrated in the lowest paying jobs; that jobs traditionally held by women pay less; and that women entering the labor force for the first time are channeled into less valuable and less demanding jobs which pay less. In explicating this claim, they allege that women are "cooks" while men are "chefs"; women are "secretaries" while men are "administrative assistants"; and women are "hostesses" while men are "maitre d's." This is described as *occupational segregation* or *job segregation*.

To compensate for this, the proponents of comparable worth propose that wages should be set on the basis of the comparable worth of a job. That is, they propose that compensation should be determined and pay equity be maintained by paying men and women equally for dissimilar jobs where skill, effort, and responsibility requirements can be shown to be substantially comparable.

The value of a job in a comparable worth scheme is determined internally, pursuant to job evaluation studies which proponents claim more scientifically determine the worth of what one should be paid. Simply put, the Equal Pay Act applies to dissimilar pay for the same or similar job, while comparable worth calls for raising the pay of certain workers on the basis of comparisons of dissimilar jobs.

Another distinction that should be made is that between the Equal Pay Act and Title VII of the Civil Rights Act. The main provision of Title VII of the Civil Rights Act makes it an unlawful employment practice for a covered employer to fail or refuse to hire or to discharge any individual or "otherwise to discriminate against any individual with respect to his or her compensation, terms, conditions, or privileges of employment because of such individual's . . . sex . . . ." The Equal Pay Act of 1963 likewise prohibits sex discrimination, but only in the area of wage compensation.

Burden of Proof in Equal Pay Act Cases

The plaintiff in any equal pay case has the burden of proving that the aggrieved employee has performed work equal to that performed by employees of the opposite sex involving equal skill, effort, and responsibility and that the work was performed under similar working conditions in the same establishment. Once a plaintiff has established such a prima facie case, then, according to the Supreme Court, "the burden shifts to the employer to show that the differential is justified under one of the [EPA] exceptions."[7] The employer must prove as an affirmative defense that the wage differential is not, in any manner, based on sex, but rather that it is based on a nondiscriminatory seniority system, a merit system, a system that measures earnings by quantity or quality of production, or some other factor other than sex.

The determination as to whether two jobs are "substantially equal" is ascertained by looking at the job requirements and the duties actually performed by the employees involved in the comparison. Administrative interpretations define the term *skill* as including such factors as experience, training, education, and ability, each measured by the performance requirements of the particular jobs involved in the comparison. The mere possession of a skill will not justify a differential if the duty that necessitates the skill is only performed for an insignificant amount of time

Relative to "equal effort," the term *effort* is defined as "the physical or mental exertion needed for the performance of the job." It is the difference in the amount or degree of effort that is actually expended in the performance of the jobs that counts.

Finally, relative to "equal responsibility," the administrative interpretations set forth a general guideline to the effect that "responsibility is concerned with the degree of accountability required in the performance of the job, with emphasis on the importance of the job obligation."

The equal pay standards do not apply in a comparison of employees who perform otherwise equal jobs under dissimilar working conditions. The Supreme Court construed the term as encompassing the physical surroundings and hazards of a job, such as "inside work versus outside work, exposure to heat, cold, wetness, humidity, noise, vibration, hazards (risk of bodily injury), fumes, odors, toxic conditions, dust, and poor ventilation.

Record-Keeping Requirements

Pursuant to the statutes, employers are required to keep certain records. Failure to keep such records may result in sanctions, including criminal sanctions. In general, while the regulations require no particular form of records, the following data is required to be kept for each employee:

- full name, with any identifying number;

- current home address;

- birth date, if under 19;

- occupation;

- day and hour when employee's workweek begins;

- regular hourly rate of pay, basis on which wages are paid, and nature and amount of each payment excluded from regular rate;

- hours worked each workday and each workweek;

- total daily or weekly straight-time earnings;

- total weekly premium pay for overtime;

- total additions to or deductions from wages paid each pay period;

- total wages paid each pay period; and

- date of payment and pay period covered.

The regulations require that the employer preserve and keep available for inspection and transcription for a period of three years all payroll or other records containing the required data, plus union contracts and other basic employment records. In addition, for a period of two years, various supplementary records, such as customer orders and bills of lading, employee time cards, production tables, and rate schedules, must be kept. Lastly, the employer is required to display the wage and hour poster in conspicuous places.

It is important to note that accurate records are important to the employer. These may be used as a defense against claims filed. If the records are shown to be unreliable, they will be of little assistance in defending against charges filed by employees or the Wage-Hour Division. Moreover, failure to observe the record-keeping regulations is in itself an unlawful act. Such failure alone may justify civil or criminal action against the employer, even though no violation of wage, hour, child labor, or equal pay provisions of the FLSA can be proved.

Child Labor Laws
The Child Labor Laws were established both for the safety of children and to preserve work for adults by eliminating low wage competition from children who would be willing or forced to do such work.

This area is under increasing scrutiny by Department of Labor investigators. One particular target has been the use of minors in fast food restaurants. Indeed, the Solicitor of Labor has outlined the Labor Department's enforcement philosophy to target the worst actors. The Department of Labor intends to leverage its enforcement capabilities to go beyond its staffing levels by targeting defendants that have high visibility and that are able to pay. One example of such leveraged enforcement was a $16.2 million dollar fine against a grocery chain.

Many states are joining in this enforcement action as well. One of the concerns is that students who work during the school year all too often seem more concerned about their work for pay than they do their schoolwork. To counter this natural phenomenon, some states have set maximum hours of work for different age levels, which vary depending upon the day of the week and whether or not school is in session, and if so, for how many days in the school week. Also restricted is the time of day a minor can work dependent upon whether it is a school day, Friday, or non-school day that precedes a school day.

Compensating Correctly—Wage and Hour Law Compliance

Employers that are subject to both federal and state laws must comply with the most stringent of the provisions, so they must be aware of state requirements.

The following chart is an example of what one state, Wisconsin, has outlined with regard to maximum hours of work for children. This trend will spread to other states, if not federally mandated at some point in time in the future.

Maximum Hours of Work	12 - 13 year olds	14 - 15 year olds	16 - 17 year olds
Daily:			
School Days:			
Mon., Tues., Wed., Thurs.	4 hours	4 hours	4 hours
Friday and Non-School Day	8 hours	8 hours	8 hours
Day During Non-School Week	8 hours	8 hours	Unlimited
Weekly:			
School Week	18 hours	18 hours	26 hours
School Week Less Than 5 Days	24 hours	24 hours	32 hours
Non-School Week	40 hours	40 hours	50 hours
Permitted Time of Day			
School Day	7am-8pm	7am-8pm	7am-11pm
Friday	7am-9:30pm	7am-11pm	7am-12:30am
Non-School Day Preceding			
School Day	7am-8pm	7am-8pm	5am-11pm
Non-School Day Preceding			
Non-School Day	7am-9:30pm	7am-11pm	5am-12:30am
Day During Non-School Week	7am-9:30pm	7am-11pm	Unlimited
Newspaper Delivery:			
Day Preceding School Day	5am-8pm	5am-8pm	5am-9pm
Day Not Preceding School Day	5am-9pm	5am-9pm	5am-11pm
Street Trades:			
Day Preceding School Day	7am-8pm	7am-8pm	6am-9pm
Day Not Preceding School Day	7am-9pm	7am-9pm	6am-11pm
Maximum Days Per Week			
Newspaper Delivery and			
Agricultural Work	7 days	7 days	7 days
Other Work	6 days	6 days	6 days

In addition, because of its hazardous nature, some work has been declared prohibited work to minors of certain ages. Again, this concept is administered on both the state and the federal level. Examples of the kind of employment prohibited to minors between the ages of 14 and 16 years old are the following:

- Manufacturing, mining, or processing that requires the performance of any duties in workrooms or workplaces where goods are manufactured, mined, or otherwise processed.

- The operation or tending of any hoisting apparatus or of any power-driven machinery other than office machines.

- The operation of motor vehicles, or service as helpers on such vehicles.

- Outside window washing that involves working from windowsills or requires the use of ladders, scaffolds, etc.

- Setting up, adjusting, cleaning, oiling, or repairing power-driven food slicers and grinders, food choppers and cutters, and bakery-type mixers.

- Work in freezers or meat coolers.

- Work in warehouses, loading and unloading goods to and from trucks, railroad cars, or conveyors, except office and clerical warehouse work.

- Construction work, including demolition and repair-type work.

For minors ages 16 to 18 years old, prohibited employment includes work that involves the operation of power-driven woodworking machines, circular saws, and guillotine-action veneer clippers; operating an elevator, crane, derrick, hoist, or high lift truck; riding on a man lift or freight elevator; or operating, setting up, adjusting, repairing, or cleaning any hazardous machinery such as bakery machinery, printing or die-casting presses, paper cutting or shear devices, and the like.

Below is a checklist that can be used to determine whether an employer is in compliance with sound employment practice rules if it employs individuals under the age of 18. It is important to note that it is mandatory that employers have on file a work permit for each employee under the age of 18. Failure to do so may result in additional damages, often including treble damages for workers' compensation injuries should a minor be working without a work permit.

Compensating Correctly—Wage and Hour Law Compliance

Child Labor Law Checklist

Are all employees 18 years old or over?

Yes____ No____

If "no," complete the following:

Is there proof of age on record for employees under 19 years old?

Yes____ No____

Are all occupations which are included in the 17 Hazardous Occupations Orders performed only by employees who are 18 years or older?

Yes____ No____

If under age 16, do employees work only between 7:00 a.m. and 7:00 p.m. in any one day, except during the summer (June 1 through Labor Day), when the evening hour is 9:00 p.m.?

Yes____ No____

If under age 16, do employees work three hours or less per day when school is in session or eight hours or less a day when not in session?

Yes____ No____

If under age 16, do employees work 18 hours or less per week when school is in session or 40 hours or less per week when not in session?

Yes____ No____

Are 14- and 15-year-old minors employed in only the permitted occupations?

Yes____ No____

Have all employees or agents of the company been instructed not to hire helpers on motor vehicles who are under 18 and could be considered employees of the company?

Yes____ No____

Are all minors paid the applicable minimum wage?

Yes____ No____

If not, are they employed at special minimum wages under the appropriate certificate?

Yes____ No____

Do all minors receive proper overtime pay?

Yes____ No____

Are current child labor permits maintained in the company's files for each minor?

Yes____ No____

Are male and female minors paid the same for equal work?

Yes____ No____

Is wage and hour law an important subject? I was tremendously surprised at how this topic seemed to light up the switchboard every time I talked about it while speaking across the country. In a speech to the Association of Legal Administrators in Chicago this topic lasted over one and one-half hours with spontaneous questions and answers alone!

It has been reported that in the United States as many as four million employees are paid at or near the minimum wage. Beginning April 2, 1990, such workers' wages were boosted by federal law to $3.80 from $3.35 per hour. On April 1, 1991, the minimum hourly wage was raised to $4.25 per hour. It is now $5.15 per hour with proposals in this election year of 2000 to carry it in stages higher still despite acknowledgment by both political parties that increasing wages from the bottom up has an inflationary impact. Of course, in this era of the lowest unemployment rate in three decades, the true minimum wage is determined by what an employer *must* pay to recruit employees, usually a higher figure for even fast food restaurants requiring little education and training to start.

However, with the passage of NAFTA, is it in the federal interest to increase the minimum wage, particularly in states that border Mexico, to further increase the distance between the minimum labor rate in the United States and in Mexico? Of course, the answer to this question gets into broader philosophical and political science arguments, which are the subject of much debate. Additionally, there are many that feel that increasing the minimum wage instead of spreading work around, and insuring a decent wage over the poverty level of existence in the United States as our society defines it, actually reduces opportunities for those willing to work at those wages. As we know, individuals gain much more than just wages when working—they gain training and experience, too.

It was interesting to read about the 1988 testimony before Senator Kennedy's Labor and Human Resources Committee. Senator Tom Harkin (D-Iowa) asked then Labor Secretary William E. Brock whether he thought people had a right to seek a job or whether they had a right to be provided with one. The Labor Secretary for the Reagan Administration responded by saying, "I don't recall in the Constitution that there's anything establishing the right to a job." However, Harkin was unsatisfied with Brock's answer and asked what he thought about reducing the length of the standard workweek from 40 hours to 32 or 35 hours as a means of spreading available jobs among the people. The question was ducked when Brock asked Harkin if the reduced workweek would be accompanied by reduced pay. Saying that it would not, Harkin suggested that the extra day off under the reduced workweek would be used for educational purposes. "We ought to take a look at the old myth that the 40-hour workweek is written in stone," Harkin said.

Additionally, it would appear the most significant change being proposed would be to change the basic standards of the FLSA as we have known them since 1935, by mandating such things as double-time pay for all hours worked over 40 in a week and time and one-half for all hours after eight in a day. Changes such as these would truly affect inflation, in my opinion, and are unnecessary in a time when we suffer labor shortages as opposed to having to spread available work around, as during the Great Depression when this law was originally passed. Let the market-place set wages, and all will be better off.

Endnotes

1   USDL 98-185, Office of Publications, Washington, D.C.

2   *Fleming v. Hawkeye Pearl Button Co.,* 113 F. 2d 56 (8th Cir. 1940).

3   *Mitchell v. Kentucky Fin. Co.,* 359 U.S. 290 (1959).

4   *Arnold v. Ben Kanowsky, Inc.,* 361 U.S. 388 (1960).

5   *Skidmore v. Swift & Co.,* 323 U.S. 134 (1944).

6   *Armour & Co. v. Wantoch,* 323 U.S. 26 (1944).

7   *Corning Glass Works v. Brennan,* 417 U.S. 188 (1974).

Answers to Chapter Three Test Your Knowledge

1. False. There is no federal law that requires the payment of over-time wages after so many hours in a given working day. Some union contracts require time and one-half after eight hours in a day of work, but this is an agreement that the employer voluntar-ily makes with its union rather than under federal law.

2. True. An employer must begin to pay overtime wages only after 40 hours worked in any particular 168-hour workweek.

3. In order for a lunch period to remain unpaid, the employee must be free from the obligation to work and must actually not work, and the period must last at least 30 minutes in most circumstances by state law. Federal case law mandates a minimum of 22 minutes.

4. e, all of the above.

5. True. The most important factor in determining whether on-call time must be paid is the relative freedom of the employees to engage in their own personal endeavors. If employees are not re-quired to remain on the employer's premises, but are only re-quired to leave word at their homes as to where they may be

reached or even to restrict their movement within the zone of a beeper, such time is not considered to be working time while the individual is on call.

6. True. In order to qualify as exempt from the overtime requirements, employees must be paid on a salaried basis.

7. The paying of compensable time is not permissible in the private sector. It is not permissible to bank hours in one week and have employees take an equivalent amount of time off in another week in order to allow the employer to avoid paying overtime.

8. An employee is suffered or permitted to work when the employer accepts the benefit of such work even though it did not authorize the employee to be at work under wage and hour law.

9. Work that is managerial in nature such that it is considered to be exempt from the payment of overtime includes the following kinds of work:
   a. interviewing, selecting, and training employees.
   d. setting and adjusting pay rates and work schedules.
   i. evaluating employees' efficiency and productivity.
   j. disciplining employees for improper conduct or poor performance.

10. If a complaint is filed about an employer, the resulting audit can cover all of the employees and need not be limited to the issues of the complaining employee.

CHAPTER FOUR

Hiring Legally and Right

The Ten-Step Audit of Hiring Practices

Legal Aspects of Interviewing

Reference and Background Checks

Test Your Knowledge
_____

# of Hiring Issues

1. True or False? In the hiring process, a "neutral" screening method such as requiring a certain score on an intelligence test may be evidence of discrimination if the test does not relate to the job opening and the impact of the test eliminates a disproportionate percentage of individuals in a class protected by the Civil Rights Act of 1964, as amended.

2. True or False? If the job description for an opening requires "heavy lifting" of fifty pounds or more on a regular basis, employers should ask the applicants in the pre-hire interview if they have had a history of back problems or ever filed a worker's compensation claim to screen out those who might be likely to injure themselves on this kind of job.

3. Which of the following interviewing questions may potentially lead to an inference of discrimination because the answer may reveal information that could be used for the purpose of excluding an individual in a class protected by the Civil Rights Act of 1964, as amended, or the Americans with Disabilities Act?
   a. Do you have AIDS?
   b. Can you handle stress on the job?
   c. Are you available for Saturday or Sunday work?
   d. Are you pregnant or planning to have children?
   e. None of the above.
   f. All of the above.

4. True or False? In matching demonstrated job-related behavior to the job opening, the best predictor of future success is relevant past experience.

5. True or False? By including a reference and background check for any candidate being seriously considered for hire, the employer is demonstrating action that a prudent person would take in the hiring process.

6. Which of the following elements are important to include in an offer of employment letter?
   a. The agreed upon starting annual salary.
   b. The agreed upon health insurance coverage and vacation allotment.

  c. Any covenant-not-to-compete agreement that will be required.

  d. That the offer is contingent upon the successful passing of a company-paid physical exam.

  e. All of the above.

7. True or False? It is illegal to include a credit or consumer investigation as part of a background and reference check unless it is first disclosed to the applicant and the applicant consents in writing to allow it.

8. True or False? The Immigration Reform and Control Act of 1986 places an affirmative duty on the employer to verify the identity and employment eligibility of any new hire within three working days of the individual's start date.

9. True or False? Written tests that can be demonstrated as being job-related, valid, and reliable indicators of performance are permitted if the results are used in a nondiscriminatory way.

The answers to these questions are at the end of this chapter.

Sue Jeffers, owner and operator of Stub And Herbs, a University of Minnesota campus restaurant and bar, replied without hesitation when asked the secret of the success of her establishment: "I take great care in hiring my crew, and the crew takes care of the rest. This even extends to the training and disciplining of their fellow employees because of the pride of the crew. The crew won't tolerate the slackers, and weeds them out for me."

Hiring is the key to successful employment practices. It is the one area of the employment relationship over which the employer has total control. Employers who make the right hiring decisions enjoy relationships with employees that will be both profitable and long-lasting for both parties. Making a mistake by hiring an individual who turns out to be a poor performer can cost a bundle.

For example, a client of mine once hired an individual he later described as the "employee from hell" for an engineering sales position. The individual possessed a master's degree in engineering from a reputable educational institution and had ten years of experience in engineering sales for a foreign-owned operation. However, once hired, he proved so inept that the company had to move him to an inside sales/order-taking job. He then fouled up that position as well. When he received a negative performance appraisal, he threatened to sue my client unless his ratings were modified upward! Additionally, he deceitfully manipulated the health insurance by making false disclosures and came close to blowing up this small business's health insurance for all the employees. How did the company ever decide to hire the "employee from hell"? His hiring was based on the employment interviews and decent references. However, the truth of the matter was that his former employer, the foreign-owned company, never adequately supervised his work. When that company went out of business in the United States, it didn't really care about the reference it gave its former employee.

There was only one ingredient of the candidate's pre-employment evaluations that demonstrated quite clearly that the company should not have hired him. An industrial psychologist, who interviewed and tested the candidate, strongly recommended against his hiring. However, the company ignored this dissenting opinion to their regret. He just seemed too good a candidate to pass up given his education, experience, and charming interviewing manner.

When the "employee from hell's" discharge became imminent, he engaged an attorney who threatened to sue the company for wrongful discharge. Fortunately for my client, the employee, prior to his hiring, had signed an employment contract which stipulated that his employment could be terminated with no notice if the employer had good cause, or with 30 days' notice if the employer had no cause. Accordingly, we advised the employer to exercise the 30-day no cause provision in the employment contract, and the employee's lawyer choose not to challenge it. In my opinion, absent such a contractual provision under the facts of this particular case, my client might have been tied up in courts for years. While it could have been worse, the employer lost the time, salary, and training invested in this individual as well as one-month's pay for no work and his own attorney's fees. However, some small business owners are not as fortunate at limiting their losses from a hiring mistake.

This chapter describes a ten-step audit of hiring practices. It will include hiring techniques to help attract, select, and ultimately hire quality applicants that become heroes on the job. Later the chapter outlines what employers should avoid in the hiring process to prevent lawsuits. Also covered is how the Americans with Disabilities Act (ADA) interfaces with other equal employment opportunity laws in the hiring process. The all-important interview and the emerging legal liability of negligent hiring will be discussed. Lastly, there is a discussion of immigration law requirements.

The Ten-Step Audit of Hiring Practices

As of January 2000, the U.S. Department of Labor (DOL) reported that the nation's unemployment rate was four percent, the lowest rate in thirty years. It estimates that 135.2 million people are now working in the United States. The economic boom has produced so many job opportunities that many people who either could not get jobs in the past or chose not to look for them are now looking for them and finding them. A separate survey showed that U.S. employers added 387,000 employees to their payrolls in January 2000 alone! According to a projection by the U.S. Bureau of Labor Statistics, employment in the United States will rise by 20.3 million jobs, or 14 percent, between 1998 and 2008. Because of the keen competition for people to fill these new jobs, let alone the vacant existing jobs, the strong temptation is to just find warm bodies with a pulse capable of "fogging mirrors with their breath" and attempting to train them.

To make matters worse, according to an article in the February 18, 2000, issue of USA *Today*, among Society for Human Resource Management (SHRM) hiring experts who use references to verify length of employment, 53 percent reported that when doing so they discovered falsified information from prospective hires. The CEO of an expanding Silicon Valley firm estimated that 20 to 30 percent of job candidates misrepresented information on their applications. A recent Wall Street Journal column reported that in its annual unscientific review of resumes, a headhunting firm noted that the percentage of candidates falsifying academic credentials had risen again, to over 16 percent of those it received during the last year, continuing the increase in its "Liar's Index" for every year it has done the survey.

Employers must remain vigilant about who is brought onto the payroll. Hiring is almost the only time in the sequence of the employment relationship that the employer has real control. There is no question that counterproductive employees can cost a business enterprise more than just the training time, money, and energy invested when they have to be discharged from employment. A manager who must closely watch substandard employees could be more productive doing something else. Although a marginal employee may be able to improve to a certain level with training, some employees will never be able to perform. Substandard employees can also hurt a business by their effect on others. It is important to hire right because only with great effort can a serious hiring mistake be transformed by training and supervision into a productive, satisfied, competent, energetic, income-producing employee.

The advantages of selecting the right person to fit job needs are many. First, in the competitive business world of today, no employer hires someone as a social service. There is work to be done, and hiring the right employee gets that work done. Moreover, industrial research has shown that the most productive employee in any particular job can be as much as twice as productive as the least qualified. In addition, better-qualified employees get up to speed faster, require less training, are more motivated to improve their skills, and require less supervision. This will give a manager more time to actually manage. Hiring the right person for the job reduces turnover, which saves training costs. Finally, hiring the right employee may keep the company out of legal trouble. Often, legal troubles begin when the poor performer must be disciplined or discharged.

There is no question that hiring is difficult. Indeed, it is made even more difficult by today's litigious society when it seems impossible to get honest referrals from employers who fear defamation actions by employees with poor records. However, there are systematic methods for predicting the future success of an applicant for employment. These systems predict future performance by concentrating on behavior, past performance, and qualifications related to the requirements of the job. Accordingly, let us go through the steps for auditing hiring practices. The first step in hiring legally and right is reviewing the applicable laws that relate to the hiring process.

Audit Step 1: Knowing the Laws That Govern the Hiring Process

There are many laws and legal theories that interact with the act of hiring. For example, the National Labor Relations Act (NLRA) makes it an unfair labor practice to refuse to hire an individual because of his or her union beliefs, and asking questions of applicants to ascertain the extent of union sympathies is construed as interference with an individual's protected right to engage in union activity.

However, probably the most extensive rights of an individual are the federal, state, and sometimes municipal ordinances concerning equal employment opportunity. Title VII of the Civil Rights Act of 1964 was originally passed according to the legislative history to prevent discrimination in hiring and to increase minority representation in the workforce. Sometimes this idea gets lost when the overwhelming number of lawsuits pursuant to the Act pertain to allegations of discriminatory discharge from employment instead of discrimination in hiring, but such was the case when the Act was passed. One of the first cases to be heard by the U.S. Supreme Court was a hiring case, *McDonnell-Douglas Corporation v. Green.*[1] It defined the concept of disparate treatment by stating that an individual can prove allegations of unlawful discrimination when the individual has been treated differently because of his or her membership in a "protected class" of individuals. While the burden of proof is on the plaintiff at all times, a "burden of persuasion" was established. This burden is defined as follows. Individuals filing discrimination complaints must first establish their *prima facie* case. This consists of proving four basic elements: (1) the individual is a member of a class of individuals protected by the statute; (2) the individual was somehow connected with the defendant/employer by having applied for either a position or promotion; (3) the individual was "qualified" for the position or promotion; and (4) someone else not a member of the protected class was hired or promoted instead.

Once the *prima facie* case has been met, the burden of persuasion shifts to the employer-defendant to establish a legitimate business reason or a bona fide occupational qualification for its failure to hire or promote the plaintiff. Once this has been established, then the burden of persuasion returns to the plaintiff to prove that the reason being given by the employer is actually a pretext masking its true discriminatory action. No matter how the burden of persuasion may shift, the ultimate burden of proof always remains on the plaintiff alleging unlawful discrimination.

In another U.S. Supreme Court case, *Griggs v. Duke Power,*[2] another theory of discrimination was established. This was labeled *disparate impact.* Discrimination in violation of the law, the Court said, can also be found where an otherwise neutral policy of an employer has the effect of discrimination by its use in the particular context. In this case the plaintiff had applied for a position as a janitor. However, the employer required all applicants to pass a standardized intelligence test prior to employment. In this particular situation it was found that the standardized test did not apply to the actual job duties required in the janitor job, and had a disproportionate, or disparate, impact on minority applicants.

The Americans with Disabilities Act (ADA), 42 U.S.C. Section 12101 et seq., is another law that impacts the hiring process. In general, its purpose is to eliminate discrimination on the basis of an individual's disability. In broad terms it provides protection for disabled job applicants, those offered a job but who have not yet started it, and existing employees who are or become disabled. Its provisions limit employers from making employment decisions regarding hiring, promoting, or terminating from employment qualified individuals with a disability unless those decisions are job-related, a business necessity, or cannot be avoided by reasonably accommodating the individual's disability. Accommodations are not required to be made if they would create an undue hardship on the employer.

The ADA defines a disability as (a) a physical or mental impairment that substantially limits one or more of the major life activities of such individual; (b) a record of such an impairment; or (c) being regarded as having such an impairment. The EEOC has also set out additional regulations further defining those conditions that qualify as disabilities. According to the EEOC, a physical impairment encompasses "any physiological disorder, or condition, cosmetic disfigurement, or anatomical loss affecting one or more of the following body systems: neurological, muscular, skeletal, special sense organs, respiratory (including speech organs), cardiovascular, reproductive, digestive, genito-urinary, hemic and lymphatic, skin and endocrine."[3]

The law has specific applications in the hiring process to prevent employers from making inquiries in the pre-employment process that will unduly expose an individual's disability and contains provisions that mandate accessibility to the hiring process. This will be covered in more detail below (and in Chapter Nine), but to provide some insight into the analysis a court might make, the West Virginia Supreme Court set forth the following legal framework regarding employment-related disability lawsuits in a recent decision, *Skaggs v. Elk Run Coal Co., Inc.*[4]

The court defined "reasonable accommodation" to mean reasonable modifications or adjustments to be determined on a case-by-case basis that are designed to enable an individual with a disability to be hired or to remain in the position for which he or she was hired. The "duty to accommodate" is that an employer is not required to offer the precise accommodation an employee requests, so long as the employer offers some other accommodation that permits the employee to fully perform the job's essential functions. To state a failure to accommodate claim, the plaintiff must allege that: (1) the plaintiff is a qualified individual with a disability; (2) the employer was aware of the plaintiff's disability; (3) the plaintiff required accommodation in order to perform the essential functions of the job; (4) a reasonable accommodation existed that met the plaintiff's needs; (5) the employer knew or should have known of the plaintiff's needs and of the accommodation; and (6) the employer failed to provide the accommodation.

The court further stated in its analysis that an employer may defend against a claim of failure to accommodate by disputing any of the essential elements of the employee's claim or by showing that the accommodation would impose an undue hardship on it. Undue hardship, however, is an affirmative defense for which the employer bears the burden of persuasion. Once an employee requests reasonable accommodation, an employer must assess the extent of the employee's disability and how it can be accommodated. If the employee cannot be accommodated in his or her current position, or the position being applied for, regardless of how it is restructured, the employer must inform the employee of potential job opportunities within the company and, if requested, consider transferring or hiring the individual to fill the open position. Proof of pretext when the employer refuses to do so, claiming a legitimate business reason, can by itself sustain a conclusion that a defendant employer engaged in unlawful discrimination. Therefore, if a plaintiff raises an inference of discrimination through his or her *prima facie* case, and the fact finder disbelieves the defendant's explanation for the adverse action taken against the plaintiff, the fact finder justifiably may conclude that the logical explanation for the action was unlawful discrimination.

In cases where the defendant employer establishes a legitimate business reason for a discharge, it can prevail if it can prove by a preponderance of the evidence that the same employment action or result would have occurred even in the absence of any discriminatory motive. However, a plaintiff can create a triable issue of discrimination through direct or circumstantial evidence. The question then is whether the evidence, direct or circumstantial, was strong enough to meet the plaintiff's burden of proof.

Some of the provisions of the ADA have specific applications to the hiring process. For example, regarding the testing of applicants for employment, using qualification standards, employment tests, or other selection criteria that screen out or tend to screen out an individual with a disability or a class of individuals with a disability is a violation of the ADA unless the standard test or other selection criteria, as used by the employer, is shown to be job-related for the position in question and is consistent with business necessity. Tests administered to a job applicant or employee with a disability that impairs sensory, manual, or speaking skills must have results that accurately reflect the skills, aptitude, or whatever other factor such test purports to measure rather than merely reflecting the disability impairment. Accordingly, wherever possible, reasonable accommodation should be offered to all applicants who may need to take the tests that may qualify them for the job they seek.

One of the most critical provisions of the ADA relates to the use of physical exams in the hiring process. Specifically, pre-employment medical exams and inquiries are prohibited. An employer may not make pre-employment inquiries into the ability of an applicant's performance of job-related functions. However, the Act specifically states that an employer may make post-employment offer inquiries, including medical exams, to determine an applicant's ability to perform job-related functions and may disqualify someone if the inquiry reveals an inability to perform those essential job functions. Any information acquired in the medical exam must be kept confidential, and all entering employees in the same job category must be given the same physical exam. If an exam rules out an otherwise qualified individual with a disability, the exclusionary criteria must be job-related and consistent with business necessity. The employer must be able to demonstrate that the essential job functions could not be performed with reasonable accommodation. The employer's physician can provide this opinion after taking a medical history as part of the physical exam.

In other words, as will be discussed in more detail below, employers should not inquire into an individual's workers' compensation or other injury history (such as "bad back problems") during a pre-employment interview. Instead, make all offers of employment contingent upon successful passing of a physical exam where such inquiries can be made in the context of a confidential medical exam. Equal employment opportunity law and the ADA are discussed in greater detail in Chapter Nine.

Another important area of law impacting the hiring process is common law tort theory and the doctrine of negligent hiring. *Negligence* in the law is defined generally as "failure to exercise care that a prudent person usually exercises." Employers who fail to follow ordinary care in their hiring procedures may put themselves at risk not only for a hiring mistake, but also for liability to third parties in the event the person hired causes harm to another's person or property. For example, in a very sad situation, one of the early cases in which this legal theory was successfully prosecuted involved a diaper delivery service. The company hired a delivery driver who proceeded to rape and murder one of the young mothers on the route. The family of the victim sued and won a large judgment after proving that if the employer had done any screening whatsoever in the hiring process it would have discovered that the route man it hired had been previously convicted of rape and was only recently released from prison for the crime.

To prove such a claim for negligent hiring, generally a plaintiff must establish that (1) an individual was hired with a history or criminal record involving problem behaviors, (2) the employer knew or should have known that the individual was unfit for hiring in the position, and (3) the employer's negligence was the proximate cause of the plaintiff's injuries. Examples of negligence in the hiring process include such fault as failing to adequately examine the information submitted on an employment application, failing to contact an employee's prior employer to inquire as to the employee's reason for leaving, failure to properly train company representatives doing employment interviews, failing to conduct a proper interview which would have revealed inappropriate conduct, and failing to follow proper hiring protocol.

Other examples of actual cases include *Connes v. Molalla Transportation Systems, Inc.,*[5] where an employer was held not liable for the negligent hiring of a truck driver who had assaulted a motel clerk. The favorable finding for the employer was due to the facts that before hiring the driver it had met its duty of ordinary care by investigating the driver's background through checking his driving record and references, had asked the driver if he had any criminal convictions related to the job for which he was being hired, and had established a company policy that required the drivers to limit contact with the public while on the road.

The opposite happened in *Tallahassee Furniture Co. v. Harrison.*[6] Here the employer was found liable for $2.5 million when it failed to conduct an interview, did not ask for references, and did not ask for an application for employment from a deliveryman it hired. The facts established that the employee returned with a knife to one of his delivery stops and severely injured a female customer. A subsequent investigation established that the employee had a juvenile record of robbery and burglary, a conviction for knife slashing his wife, and several medical hospitalizations for psychiatric disorders with reports of hearing commands to kill others. It is a sad and egregious case, yet failure to follow prudent hiring procedures resulted in a justifiable verdict.

However, if an employer follows certain regular procedures such as those described in this chapter, it should be able to establish that its hiring process was designed to legally select the best candidate for employment, and thereby position itself to defend any claim that the employer negligently hired an individual.

With this brief legal background as the backdrop against which hiring decisions are to be made, the next step in designing a successful hiring protocol is to design the application form.

Audit Step 2: Designing the Employment Application

In the case of *Barbano v. Madison County*,[7] an award was upheld upon review for a woman who was denied a job with the county veteran's office following an employment process that impermissibly focused upon her gender, including questions on the application itself about her plans to have a family. Job applications should not include statements that make any suggestion of identification of protected classes. Questions or references to age, sex, race, marital status, children, U.S. citizenship, birthday, "relative" to notify in case of emergency, hair color, request for photograph, etc., should be eliminated. Any of this kind of information if necessary for affirmative action or other such requirement can be collected *after* an individual job candidate has been hired, in a Post-Employment Information Form.

For example, substitute "individual" for the word "relative" if the identity of an emergency contact is necessary. Instead of asking for citizenship, ask, "Can you after employment submit verification of your legal right to work in the United States?" Instead of inquiring about maiden name, ask whether any additional information relative to change of name, use of assumed name, or nickname is necessary to enable a check on an applicant's prior work or educational record. Asking whether an applicant is planning to have children has been found to not be a job-related question.

Other items should be included on an application. These include disclaimers, such as an Equal Employment Opportunity Statement, which can be phrased as:

> We are an equal employment opportunity employer. No question is asked for the purpose of excluding any applicant for employment due to membership in any class protected by the equal employment opportunity laws such as race, color, creed, national origin, religion, age, sex, handicap, veteran status, disability, or any other class of individuals protected by law.

Another good way to limit exposure to liability is to publish that, "This application will be current for 45 days only. If you have not heard from the company at the end of 45 days, you must contact the company to determine if you must reapply for the position you seek." Some companies use a "stamp" to put in a date after which the application is void. While it is always best to notify job applicants if they are no longer being considered, sometimes it is simply impossible to do so because of the number of applicants. It is generally advised that to limit exposure a company should not accept applications unless a specific position is open. This will help defend against individuals who charge that they were illegally not considered for a position when in reality they never applied. The employer is best advised to control the application process so as to be able to affirmatively establish the extent of applications that were timely submitted for consideration.

Lastly, above the signature line on every application should be "release of liability" language certifying that the information submitted on the application is true and complete, that it authorizes the employer to investigate that information, and that it releases all concerned from liability for asking or providing information about the application for employment. Such a release can also confirm the employment relationship as employment at-will if the applicant is hired. Also, if an agreement to arbitrate any and all claims related to the employment relationship is to be included, it can be put here, too.

A sample application form follows.

Application for Employment

We are an Equal Employment Opportunity employer. No question is asked for the purpose of excluding any applicant due to race, creed, color, national origin, religion, age, sex, handicap, veteran status, disability, or any other class of individuals protected by law. This application will be current for only 45 days. If you have not heard from this company and still wish to be considered for employment at the end of 45 days, you must fill out a new application.

Date
Name   last   first   middle
Street address
City   State   Zip Code
Telephone (   )   Social Security No.
Position Applied for:
Position Application Period Ends:
What source led you to make application with us?

Employment History (List present or most recent employer first)

Employer	Address	Telephone
Dates Employed	Job Title/Salary	Reason for Leaving

Employer	Address	Telephone
Dates Employed	Job Title/Salary	Reason for Leaving

Employer	Address	Telephone
Dates Employed	Job Title/Salary	Reason for Leaving

Employer	Address	Telephone
Dates Employed	Job Title/Salary	Reason for Leaving

Education (List most recent educational experience first)

Name & Location of School	Course of Study	Dates Attended
Diploma or Degree		

Name & Location of School	Course of Study	Dates Attended
Diploma or Degree		

Name & Location of School	Course of Study	Dates Attended
Diploma or Degree		

Personal Information

Are you prevented from lawfully becoming employed in the U. S. because of Visa or immigration status? (All individuals hired must supply proof of citizenship or immigration status according to federal law upon employment.)
Yes _____ No _____

If you are under age 18, can you provide proof of employment eligibility?
Yes _____ No_____

Have you served in the United States Armed Forces?
Yes_____ No_____
Dates of service: From _____ to _____

Briefly describe skills acquired while in the United States Armed Forces._____

If you are an experienced operator of any office machines or equipment, please list them. _____

Do you have any other skills you wish to mention?
_____

Are you presently employed?
Yes____ No____
If so, may we contact your present employer?
Yes____ No____

What is the best time to contact you? _____

If hired, when would you be available? _____

What are your minimum salary requirements? _____

Is any additional information relative to change of name, use of assumed name or nickname necessary to enable a check on your prior work or educational record? If so, what? _____

References

Name of reference_____
_____

Occupation_____

Address_____
_____

City, State, Zip_____

Telephone_____

I certify that the answers given by me to the foregoing questions and statements are true and correct without omissions of information. I agree that the company shall not be held liable in any respect if my employment is terminated because of false statements, answers, or omissions made by me in this application. I also authorize the companies, schools, or persons named above to give any information requested regarding my employment, character, and qualifications. I hereby release said companies, schools, or persons from all liability for any damage for issuing this information. I understand that any misleading or incorrect statements may render this application void and, if employed, may be cause for termination.

I understand that no personnel recruiter, interviewer, or other representative of [Name of Employer] other than (specify title) has any authority to enter into any agreement for employment for any specified period of time. I also understand that if employed, my employment can be terminated with or without cause, and with or without notice at the option of myself or of [Name of Employer]. I further understand that any employment manuals or handbooks that may be distributed to me during the course of my employment shall not be construed as a contract or contract by implication.

I understand that any offer of employment may be conditioned upon the results of a physical exam.

Signature _____

Date _____

Audit Step 3: Creating the Job Profile

The next step in successful hiring is the construction of a job profile. The profile identifies the work requirements of a particular job. Matching an applicant's demonstrated behavior with the behavior demands of the open job leads to the right hiring decision. After all, if an employer can't define what is being sought, how will it recognize the best applicants? By identifying a specific list of qualities necessary for the open position, it will be easier to elicit the information required for decision-making from the interviews, testing, and work record investigations.

Establishing a job profile also makes the hiring process more uniform. Seeking similar information from each applicant will result in a better basis upon which to evaluate the information received. Using a job profile may also help an employer avoid accusations of making decisions prejudiced by factors unrelated to the job. These kinds of hiring decisions can cause trouble with equal rights law. By making a thorough job analysis and then soliciting the appropriate information so that an intelligent decision can be made, the hiring process is less likely to waste time and money or expose the company to a lawsuit. Most important, the employer is more likely to hire the best applicant.

How Jobs Are Analyzed

Job analysis is often used in setting pay levels for a job by determining the demands that a job places on the person who holds it. Of course, the more demanding the job, the higher the level of pay that will be needed to attract qualified applicants. However, analyzing a job for the purposes of making a hiring decision has a somewhat different objective. Here, the goal is to determine what knowledge, skills, and behavior will be needed to succeed at the job.

CHAPTER FOUR

The first step in the job analysis process is to define the specific behaviors needed for successful performance. The existing job description is reviewed and the desired behavior and the critical requirements of an applicant for that job are identified. For example, an entry-level clerical position may have only a few requirements, such as demonstrated typing ability at a certain performance level, demonstrated attendance record, and a demonstrated ability to interact and communicate with others. For a management position, many skills may be required because managers are dependent not only upon their own abilities but also upon their capacity to motivate others to work. This list could include both objective and subjective attributes, such as character traits that have been recognized as leading to success on the job.

The next step is to check if the job description itself needs updating so that it matches the vision the employer has for the job. With every new hire, take time to review the job description to see if it still fits. A carefully constructed job description is accorded substantial weight under the ADA. Conversely, inaccurate or poorly drafted job descriptions can present major problems. Indeed, it might even be evidence of discrimination itself. The key is determining what tasks are essential to performing the functions of a job. It may seem unusual, but the amount of time spent on any particular function is not necessarily in and of itself the most important criteria. Some essential functions might be performed only rarely or infrequently. Generally speaking, reasons cited for classifying a function or job task as essential are: (1) performance of the task is the reason the position exists, (2) a limited number of employees are available to perform the task, and (3) the task itself may require highly specialized expertise calling for specific skills or training.

As previously mentioned, employers should also distinguish between essential and marginal functions of a job. For example, the ability to drive an automobile may be essential for a position as a bus driver, but it might not be an essential function for a retail store clerk who is only called to drive a company vehicle to pick up parts at a warehouse on an infrequent basis and where other employees are available to drive as well. In the latter example, ability to drive would be classified as a marginal job function. Where included in the job description, marginal or nonessential functions should be properly identified as such.

It is also important to provide an adequate amount of flexibility in a job description. A job description should avoid designating specific procedures that an employee must use to do the job, but instead focus on the outcome. Whenever possible, the designation of particular equipment or general references to following established procedures should be avoided. It might be easier for ADA purposes to prove that a specific procedure could be modified to accomplish the same result instead of putting the focus where it belongs, that is, on exactly what needs to be accomplished.

It is permissible and recommended to include "standards of performance." For example, a job description may include the ability to lift a certain amount of weight or the ability to effectively understand written instructions and communicate in writing to others. However, such standards should be examined to ensure that they are appropriate to the position being described. General standards applying to every job may be inapplicable to some positions. Also, if the job result can be accomplished with an accommodation reasonable to the employer, then such standards cannot be used to deny employment to an individual with a disability. An employer should be ready to show that any standards are required of all employees in the position and not just those with disabilities. This would include educational prerequisites such as a law degree for a lawyer, a medical degree for a doctor, etc. Such prerequisites usually revolve around the appropriate educational background, employment experience, skills, or licenses necessary to do the job.

If possible, in creating or modifying job descriptions, the employees themselves should be involved. This could serve to prevent employees from later challenging the contents of the description. While job descriptions should not be padded by including immaterial or unimportant functions, if an essential function is missing it cannot be relied upon in a contested case as a reason to exclude someone from being hired. Employers should be careful not to mix functions of some categories with others if they are not appropriate to the job. Lastly, it is important to include a catchall disclaimer that employees may be assigned other duties in addition to those listed and that the employee's duties may change according to the changing needs of the company.

The following is a sample form for a job description.

Job Description Form

TITLE OF POSITION_____ Date _____

Approximate number of Employees in classification or with same job title _____

Div./Dept. _____ Location _____

Employee Reports to (job title)_____

Purpose of position_____

Fundamental job duties:
    Essential functions_____

    Marginal functions_____

Physical demands of essential functions_____

Working conditions while performing essential functions _____
_____

Qualifications needed (education, skills)_____

Performance and/or Production standards: ·
    (qualitative and quantitative, as long required for all employ-
    ees in this job title) _____

Collective Bargaining Agreements, if applicable_____

The above duties and functions may be changed to keep them current
with changing company needs.

These requirements in the job profile and the job description become the
focus for the remainder of the hiring process. This approach concentrates
the interviewing on the actual needs for which one is hiring and helps to
avoid considering character traits that may be irrelevant and prejudicial, not
to mention illegal. It will help bring successful results from the hiring process.

Audit Step 4: Recruiting a Pool of Applicants

In order to improve the chances of hiring people who will become heroes
and heroines on the job, the employer should recruit as many applicants
as possible for the pool of applicants. However, the best advice is to have
at least two applicants for every position. Not only does this allow for
"comparison shopping," it will provide confidence in the final candidate
chosen for the job. Further, and most significantly relative to the defense
of cases brought by individuals not accepted, it allows the employer to
defend its choice by saying in comparing the two final candidates, the
one awarded the position was chosen because he or she was the better
candidate. There will almost always be easily identifiable and legitimate
business reasons why one individual was chosen over another.

However, in a tight labor market, the temptation is to use the "pass-fail"
method. That is, when there is an opening to be filled, each applicant is

judged as to whether he or she is fit for being hired—pass or fail. If the individual is not hired, then the employer waits until it finds another candidate to judge pass or fail. The problem with this approach is that if a failing individual complains that the real reason for not getting the job was because of membership in a protected class, all the applicant needs to show is that he or she met the minimum qualifications for the job to establish the inference of discrimination. The burden of proof, and potentially a much more difficult burden to establish, is that there was some legitimate business reason for not hiring a person qualified to do the job, or that the person was not qualified in the first place. This burden of proof can be much more difficult to prove than establishing that candidate A was chosen over candidate B because in comparison of their qualifications A was the better choice.

Employers can use many methods of getting the word out that a position needs filling, including word of mouth, walk-in applications, job posting, outside advertising, and use of employment agencies. In fact, the best method of recruiting a pool of at least two candidates for every opening is usually a combination of some or all of these. Although it can be successfully argued that word-of-mouth recruiting results in current employees informing only friends and relatives (typically of their same racial group) about a position, thus perpetuating a single-race workforce, in my opinion the most exposure to potential liability comes when publicly advertising for an open position.

While an employer has the right to set whatever qualifications it wants and to use any hiring method, it should exercise care not to utilize arbitrary, artificial, or discriminatory standards that may have the result of restricting employment opportunities of protected classes of people. The idea is to avoid wording in any advertising that may be indicative of discriminatory preference. For example, avoid using gender descriptions unless the employer can demonstrate a bona fide occupational qualification or limitation for it. Do not state a preference for marital status or show a preference for individuals outside a protected class, such as "the perfect job for young, strong men."

However, there is nothing wrong with describing the nature of the job and letting applicants decide for themselves what is fit for their various abilities and talents. For example, if there are physical requirements for the job such as weight-lifting requirements, there is nothing wrong in stating them. If the job requires long hours or frequent travel or weekend work, state it upfront. If there is a specific location for the job, or if it may require a second language, put it in the advertisement. Lastly, affirm in every public advertisement, "We are an Equal Opportunity Employer."

Audit Step 5: Matching Behavior to the Job

Once a pool of at least two candidates is gathered, they must be evaluated. Employers typically use three main methods to evaluate applicants:

1. interviews,

2. reference checks, and

3. tests.

For any method to prove useful, it should display four key qualities. The screening method used should be:

1. job-related,

2. valid,

3. reliable, and

4. used in a nondiscriminatory manner.

A job screening method that is *job-related* is one that evaluates candidates on whether or not they can carry out the duties of the job, typically as defined in the up-to-date job description. Second, a job method is *valid* if it accurately predicts what it professes to predict. For instance, if a screening method aims to predict a job applicant's skill on a particular job function, how accurately does it do so?

Third, is the screening method *reliable*? For instance, it is quite common for two managers to interview the same applicant but arrive at different predictions of how the person may carry out the requirements of the job. Such an interview is *unreliable*, since two interviewers came to differing conclusions about the same candidate. In contrast, if two managers both score an interview or test in the same way, then such interviews and tests may be reliable predictors of success or failure. A job screening method is reliable if it provides similar results each time the same candidate is tested using the same screening method. Often, tests that are objective in their scoring procedures are more reliable than face-to-face interviews because such interviews are naturally subjective. Usually the creators of such tests will have documented statistical proof that their psychological tests are reliable.

Finally, a screening method to determine who to hire is to be *used in a nondiscriminatory manner*. It is nondiscriminatory if each person's test results are analyzed and applied in the same way, regardless of the candidate's race, gender, or membership in any other protected class for equal employment opportunity law purposes. In this regard, the EEOC follows the 80-Percent Rule, which says, "an employer should hire qualified minority candidates at least 80 percent as frequently as the company hires qualified non-minority applicants," using any particular screening method.[8]

Generally, tests that aid in selecting the right candidate and avoiding the "employee from hell" fall into four main types: behavior tests, abilities tests, integrity tests, and technical skills tests.

Behavior tests usually include questionnaires that predict how a person may act on the job. For example, a behavior test may evaluate candidates on interpersonal skills such as friendliness and teamwork; personality traits such as a tendency to follow rules and handle criticism; and motivation, such as a desire to help people and earn more money.

Abilities tests generally measure a candidate's aptitude at handling mental challenges posed by a job. For instance, such a test could evaluate a candidate on his or her ability in problem-solving, vocabulary, arithmetic, grammar and spelling, and speed and accuracy in handling small details.

Integrity tests are generally paper-and-pencil tests that delve into a candidate's character as it may relate to key workplace concerns. This type of test may help pinpoint a candidate's crucial opinions on drugs/drinking, work ethic, and honesty.

Lastly, *technical skills tests* evaluate a candidate's ability to carry out skills necessary to do a specific job. Common examples include typing tests or tests to see if an applicant can operate certain kinds of machinery that might be used on a particular job.

Almost invariably, these testing instruments have been developed using scientific research procedures. Such research, which often takes years to conduct, helps objectively establish the validity and reliability of the testing. When used in conjunction with other screening methods and the all-important face-to-face interview, such testing is both cost effective and legal.

Many employers are concerned with whether testing complies with the ADA. The key to understanding equal employment rights shaped by the ADA requirements is that so long as the tests are not designed or used in a manner to screen for physical or mental impairments—but rather, to test for job-related character attributes—the tests are legal. If such tests are not selectively applied or utilized, but used on an equal basis to applicants in a nondiscriminatory manner, they are legal and effective.

Of course, employers should only use tests that have been thoroughly researched to establish validity and reliability. Such tests are generally developed by industrial psychologists who possess expertise in workplace testing to predict on-the-job performance. Employers should ask about a particular test's research base and feel free to demand a copy of the test's technical manual that describes research results establishing the test's validity and reliability. It may come as a surprise that the use of such tests is actually easier to defend in court than the reliance on typical face-to-face interviews alone.

Most commonly, testing is used as only one component in a framework of other legal hiring procedures. The best advice for employers is to collect a pool of candidates and then screen out those unqualified using consistent, job-related criteria. Then interview, test, and check references for candidates who seem the most qualified to do a good job. This also might include face-to-face interviewing with licensed psychologists, who will help determine whether or not the candidate is likely to fit in with the company culture and work well with its customers.

Most importantly, employers should not rely solely on one screening method. Instead, choose candidates who, based on *all* of the screening methods, seem most likely to succeed. Take into account the predictions made about each applicant by all the methods.

In order to comply with the ADA requirements, candidates should be advised that there may be alternative ways to take the tests if they have a disability that may make taking the tests difficult without reasonable accommodation. For example, a dyslexic candidate may have a hard time reading certain tests. In this regard, the ADA specifies that the candidate must tell the employer if he or she has a disability that prevents him or her from suitably handling an interview, test, or other screening method. Accordingly, it is appropriate for employers to inform applicants that alternative testing methods can be made available, if necessary. If the applicant does not request alternative procedures, there is no duty to provide them. This should be handled on a case-by-case basis.

Audit Step 6: The Legal Aspects of Interviewing

The next step in the hiring process is the pre-employment interview. It is important to understand the legal aspects of an interview as they relate to equal employment opportunity law because improper inquiries can be used as evidence against an employer to establish a violation of the state and federal equal employment opportunity statutes. Many questions are not by themselves per se illegal and will not automatically lead to the jailhouse. However, inventive and imaginative plaintiffs' lawyers utilize such questions, even when the employer does not use the information in the answers, to be probative of establishing that the employer's reason for alleged discrimination is really a pretext. The theory presented to the judge, jury, or administrative law judge is that if the question doesn't relate to the job, why is it being asked if not to be used as a basis for discrimination?

The key to employment inquiries is to ask about areas that will provide information about the person's ability to do the job. Indeed, the questions should, for the most part, be substantially the same for all applicants. In this way, the employer can avoid being charged with probing into one area with one applicant and not doing the same with another, and thereby discriminating.

Basic Questions to Avoid
1. Age and date of birth?

    The answer to the question does not relate to the ability of the job applicant to perform the job. Knowing the exact age of an applicant does not normally help to determine whether an individual is qualified. If the information is needed for insurance purposes, the forms, with the pertinent facts, can be filled out after the employee is hired.

2. Arrests and conviction records?

    Under some state laws, a past arrest that did not lead to a conviction should not be given any consideration since the person was not proven guilty. Relative to a conviction, one may inquire, but should do so only with the disclaimer that unless it is related to the job information given in response, it will not be used in determining the applicant's employability. Also, to further muddy the waters, in some states there is a duty to *include* a criminal background check for health care employees, as well as a corresponding obligation on the employer not to discriminate unless a violation discovered substantially relates to the job being performed by the individual. To keep such individuals whose background check reveals a prior arrest and conviction, an employer may affirmatively certify on a case-by case basis that in its opinion either the offense does not relate substantially to the job or it is too remote in time to be a substantial concern.

3. Available for Saturday or Sunday work?

To prohibit discrimination on the basis of religion, employers are required to reasonably accommodate a person's religious beliefs and practices. Certain religions prohibit their members from working on a Saturday or a Sunday. If a question in this area needs to be asked, the employer should indicate that a reasonable effort is made to accommodate religious requirements of employees. The better tack on this dilemma is to include the fact that weekend work is an essential function of the job upfront in the advertisement instead of during the interview. However, when doing so be sure to include the disclaimer that the employer "will accommodate up to the extent such accommodation does not create an undue hardship."

4. Citizen of what country?

    Because this question asks of which country the applicant is a citizen, in theory, it is then possible for the employer to use the information to discriminate on the basis of a particular national origin. Again, this knowledge does not relate to the applicant's ability to perform the work. Lawfully immigrated aliens may not be discriminated against on the basis of their citizenship.

5. Height and weight?

    Height and weight may be a protected handicap under the equal opportunity laws. Before asking such questions in a pre-employment context, analyze how the answers to these questions are going to help to successfully predict future performance from the candidate for employment. If imposing minimum height or weight requirements, be sure these are related to the job to be performed.

6. Marital status?

    Marital status is defined as a state of being married, single, divorced, separated, or widowed. The asking of such a question may be used as evidence against the employer where it can be proved that the real reason for refusal to hire a person was because of the employer's beliefs concerning morality, or parental or family responsibility, or because of the belief that a woman's pay represents a second family income while a man's pay does not.

7. Pregnant or planning to have children?

    An employer may not refuse to hire a woman because she is or might become pregnant. Like all the above questions, even if the decision not to hire was made on other grounds, one only increases the likelihood of being charged with discrimination when the question is asked.

There are other questions to avoid, but the idea is that an interviewer should never ask a question that does not relate to the job for which the candidate is being interviewed.

Interviewing in Compliance with the Americans with Disabilities Act

The EEOC has issued rules for what can and cannot be asked in a job interview in order for an employer to be in compliance with the ADA.

This is important because the Americans with Disabilities Act is unique in that it flatly prohibits certain inquiries at the pre-offer stage of the hiring process. These provisions of the law reflect the intent of the Statute to prevent discrimination against individuals with hidden disabilities. The theory is that if applicants are asked about their mental condition at the time they submit their applications, applicants who disclose a disability and are then rejected may not know whether or not the rejection was because of this disclosure.

The protocol required by the ADA in general is one that employers sensitive to the legal subtleties of hiring process have used for many years. That is, first gather a pool of candidates from job applications, posting, advertisements, etc. Initially reduce this pool of applicants to a workable number of finalists by analyzing their resumes, applications, and any other information on hand.

Apply the screening methods of testing, interviewing, and reference and background checks to the group in the same manner for every final applicant. Then select the best job candidate based on these measures. Once the best person is determined, make an offer of employment, but condition the offer on the successful completion of a medical examination administered by the company physician. It is in the context of a private medical exam that the physician can test for drugs, take a complete medical history, and determine whether or not the individual can, with or without reasonable accommodation, physically perform the job as defined in the job description without causing undue hardship on the employer.

It is in this exam that the doctor can legally ask if the candidate has a bad back or some other physical restriction, perhaps even an injury in a past job. Only a physician is qualified to render the medical opinion that will provide a defense to future legal claims if the employer then changes its mind and refuses to hire the candidate. Also, if the candidate lies about his or her medical history to the doctor and the lie is discovered later, such dishonesty can become the legal basis for discharge from employment.

Accordingly, an employer may not ask about the existence, nature, or severity of a disability and may not conduct medical examinations until after it makes a conditional job offer to an applicant for employment. In theory, this insures that any hidden disability will not be considered before the assessment of the applicant's non-medical qualifications. As always, employers *may* ask about the ability to perform job-related functions.

After a conditional offer is made, an employer may require medical examinations and may make disability-related inquiries if it does so for all entering employees in the job category. If an examination or inquiry screens out an individual because of a disability, this criterion must be job-related and consistent with business necessity. The employer must be able to show that the essential functions of the job cannot be performed even with reasonable accommodation.

If an individual is screened out for safety concerns, the employer must be able to demonstrate that the decision was based on objective factual evidence that the individual would pose a significant risk of substantial harm to himself and/or others, and that the risk cannot be reduced below the level of a direct threat through reasonable accommodation.

In the interviewing process then, an employer is not to ask the job candidate about disabilities. An inquiry concerning the existence, nature, or severity of a disability is an inquiry that is likely to elicit information about a disability. The EEOC prohibits an employer from making inquiries about whether an individual has a particular disability or making inquiries that are so closely related to the disability that the individual's response is likely to elicit information about it.

For example, "How well can you handle stress?" and, "Do you work better or worse under pressure?" are inquiries that are permissible *if they relate to the job duties as defined in the job description*. However, to follow up these permissible questions with a question such as, "Have you sought treatment for your inability to handle stress?" would be improper because it is likely to elicit information about whether or not the applicant has a mental disability. This is something for the doctor to ask in the medical exam, not for the interviewer to ask before a job offer.

It is important to understand that information volunteered by an individual in response to a non-disability related question would not be a basis to conclude that the inquiry was disability-related. For example, suppose an applicant is asked whether or not he can perform a particular job function, and in answering that question the applicant states that he has multiple sclerosis. The employer has not made a prohibited pre-offer inquiry. Rather, the applicant has volunteered information about a disability, which was unsolicited by the question. However, in such cases, the employer may not make follow-up inquiries concerning the disability at this pre-offer stage. Questions of a follow-up nature would be prohibited such as, "How debilitating is your multiple sclerosis?" "Does it limit your ability to work?" "Do you expect your condition to get worse?" These are questions that would only be permissible in the context of a post-offer medical exam to determine whether or not the employee could with or without reasonable accommodation perform the job duties as expressed in the job description.

Direct inquiries about a disability are specifically prohibited during the employment interview. These are questions such as, "Are you an alcoholic?" or "Do you have AIDS?" This would even include, according to the EEOC, questions asked to avoid violations of federal law, such as asking a candidate for an interstate truck driver position whether he or she has epilepsy. Even though hiring an epileptic may violate federal law, a trucking company still may not ask at this pre-offer stage whether a truck-driver applicant has epilepsy. Such an inquiry would have to wait until the post-offer medical exam. Another key example given by the EEOC is the question, "Do you have a disability that would prevent you from performing the essential functions of the job with or without reasonable accommodation?" This inquiry is about disability and is prohibited at the pre-offer stage even though the employer may, in fact, be able to refuse to hire an applicant who cannot perform essential functions with or without reasonable accommodation.

However, Congress did not intend to disallow all inquiries about the applicant's ability to perform job functions. For example, an employer may ask an applicant, "This job requires an employee to transport 20 pound bags of frozen fish from a loading dock, down two flights of steps, to a processing machine. Can you perform this function with or without reasonable accommodation?" In addition, an employer may inquire about an applicant's ability to perform both the essential and marginal functions of a job. For example, if a secretarial job involves typing as an essential function and driving as a marginal function, the EEOC says that the employer may ask about an applicant's ability (with or without reasonable accommodation) to both type and drive.

In addition, as a general rule employers should not ask open-ended questions on an application form or in a pre-offer interview about whether an applicant will need reasonable accommodations to do a job and, moreover, in particular what particular accommodation might be necessary.

To this general rule, there are two exceptions. First, in the hiring process, employers may explain to applicants what duties a job involve and then ask if any reasonable accommodations will be needed by the applicant to do them. If the applicant requests an accommodation, and the need for it is not obvious, then the employer may ask for documentation about the disability itself.

The second exception to the general rule is where the employer reasonably believes an applicant will require reasonable accommodation because the disability is obvious or where the application has voluntarily disclosed a hidden disability and/or the need for accommodation for it. In this circumstance, the employer may then ask if reasonable accommodation may be needed and what type of reasonable accommodation it may be.

Questions about impairments are treated somewhat differently by the EEOC rules and regulations because the impairment may or may not be a disability. A distinction is made because an impairment is a disability only if it substantially limits one or more major life activities. Thus, inquiries about impairments are unlawful at the pre-offer stage only if they are likely to elicit information about an applicant's disability.

For example, suppose an employer is hiring a word processor to type information into a computer. The employer asks the applicant with a broken arm how he broke his arm. This is not a prohibited pre-offer inquiry, because it focuses only on the manner in which the arm was broken and is not likely to disclose whether the applicant has a disability such as the extent of the break or the duration of the healing period. However, if the employer follows up with questions such as how extensive the break was and whether or not the applicant will have full use of his arm in the future, these kinds of inquiries are likely to disclose whether the applicant has a disability and are, therefore, improper at the pre-offer stage of the employment process.

Another kind of inquiry that may not be asked are those relative to the ability to perform major life activities and about substantial limitations on such major life activities. For example, asking applicants for a clerical position questions such as, "Can you stand?" or "Can you walk?" are broad questions about the ability to perform major life activities and are likely to elicit information about disabilities. In addition, says the EEOC, they are probably not specifically about an applicant's ability to perform job functions and, therefore, they are prohibited at the pre-offer stage.

Requests for applicants to describe or demonstrate performance of job-related functions are not considered disability-related because they are not likely to elicit information about a disability. Accordingly, employers may ask applicants to demonstrate their ability to distinguish colors if distinguishing between color-coded wiring is a job function. Employers may ask applicants to demonstrate their ability to lift 10-pound boxes of finished metal parts if such lifting is an actual job duty. Employers may ask applicants to retrieve lumber from shelves that are four feet high if this is an actual job duty. If, in response to an employer's request to demonstrate performance, an applicant indicates that he will need a reasonable accommodation, the employer must either: (1) provide a reasonable accommodation that does not create an undue hardship so that the applicant can demonstrate job performance, or (2) allow the applicant to simply describe how he would perform the job function.

The EEOC feels that inquiries concerning attendance are not likely to elicit information about a disability because many reasons unrelated to disability may come into play as to why someone cannot meet attendance requirements. However, at the pre-offer stage, an employer may not ask how many days an applicant was sick at a previous job, because such inquiries are likely to elicit information about a disability. In addition, at the pre-offer stage, an employer may not ask about how much time the applicant would need off from work on account of his disability because these inquiries are likely to elicit information about the nature and severity of the disability. Again, these are questions that must be left to the medical examination, which should be a part of the hiring process once a conditional offer is made.

The same is true for questions regarding workers' compensation history. The ADA prohibits an employer from asking an applicant at the pre-offer stage about job-related injuries or workers' compensation history because these inquiries are likely to elicit information about an applicant's disability. Again, leave these questions for the doctor to ask during the medical exam.

As discussed previously, after an applicant has been offered employment, but before employment has begun, an employer may require medical examinations and may inquire about the existence, nature, or severity of a disability. Employers may condition the employment offer on the results of the examination as long as:

● All entering employees in the same job category are subjected to the examination/inquiry, regardless of disability; and

● The information obtained is kept confidential.

For example, at the post-offer stage, the employer asks entering employees whether or not they have had back injuries and learns that some of the individuals have had such injuries. The employer may then give medical examinations designed to diagnose back impairments to persons who stated they had prior back injuries as long as the follow-up medical examinations are medically related to those injuries.

If an examination is used to screen out a disabled individual as a result of the disability, the exclusionary criteria must be job-related and consistent with business necessity, and the employer must demonstrate that the essential job functions could not be performed with reasonable accommodation. This is an opinion that the company physician should be in a position to give after the examination.

Where safety considerations are implicated, the individual can only be screened out because he poses a *direct threat*. This, too, is an opinion that can only be rendered by a medical doctor. Medical information obtained in the course of a post-offer medical examination or inquiry may be provided to and used by the appropriate decision-makers involved in the hiring process in order to make employment decisions consistent with the ADA. This may include supervisors, managers, and safety personnel where appropriate.

If an individual reveals medical information in response to inquiries, the information obtained must be kept confidential. The employer must be sure that medical information is not included on any personnel documents that are to be distributed to individuals beyond those permitted under the ADA to receive an individual's medical information. Individuals such as an immediate supervisor, manager, or human resource director are examples of those who may have a need to know about such medical information based on their legitimate job functions.

Appraising the Candidate in the Interviewing Process

Hiring right takes hard work. It calls for decision-making based upon both objective and subjective criteria in an attempt to predict future performance from past behavior. This takes judgment, maturity, thinking, and evaluation skills that often do not just come from a book. Employers must "read between the lines." This includes studying both what is presented on paper and information discovered from others, including the applicant, orally.

The first thing for an employer to do is to try and evaluate a candidate's relevant past experience, because it is the best predictor of future success. The key words here are *relevant experience*. Often, an applicant will not have specific experience in the job that is open, but may have independent experience that will fit the analysis of that job. For every critical job requirement, what the applicant has done in the past to meet this kind of requirement will be the best predictor of future performance. Of course, the strongest consideration is then given to those who have met these requirements often and well. In this way, past relevant behavior is used to predict future success.

In studying resumes and other documentation, remember that people prepare them to put their work history in the best possible light and to sell themselves. Good resumes show accomplishments in addition to job responsibilities. They should also include facts that can be verified, such as where the applicant has worked, what job titles have been held, and what was done while employed. However, sometimes these may be described only in general terms. The key is to look for meaningful specific information that can be verified. Pay little attention to statements on a resume that are vague, but sound and look impressive, such as "deep involvement" and "thoroughly involved in planning and implementation." Look for results, such as "responsible for the hiring of personnel for manufacturing positions which reduced turnover in the department and resulted in a 30-percent reduction in the training budget."

What should be in a good resume? First of all, a resume should give an accurate chronology of the individual's experience in the working world. If there are gaps in employment, these may be explored during an interview with the applicant, who otherwise may be qualified. A good resume should describe the candidate's educational qualifications for the job. Employers should remember to screen individuals who are overqualified for the job.

However, this should be done with caution because in some cases the word *overqualified* has also been held to be a code word for age discrimination. Nevertheless, if true, such overqualified individuals may become bored if the job entails elements of the routine or mechanical application of an already designed function. Boredom usually leads to dissatisfaction and ultimate turnover in the job. For example, at my law firm, sometimes the duties of the receptionist, although very important, are quite routine. Often when filling the job, I encounter individuals who are legal secretaries and interview for the receptionist position hoping to use it as a stepping-stone to a legal secretarial position in the future. Unless I know there may be such a position opening up, I will not hire a legal secretary for this position, because experience has shown I will be doing both the legal secretary applicant and the law firm a disservice in the long run.

The resume may also state the applicant's hobbies, which might show an aptitude for the job. For example, if the job requires leadership skills, does the resume show leadership positions in civic organizations?

Good resumes generally should be accompanied by cover letters. This shows that the applicant is truly interested in a specific employer and is a career-oriented candidate motivated to excel.

Since the interviewing process can become an administrative, time-consuming nightmare, it must be controlled. Once applications and resumes have been received, they should be screened effectively in order to allow time to interview the most promising prospects.

In general, when interviewing to hire for a position, employers should try to limit the number of candidates to no more than five people, but always more than one. If an employment agency is used, it can assist in the initial screening.

For some companies, successful screening can also be done through the state Job Service. Also, many private job agencies contact employers on a regular basis concerning any openings for employment. When an opening occurs, job agencies can screen applicants and send their best candidate to interview for the position available. Job agencies know that their reputations depend upon the quality of the individuals they send to be interviewed. By starting out with the best candidates screening agencies can send, selection of a qualified, competent, and successful employee usually results.

Choosing a new employee after a face-to-face appraisal is one of the most important management responsibilities. The value of the employment interview itself cannot be over-emphasized. Matching candidates with the work required is essential in creating the best possible corporate culture. During an interview, the interviewer's objective is to obtain as much information about the applicant as possible, while still selling the company as a good place to work. This obligation cannot be taken lightly. Accordingly, interviewers should strive to have the applicant for employment do most of the talking—at least 75 percent of it.

The information upon which decisions will be made must be pertinent and believable. It should focus on the candidate's experience, qualifications, and, most importantly, the probability of success in the vacant position.

The candidate's major purpose is to receive a job offer, so he or she will try to present him- or herself in the most advantageous manner possible. In pursuit of the job, candidates will say what they think the interviewer wishes to hear. The key is for the interviewer to be able to separate substance from embellishment. That takes preparation, structure, and technique. Asking the right questions should elicit the information needed to decide whom to hire.

The environment in which the interview itself will take place should be considered before beginning the interview. Will the layout of the room influence the amount of information being received from a candidate? If the environment is too formal, will it create stress in the applicant? Usually, interviews are best conducted in private areas, away from possible interruptions, with the interviewing room as neutral as possible to avoid influencing or restricting the candidate's answers to the questions.

Often, candidates give the most spontaneous answers when standing, as opposed to the formal seated interview in a room or office, for example, when they are given a visual tour of the company and shown the environment in which they may be working, Of course, this is unique to each job environment. The point here is to give the overall location of the interview consideration when developing an interviewing technique.

One objective of an employment interview is to predict the candidate's future behavior, which can best be accomplished by listening to the candidate, remembering that past behavior will probably be repeated.

In preparation for an interview, the interviewer should create a composite or profile of ideal candidates and include an understanding of their education and training, experience, past successes, and career goals. Ask questions of applicants to discover if they fit the profile. Remember that asking good questions is only half of the process; the other half involves real listening.

To start an interview sometimes it is best to ask certain fact questions that have a yes or no answer. Generally these relate to screening candidates about their ability to perform job requirements. One question in the hiring of a clerical person might be phrased, "Have you operated a word processor?" The answer will be yes or no because it relates to a specific job requirement.

Once past the specific job requirement questions, the open-ended questions begin. These are the best questions and help the interviewer learn about the individual being interviewed. These questions do not suggest an answer to the applicants or lead them to discovering the correct answer. Generally, they are not questions that can be answered by yes or no. They usually start with the familiar how, when, what, and why. Another open-ended method involves questions that begin with the words, "Tell me about . . . "; for example, "Tell me about your last job," or "Tell me about your past successes and how you achieved them," or "If I were to call your last supervisor and ask him about you, what would he tell me?"

The following are the kinds of questions you may wish to include in an interview:

- What is your reason for leaving your current position?

- What do you most enjoy in your current work?

- What do you least enjoy in your current work?

- What specific strengths do you have that you hope to bring to this job?

- What attributes do you think a person needs to have to be successful in this job?

- In what area do you feel you are weakest in your current position?

- Describe to me your vision for yourself three years from now.

- If you are having trouble in doing your work, what do you do?

- Have you ever had to deal with a difficult personality? What did you do about it?

- Tell me about the best person you ever worked for and why you feel that way.

- Describe for me what it is you do now.

- What does your boss do?

- How would you describe your management style?

- What do you do in a typical workday?

- Describe for me what you know about our company.

- Why do you think you would be good for the job here?

- What would you say is your most significant contribution to the business of your current work?

- What has been your biggest failure? What have you done to prevent it from happening again?

● What is the most important factor to you in choosing to apply for the job here?

Lastly, remember that the interviewing process is a two-way street and that desirable candidates are also interviewing the company at the same time. When a candidate appeals to the interviewer, the tables may be turned so that the interviewer may then want to sell the job to the applicant.

The best results are obtained when the interviewer is prepared with an interview form. This will insure consistency in the process such that each job candidate was asked the more or less the same questions. Such preparation will help insure as well that all questions asked were job-related and that the interview was thorough.

In summary, a hospitable interviewing environment lends itself to eliciting honest and helpful information. If the interview has been properly prepared, and ethically conducted by avoiding questions that do not relate to the candidate's ability to do the job, the interview will succeed in giving the information needed to make the right choice.

Audit Step 7: Reference and Background Checks

Once the screening and interviewing process has reduced the pool of qualified candidates to two or three finalists, the last step is to perform reference and background checks.

It is important to perform a reference check. Doing so establishes that the company made a good-faith effort to find out if there was any problem with the applicant's background that might have easily been discovered. In fact, there is potential risk in the hiring process for failure to make such normal, usual, and customary efforts to check out the background of any new hire.

Indeed, counter to a once popular trend to avoid exposure to defamation lawsuits, it may come as a surprise to find that more and more companies are abandoning the idea to give only "name, rank, and serial number" in response to bona fide inquiries. This is especially true when the prospective employer can provide the past employer with a signed *release of liability* from the job candidate. This can either be put directly on the application for employment itself or on a separate form. It need say nothing more than:

> I authorize [the employer] to make any investigation of my personal or employment history and authorize any former em-

ployer, person, firm, corporation, or government agency to give the [employer] any information they may have regarding me. In consideration of [the employer's] review of this application, I release [the employer] and all providers of information from any liability as a result of furnishing and receiving this information.

Often the best person to do a background check is someone with experience doing it. Using professional private investigators or the services of employer associations can be the most efficient and effective way to do employment background checks. Such private investigators are normally listed in the yellow pages of any telephone book, as are employer associations who may employ individuals to provide this service as well. Such a professional knows what to ask and where to look to both verify resume statements and legally probe into past conduct related to the job.

Prior employers can be asked questions relating to the job in the same manner as in the employment interview: questions relating to job functions, tasks, quality and quantity of work output, attendance, and experience. As in the interview, preparation of a reference question form is helpful in attaining consistency among applicants. This could also be done in writing or e-mail as well as by telephone. Sample questions to ask include:

- What was the applicant's former job title?

- What was his or her rate of pay?

- From what dates was the applicant employed?

- What were his/her job duties?

- How would you rate his/her work?

- What was the reason for leaving?

- What would describe his/her strong points?

- What would describe his/her weak points?

- Would you re-employ the individual?

- What else, if anything, would be helpful information?

Depending on the level of the job, such background checks can be adjusted for thoroughness and cost. However time-consuming and costly this may first appear, catching one applicant falsifying credentials or hiding criminal job-related activity will justify this extra precaution.

Obtaining Credit Checks or Consumer Investigation Reports

Effective September 1997, the Fair Credit Reporting Act, 15 U.S.C. Section 600-624, 1681, was amended to require steps be taken when an employer uses credit and consumer reports as a part of its background check with an applicant for employment.

There are two main requirements for compliance with the Act. First the employer must clearly and conspicuously inform the job candidate that a report may be obtained in the employment hiring process. This disclosure must be made in a separate document from the application itself. The employee must indicate the authorization to conduct such an investigation. No consumer credit reporting agency is to provide such a report without certification from the employer that it has disclosed its intent to receive a report and that the job candidate authorizes such an inquiry.

Second, an employer cannot use the report to make an adverse decision without providing the job candidate with a "pre-adverse action disclosure," which includes a copy of the report and a written description of the candidate's rights. If using such report to deny employment, the employer must allow the applicant to challenge the report and provide the applicant with the name, address, and telephone number of the agency that gave the report. If the agency providing the report cannot explain its report, it must reinvestigate the accuracy of any disputed information within 30 days without cost to the individual. If the report is determined to be inaccurate, no adverse decision can be made because of the report. Accordingly, in disputed cases employers are well advised to wait before making their final employment decision until the dispute is resolved.

Employers found guilty of violating their obligations under the Act are subject not only for actual damages, but punitive damages as well, plus costs and reasonable attorney's fees.

Employers that choose to use consumer report information should have applicants sign the following disclosure form.

Applicant Disclosure and Consent
to Request Consumer Report Information

I understand that the Company may utilize the services of a consumer reporting agency as part of the procedure for processing my application for employment. I also understand that if hired, the Company may obtain further information through subsequent investigations by a consumer reporting agency so as to update, renew, or extend my employment, or for consideration for reassignment or promotion.

I understand that information obtained from a consumer reporting agency's investigation may include information from the previous seven years. This information may include credit background, references, past employment, work habits, education, judgment, liens, criminal background, character, general reputation and driving records. Information regarding bankruptcy filing(s) may include information from the previous ten (10) years. [Information obtained from a consumer reporting agency's investigation for employees with a salary which equals or which may reasonably be expected to equal $75,000 may extend back indefinitely.]*

I understand that such information may be obtained direct or indirect contact by a consumer credit agency with former employers, schools, financial institutions, landlords, and public agencies or other persons who may have such knowledge.

I also understand that, pursuant to the Fair Credit Reporting Act, 15 U.S. C. Sec. 1681a, et. seq., (FRCA), before I am denied an assignment, extension, reassignment, or promotion of employment, or other benefit of employment, based in whole or in part, on information obtained in the report, the Company will provide me with a copy of the report and a description in writing of my rights under the FCRA.

I understand that if I disagree with the accuracy of any of the information in the report, I must notify the Company within five (5) working days of my receipt of the report. If I notify the Company that I am challenging information in the report, the Company will not make a final decision on my status until after I have had a reasonable opportunity to address the information contained in the report.

I hereby consent to this investigation and authorize the Company to procure a report of my background as stated above from a consumer reporting agency.

Applicant's name (print): _____ SS#_____

Signature: _____ Date: _____

* This information can be removed if not applicable to the specific applicant or employee.

Audit Step 8: The Employment Offer

Once the interview and reference check are over, the manager has acquired the information necessary to make the best possible choice. The next step is to make the offer of employment. Typically, I suggest that one personalize the offer by presenting it in person or in a telephone conversation. It is a "golden moment" for both parties. However, the employer should include in the conversation that the verbal offer will be confirmed in writing. Having concepts in writing minimizes surprises. If there are special considerations involved, such as employment contracts to be signed that contain covenants not to compete or trade secret protection language, they should be mentioned, even if the actual documents will be drafted and signed later. Mention as well that the offer of employment is *contingent* upon the successful passing of a medical exam. If this exam will include drug testing, mention that too. Also include the salary offer and when the company must be notified if this offer is accepted.

In some situations it can be useful to state in the written offer the appropriate period for notice of termination by either party. This is especially true in the professional setting. It will again serve to minimize surprises when such time comes.

An example of such an offer letter follows.

Dear _____,

Congratulations. We welcome you to _____, Inc.

This letter is to confirm our telephone conversation yesterday and our offer of employment to you to become our Executive Vice President of Marketing. Based on our conversation, it is my understanding that you accept our offer, and will be able to start April 1. It is exciting to have you on board with our marketing team.

As we discussed, your starting rate of pay is at an annual salary of $75,000. During your first year you can anticipate receiving a six-month and twelve-month performance and salary review.

Also, it is my understanding that you will receive our standard family health insurance plan effective your first day of work. Relative to your vacation benefits, we agreed that because of your experience you will receive three weeks' paid vacation, and that one of the weeks will be taken beginning June 1 because of the arrangements you have previously made to attend your family reunion in Bar Harbor, Maine.

Relative to the rest of our company benefits and policies, enclosed is a copy of our company employee handbook. We hope it will serve to introduce you to our company and answer many of the questions you and your family may have about the way we strive to do business. Please do not hesitate to contact me directly at any time to answer any question or concern you may have about our company and how we operate. We ask that you return the employee handbook receipt form enclosed with it to our human resources department at your earliest convenience prior to your starting employment.

As we also discussed, your employment relationship with the company can be terminated with 30 days' notice without cause or without notice for cause at the discretion of the company. Further, because of the sensitive nature of your position, you will be asked to sign a covenant not to compete and trade secret protection agreement before you may start work. You can anticipate receiving these agreements in the mail by May 15.

Lastly, please understand that this offer of employment is contingent on the successful passing of a physical exam conducted by our company physician. As we discussed, this exam is paid for by the company and will include a drug screening test. You may make your appointment at your convenience through our human resources department.

If you agree with the above terms of employment, please signify by signing, dating, and returning to me in the business reply envelope provided the duplicate copy of this letter enclosed herewith.

Congratulations again on being selected as our new Executive Vice President of Marketing. On behalf of our company and its great staff of employees, let me wish you the best of success in your new position with us. I look forward with confidence to the realization of mutually beneficial employment relationship in the time to come.

Sincerely,

I. M. Ready Forue

President and CEO

I, _____, this _____ day of _____, 2000, hereby accept the offer of employment tendered to me and I acknowledge and confirm that the above represents my understanding of my employment relationship with the Company.

This may appear as a giant case of overkill, but if the individual wanted the job and agreed to the salary, what should be the objection to the rest of it? While such measures may not be appropriate for nonexempt positions, this kind of a hiring letter clearly sets out the company's expectations. If the new hire is a success, there will not be a problem with any of these terms. If the employment relationship fails, the company's interests have been protected. If the employee objects, and the objections cannot be ironed out in the negotiation of hire, both parties are better off not to have ever begun the relationship in the first place.

Audit Step 9: Physical Exams That Comply with the ADA
Pre-employment Physicals and Medical Examinations
As discussed above, general employment physicals before an offer of employment is made are prohibited by the ADA. However, all offers of employment may be made conditional upon the successful completion of a medical examination if such physical examination is required of all the applicants in any certain job title or job classification.

It is here, in the context of a confidential medical exam, that a medical history of the applicant is taken and drug and alcohol tests to determine current use are permitted. The physician will be asked to provide a medical opinion as to whether or not the job candidate with or without reasonable accommodation is physically fit to perform the job duties as defined in the job description.

Information regarding the medical condition and history of the candidate can be included in the medical determination, although such information must be maintained on separate forms and in separate medical files from the typical employee personnel file. It is also permissible in the context of the confidential medical exam for the examining physician to inquire about past workers' compensation claims and occupational injury. It is important to note that falsifications by the job candidate to the physician of this history, if discovered later in the course of employment, may be used to constitute a legitimate business reason for the employment termination of the employee. When such medical information is obtained, strict confidentiality is required. However, supervisors, managers, and first-aid and safety personnel who need to know about necessary restrictions and accommodations may be informed of the individual's medical data.

It may be helpful to provide the following form to the physician doing such examinations.

Physician's Medical Review

I have reviewed the medical qualifications of [Name] and I understand that he/she is being considered for the position of [position applied for/being considered for].

1. Are there any job functions the individual cannot perform?

Y_____ N_____ Comment_____

2. Are there any functions of the job that the individual can perform only by posing a direct threat (i.e., a significant risk of substantial harm to self or others)?

Y_____ N_____ Comment_____

3. In determining that there is a significant risk or high probability of substantial harm to the individual should he/she perform the function in question, I have considered:

   a. The duration of the risk

Y_____ N_____ Comment_____

   b. The nature and severity of the potential harm

Y_____ N_____ Comment_____

   c. The likelihood that the potential harm will occur

Y_____ N_____ Comment_____

   d. The imminence of the potential harm

Y_____ N_____ Comment_____

4. Does the individual have a mental or emotional limitation that would prevent the individual from performing the functions of this job or pose a direct threat to the health and/or safety of self or others?

Y_____ N_____ Comment_____

5. Has the individual suggested any reasonable accommodation(s) that would allow him/her to perform the function without any significant risk?

Y_____ N_____ Comment_____

6. Am I personally aware of any accommodation that would allow the individual to perform the functions without significant risk of harm to self or others?

Y_____ N_____ Comment_____

7. Does the individual fail to meet applicable federal regulatory requirements, such as those required by the Department of Transportation?

Y_____ N_____ Comment_____

8. If any of the answers above (except item 3) are yes, please explain the medical and/or factual basis for your answer:_____

_____

_____

_____

[Name] Please Print   Date

_____

Signature

Audit Step 10: The Immigration Reform and Control Act of 1986

The Immigration Reform Control Act of 1986 (P.L. 99-603) requires an employer to verify that applicants for employment are not unauthorized aliens. This law applies retroactively to any employee hired on or after November 7, 1986. Why compliance with the law is important, how it can be achieved, some of the pitfalls to avoid while complying, and a review of some of the challenges employers face with the immigration laws in general will be covered here.

Why is compliance important? The law adopts a new approach at stemming the flow of illegal aliens into the United States by removing the main incentive (jobs) for illegal immigration and punishing employer violators.

In addition to the cost of paying legal fees to defend against allegations, employers guilty of hiring violations can be subject to civil fines from $250 to $2,000 for first offenses, $2,000 to $5,000 for second offenses, and $3,000 to $10,000 for subsequent offenses for each illegal alien. Furthermore, pattern or practice violations subject employers to criminal sanctions of up to $3,000 for each illegal alien and/or six months in jail. Even paperwork violations may subject employers to fines from $100 to $1,000 for each individual involved.

Compliance Regulations

In order for employers to comply with the law, employees must attest to the employer on a special form both their identity and authorization to work in the United States. Then, employers must attest on the form that they have actually seen the required documentation and that the documentation reasonably appears on its face to be genuine.

The law places an affirmative duty on the employer to verify the identity and employment eligibility of any new hire. Moreover, these forms must be completed within three business days after employment begins, although an extension to 21 days is permissible for prospective employees who indicate that the application process required for documentation already has begun.

Identity and employment eligibility certification appears relatively straightforward. Two types of proof must be provided: proof of identity and proof of employment eligibility. Documents currently authorized as acceptable by the Immigration and Naturalization Service (INS) as proof of an employee's eligibility to be legally hired in the United States are shown below.

Documents that Satisfy Both Identity and Employment Eligibility
- U.S. passport,

- Certificate of U.S. citizenship,

- Certificate of naturalization,

- Unexpired foreign passport with attached employment authorization, and

- Alien registration card with photograph.

Documents that Satisfy Identity Only
- State-issued driver's license or identification card with photograph or identification information,

- U.S. military card, and

- Other identifying information, if it proves identity.

Documents that Satisfy Employment Eligibility Only
- Original Social Security Number card unless coded as not valid for employment,

- Birth certificate issued by state, county, or municipality bearing a seal or other certification, and

- Unexpired immigration and naturalization service employment authorization.

If the applicant for employment cannot produce a document that certifies both identity and employment eligibility, then two documents are required identifying each. Employers may accept as valid only those documents presented by applicants for employment that " . . . reasonably appear on their face to be genuine." Employers may retain on file a copy of the documents presented by applicants.

There are three basic categories of individuals to be considered in determining the verification compliance.

1. For individuals hired before November 6, 1986, no verification of identity or of employment eligibility is required.

2. No verification of identity or employment eligibility is required for employees who are hired after November 6, 1986, but are no longer employed after June 1, 1987.

3. Individuals hired after November 6, 1986, and who continue to be employed after June 1, 1987, must be verified as to their identity and employment eligibility within three days after employment begins.

Forms and Paperwork

Required paperwork includes Form I-9 of the U.S. Department of Justice and the INS. All employers must make this form available for inspection by United States INS or Department of Labor (DOL) officers upon a maximum of three days' notice. Failure to provide all of the requested information on the form may result in a determination that the applicant is ineligible for employment in the United States and subject the employer to penalties. The information on the form must not only be certified by the individual applicant, but also signed with address information by the individual designated by the employer to take such information.

It is now standard procedure that every wage and hour investigation audit performed by the DOL and its Wage and Hour Division includes a review of an employer's I-9 record-keeping and paperwork.

Both certifications are under penalty of perjury for falsification. The Form I-9 must be completed within three days of the start date, or one day if the individuals being employed are expected to work only three days or less. The form must be kept on file for at least three years, or for one year after the employee has terminated employment, whichever is longer.

Questions of Discrimination

Interestingly, the equal opportunity laws against natural origin discrimination contain one section which specifically states that employers may prefer citizens over aliens when the two are equally qualified, while another section says that it is illegal to discriminate against aliens because of their national origin or citizenship status. The answer to reconciling these two conflicting provisions is unclear. However, employers that select citizens over aliens should be prepared to prove that the citizens were at least as well qualified as the aliens.

Also, company work rules against the employment of non-citizens must be based on provable business necessity if employers can hope to prevail in any civil rights actions against them. It seems that job discrimination lawsuits are likely to grow out of the new law as employers tread the narrow path outlined between the pillars of the Immigration Reform and Control Act (IRCA) and the equal employment opportunity anti-discrimination guidelines.

Common Immigration Law Compliance Challenges

It is important to note that an employer who looks at the eligibility documents of an applicant before making an offer of employment is not complying with the Act and, indeed, may be exposed to charges of discriminatory hiring practices. The time to look at such documents is after making an offer of employment. While it is not *per se* discrimination to do so, it is not uncommon for these documents to include information about the perspective employee's race, religion, national origin, or age. Once an employer has knowledge of this information and then later chooses not to employ the individual, the possession of such knowledge might be evidence that the employer used it improperly in making its hiring decision.

It is important that employers be consistent in their hiring procedures to avoid claims of unequal treatment of all job applicants. In this regard, each perspective employee should not start work until the verification process has been completed, or everyone should be given three days after starting work to produce the documents (or up to 90 days if the new employee can show receipts of application for qualifying documents). In the same manner, it is advisable to have a consistent practice regarding how long any job offer will remain open. Having different rules and timelines for different positions could lead to allegations of unequal treatment because of discriminatory reasons.

Also, employers must not confuse the importance of possession of a green card and/or the requirement of U.S. citizenship for a job applicant and compliance with Immigration Reform Control Act. The Immigration Act of 1990 prohibits an employer from refusing to accept documents that may be genuine on their face or insisting upon more documentation than the law actually requires. Remember, certain residents are still protected under the Act even though they do not have a green card or U.S. citizenship.

Employers should make hiring decisions based upon an applicant's ability to do the job, and therefore not ask job seekers about their employment eligibility before making offers of employment.

Employers are duty bound to accept any document or combination of documents that fulfill the verification requirements. Policies that limit verification to only specific documentation from employees place themselves at risk for complaints. For example, requiring only INS-issued documentation is one example of a practice that could put an employer at risk of violating the statute.

Lastly, it is a violation to refuse to hire protected aliens that have only time-limited work authorizations. This is particularly true for refugees, temporary residents, conditional residents, and certain permanent residents who do not possess a green card, but instead may have a stamp on their passport serving as temporary evidence of the granting of permanent residence. This is not to say that if the job requires more than the ability to work for a limited period of time, this may not be used to justify a no-hire decision. However, employers should be careful when making such decisions to establish that this is reasonably necessary for the job in question.

Finally, it is impermissible for employers to charge special fees for employees to complete the verification process.

The IRCA is a complex change in U.S. law. This legislation necessitates substantive changes in employee selection and employer record-keeping requirements. If not in place already, employers must develop and implement an employment verification system for all new employees, even known U.S. citizens.

In this litigious era in America, the cost of a hiring mistake that turns into a lawsuit is too expensive to ignore. When one considers how much research may go into the purchase of a computer system or even a copy machine, the price of hiring legally—and right—pales in comparison to the expense of making a mistake.

Endnotes

[1] 411 U.S. 792 (1973).

[2] 420 F.2d 1225, 401 U.S. 424 (1971).

[3] 29 CFR Section 1630.2(h)(1).

[4] 3 ADD ¶3-136 (CCH).

[5] 831 P2d 1316 (1992).

[6] 583 SO2d 744.

[7] 992 F.2d 139 (2d Cir. 1990).

[8] See EEOC Uniform Guidelines on Employee Selection Procedures, Sec. 4D.

Answers to Chapter Four Test Your Knowledge

1. True, 2. False, 3. f, 4. True, 5. True, 6. e, 7. True, 9. True, 10. True.

CHAPTER FIVE

Proper Supervisory Methods

The Importance of a Good Employee Orientation

How Supervisors Should Act

Performance Evaluations

Dealing with Cultural Diversity

Test Your Knowledge

# of Proper Supervisory Methods

1. Name three benefits of a planned "New Employee Orientation."

2. True or False? The legal significance of being a supervisor means that as a representative of management whatever a supervisor says or does is binding on the company.

3. What are the three levels of supervisory authority to make decisions in the workplace?

4. Which of the following should be considered when deciding what is appropriate discipline for work rule violations?
   a. The results of an investigation, which includes listening to the side of the story of the employee who violated the work rule.
   b. Whether certain allowances for special circumstances are appropriate.
   c. Whether certain allowances for special people are appropriate.
   d. Whether it is necessary to discharge an employee on the spot because of the seriousness of the incident.
   e. All of the above.

5. When dealing with acts of an insubordination where an employee refuses to obey a supervisor's order, in deciding whether discharge from employment is the appropriate discipline, which of the following should be considered?
   a. Was there a direct order given or was there merely a suggestion or hint given by the supervisor as to what the employee was to do?
   b. Was the order given by a person with the authority to command it?
   c. After the order was given, did the employee understand it and clearly refuse to follow it?
   d. Was the duty to follow the order clearly within the scope of the employee's job?
   e. Did the employee know the full consequences of disobeying the order?
   f. What was the employee's reason for refusing to obey the order? Did it involve a safety issue?
   g. All of the above.

6. True or False? In a successful disciplinary conference with an employee, the employee should be given a chance to explain his or her perspective, a memo should be prepared to memorialize what was said, and that memo should be given to the employee as well as placed in the personnel file.

7. Which of the following are expected of a supervisor by his or her allied supervisors?
    a. To cooperate with them.
    b. To share ideas for the good of the company.
    c. To talk positively about company affairs.
    d. To help each other look good in each other's work.
    e. All of the above.

8. When evaluating employees, which of the following are common complaints from employees?
    a. Performance evaluation forms do not ask for ratings on what is really important in doing the job.
    b. The supervisor's low ratings exhibit personal bias.
    c. There is too much reliance on small incidences to justify reduced ratings.
    d. Ratings do not reflect efforts at improvement once a supervisor's mind is made up.
    e. All of the above.

9. True or False? Once an employee quits a job, he or she is automatically denied unemployment insurance and cannot sue the company for equal rights claims.

10. Which of the following behaviors can amount to misconduct justifying discharge from employment for a single offense?
    a. Dishonesty, such as theft or falsification of work records and employment applications.
    b. Insubordination, such as direct disobedience of valid work orders.
    c. Negligence, such as neglect of duty or carelessness in the performance of work.
    d. All of the above.

The answers to these questions are at the end of this chapter.

The Importance of a Good Employee Orientation

Getting an employee off to the right start is crucial in establishing a sound employment relationship. On the first day of employment, at a time when the employee is most attentive and will learn most about the operation, he will form his first impression of the company. These impressions may last a career. A good employee orientation program often serves to create a positive rapport between management and employees. Indeed, the costs of laying a poor foundation and eventually losing an employee can be great, considering the costs and risks associated with recruiting new employees.

The way employees are treated between the day they are hired and the day they report to work is extremely important. The attitudes of new employees often reflect what they perceive to be the attitude of the company toward them. Introduce new employees to the rules and regulations, as well as the company's vision, and they will more likely feel a part of the effort in reaching the goals being set. Indeed, the more personal the goals and values of the company become, the more likely such goals and values will be assimilated.

As part of the new employee orientation, the new job function and how it ties in with total productivity should be explained. It is important here to illustrate that the overall success of a company depends on individual and team effort. The relationship to goals and current priorities, other departments, customers, jobs within the department, the organizational structure, and more, must be covered. Without this information, a new employee may develop an improper attitude based on misinformation acquired in casual conversation.

Most new employees want to know what the supervisor expects, how employee evaluations are done, and by what measures such evaluations are made. It is important to make employees feel that they are special in some way. A program to accomplish this may make new employees more productive and satisfied in the work they do.

Many supervisors use the first day of employment to give a detailed explanation of the job, using a current job description and detailing the expected level of performance. Explaining why the job is important and how the duties of the job affect the final result seems to help motivate the new employee to strive for such results. Often, a discussion of the common problems of the job and their solutions is very helpful on the first day. In this regard, an examination of an employee evaluation form can help direct the employee to the kind of quality, productivity, attendance, and work habits the employer has a right to expect.

The most important elements of the employee orientation include a substantive review of the job description linked to employee evaluation forms and a page-by-page explanation of the employee handbook. The employee should sign the employee handbook receipt form.

Many companies like to use a new employee orientation checklist form, such as the one below. This form can be helpful (in court, if necessary) in showing that the employee knew or should have known the company rules and regulations. The supervisor should manually check each subject after explaining it to the employee.

New Employee Orientation Checklist

Employee Name: _____

☐ Explained job function and how it ties in with total company operations

☐ Explained importance of each employee to the overall success of the company

  ☐ Teamwork concept

  ☐ Attendance, punctuality

  ☐ Working where required

  ☐ Received and signed for Employee Handbook

☐ Told about the hours of work

  ☐ Workweek

  ☐ Starting and quitting time (1st shift, 2nd shift, rotation, nonrotation)

  ☐ Told how to use time card

  ☐ Lunch period and paid break periods (punch out when leaving premises)

☐ Told how he/she gets paid

  ☐ When

  ☐ Where and by whom

- ☐ Rate of pay

- ☐ Overtime policy and pay

- ☐ Future salary/merit compensation

- ☐ Check deposit option

☐ Sixty-day trial period explained

☐ Told about company safety policy

- ☐ Safety policy (received)

- ☐ Safety rules (received "Basics" and "Safe Work Manual")

- ☐ Told to be alert for accident hazards

- ☐ What to do in case of an accident (appraise, first aid, get help, comfort)

- ☐ Informed of dust mask and filter/ear plugs

- ☐ First aid courses

☐ Told about company rules

- ☐ Parking area

- ☐ Smoking

- ☐ Personal phone calls; phone policy

- ☐ Leaving work section

- ☐ Absences; when and where to call daily (received plant phone number, snow policy)

- ☐ Where to leave personal property (locker number; right to inspect)

- ☐ Enter and leave through receiving door

- ☐ Report all changes in address, telephone number, marital status, dependent status, or change of name in writing as soon as the change occurs

- ☐ Two-week written notice requested when leaving

- ☐ Bulletin boards; consult regularly

☐ Employee Benefits

  - ☐ Company profit-sharing plan (all contributions made by the company; employee pays nothing)

  - ☐ Company-paid sickness and accident insurance

  - ☐ Company-paid group life and accidental death & dismemberment insurance ($10,000), plus term life insurance valued at twice your salary

  - ☐ Hospitalization plan (starts 1st of month following 60 days of employment)

  - ☐ Sick leave plan

  - ☐ Paid vacation plan

  - ☐ Paid holidays (attendance requirements)

  - ☐ Funeral leave

  - ☐ Jury duty

  - ☐ Leaves of absence—personal, medical, military (maximum two weeks' pay, same as jury duty)

  - ☐ Workers' compensation

  - ☐ When benefits go into effect (insurance benefits are effective the 1st day of the month following 60 days of employment; holidays, sick leave, etc., after 60 days)

☐ Shown physical layout of plant

  - ☐ Shown how to punch time card

- ☐ Shown use and location of nearest fire extinguisher

- ☐ Washrooms and restrooms

- ☐ Lunch facilities

- ☐ Shown location of workstation

  - ☐ Introduced to fellow employees

  - ☐ Introduced to machine

  - ☐ Introduced to supervisor and/or leadman

- ☐ Leaving before probation completed

  - ☐ Please return all items handed out during orientation

  - ☐ Remember to read handbook and sign form in back of book and return tomorrow

I have been given a general orientation covering the policies described above at XYZ Company. I understand that violations of the rules and regulations can and will be grounds for termination of employment.

Employee Signature: _____ Date _____

Supervisor Signature: _____ Date _____

To be fully effective, the orientation program should use a variety of methods to inform employees. Programs may include a videotape, overhead projections, computer programs, lectures from highly placed company officials, personal demonstrations to make sure everything is clear, and documentation to memorialize what was done. At the conclusion of the orientation presentation, many companies assign a veteran employee to the new employee as a sponsor. The sponsor not only establishes a friendly working environment with the supervisor by introducing the new employee to fellow workers and other supervisory staff, but also gives a "word to the wise" when necessary during the initial phase of employment. When time is spent with new employees, healthy precedents are set when the employee is most eager to learn and attentive to the company's leadership. It is a mistake for a supervisor to ignore the opportunity to make this first impression memorable and to help shape the beginning of long-term relationships.

How Supervisors Should Act

It is clear that the treatment of employees by management will determine not only how productive employees may become, but also how well they will identify with the company and its goals. In the long run, this will determine how well the company succeeds in serving its customers. The issue, then, is how management should act. Supervisors, who represent management to employees, should understand the parameters of appropriate supervisory conduct.

Generally, there are three levels of supervisory authority. At the first level, supervisors decide what to do and then do it, reporting to no one. At the next level, supervisors act, and then report to higher management what was done and why. At the last level, supervisors must first obtain approval from management before acting.

Good supervisors know exactly where the lines are drawn in deciding what level of authority to use in a given situation. In the decision-making process, good supervisors understand that their value to an operation is measured by what they are able to motivate their employees to do, rather than by how hard they work. Therefore, authority to discipline must be used with discretion, and not as a club. In many instances, what may seem to be stubbornness on the part of an employee may only be uncertainty about how to act.

Employee Discipline

Discipline is often confused with punishment. Supervisors can easily become emotionally involved in work problems, which can lead to an obsession with retribution. The proper approach to discipline is to simply view it as a means to an end—proper employee behavior on the job. Reinforcing and encouraging proper behavior often eliminates improper behavior and thus the need to punish. If labor costs, scrap, quality of service, attendance, etc., are satisfactory, then discipline is unlikely to be a serious problem. If satisfactory results are being obtained with an informal form of discipline, it is wise to leave well enough alone. However, if company work objectives are not being met or are falling off, then it is important to take steps to reverse the unfavorable trends and bring results up to where they should be.

There are two basic forms of discipline. One is *informal control*, where guidelines for proper conduct are loosely structured. Informal control is the most desirable kind of control.

The second basic form of discipline is *formal control*, which is embodied in formal disciplinary procedures described in work rules that are usually contained in an employee handbook. The widespread belief is that a set of work rules automatically results in complete control, but the rules must also be enforced. Rules without enforcement are worse than no rules at all. Proper enforcement of a reasonable standard of conduct that has been properly communicated to employees will promote the best possible work environment.

Enforcing the Work Rules

For the most part, it is up to the supervisor's discretion to determine when work rule violations will be followed with formal punishment. It is important to be firm but fair and to impose punishment only after a complete investigation of the facts that gave rise to the incident.

For example, two men report for work looking obviously unfit to work. The result is the same in each case—a missed work assignment. However, upon investigation, the facts reveal that while one employee was on an all-night carouse, the other had been up all night because of a medical emergency. To treat each with the same corrective disciplinary punishment would be unreasonable.

Supervisors must remember to make allowances for circumstances, but not for people. If possible, make the same allowances for everyone under the same circumstances.

If an incident is serious and requires immediate action, it is best to indefinitely suspend employees and send them home, pending investigation and consideration in the disciplinary decision-making process. It is never necessary to discharge on the spot. Conduct a complete investigation and talk the matter over with central management before making a final decision.

Handling Acts of Insubordination

In making a discharge for insubordination, which is a direct challenge to a supervisor's authority, the following items should be considered in order to decide whether a discharge is appropriate.

Was an order given? It is important to distinguish whether or not what was asked of the employee was merely a suggestion to the employee or perhaps a hint made to the employee in an ambiguous manner.

After this order was given, did the employee make a clear refusal to follow it? In line with this, the supervisor must make sure that the order was fully understood by the employee.

Was the person who gave the order a recognized supervisor? The line should be clear as to what authority a person has to give an order. Some lead-workers have responsibility to get the job done, but are not authorized to impose orders on the individuals who work with them. They only have the authority to recommend disciplinary punishment to someone else.

Was the order part of the employee's job? It is also necessary to decide whether the duty to perform the order was within the regular scope of the job of the employee involved. If it is not, then the individual employee should be advised of the "work now, grieve later" procedure. For example, in one recent incident at a printing operation, a material handler objected on moral grounds to working with a new magazine printed at the company that contained explicit, prurient material. In this case the supervisor correctly informed the employee that he should perform the work, but file a complaint or grievance concerning the matter. This gave the supervisor time to devise an equitable solution that worked for both the company and the employee. However, if the employee stopped working entirely, the supervisor would have been authorized to issue corrective disciplinary punishment pursuant to normal labor law arbitral decision-making standards.

What was the employee's reason for disobeyng the order? Lastly, determine why the individual refused the order. Did the individual employee know (not "should have known") the full consequences of disobeying the order given? Did the employee feel that by its performance a dangerous or unsafe situation might result? If so, the employee may have certain rights to refuse the order pursuant to OSHA regulations or NLRB "protected concerted activity" (unionized or not). As is always the case, the little time spent investigating a situation may save much grief later in the form of actions by the employee against the employer for wrongful discharge or other claims.

Handling Poor Work Habits

Sometimes even good employees may develop poor work habits that can undermine the morale or effectiveness of the other employees. Often, discharge is not necessary, but corrective disciplinary action or constructive criticism is more appropriate. If productive employees begin to do things like leave early, spend excessive work time on personal phone calls, or frequently take long lunches, the supervisor may feel stymied by a delicate situation. Moreover, the employees may feel that their excellent job performance deserves a few extra privileges. This problem must be solved without damaging the employees' willingness to perform.

Some managers may choose to avoid dealing with the poor work habit in the hope it will disappear. It seldom does. However, using an authoritarian approach may change an individual into a resentful employee who will get even by doing the least possible. While problems of attitude and behavior may be personal and hard to change, managers must take action before coworkers begin to resent the supervisor's failure to act and begin to develop poor work habits of their own.

Guidelines for Corrective Action

When corrective disciplinary action or constructive criticism of an employee becomes necessary, the following guidelines are suggested.

First, when talking to the employee, be sure to get to the point. Many supervisors make the mistake of being too friendly and familiar in corrective discipline encounters. This is counterproductive, and tends to make the employee uneasy.

The next step is to describe the situation. Relate only the facts when attempting to correct the employee's behavior. Present criticism logically and constructively; do not make value judgments that only demean or belittle the employee personally. Remember that the goal is to persuade the employee that the criticism is a valid evaluation of the existing situation.

Subsequently, be sure to *listen* to the employee's response to your criticism. Encourage the employee to explain his or her actions. Willingness to hear the employee's story makes the employee less defensive and helps to clarify the situation that led to the discipline. Lastly, the employee will be encouraged to think through the problem in order to understand and correct the mistake.

Try to ask open-ended questions that cannot be answered with a simple yes or no. Such questions often begin with the words "what" or "how." Also, remember that silence acts as a magnet; it will draw information from the employee. Silence after a question gives the employee time to respond.

The successful supervisor in discipline conferences helps the employee isolate and then understand the causes for the discipline. If agreement on the true source of a problem can be reached, its solution and improved behavior on the part of the employee can be better accomplished.

Once the source of the problem is found, focus on the solution. If possible, have the employee sum up the conference meeting. If a program or goal for the employee has been agreed upon, such as perfect attendance for the next month, set up a future appointment with a specific date, at which time progress can be assessed.

No one likes rules or regulations, but they are necessary to maintain order in groups. Standard disciplinary procedures help facilitate consistent application of penalties for similar offenses. Consistent fair treatment helps reduce accusations of favoritism. Therefore, rules have to be in place and they have to be acted on consistently. If consistent action is not taken to correct problems, the employer is likely to experience a negative impact on morale, productivity, and profits.

Lastly, make notes after each disciplinary conference that include the date, time of day, what happened, who was involved, and what disciplinary action was taken. Sign and date these memos and make them a part of the personnel file. These notes may help provide information at some later time if there is a question about any action that has been or may be taken. Another helpful practice is to give the employee a copy of the memo to memorialize the conference. Let the employee know that if the memo is inaccurate, the employee can correct it. This will let the employee know that there will be no "surprises" in the personnel file. It will also help establish that the company's actions were fair and in compliance with general due process standards.

Such information may be important in winning denials of unemployment benefit claims or defending against unfair labor practice, equal employment opportunity, or wrongful discharge claims in the future.

Procedures in Discipline Situations

What procedures should supervisors follow when they find it necessary to administer discipline or discharge an employee? Remember that it is never necessary to discharge an employee on the spot and that it is always appropriate to investigate before administering corrective discipline. It is important to document the results of the investigation and disciplinary conferences by making notes as soon as possible. These notes should include the date, time of day, what happened, who was involved, what the employee said in response to the incident, and what final corrective disciplinary action was taken. The notes form a memo that should then be dated, signed, and placed in the employee's personnel file while the issue is fresh.

However, there are methods that the supervisor can properly and legally use to maintain discipline and stop potential trouble before official action becomes necessary. By successful informal control, some supervisors can obtain satisfactory results. Informal control is the more desirable kind of control. A supervisor can be an effective motivator without formal discipline by actively listening to employee complaints.

There are bound to be misunderstandings and grievances even in the best-managed companies. Unless employees can have justified grievances corrected, morale will become low and labor trouble a possibility.

Supervisors should listen to employee complaints even if they seem trivial. Once they gather information from the employee, they need to correct mistakes if possible and report back to the individual. They should tell the employee whether corrective action is appropriate, necessary, and possible. If supervisors do not work with employees to correct problems, employees may feel that it is necessary to resolve their issues using in-house grievance procedures or even outsiders such as unions. An important part of a supervisor's job is to learn about the causes of dissatisfaction and act on them in each case.

Avoiding Misunderstandings

There are three excellent methods to avoid misunderstandings in the workplace and to help the supervisor become aware of potential problems before they arise. A supervisor should:

- Circulate among employees regularly. Daily circulation is preferred, but every other day or at least once a week is acceptable. An open-door policy is not enough. Employees may be reluctant to come into an office, but they usually feel free to say what is on their minds at their workstations.

- Find reasons to talk with each employee at specific times, such as the anniversary of the first day of employment at the company. Not only is it a nice personal touch, but it provides opportunity for improved employee communication without giving the employee instructions or orders.

- Make an effort to talk to an employee who seems upset. Stopping at the workstation may get an employee to talk; however, if a situation seems serious and the employee does not "open up," mention to the individual that he or she seems upset and extend an offer of help. An employee usually will not want to talk where others can hear, so if there is no privacy in the work area, an office or other room should be used for discussion.

Patient listening to employee complaints is one of the surest ways to avoid labor problems. It may take time but usually pays off. Supervisors who are always too busy to speak with employees are likely to have trouble with the employees they supervise. This does not mean that a supervisor must drop everything in the middle of an important job to hear an employee complaint. Instead, make an appointment for a mutually convenient time.

Supervisory success depends upon an ability to motivate people to do with enthusiasm what the supervisor wants them to. More supervisors fail

CHAPTER FIVE

for lack of ability to deal with people effectively than for lack of technical know-how. Good supervisors know the sensitivities of each employee, that no two employees can be successfully handled alike, and that some employees show their reactions while others do not. The successful supervisor senses when employees are disturbed and helps them verbalize their feelings.

Remember that it is possible to discharge an employee and be thanked, or to give a raise and be criticized for it. How a supervisor treats an employee and his or her degree of interest in the employee's well-being will be evident to each employee from the start.

It sometimes seems astonishing that a genuine interest in employees, rather than a concentrated drive for more work, actually results in improved productivity. Showing confidence in people often encourages them to respond beyond expectations. Indifferent or incompetent employees need not be retained, but each employee should be treated individually and given a fair opportunity to succeed. Successful supervisors do everything in their power to help employees develop into good workers, and they do not merely sort out the good from the bad.

Employees feel free to confide their problems to supervisors who have respect for and confidence in them. Successful supervisors will check into a justifiable work complaint and follow up with an answer. They do not make or imply promises they cannot keep, but only research problems and report back.

Unfortunately, many people hear what they want to hear and see what they want to see. At times, employees may appear to lie. Usually they do not intend to lie but unconsciously slant things in their favor. For this reason, supervisors cannot always accept what employees say without investigating. In doing so, never tell employees what other employees have said about them or about the incident itself. Be sure of the facts, and then the error in the job that gave rise to the complaint can be accurately corrected or an explanation of why nothing can be done about the complaint can be given.

Good supervisors maintain their integrity. This is the only way to foster employee dedication, especially during emergency situations. Keys to maintaining integrity are as follows:

- Admitting a mistake rather than passing the blame onto company headquarters or someone else.

- Recognizing and giving credit to an employee who presents a good idea, rather than claiming the credit.

- Meeting issues squarely, leaving no doubt as to whether an answer is yes or no. Not straddling the fence to avoid being charged with a mistake.

- Working in the best interest of the company rather than in the best interest of oneself.

Good person-to-person relations act as a lubricant, enabling people to work together without friction. Where relations are good, work progresses smoothly, safely, and effectively without confusion or waste. Everything is neat, clean, and in order when potential customers tour the plant. People are relaxed and the work completed. Productivity and quality are high and costs low.

Where employee relations are good, the supervisor knows what is going on, but has no need to constantly prod people. The supervisor has time to listen, observe, control, and plan ahead. Not only does the supervisor do a better job, but also derives more pleasure from the work.

Employees have confidence in and respect for a good supervisor and the company for which they work. Employees like their jobs and brag about their work. They have no need or desire for outside union or governmental help.

Being a Good Investigator

An investigator must know the legal principals involved in the subject matter of the investigation—for example, sexual harassment and discrimination. There are several purposes to an investigation. First, investigations are an important tool in identifying and resolving challenges important to the life of the parties involved, the immediate work team, and the organization as a whole. A good investigator is cognizant of the background between the parties involved and any labor relations and professional rivalries as well. This is critical because all emotions will be heightened in the course of an investigation.

The investigator's success will have an impact upon the ultimate outcome of the claim or complaint in terms of the satisfaction of the parties, decisions to proceed further, and amenability of the parties to settlement.

Good investigators are aware of the limitations of human communication. For example, investigators may have "selective memory," meaning that one's own identity can result in a filtering of information. An investigator's own natural biases may distort understanding and perception. The relationship of the investigator to the parties may also affect decision-making.

There are several key concepts for the good investigator to keep in mind. First, harassment claims can build over time, each incident adding to the limit of what an individual may be able to tolerate. The expectations of the parties involved are likely to be unrealistic, and these can be further exacerbated by the media, internal policy statements, reports of other people's experiences and the employee's own interpretations of his or her rights. A good investigator must acknowledge that not every investigation will result in satisfaction. However, well-conducted interviews will always manifest fairness. Evenhandedness and compliance with employer policies are the best insurance that all involved will feel the process was fair. Investigators must recognize that they themselves often play multiple organizational roles, which can lead to confusion.

Furthermore, it is not uncommon in harassment cases that the improper behavior is occasional rather than frequent, may not appear to be targeted or intentional, and may often represent simple ignorance, insensitivity, or a learned "bullish" habit. Most harassers are regular people whose behavior has merely gone over the line. They are not necessarily malicious or socially maladept.

Unfortunately, it is also important to understand that employees do not usually trust that human resource problems can be corrected. For example, some employees may feel that the last place they would go with a problem is to a manager or human resources personnel. Most individuals who complain of harassment fear being disbelieved and are concerned that they may be treated as "complainers" or "whiners." Accordingly, it is imperative that the investigator do everything possible to build faith and maintain credibility.

Levels of Complaints

There are typically three levels of sexual or racial harassment complaints. The first level is more of a "warning shot" or "word to the wise" from an employee complaining on a "for your information" basis about conduct that may be of limited apparent impact. The second level is a complaint of concern from an employee who exhibits characteristics of stress. The behavior the employee complains about is intrusive and the employee "has a problem." The third level is the official complaint. This is a full alert where the employee's emotions are overwhelmed and he or she is in effect saying, "This has to stop." The level of complaint dictates the investigator's involvement.

Interview Preparation

A good investigator is prepared. This means the investigator is aware of his or her own mindset and is careful not to develop a clouded perception of the facts. Good investigators must appraise themselves objectively. Can the investigator stand by the outcome no matter what the findings may be? If the investigator decides he or she has any hint of conflict of interest, then he or she should withdraw. Otherwise, the investigator may become the issue, instead of the complaint.

In addition, a good investigator should clear his or her "emotional desk." Investigations involve a great deal of stress, and high levels of intervening emotional turmoil will make an investigator ineffective. An investigator must also make sure that he or she is given the proper time and authority to do a thorough job.

A good investigator should be prepared for tough, substantive and procedural questions from the individual being questioned. Such questions may include:

"What are my privacy rights?"

"Could my cooperation result in discipline to me?"

"Do I have to talk to you?"

"What if I do not cooperate?"

"Could I lose my job over this?"

"Can I record this interview?"

"Should I/can I have an attorney present?"

"Should I have someone from the union here?"

"Who else will you be talking to besides me?"

"Will you tell anyone else what I tell you?"

The investigator should always strive to maintain professionalism and neutrality. This does not mean officiousness or condescension. The interviews with the parties involved should be non-adversarial and accommodating. Use formality to distance oneself from the individual being interviewed. This hopefully will feed into an assumption that the investigator is there primarily to serve the system, and not because he or she is taking a personal interest in the case itself. Good investigators demonstrate receptiveness through body language and body posture, willingness to engage in "small talk," and active listening.

The challenge is to be empathetic and interested without telegraphing the acceptance of facts as they are being described. An investigator can be sorry, but only about feelings, not about the facts. The investigator's role is to find the facts. One may recognize the difficulty of the situation, but not each individual incident. Sometimes, using unbelievability is a device for feedback. For example, asking questions such as, "How would you respond to someone who told you that you did not appear to be upset?" Lastly, investigators should remember not to use self-disclosure or emotion that may be interpreted as being "manipulative" by the person being interviewed.

The setting for an interview can have an effect on the investigation. The location should be neutral, such as a conference room or off-site room. However, in some instances, the interview may have to take place at the offices of the witnesses under less than the best conditions. Strive to keep the location private, well lit, and well ventilated, and outside the regular work area, if possible. There should be no interruptions, such as telephones or pages. Water, tissues, copy machines, and a calendar should be handy, and a restroom nearby.

The investigator should ask interviewees in advance to bring any letters, notes, diaries, calendars, or any other documents that may be helpful in obtaining a full understanding of the situation. The person being interviewed should also be asked to refrain from discussing the appointment with other people.

It is good advice to prepare a checklist before beginning any interview. This list could include any appropriate notices and warnings; a preamble, which would include the purpose of the interview and the investigator's role in it; who has requested the investigation; and that the investigator's stance is to gather the facts. Such a preamble may also include a description of what is being investigated, and explain to the interviewee the investigator's intent to make notes and how such notes will be used. Further, interviewees should be advised that reprisal will not be tolerated against them for any information they may provide. It should also be stated, where appropriate, that disciplinary action might be taken as a result of the statements made in the interview. In conclusion, the interviewee should be informed that he or she should not discuss the matter with anyone else and that you may need to talk with him or her again. It is prudent to let the individual know that you will maintain confidentiality as much as is practicable.

Interviewing Techniques

In any interview there are certain "boilerplate" questions that should be asked before delving into the specifics. Such preliminary questions might ask about the employee's familiarity with the company's policy prohibiting sexual or racial harassment, length of time worked with the company, position in the company, and why the individual has been asked to participate in the interview. One way to phrase these questions is to ask the employee, "Do you know why you are here? What do you know about why I am here?"

Good interviewers are always aware of the interviewee's thinking process. That is, they let the individual talk by allowing time for narrative responses. Be "mute" and affirming, and use verbal prompts to keep the individual speaking in such instances. Often, beginning with general questions allows the individual being interviewed to give positive responses at first. Ask questions in a chronological order. Do not be confrontational when dealing with factual inconsistencies. Try not to categorize or judge responses. For example, never use the word "harassment" when asking about specific behavior. Always be fair.

Many good interviewers also try to avoid certain complications. For example, do not appear to be too accepting of the interviewee's version of events. In other words, avoid nodding, being sorry about what happened, suggesting that "something will be done about this," or saying, "That explains a lot." Also try to avoid appearing to disbelieve what is being said. Do not act cold or arrogant, but take time to listen. Avoid asking, "Why did you do that?"

Lastly, do not assume that the individual has a certain education or intelligence level. Use the appropriate vocabulary, talk slowly, and confirm understanding of information. Expect powerful emotions, but do not overreact to them. Avoid making promises or appearing to make commitments.

Good interviewers recap the interview in its entirety at the end of an interview. One can ask for confirmation of understanding with questions such as, "Did I get that right?" Also tell the interviewee that if he or she remembers something else after the interview is over, to get back to you. In addition, ask what other people you might speak with to get a better understanding of the situation. Invite the individual to talk to you again, and remind the individual that he or she will not be retaliated against or punished in any way for participating in the process.

Some good investigators also have a prepared closing. It might include questions such as:

"What do you think should happen now?"

"Is there anything else that is happening right now that I should know about?"

"Will you need any support for yourself while the process continues?"

"Are there any questions I have failed to ask you?"

"Have you told me everything you know about this situation?"

"Is there anything else you would like to say?"

Conducting a proper, fair, and thorough investigation is an employer's best line of defense. For example, in a California case, *Cotran v. Rollins Hudig Hall International, Inc.,*[1] a jury awarded the plaintiff $1.78 million on the theory that he had been wrongfully discharged and that the company had breached an implied contract. In reversing the jury award, the California Supreme Court understood the predicament of employers when accusations of harassment are made. In making its determination that employer defendant Rollins Hudig Hall had acted properly in terminating the employment of the plaintiff, the California Supreme Court adopted what has become the majority rule for employers. This is that the employer has a right to impose discipline without having absolute certainty about the underlying facts. Employers will retain this right as long as they are acting in what has been called "good faith." The standard for a good faith belief is determined by the facts as developed by the investigator. In *Cotran,* the company had conducted a thorough investigation, it had done so in a manner that was neither arbitrary nor capricious, and the decision to impose discipline had not been based on illegal or impermissible reasons.

The *Cotran* court acknowledged that one of the important needs of employers is to have some degree of autonomy in the workplace in order to accomplish underlying business objectives. It recognized that exercising such autonomy can be consistent with the employer fulfilling its legal obligations with respect to the strong national public policy against sexual harassment. The court stated this in the following way:

> If an employer is required to have in hand a signed confession or an eyewitness account of the alleged misconduct before it can act, the workplace will be transformed into an adjudicatory arena and effective decision making will be thwarted. Although these features do not justify a rule permitting employees to be dismissed arbitrarily, they do mean that asking a

civil jury to reexamine in all its factual detail the triggering cause of the decision to dismiss—including the retrospective accuracy of the employer's comprehension—months or even years later, in a context distant from the imperatives of the workplace, is at odds with an axiom underlying the jurisprudence of wrongful termination. That axiom ... is the need for sensible latitude for managerial decision-making and its corollary, an optimum balance point between the employer's interest in organizational efficiency and employee's interest in continuing employment.[2]

The current trend is to continue to allow employers the discretion to make appropriate business judgments up to and including termination of individuals who engage in inappropriate conduct in the workplace. Employers should not become fearful of exercising these rights.

Resolving Complaints Where Appropriate

Can you give the complainant what he or she wants? Remember that what is "desirable" is certainly in the eye of the beholder. If you offer a transfer, try to get the complainant's consent. Make sure the transfer position is substantially similar to the complainant's prior position, if possible. This way, there will be no legal liability because the complainant has not suffered. If possible, make sure the complainant does not come away from the situation frustrated by the result or unsatisfied with the confidentiality or the fairness with which the process was handled by the employer.

There are many concerns about the person accused of harassment. Of course, the severity, frequency, and pervasiveness of the conduct complained of is important when deciding whether or how to discipline the accused harasser. Management discretion options include oral and written warnings, formal reprimand, suspension with or without pay, probation, or, depending upon the severity of the problem, even the transfer, demotion, or discharge of the accused. Of course, if the discipline is less than discharge, the complainant should be told in no uncertain terms that similar misconduct in the future may result in immediate discharge from employment, i.e., his or her job is in jeopardy.

Lastly, be sure to conduct personal follow-up interviews with all the parties individually to inform them of the company actions.

What should be done in a situation where it is one employee's word against another's? In such a case, the proper resolution of the matter depends upon the believability and credibility of the parties. Do not assume that merely because there are no witnesses that this precludes a finding of sexual harassment. The courts and the EEOC have the power to determine what happened based upon their view of the witnesses who testify. They can pick one person's story over the other. Look for the lack of supporting evidence when, in your opinion, such evidence should really exist. On the other hand, a general denial by the alleged harasser will normally not be persuasive with the finders of fact. A thorough investigation should answer questions concerning whether or not coworkers had any knowledge of the conduct and whether anyone observed the employee's behavior shortly after the alleged incident of harassment. Did the employee talk about the matter to anyone? Was there any change in the behavior of the employee at work or in performance at work? Were any other employees similarly harassed?

If it is impossible to tell what really happened, what should management do? First, the company can re-emphasize to everyone involved in the complaint that the company's policy is to prohibit sexual or racial harassment and that it will thoroughly investigate any complaints. Documentation should be made that a complaint has been received and that an investigation took place, but that the result was that it could not be determined if unlawful sexual harassment actually occurred in violation of the company policy. The complainant should be reassured that his or her employment conditions will not be adversely affected by the bringing of a complaint.

In some cases, the victim of harassment does not want any action to be taken. However, once management has been made aware of a situation, it has no alternative but to investigate it. This should be explained to the employee. The employee can be assured that the matter will be handled as discreetly as possible. If the employee refuses to give any further information on the conduct, that is fine, but the investigation must proceed. While it is obviously going to be difficult to discipline the person complained about, this fact alone must not halt the investigation. It should be documented that the investigation unearthed no evidence of a violation of company policy. However, a note could be made to suggest that the company re-emphasize its no sexual harassment policy and perhaps renew the supervisory training to emphasize that the policy is important to the company.

There can be no underestimation of the power of the sexual harassment issue in the workplace today. Skeptics as well as those ready to sensationalize what once may have been normal day-to-day conduct in the environment of the workshop, with no intention to harass anyone, must acknowledge there is a middle ground where trouble is brewing. While there will always be a certain percentage of individuals who attempt to legally take advantage of situations either for protection or profit, there are far too many sincere situations that have led to unfortunate results for everyone involved. This area of human behavior, and of the law that regulates it, is certainly all too susceptible to fabricated or exaggerated complaints, but also to fabricated or exaggerated denials.

In one particular case, the story followed a destructive pattern in which everybody lost. A female medical technologist worked in a health-care laboratory supervised by two male physicians. It was the habit of the physicians to tell dirty jokes and make innuendoes of a sexual nature. On one occasion, the doctors went so far as to inquire of the medical technologist, "Did you get any last night?" Of course, to the physicians, they thought it was all good-natured fun and convivial personal relations. To the female under their supervision, it was a nightmare. In the investigation after she complained to the human resources department, coworkers not only confirmed her allegations, but echoed her distaste and frustration at the behavior. The hospital president took the confidential report to the hospital board of trustees for action. The board decided to admonish the physicians, and that was done in a private session. However, this is not the end of the story.

After the investigation, the atmosphere in the laboratory became markedly cold, causing more stress for the medical technologist than before. She was the first to admit that it affected her work performance, which steadily declined. Mistakes began cropping up on laboratory reports. Her performance evaluations from the doctors reflected her poor performance. Eventually, they recommended her termination from employment.

After her discharge for poor performance, the medical technologist filed a lawsuit with the state Equal Employment Opportunity Agency. Her claim was eventually settled in a monetary settlement. But this is not the end of the story.

The fact that a settlement was needed to resolve her complaint made the board of trustees angry at the doctors involved. At year-end bonus time, the amount of the settlement was removed from the doctors' discretionary bonus, which angered the doctors. In a very short time, they left their residency at the health care institution and went to a competing provider, taking their patients with them.

In complaints of harassment, the issues are many and the people involved are typically extremely sensitive. Projecting firmness and fairness is key to defusing complex workplace issues, especially those as emotionally charged as complaints of harassment.

Supervisory Methods Checklists
In discussing supervisory methods, the most important point to remember is that supervisors are part of *management*. This means that the

supervisor is the front-line commander of the business, the person who really makes it work. The supervisor is the primary leader to whom the employees look for guidance and direction, pay raises and promotions, fair scheduling of work, special treatment in cases of personal hardship, and impartial treatment in cases where corrective disciplinary punishment is necessary. Employees consider the supervisor as the connecting link between central management and the plant floor or office. In addition, under the National Labor Relations Act, the supervisor is the legal agent for all of management. This means that what a supervisor says or does carries the same weight under the law as what is said or done by the president of the company. Clearly, being a supervisor is one of the most important positions an individual can hold in any company.

It has been stated previously that a genuine interest in the employees who work for a supervisor allows for better contingency planning and results in more and better work than does concentrated driving, prodding, and pushing. In performing this important job, a good supervisor possesses many skills. The following list gives a sample of some of these attributes.

- When a reprimand is necessary, good supervisors do it in private to save face for the employee rather than reprimanding the employee in front of others. Good supervisors emphasize *what* is right rather than *who* is right.

- When changes are necessary, good supervisors explain the changes in advance and ask for suggestions.

- Good supervisors settle differences between employees.

- Good supervisors lead by persuasion rather than through fear. Good supervisors explain why and ask for cooperation rather than giving abrupt and arbitrary orders.

- Good supervisors show confidence in their people, encouraging them to develop and to qualify for promotion.

- Good supervisors compliment for work well done rather than taking it for granted, commenting only on mistakes.

- Good supervisors listen patiently, even to small talk or complaints, rather than always being too busy.

- Good supervisors welcome good suggestions and complaints and ask for advice rather than ignoring employees.

- Good supervisors see that good employees are promoted, even if it means losing them, rather than blocking employees' progress just to make it easier on themselves.

In the course of their work, supervisors develop many relationships. These include their relationship to the company, the employees they supervise, their allied supervisors, and their immediate superior. The following provides guidance on how a supervisor can develop these relationships.

Company Expectations
In relationship to the company, supervisors are:

- The front-line commanders of the business, the people who really make it work.

- Considered by employees as a connecting link between central management and the plant office or floor.

- The primary leaders to whom the employees look for guidance, direction, pay raises, promotions, fair scheduling of work, special treatment in cases of personal hardship, discipline, and impartial treatment.

- Legal agents of the company under the National Labor Relations Act, which means that what a supervisor says or does is the same under the law as if it were said or done by the president of the company. Accordingly, supervisors are expected to:

    - Enforce and practice all safety rules and regulations.

    - Support with honesty the policies laid down by the company.

    - Protect and preserve company property at all times.

    - Help develop a good organization by hiring employees who can carry on the business in the future.

    - Promote the company by speaking well of it to employees and outsiders.

    - Maintain the highest standards of efficiency.

    - Be morale-builders.

    - Be good citizens off-duty as well as on-duty.

- Promote economy and prevent waste.

- Make suggestions concerning the improvement of efficiency and personnel relations.

In dealing with their employees, company management expects supervisors to:

- Treat employees with consideration, remembering at all times to respect their feelings.

- Honestly represent employees to upper management when necessary.

- Interpret company policies for employees.

- Be good examples, both on-duty and off-duty.

- Be generous with praise where deserved.

- Be considerate and positive with corrective discipline.

- Be consistent in the treatment of all employees.

- Help employees to develop themselves.

- Study employees carefully and judge them honestly. Never let personalities enter into judgment.

- Develop the confidence of employees by being fair and loyal to them.

- Try to place people according to their ability and temperament.

- Support workers by assuming full responsibility for their work.

- Be interested in and sympathetic to their personal problems as well as their work problems.

- Always avoid favoritism.

Employee Expectations of Supervisors
The supervisor must understand what employees expect from a good supervisor. Employees expect supervisors to:

- Keep them busy without prodding them.

- Know their individual capabilities and judge them honestly.

- Teach them thoroughly and correctly.

- Maintain discipline.

- Insist upon safety in every detail.

- Be willing to discuss individual grievances and handle them fairly.

- Insist upon high standards of work.

- Be good workers as well as good supervisors.

- Be well-liked and have the respect of upper management and allied supervisors.

- Know the job thoroughly.

Expectations of Allied Supervisors

In relationship to one another, it is important to understand what allied supervisors expect. They expect supervisors to:

- Cooperate with all supervisors on the same level.

- Exchange ideas for the good of the company.

- Talk positively about all company affairs.

- Treat each other with courtesy, respect, and tolerance.

- Consult on personal matters, if invited.

- Help each other look good in their work.

- Never belittle other supervisors for the sake of personal gain.

- Show confidence in each other's ability.

- Act fairly and honestly.

Expectations of Immediate Superiors

Supervisors also have relationships with their immediate superiors and need to know what the expectations of their superiors are in these relationships. In this regard superiors expect supervisors to:

- Cooperate with them.

- Obey orders and carry out instructions in detail, informing them of changes in conditions immediately.

- Prepare for advancement and train subordinates to step into the position.

- Report results fully and accurately.

- Be courteous and respectful of the position of superiors.

- Make suggestions for improvements.

- Try to relieve superiors of as many details as possible.

- Assume full responsibility for the work unit or department.

The supervisor's position is action-oriented and critical in any business. While it is impossible to cover every imaginable situation that may occur, proper methods generally allow supervisors to successfully administer the philosophy and policy of the management on a day-to-day basis with their employees. In sum, it is the supervisor's competent administration of the company's policies that insures the continued success of a business in the competitive world today.

Performance Evaluations

Performance evaluations are difficult to administer properly because they must be presented to individual employees in an accurate and balanced way. There are legions of cases and occasions where a review of performance evaluations in a poor performer's file reveals only excellent, superior, or above average performance. Often in these cases, the individual supervisor states as he or she recommends discipline or discharge that it is a wonder the company was able to put up with this employee for so long. On the opposite end of the issue is the supervisor who does nothing but point out an employee's weaknesses, thereby destroying morale, trust, and teamwork?

In theory, employees want to know where their performance is lacking so they can make improvements and earn rewards. The difficulty presents itself in the communication of the performance evaluation. Some supervisors use what some like to refer to as the *sports model* or *screaming coach* performance evaluation. For athletes under this type of supervision, "the time to start worrying is when the coach stops yelling." This model meets with plenty of criticism in athletics and much more in business, where finding and especially retaining the services of competent employees is a great challenge. Supervisors are challenged by the immediate need to improve their employees' performance via honest constructive criticism and at the same time retain loyal and motivated employees. These two distinct needs meet in the performance appraisal.

It is difficult to provide effective performance evaluations. The following checklist details some of the problems every supervisor encounters in this delicate task.

Common Performance Evaluation Complaints

- It takes too much time.

- It is too complicated to be meaningful.

- The appraisal form is outdated and does not ask the supervisor to measure what is important.

- Everyone expects an exemplary evaluation and anything less is a devastating blow to an employee's morale and career so supervisors cannot say what really needs to be said.

- Performance evaluations do not produce changes for the better.

- Ratings are so subjective that they reflect the individual supervisor doing the rating more than the employee being evaluated.

- Lack of training on *how* to evaluate performance results in lack of consistency in ratings.

- A poor rating often results in accusations from the employee of personal bias.

- There is very little information to help anyone interpret the difference between the levels of ratings.

- Employees feel that managers dwell unnecessarily on small incidents to justify reduced ratings.

- Ratings do not reflect efforts at improvement once performance levels in the minds of the evaluator have been made.

- No one tells the employee in the process what to do differently and how to do it in order to improve performance.

Giving feedback is probably the most important element in improving anyone's performance on any task. However, the employee evaluation process in itself does not motivate employees effectively, especially when given only once a year. For feedback to be effective, it must be specific and given on a day-to-day basis. Supervisors who believe that the annual evaluation process fulfills their performance appraisal responsibilities effectively are mistaken.

Effective performance evaluations in combination with day-to-day feedback can help improve performance. In addition to combining formal evaluations with frequent informal feedback, it is also important to identify the kind of behavior that leads to success or failure in the job being evaluated. In determining which behaviors are critical to the job and therefore which behaviors should be measured, supervisors should involve the employee who is closest to the job in the identification process. Once important behaviors are established, they can be further prioritized by how often they occur on a scale from frequent to seldom. In this way, a seemingly less significant behavior takes on added importance if it occurs frequently in the workplace, and a seemingly significant behavior may be reduced in importance if it seldom is required. The list of important behaviors and their relative importance should be evaluated annually to make adjustments in line with developing business needs.

There are probably as many ways to rate performance as there are management consultants in the business of designing performance evaluation systems. One popular rating method, frequently used for exempt positions, is the *essay format*. In a management by objectives (MBO) appraisal process, the essay format could be a single question, such as, "describe this individual's performance as it relates to his or her primary responsibilities." One of the criticisms of this method is that the evaluator often makes the mistake of writing about relatively unimportant but interesting items because there are no guidelines and the writer has little feedback from anyone about what is being written. Sometimes a more direct question is added, such as, "Describe three strong points and three weak points of this individual." Of course, this method is subject to the criticism of personal bias for negative ratings more than any other. Its strength is that the manager's ability to rate performance comes through clearly and the manager is not limited by the form itself.

The other end of the spectrum is the *checkmark system*. In this system, employees are rated on forms that rank performance on number scales from one to four or five or seven. Here the supervisor lacks any individual input into what is being rated and how, but the marks go on the paper nonetheless, for good or for ill. However, this method takes less time and leaves less to the imagination and, therefore, some supervisors prefer it.

Another problem is defining on a consistent basis how the evaluator thinks. For example, one rating could be from one to four with one being fair, two being good, three being very good, and four being superior. What these numbers mean, and corresponding categories, can be anyone's guess. For some people, "excellent" is average, and for others it is the reverse. However, most employees don't want to be considered average; they want to be considered excellent. Another rating that causes confusion is *meets minimum requirements*. While this certainly would be less than *exceeds minimum requirements*, it still hinges on how one defines the requirements, and what is meant by "minimum."

For performance evaluations to work in improving employee performance, they should be designed to only list behaviors related to success on the job. They should also provide a basis for giving specific and measurable feedback relative to the actual ways an employee behaves. This should focus a manager's time and attention on improving an employee's performance on those areas that are most important to such success. In other words, the behaviors described should be important, observable, and measurable. Then, when meeting an individual employee, the manager can talk about what the employee is doing better than expected, what he or she is doing in an acceptable manner, and what he or she must improve upon. Being simplified in this manner, the supervisor and employee can mutually discuss what can be done to improve performance.

If the meeting is meant to improve an employee's performance, no time should be spent discussing an employee's potential for future promotions or what monetary compensation might be in the offing as the reward. Also, these discussions should take no longer than 30 minutes. Time spent beyond that is normally unproductive.

In discussing those areas that must be improved, it is important to develop a plan of doing so. Such a plan should clearly identify the challenge to the employee, what the employee must do to change, how the supervisor can help the employee change, and when the next meeting to discuss progress concerning the change will take place.

In summary, the performance evaluation process is a tricky proceeding. While it can enhance an employee's understanding of where he or she stands, it can also be harmful to the employment relationship if care is not taken to properly assess and discuss performance issues. Below is one format used by a manufacturer to perform this delicate task.

Sample Employee Performance Evaluation Form

Employee Name:_____

Clock Number:_____

1.0 Quality
1.1 Documentation: Are forms complete and accurate?

_____

1.2 Inspection: measurements accurate, follows procedures.

_____

1.3 Observation: notices and reports changes in process and/or parts.

_____

1.4 Product Conformance: produces parts within specification limits.

_____

1.5 Suggests Improvements: offers ideas for enhancing product quality.

_____

Subtotal_____ x 1.5 = _____

2.0 Productivity
2.1 Documentation: labor and routing tickets complete and accurate.

_____

2.2 Efficiency: organizes workstation, manual operations match machine.

_____

2.3 Procedure: adheres to operation procedures and instructions.

_____

2.4 Rate: achieves or exceeds standard for operation.

_____

2.5 Suggests Improvements: offers ideas for enhancing productivity.

_____

Subtotal_____ x 1.5 = _____

3.0 Attendance (Absences pursuant to company's Family & Medical Leave Act policy not included for the purpose of this evaluation)
3.1 Leave Early

_____

3.2 Sick Leave

_____

3.3 Tardiness

_____

3.4 Unexcused Absence

_____

Subtotal_____ x 1.0 = _____

4.0 Work Habits

4.1 Attitude toward company, customers, and coworkers.

_____

4.2 Dedication to job throughout shift.

_____

4.3 Housekeeping and safety conscious.

_____

4.4 Responds to supervision/training.

_____

4.5 Proper use of tools and equipment.

_____

Subtotal_____ x 1.0 = _____
Total Score = _____

Here is another example.

Second Sample Employee Performance Evaluation Form

Date:
Employee:
Department:
Job Title:
Supervisor:

Kind of Evaluation: ___ Annual ___ Trial and Training ___ Termination ___ Other

Date of Last Review: _____

Next Scheduled Review: _____

Performance Ratings:
1 — meets orexceeds expectations
2 — needs to improve

Rating Job-Related Criteria
_____ Job Understanding: Employee possesses a clear knowledge of the responsibilities and the tasks he or she must perform.

_____ Job Performance: The thoroughness, neatness, efficiency, and accuracy of employee's work.

_____ Job Productivity: The quality and quantity of employee's work in terms of volume and accomplishments.

_____ Dependability: Can supervisor rely upon employee to timely complete assigned tasks?

_____ Cooperation: The ability of employee to work willingly with associates, subordinates, supervisors, and others.

List general comments as to employee's strengths, weaknesses, and action to be taken to improve job performance. (Attach additional sheets if necessary.)

Employee Comments (attach additional sheets if necessary):

Reviewed and discussed with employee

_____

Employee   Date

_____   _____

Supervisor   Date

_____   _____

Managers and administrators can be part of the evaluation process too. A "self appraisal" that includes a goal setting segment is especially valuable. The following example has been used in the non-profit sector for an executive director position. It is in two parts, the first being the self-appraisal and the second being the actual fiscal year-end performance evaluation.

Self-Appraisal Form

Name: _____

Date: _____

Appraisal Period: _____

Purpose:

1. To ensure that your perception of performance is understood.

2. To help make performance and development discussion more productive.

3. To assist you in evaluating your past performance.

Instructions: Complete the self-appraisal and return the form to your supervisor. This form is for discussion purposes only.

Significant Contributions: Note significant contributions you have made during the year (problems solved, decisions made, improvements, specific examples of outstanding performance.)

_____

_____

_____

Overall Performance Perception: Overall, how would you rate your performance during the year? Please explain.

_____

_____

_____

Performance Improvement Areas: Identify areas that could be improved to enhance your effectiveness. Identify other barriers (e.g., the environment, staff, board, etc.) That inhibit growth and improvement.

_____

_____

_____

Goals: Specific goals from your last appraisal are identified below. Indicate the progress you have made toward meeting these goals. Include specific measures you have taken where appropriate. If a goal has not been met, explain.

GOAL   STATUS

1. Goal #1

2. Goal #2

3. Goal #3

Future Goals: What are your future goals? How do you feel these goals support overall agency goals?

GOAL   IMPORTANCE

1.

2.

3.

PERFORMANCE APPRAISAL FORM

Employee's Name: _____

Evaluation Period: _____

Evaluation Date: _____

Rating Scale:

NA = Trait not applicable to this job or person.
1.   = Performance meets or exceeds expectations.
2.   = Performance below expectations.

Decision-Making /Judgement

–Judgements are consistently wise and appropriate. _____

–Input from staff and/or peers is sought, when appropriate. _____

–Management input is sought, when appropriate. _____

–Decisions are well thought out and backed by factual information, when available. _____

–Decisions are made on a timely basis, when necessary. _____

–Employee is adaptable to changes which may be required. _____

Other relevant factors: _____

Comments:
_____
_____

Job Productivity/Quality

–Completes job tasks, as requested, on a timely basis. _____

–Carefully analyzes all work for accuracy, compliance and thoroughness. _____

–Consistently generates high quality work. _____

–Responds promptly and appropriately to requests. _____

–Keeps internal and external contacts aware of status of pending requests. _____

Other relevant factors: _____

Comments:

_____
_____

Planning/Organizational Skills

–Consistently exercises effective planning techniques. _____
–Submits challenging goals and objectives _____
–Utilizes a structured and organized approach to completing job tasks.
_____
–Demonstrates good forward thinking/planning skills. _____
Other relevant factors: _____

Comments:

_____
_____

Communication Skills

–Demonstrates effective written communication skills. _____
–Demonstrates effective oral communication skills. _____
–Keeps employees/peers informed of issues. _____
–Keeps management/board informed of issues. _____
–Maintains effective communication with internal/external contacts.
_____
Other relevant factors: _____

Comments:

_____
_____

Leadership

–Provides strong leadership; instills trust, confidence, etc. _____
–Seeks opportunities to lead various activities and projects.
_____
–Effectively gains cooperation of subordinates/peers/board.
_____
–Effectively delegates activities that can be completed by others.
_____
–Promotes teamwork within agency/peers/board. _____
–Functions successfully under stressful conditions. _____
Other relevant factors: _____

Comments:
_____
_____

Financial Management

–Adequately develops departmental and agency budgets. _____
–Ensures the operation of departments and agency within budgets.
_____
–Ensures the security of financial resources and assets. _____
–Investigates appropriate cost reduction strategies. _____
Other relevant factors: _____

Section II- Narrative

1. Summarize employee success in achieving most recent goals.

2. Provide overall summary employee's job performance.

3. Summarize performance areas to be improved and provide action steps to be taken.

4. Employee Input.

Employee Signature: _____ Date: _____

Supervisor Signature: _____ Date: _____

Dealing with Cultural Diversity

It is an undeniable fact that the cultural makeup of the American workforce is changing rapidly. Estimates are that in the near future minorities, women, and immigrants will comprise approximately 85 percent of the American workforce. If current trends continue, the highest rate of increase in the workforce will be among Asian Americans and Hispanics. Women will continue increasing their representation in the workforce. The number of workers between the ages of 35 and 54 are increasing as well. It is estimated that white males will soon constitute only about 15 percent of the new entrants to the labor force.

In addition to the numerical changes in the makeup of the workforce, individuals are starting to celebrate their cultural differences and have become less amenable to comprising the characteristics that make them different. Employees are now inclined to believe, "I'm different and proud of what makes me different." Part of the reason for this is that minority employees have observed that their predecessors who attempted to assimilate or fit in with their perception of the reigning corporate culture lose some of their minority identity. The same is true for female employees who wonder if they lose some of their femininity when they try to "fit in with the boys." To many, the price of attempting to be a part of the cultural mainstream is too great a price to pay for success. Employees are now more certain that if they are too busy focusing on adapting their personal styles, they cannot focus on their personal strengths or productive ideas. In addition, industrial psychological research has shown that the best teamwork comes from the recognition that we all are different. When we can understand and accept our differences, we can better draw upon our respective strengths to achieve overall success.

However, some studies challenge whether attitudes towards minorities and women have really changed. For example, pollsters for ABC News and the *Washington Post* asked a random sampling of whites, "Do you happen to have a close friend who is black?" When the question was asked by a black interviewer, 67 percent of the white respondents answered "Yes." When a white interviewer asked the same question of the same group, the percentage dropped to 57 percent. Conversely, the same occurred with African Americans. Sixty-seven percent of blacks in the random sampling told a black interviewer that they had a close friend who was white. Seventy-nine percent gave the same answer to a white interviewer.

When survey participants were asked: "Are the problems faced by blacks brought on by blacks themselves?" Sixty-two percent of the white respondents said yes to white interviewers. When the same white respondents were asked the same question by black interviewers, the number dropped to 46 percent.

Dr. John Fernandez, in his book, *Managing a Diverse Workforce*, noted the following comments from surveys of over 4,000 managers:

"I fear blacks. I think of women as mothers and homebodies. I don't understand Asian culture." (White male.)

"I have a hard time listening to Asians with heavy accents. I distrust white males in groups." (Hispanic female)

"I fear situations where I am the minority." (White male)

"I stereotype people. I believe that Orientals are smart, southerners are slow and minority groups have gotten help because of race." (White female)

"I have a wife at home, a mother at home, and I see women in those roles." (Black male)

"I am concerned about the skill level of someone from a predominantly black college." (Asian male)

"I have a difficult time dealing with people with accents." (Black female)

"You must assimilate to move up in corporate America." (Asian female)

"I feel that I perform my job well, but I do not feel that I receive any support from upper management." (Black female)

"People of color have to be three times as competent as whites in order to be recognized as competent and capable." (Asian female)

The first step toward managing in a diverse workplace may be not to ignore diversity, but rather to recognize it, understand it, and adapt to it. While this may require a change of thinking and communicating, it may be possible to do so without being seen as patronizing or phony.

It is important to recognize first that there may be hidden meanings in our choice of words. Some words, phrases, or ideas may be interpreted by sensitized individuals to imply that certain racial or ethnic groups, women, or other cultures may be felt to be superior or inferior to others. In other words, watch your language—biased communication can be unbelievably harmful even if the supervisor lacked any biased intent. However, the listener can be offended and one's true message accordingly tuned out. Responsible communicators make every effort to end biases that often invade unintentionally written, visual, and face-to-face exchanges.

While the following may seem obvious, here are some suggestions for words to help a supervisor maintain biased-free communication.

Words	Unbiased Word
Handicapped	Individual with a disability
Negro	African American or Black
Jew	Jewish person
Boy, Girl or Gal	Use of the person's real name
Cop	Police officer
Fireman	Firefighter

Mailman	Letter carrier
Stewardess	Flight attendant
Ladies, Girls	Salesperson
Deaf and dumb	Hearing and speech impaired
Chairman	Chairperson or Chair

There is no mistaking that there are cultural differences in the way people communicate. At times these differences may seem like an extension of stereotypes. However, it's important to have a sense of just how cultures differ as we go forward into the global marketplace. Understanding cultural differences should lead to a more tolerant attitude towards others and may help us get past either being misinterpreted ourselves or misinterpreting someone else's culturally learned behavior. However, it is just as important to be open-minded in reviewing the following materials and understand that people are individuals who may or may not follow a particular cultural behavior. The following list outlines general cultural beliefs and behaviors.

Shaking Hands

- Arabs, Hispanics, and Greeks may shake hands repeatedly.

- The French may feel it inappropriate to shake hands with a superior; furthermore, they may shake hands lightly and quickly.

- Japanese, Arabs, Native Americans, and some women have relaxed handshakes; thus, be careful of the strength of your grip.

- Be alert to cultural variations with respect to shaking hands with women.

- With Germans, it is appropriate to shake hands with everyone upon arriving and leaving.

Touching

- Many Americans dislike touches on arm, shoulder, or back (personal preference). Thus, these public displays should be generally avoided.

- Arabs object to touches with the left hand.

- Do not pat Koreans on the back.

- Be cautious about touching Asians and persons from Israel, Puerto Rico, or Great Britain because it is considered to be too familiar.

- Do not touch children from Thailand or from many areas of Asia on the head or shoulders. The head is considered sacred.

- Some Arabs may want to touch your arm, lapel, or hand during conversation.

Eye Contact

- Persons from the Middle East feel it appropriate to keep very direct eye contact, especially with someone of the same sex. This is not meant as an aggressive gesture and it would be offensive for one to look away.

- Some Asians, particularly the Japanese, feel that direct eye contact is rude and intrusive.

- Hispanics and Europeans generally prefer to maintain direct eye contact.

- Native Americans may not maintain eye contact.

- Others may make eye contact or even stare while talking and then look away while listening.

Language

- Many foreigners can understand far more English than they can speak.

- There may be a tendency to pretend to understand what has been said.

- In some Asian cultures, it is impolite to say no. Smiling and the nodding of the head may indicate comprehension, rather than actually meaning "yes." Moreover, the word, "yes" as a response may only indicate that your question was heard and not agreed to.

- Utilize written documents because it may be easier to read English than remember it.

- Increase use of understandable nonverbal communication methods, because these signals represent 55 percent of what is actually understood.

- Watch for nonverbal signs of misunderstanding (repetitive "yes," repetitive nodding and smiling) in the absence of questions. Nonverbal and verbal communication systems may vary.

- Even with a given language, accents, usage, and differences may create communication barriers.

Family Roles and Relationships

- Some cultures have very traditional family roles for males and females.

- Some cultures place a higher priority upon family than upon business.

- Hispanics and Asians generally feel strongly about conducting business with people they know rather than with strangers.

Personal Achievement and Competition

- These traits are highly held in the United States.

- Native Americans may place a higher priority upon sharing and community than possessions and competition.

- Other cultures may place a higher priority upon family rather than competition, success, initiative, and material possessions. Also, modesty and patience are highly valued traits.

- Vietnamese and Asians generally discourage aggressive behavior, as opposed to teamwork and consensus building.

- Asians, Hispanics, and some Europeans may feel that the use of initiative is disrespectful.

Social Behavior

- The need for an Asian to *save face* may be related to a lack of knowledge as opposed to misunderstanding.

- Some Asians, in particular, and other cultures in general may feel uncomfortable or ridiculed when they are the source of laughter, jokes, or humor.

- Some Asians and Arabs may have noisy eating habits, such as belching.

- In some cultures, it is considered rude to leave food on your plate.

- Some cultures feel it would be interfering to interrupt someone in mid-sentence.

- Other cultures have a more relaxed view of posture.

The list of differences is endless. What is important is what is done and what is said, rather than who is saying it and how he or she may express

CHAPTER FIVE

it. Other areas of cultural differences include hobbies and interests, body language, small talk, expression of emotion versus control of emotion, sense of humor, appearance and dress, and the importance of individuality.

In summary, there is really little difference among people in terms of human desires, emotions, and feelings. However, the differences can be vast in terms of beliefs, experiences, and values. While we cannot live someone else's experiences, we may be able to change our own by listening to and learning from those around us. The acceptance of cultural differences should diversify our own experience and may change our beliefs and broaden our values. In my opinion, when we limit ourselves by spending time only with others whose beliefs, experiences, or values mirror our own, we eliminate the rest of humanity and thereby limit our own education. The successful supervisor in the future will be the one who can engage, lead, and motivate those of different cultural backgrounds.

Constructive Discharge

Supervisors who are tempted to avoid an employment lawsuit by making an employee's job so bad that he or she will quit do so at their own peril.

They might think that once an employee quits, the company is not only off the hook for unemployment compensation benefits, but also for any liability for equal employment opportunity discrimination claims, wrongful discharge actions, and any other employment law related cause of action. After all, they might think, "how can I be held accountable if the employee is the one who decides not to work for me? Isn't that *the employee's* decision not to work?"

However, under the legal doctrine of *constructive discharge*, even though it may be good advice to ask an employee who says he or she wants to quit to "put it in writing," and never to talk an employee out of quitting, you must understand that the employee can still file a lawsuit against the company and be *excused* from being the one to sever the employment relationship.

The courts have consistently ruled that when an employer makes a job so unbearable for an employee that he or she finally decides to quit rather than suffer more abuse, the employee has been unfairly discharged. Reinstatement and back pay are the usual remedies. However, most courts and Equal Employment Opportunity Agencies would rule that it would be unfair to put the employee back into such an environment of abuse, and that, therefore, *front pay* is a possible award available to the employee. This trap can be avoided by disciplining and counseling employees for cause rather than doing things that will cause an employee to quit if his or her performance or behavior is substandard.

Understanding the Law of Constructive Discharge

In most jurisdictions, all that an employee is required to show a jury or judge is that working conditions were so difficult or unpleasant that a reasonable person in the employee's shoes would have felt compelled to resign. Another case put it this way, "A discharge, within the meaning of the Age Discrimination and Employment Act (ADEA), may be *constructive* if a reasonable person in the employee's position would have felt compelled to resign under the circumstances." In other words, if the employee can show that the employer has deliberately made an employee's working conditions so intolerable as to *force* the resignation, then a finding of liability against the employer is appropriate.

Whether conditions are so intolerable that a reasonable person would be forced to resign is generally a question of fact that will be up to a jury to decide. However, the burden of proof is on the employee. The plaintiff must show some aggravating factors, such as a continuous pattern of discriminatory treatment, in order to prevail. In California, for example, a plaintiff must show "actions and conditions so intolerable or aggravated at the time of the resignation that a reasonable person in the employee's position would have resigned, *and* that the employer had actual or constructive knowledge of the intolerable actions and conditions and of their impact upon the employee and could have remedied the situation, but did not."

The cause must be objective. There is some good news under this theory. The reasons for quitting, in order to establish liability under this doctrine, must not be merely *subjectively* intolerable by the employee, but must be *objectively* so bad that the employee had no real alternative but to quit. In other words, it must be some cause attributable to the employer; some act or omission to act by the employer that justifies the employee's quitting. This usually involves some fault on the part of the employer that is real and substantial and not just a compelling personal reason.

Kinds of Acts by an Employer That Justify Quitting

These situations will be dealt with by the court on a case-by-case basis. However, some examples are clear. In one case, the evidence showed that the plaintiff was demoted from a managerial position to a sales position and was asked to train his younger successor. His salary was then decreased and his duties were cut back to the point where the employer did not allow the plaintiff to act alone in any respect. Finally, each time a new restraint was imposed on the plaintiff, the evidence showed that the employer would ask, "Are you going to quit your job yet?" The Court held that the combination of the demotion, continuing limitations on his salary and responsibility, and the company's repeatedly asking him whether he was going to quit his job, made working conditions intolerable and allowed plaintiff's claim to proceed even though he quit.

In the context of an unemployment compensation claim, an employee quit after his hours were unilaterally increased from 10 to 12 hours a day, despite his complaints. It was reasonable for him to have believed that a transfer would not have alleviated the problem. It was held that that he quit with good cause and was awarded unemployment compensation benefits. In another situation, an employer unilaterally reduced an employee from full-time to part-time and eliminated all fringe benefits. It was held the employee had good cause for quitting and was, therefore, eligible for benefits.

In general, reasonable criticism and a denial of benefits based on merit are the prerogatives of management. However, if an employer's discipline is improper or abusive and the employee quits because of it, it may amount to a constructive discharge. This is particularly true where the abuse is connected to membership in an equal employment opportunity protected class.

Defenses to Constructive Discharge Claims

One of the major defenses to these claims is that the law does not permit an employee's subjective perceptions to govern whether or not the discharge was forced by the employer. For example, in one recent case, the employee alleged that working conditions had become objectively intolerable by virtue of the employer's selective enforcement of its attendance policy when it required a doctor's note. The employee considered this an insult. However, even if the policy was selectively enforced, it still does not make the employee's working conditions so difficult that a reasonable person would be compelled to quit. Merely because an employee may take the requirement of a doctor's note to be an insult, does not make it *objectively* an intolerable condition.

Accordingly, while it may be difficult for the plaintiff to show objective considerations that are real and substantial before saying conditions are so intolerable that he or she was forced to quit, *do not think the case is closed merely because an individual does quit.* One technique is to conduct a mandatory exit interview for all employees who quit. If hard feelings are alleged because of changes in working conditions, often these differences can be ironed out *before* the employee feels so aggravated as to file a lawsuit. The best advice is, as always, to play it straight. If an employee's work is unsatisfactory, the supervisor can discipline him/her for the unsatisfactory work. Do not change conditions of employment to induce an employee to resign thinking that you will have avoided a lawsuit by so doing.

Discharging Employees

Preparation and decisiveness are the keys in discharging employees. When the time comes to discharge an employee, a supervisor should not hesitate. Counterproductive employees can cost the business much more in the long run than it costs to defend dismissals. However, it is never necessary to discharge anyone on the spot. (This is more fully discussed in Chapter Seven.) Remember that there is an increasing awareness of employee rights and avenues of legal challenge, so it is important to pay careful attention to creating responsive supervisory and personnel systems to protect management's right to act where appropriate.

When management asserts its right and discharges an employee, it seems to many employers that throughout the government's administrative hearings and investigative processes that follow, a company is judged guilty unless able to prove itself innocent of wrongdoing. This is because businesses are presumed to be responsible for and attentive to all of their operations. It means that the discharge decision is a serious matter, one that requires special thought, and should not necessarily be left to the supervisory authority alone.

There is some leeway, however, in supervisory discretion. First, there are certain types of employee misconduct that violate the standard of behavior that employers have a right to expect from employees. Examples of such behavior include:

- excessive absenteeism or tardiness without notice to the employer;

- dishonesty, such as theft or falsification of work records;

- insubordination, such as direct disobedience of valid work orders, refusal to perform assigned work, and disregard or ridicule of those in authority; and

- neglect of duty, such as sleeping on the job, horseplay, or extreme carelessness in the performance of work.

If the employee's behavior continuously shows that the employee is indifferent to the obligations, duties, and standards the employer has a right to expect, the employer should ultimately prevail in any challenge to the decision to discharge.

A company can prove continuing poor behavior using corrective, progressive discipline. This simply means telling employees when they are doing something right so that they continue to do it right, and telling employees when they are doing something wrong so that they will stop. Simple notes to a personnel file detailing supervisory counseling that are dated, and signed by the supervisor giving the counseling, establish the record of such an event. In fact, such notes may be used to refresh a supervisor's memory and may even be admitted into evidence themselves as a business record at subsequent hearings on any dismissal decision challenge.

There are a few important things to remember during this process:

- Never meet with an employee alone during counseling sessions. Supervisors should always have a witness to what is said, eliminating the problem of one person's word against another's. The presence of this witness emphasizes to the employee that the decision in process is not solely the result of the supervisor's opinions, but is, in reality, a company decision.

- Immediately after the conference, the supervisor should prepare and sign a brief memo describing the results. Although this is not mandatory, a copy can be given to the employee. In fact, this is the preferred procedure because it is not uncommon at discharge hearings for the attorney for the employee to ask if the employee was given notice of the warning that went in the employee's file. It makes sense to give the employee a copy because the reason for the meeting is to discipline him for poor performance that can be corrected.

In many cases, the governmental agencies or reviewing courts of law hold that although each individual incident in an employee's work record may not amount to misconduct, an employee's overall work record may be used to prove misconduct. It is difficult judging when discipline appears too formal to be effective. However, this should not deter supervisors from using formal discipline as a tool when it is necessary to record and preserve what happens in the workplace.

Also, remember that gross carelessness in even a single instance may be severe enough to amount to misconduct if the consequences of the act or failure to act were fairly obvious and were likely to cause serious loss to the business. For example, theft and falsification of work records fall into this category.

In establishing business reasons for discharge, the following analysis will be required

- It must be verified that there is a rule or policy prohibiting the conduct of the employee. Employee handbooks can provide the perfect communications forum for the publication of such policies.

- Supervisors should be ready to establish that the employee was or should have been aware of company policies governing standards of behavior. As discussed at the beginning of this chapter, the best time to acquaint an employee with the rules and the policies is during the employee's orientation.

- New employees should sign a form indicating that a copy of the employee handbook and work policies have been received.

    Most adjudicative review bodies will ask an employer to establish that its rules and policies are reasonable. This can be done by showing that violations of these rules harm the interest of the employer. However, employers are best advised to be specific in this effort in proving their case and show how the misconduct or rule violation harmed its interest.

- Lastly, after the business has established the above points, verify through direct testimony that the employee actually violated the company's rules. At administrative hearings, this usually means that the employee's supervisor will be testifying. Although this results in lost work time for a management employee, discharge decisions are seldom upheld without firsthand sworn testimony.

With each passing day, we read about more and more cases of employers being held liable for thousands, if not millions, of dollars in back pay and other costs associated with discharges. However, most challenges to discharge decisions can be won or avoided altogether through proper attention to basic personnel operations and proper supervisory methods.

Making Peace with Employees

Imagine that two employees are vying for a promotion. One is young but qualified; the other is a long-time employee with a good performance record but a reputation for being difficult. The younger worker gets the job, and the veteran employee promptly files an age discrimination lawsuit. Uneasiness settles across the company as the long, slow, expensive legal process of deciding who is right grinds on and on.

In recent years, as more and more such cases crowd court dockets and fuel legal expenses, employers are seeking new ways to handle employee disputes. They are turning to alternative dispute resolution (ADR) methods, ranging from in-house peer-review boards to outside arbitrators who impose an objective third-party decision. All types of employee claims—including termination, discrimination, promotion or demotion, and union grievances—have been resolved with these alternative methods.

It's easy to see why. Employees have become increasingly litigious in the past decade, and they take little risk in pursuing the many avenues of legal action available to them through state and federal equal-rights agencies and courts of law. But even one such lawsuit could put a small company out of business. An employee grievance that gets entangled in the legal system—such as an age-discrimination case—can take four years to go to trial and cost tens of thousands of dollars in legal fees. The same case heard by arbitrators might be decided in 90 days at a fraction of the cost, perhaps less than 10 percent of a regular trial.

To use ADR methods, however, employers need to overcome some obstacles. Most important, they must promote the use of procedures that may very well undercut their management authority. However, by willingly subjecting its decisions to the review of third parties, an employer can resolve disputes confidentially, head off legal costs, and preserve employee relationships.

Informal Routes

If you decide to pursue ADR methods, you'll find that they vary significantly in their formality, cost, and ability to deliver a binding decision. The most informal and least binding procedures are those conducted in-house to resolve legitimate employee complaints before they escalate to legal action. Some companies, for example, require employees to submit disputes to *peer review boards*, generally composed of employee and management representatives, before pursuing any legal course. Even a company with only 10 employees could have a three-person board that hears both sides of a case and votes on a resolution, much like a jury.

Employees are more likely to perceive this process as fair, and companies using peer review boards report that coworkers often are much harder on the employee than a manager would have been. It's best to keep attorneys and union agents out of the process, however. When they get involved, positions may harden and lead to expensive legal action.

Another level of objectivity can be achieved by hiring an independent ombudsman to serve as a mediator between an employee and manager. With this process, an ombudsman who is trained in counseling and industrial law will hear both sides of a dispute and attempt to help the parties reach a resolution. While this process is not binding, people are less likely to pursue complaints when they believe an objective third party has heard them out. To locate an ombudsman or mediator, try the Yellow Pages and local and state bar associations. In recent years, some attorneys have even given up their law practices to set up businesses to mediate disputes rather than litigate them.

However, remember that these methods generally do not prevent employees from taking a matter to court or a state or federal agency. But, in one case, a Michigan court did stop an employee from pursuing a wrongful discharge action after an employee grievance council upheld a manager's decision to discharge the worker.

The Arbitration Option

The most common ADR method used today is arbitration. Here, a neutral third party (often a retired judge, practicing attorney, or labor relations specialist) hears both sides of a case and imposes a decision.

Some companies are so determined to stay out of court that they add language to their employment applications or draw up separate pre-employment contracts stipulating that all disputes are subject to arbitration (including those that otherwise would be heard under state and federal Equal Employment Opportunity law, such as discrimination claims). Some employers also believe a pre-employment arbitration agreement prevents employees from unionizing because it gives them the benefit of a formal grievance channel, which is usually provided for in union contracts.

Again, there's no guarantee that mandating the use of arbitration will prevent an employee from pursuing the case in court or through state and federal agencies anyway. And it is still unclear how much influence arbitrators' decisions carry in the formal legal system when such claims go to trial.

Two arbitration cases that went to the U.S. Supreme Court had different results. In *Alexander vs. Gardener-Denver Co.*,[3] the court held that an employee who had submitted a discrimination charge to arbitration in a union setting could later file a lawsuit in federal court. The court said that the arbitration clause in the union contract did not include rulings related to the workers' independent statutory rights, including discrimination charges.

The opposite was true in *Gilmer vs. Interstate/Johnson Lane Corp.*[4] In this case, a securities representative agreed, during the registration process, to arbitrate any employment dispute with the New York Stock Exchange. When he later filed a discrimination lawsuit, the court found the contract to be valid and enforceable because it clearly specified that all employment-related claims were subject to arbitration.

The facts of the *Gilmer* case are unusual. The agreement to arbitrate was an integral part of the registration process, as opposed to a separate contract. However, the mere existence of an arbitration clause in an employment agreement may take the steam out of some disputes. Many disgruntled employees simply want to have their argument heard by a neutral third party. So even if the decision goes against them, an impartial process may be enough.

Indeed, the point of ADR is to give employees and managers a way to resolve their differences before positions harden and legal costs start to escalate. That's what usually happens when cases go to trial or become ensnared in government agencies. Employees may be less than perfect at times, but managers don't always measure up 100 percent either. ADR methods prevent hard feelings with employees in a relatively quick and inexpensive way.

Being a supervisor is said to be the most difficult job, and the most important for a company to fill with the right person. There is no blueprint or any one style of managing that is a surefire path to success.

However, the task of managing other people to do the work of the unit can be very rewarding. Employees depend upon the supervisor for leadership, direction, work orders, equipment, and judgment. The supervisor is their link to allied supervisors, human resources, sales, and upper management. This position puts the supervisor at the heartbeat of every successful enterprise. For those willing to accept the challenge and responsibility, what better position of importance could one want?

Endnotes

[1]   17 Cal 4th 93, 69 Cal. Rptr. 2d 900 (1998).

[2]   *Id.* at 909.

[3]   415 U.S. 36 (1974).

[4]   500 U.S. 20 (1991).

Answers to Chapter Five Test Your Knowledge

1. It helps form a good first impression. It introduces a new employee to the company culture. It informs the employee of company expectations and benefits by a review of the employee handbook. The employee's signature can be obtained easily as evidence of receipt of the employee handbook. The employee can be informed as to how his or her job fits in with product or service

offered to the company. It can help form employee loyalty to the company at a time when the employee is most attentive to company leadership.

2. True.

3. The highest level of authority is to decide what to do and then do it without reporting to anyone. The next highest level is to act, but report what you did and why to higher management. The lowest level is to recommend action, and wait for approval before acting on the decision.

4. a and b, 5. g, 6. True, 7. e, 8. e, 9. False, 10. a and b.

CHAPTER SIX

Keeping Union-Free Status

Test Your Knowledge

of Union Issues

1. True or False? Unions can become certified as the exclusive representative of an appropriate bargaining unit of employees either by voluntary recognition on behalf of the employer or through winning a majority of the unit employees who vote in an NLRB-supervised secret-ballot election.

2. True or False? Threats, promises, secret spying of union activities and of union meetings, interrogating of employees to gauge union sympathies, and the solicitation of grievances or problems from employees are examples of improper conduct by a supervisor during a union recognition campaign.

3. True or False? To petition the NLRB to hold a recognition election, a labor organization must establish that there is a significant showing of interest among the employees of as little as 30 percent of the bargaining unit defined as appropriate by the union.

4. True or False? An employer can communicate directly to employees its opinion that it would rather remain union-free without interfering with an employee's free choice to band together for each other's mutual aid and protection in a union.

5. True or False? The decertification of a certified union is almost the mirror image of the certification process in that it takes a similar showing of interest of 30 percent of the employees in a bargaining unit to ask the NLRB to hold an election. However, unlike a representation election in a previously non-union situation, such a petition can only be filed during a time limit of 90 to 60 days prior to the end of a contract term or when there is no contract in effect.

6. True or False? It is illegal for a union to "target" an employer by sending its own paid agents to apply for work and work at the targeted employer to obtain access to other employees in order to solicit signed union authorization cards.

7. True or False? It is illegal for an employer to hire and send into its own workforce employer-paid agents who while performing regular work assist in obtaining signatures of employees in an existing bargaining unit to a petition to the NLRB to decertify the union.

8. True or False? When a union exists at a company being acquired, if the new company owner retains a minimum of over 50 percent of employees from the former workforce in the new workforce, it becomes a successor to the duty of bargaining with the union that had formerly represented the employees with the prior ownership.

9. True or False? In an acquisition situation, during the time of the negotiation of a new contract there is technically no contract in effect covering the employees of the new company if the new owner makes it perfectly clear it is not adopting the former union contract.

10. True or False? Supervisors are a part of management, and therefore whatever a supervisor says or does is binding on the company as if it were said or done by the company owner.

The answers to these questions are at the end of this chapter.

Understanding the National Labor Relations Board

Since the passage of the National Labor Relations Act of 1935 (NLRA or "the Act"), which regulates labor relations and collective bargaining in this country, the National Labor Relations Board (NLRB) has administered the Act through its evolution, as amended in 1947, in 1959, and in 1974.

To give employer representatives an orientation to the "Labor Board," I found interesting the *Wall Street Journal* "Work Week" report of September 23, 1997, which quoted a survey by the Labor Policy Association, a large-employer group, that "fully 71% of 142 companies named the National Labor Relations Board the 'most aggressively anti-employer' federal agency . . . ." My personal experience is that while the NLRB and its regional offices are tremendously professional in carrying out its mission in the workplace, it is the most politically sensitive of all the governmental regulatory agency institutions. The thrust of its rulings may vary dependent upon the general orientation of the individual Board members, and the general counsel which prosecutes the labor cases before it. Accordingly, NLRB case law, even long-held precedents, may be reversed from time to time. One recent example of this is the NLRB ruling in June 2000 reversing the concept that even in a nonunion situation, an employee has a right under the Act to have a representative present, if requested, during an investigative interview.[1] This right formally only existed for an employee in a union environment.[2] While this decision is being appealed by the employer to the Federal Circuit Court of Appeal, and it may ultimately be affirmed or reversed by the U.S. Supreme Court, it is indicative of the nature of this area of law.

Therefore, it is important to understand the agency and the law within which the pitched battles of labor and management are played out on a day-to-day basis.

Purpose of the NLRA

According to the statutory language of the NLRA itself, it is in the national interest of the United States to maintain full production in its economy. The Act declares that industrial strife among employees, employers, and labor organizations interferes with full production and is contrary to our national interest. The policy of the United States is that labor disputes can be lessened if the parties involved recognize the legitimate rights of each other in their relationship. Accordingly, to legally establish these rights, Congress enacted the NLRA to define and protect the rights of employees and employers, to encourage collective bargaining, and to eliminate certain practices on the part of labor and management that are harmful to the general welfare.

The Act essentially guarantees the right of employees to organize and to bargain collectively with their employers through representatives of their own choosing, or to refrain from all such activity. It limits activities of employers and unions so that employees may exercise their statutory rights. The Act also seeks to serve the public interest by reducing interruptions in interstate commerce caused by industrial strife.

In administering the Act, the NLRB has two primary functions:

1. To determine and implement, through secret-ballot elections, the free, democratic choice by employees as to whether they wish to be represented by a union, and if so, which one; and

2. To prevent and remedy unlawful acts, called unfair labor practices (by either employers or unions).

The NLRB does not act on its own motion in either function. It processes only those charges of unfair labor practices and petitions for employee elections that may be filed with it at any of its offices around the country.

Representation Cases

A labor organization or an individual seeking representation rights for employees may petition the NLRB for a secret-ballot election. The petitioner must show that at least 30 percent of the workers involved have indicated their support for such representation by signed authorization cards, petitions, or other means.

An employer may withdraw recognition of a union or ask for a representation election if it presents evidence that a labor organization has made a claim to represent its employees or establishes by objective considerations that the union has abandoned the employees. Furthermore, 30 percent of the workers involved in any collective bargaining unit may also call for a secret-ballot election to determine whether they wish to continue to be represented by a labor organization. This is called a *decertification petition*.

If the NLRB finds that a question concerning representation exists in a unit of employees appropriate for collective bargaining, it can conduct a free-choice secret election. It certifies or decertifies the bargaining representative, depending upon the tally of the ballots cast. If a majority of the voters select the collective bargaining representative, the NLRB certifies the union as the exclusive representative of the workers in the unit at the subject employer. If the employees reject representation (50 percent or more of the workers vote against a union), then the NLRB certifies the election results.

Only one valid representation election, whether for certification of a union, rejection of a union, or decertification of a union in existence, may be held in an appropriate employee unit within any 12-month period.

Unfair Labor Practice Cases
In basic terms, the statutory provisions of the NLRA forbid an employer or a union to interfere or discriminate against employees for exercising the rights guaranteed by the Act. Examples include the failure to bargain in good faith, unlawful union picketing, and employer domination or support of a labor organization.

Protected Concerted Activity
The rights of employees are set forth principally in Section 7 of the Act, which provides as follows:

> Sec. 7. Employees shall have the right to self organization, to form, join, or assist labor organizations, to bargain collectively through representatives of their own choosing, and to engage in other concerted activities for the purpose of collective bargaining or other mutual aid or protection, and shall also have the right to refrain from any or all of such activities except to the extent that such right may be affected by an agreement requiring membership in a labor organization as a condition of employment as authorized in Sec. 8(a)(3).

Examples of rights protected by this section are:

● Forming or attempting to form a union among the employees of a company;

● Joining a union whether the union is recognized by the employer or not;

● Assisting a union to organize the employees of an employer;

● Going out on strike to secure better working conditions; and

● Refraining from activity on behalf of a union.

This is a very complex area where case law frequently affects the rights and obligations of an employer and union. Accordingly, this subject is more complex than can be adequately covered in detail here.

Relative to the fifth item, refraining from activity on behalf of a union, it is important to note that the U.S. Supreme Court has affirmed a decision ruling that Section 7 gives workers an "unfettered right to refrain from all concerted activity." In so doing, the U.S. Supreme Court eliminated the prior union right to restrict striking members from resigning from the union and returning to their jobs. Previously, an employee was allowed to resign from the union, but was barred from returning to work in a strike situation for 30 days. Now, an employee has a right to resign without penalty from the union at any time, including just prior to a strike. A union may not legally fine any employee pursuant to internal union regulations if an employee chooses to resign from the union and cross a picket line to come to work.

How the NLRA Is Administered
The law is administered on behalf of the public interest principally by the NLRB and its General Counsel, acting through more than 45 regional and other field offices located in major cities throughout the country. The General Counsel and its staff in the regional offices investigate and prosecute unfair labor practice cases and conduct elections to determine employee representatives and to decertify the same. The five-member board decides cases involving charges of unfair labor practice and answers representation election questions that come to it from the regional offices.

For employers, one of the most important sections of the Act is Section 8(c), which states that:

> The expressing of any views, argument or opinion, or the dissemination thereof, whether in written, printed, graphic, or visual form, shall not constitute or be evidence of an unfair labor practice under any of the provisions of this Act *if such expression contains no threat of reprisal or force or promise of benefit."* [Emphasis added.]

In other words, it is not an unfair labor practice for an employer to state that, in its opinion, it would rather be non-union.

Keeping Non-union Status
The percentage of union-organized workers in the United States is at its lowest level in decades, down from almost 25 percent of the workforce to less than 12 percent. Remove public sector unions involving government employees, and the figure further drops to approximately eight percent of the private-industry workforce. This is in part because historically strong union industries are employing fewer workers and unions often find it more difficult to organize employees in the service sector, which is currently where the growth of employment seems to be. In addition, unions are being decertified and ousted from companies where they have

represented workers for years. Many believe that unions have outlived their effectiveness because of misguided or ineffective leadership and that workers are now more intelligent, self-motivated, and independent and do not need the protection of a union to hold their jobs.

While there may be many reasons why unions represent only 12 percent or less of the workforce, unions still stand for approximately 20 million employees, as well as millions of dollars in dues money and billions of dollars in pension contributions. In fact, union membership in the United States actually rose in the last reported fiscal year according to the U.S. Department of Labor's Bureau of Labor Statistics.

It may be true in part that unions once served a useful purpose that is now being made obsolete by increased statutory law, and governmental agency rulemaking in safety and health, equal employment opportunity, and even proposed uniform employment termination statutes. It may also be true in part that insightful employers realize that it is in their best interest to provide a safe working environment at competitive wage rates to employees so that the employer can attract and retain valuable workers. Despite such relative "truths," unions now have a larger target market, that is, the remaining 88 percent of the workforce, which is nonunion. They also have the capital and committed intelligent manpower to organize themselves in even greater combinations than before.

Unions Have New Target Areas
Under federal law, employees have a right to be represented by unions in the collective bargaining of wages, hours, and working conditions if they so desire. Many states also have such laws to govern the public sector or employers outside the reach of federal jurisdiction as defined in the National Labor Relations Act. Furthermore, it is still the policy of the United States government to encourage and foster unions and collective bargaining. Accordingly, in union strategies of the new era, white-collar and small and family-owned businesses have become the targets of union organizing.

Managers who have worked in a unionized environment generally need little convincing of the importance of remaining union-free. All one need consider are the effects of two or three generations of unionization in industry, often seen in heavy manufacturing, the slowest growing segment of industry.

Such unionization has often created unwieldy and expensive grievance systems that leave no one satisfied, with senseless job redundancy and severe restrictions on management rights to work rules in labor contracts, job assignment procedures, and even job rewards for good performance.

In addition, unions have meant resistance to improvements and efficiency in productivity, and, of course, the ever-present threat of work slowdowns and strikes.

However, the bottom line for management is the estimated 25 percent higher average labor cost in union shops compared to union-free shops, even where wages and fringe benefits are equal. Besides cost savings, there are many other benefits to union-free status.

Many employers value the ability to communicate directly with employees rather than through some outside third party who may often know a great deal about the business of unions, but very little about the business of an individual employer. Moreover, trust in mutual enterprise can often thrive in the union-free shop where the employee is more attentive to company leadership. This may help provide a competitive edge, which is especially important in the business world today. Many people believe that it is easier to foster team spirit, which can add to the bottom line, without the union partner. Indeed, the current emphasis in unionized industry is for more labor-management cooperation. Could unions be responding to competition, not only from foreign enterprises, but also from U.S. union-free enterprises?

Why Some Employees Are Attracted to Unions

Businesses often wonder why employees would want to be represented by a union. According to industrial relations practitioners, there are generally four reasons why a worker would want to unionize. These are:

1. Poor, unsafe, or unhealthy working conditions;

2. A perceived lack of job security;

3. Inadequate wages and benefits; and

4. A need for more control over work life.

While the first three reasons may be easily understandable, they are also readily correctable within reason. However, the fourth factor is harder to understand, harder yet to neutralize, and impossible to completely avoid. Nevertheless, it is perhaps the strongest impetus for unionization today.

It frequently comes as a surprise to managers that production jobs in a factory and other non-managerial functions, even in white-collar industries, can be among the most stressful. Indeed, the major elements of dissatisfaction among the workforce relate to job content rather than terms of employment. While workers may desire to be creative, assume responsibility, and exercise control over the job environment, often the job is performed under conditions that require work utterly lacking in mobility, interest, challenge, change, or autonomy of decision. Think of the popularity of the *Dilbert* comic strip or the film *Office Space*, for example. In light of this, it should not be difficult to understand why employees may be fascinated and perhaps even committed to unionism as a means of gaining greater control over the working environment or to satisfy their inner need for leadership and advancement.

Techniques of Union Organizers

The experienced union organizer possesses considerable knowledge about devices and techniques that have proven successful in unionizing the unorganized company. Theories of unionizing have advanced from the days of the blunt use of high promises and the castigation of the employer as a "slave driver" earning his bread from the sweat of another man's brow (to paraphrase Abraham Lincoln's comments about slavery). Although the union organizer may still rely on such slogans as job security and dignity, more subtle means are now in use.

For example, the process of collective bargaining produces labor contracts that provide stated benefits for the term of the agreements. Some employers may feel secure against possible union inroads because they have copied the wages, hours, and benefits of union contracts. In these situations, the union organizer may not sell the employees on the merits of union membership because of poor wages or conditions, but may state that without a contract, such conditions may change at the whim of the employer. The argument will be to maintain the status quo by joining the union and negotiating a contract.

This argument may be especially persuasive if during periods of economic adversity the employer has reduced wages or taken away benefits previously enjoyed, even though these benefits may have been restored at a later time. In other words, the union organizer is selling unionism as insurance. Moreover, the union organizer will often state that, without professional bargaining, the employer may do anything it wants. With a union, however, the organizer can say that workers will have input into their own wages, hours, and working conditions, as guaranteed by the National Labor Relations Act. This can be very persuasive to employees already disenchanted with company management.

Other cases where unions have sold their functions as a guarantor of benefits and conditions are:

● where layoffs and recalls have been done out of line of seniority;

- where employees have been dismissed without explanation;

- where significant increases in employee contributions for group insurance were necessary;

- where jobs have been combined so that employees have been responsible for more duties, while being paid at the same rate; and

- where work has been subcontracted to other firms with consequent layoffs.

Legally, under the rules of the NLRB, it takes only 30 percent of the employees in an appropriate bargaining unit to petition the Board for the holding of an election. If the NLRB is satisfied that the union authorization card signatures are current and genuine and there is a sufficient showing of interest (30 percent), it may direct a representation election to be held. At such an election, if a majority of the voting employees vote yes to union representation, the company will be obligated to bargain with that union over workers' wages, hours, and working conditions.

While the union needs a majority of the workers who vote in order to be certified as the collective bargaining representative, one can see that it may not take much for a union to establish a drive. In an interview, the former National Organizing Director for the Teamsters Union, Vicki Sapporta, stated that businesses with employees receptive to union organizing are "ripe" because of several factors. These factors include the lack of a grievance system, favoritism, denial of promotions, and an ineffective job-posting system.

Sapporta explained that a unit is ripe for organizing because most employees seek union representation not only for monetary gain, but also to gain job security and a voice in how things are done. She also stated that she believed very strongly in the use of employees during union campaigns to organize their own company.

> There's no substitute for an organizing committee of workers in the place you're trying to organize. You can't organize a place of any size without one. Workers have to commit. A place has to be organized from the inside out.

Today, many in business are still enamored with the independent or company union concept. They believe that their employees should be organized as a unit and through representation have a voice in certain matters. These people read about alleged successes by other employers with a "company union." Some employers may even feel that liberal thinking requires that they do not contest the right of their employees to join a union, so long as the union is not affiliated with large national unions such as the AFL-CIO, Teamsters, or United Auto Workers.

However, many believe that a business with a company union is an easy target for an experienced union organizer. The employer who directly or indirectly has aided or counseled an independent or company union may have provided the impetus for big union organization. The employer has shown the employees that there are certain benefits to organization; the employer has brought all of the employees together in meetings that it does not attend; the employees have discussed their problems among themselves; the employees have become accustomed to acting through a committee instead of dealing directly with their supervisor; and they probably have become aware, to some degree, of the strength of unified action.

The only thing missing from the company union situation is a bona fide union label, and the experienced organizer will know exactly how to put that label on the independent union. The organizer will learn the identity of the president and the names of the executive committee of the independent union, and will then invite these people to a special meeting of the union members of another company. This meeting will go smoothly and will sell the benefits of the organization and union representation without company interference or domination. The union agent may even go so far as to indicate that it is an unfair labor practice for an employer to dominate or interfere with the formation or administration of any labor organization or to provide financial support for it. In short order, the virtuous company union will be transformed from a passive independent to a vocal affiliate of the AFL-CIO, Teamsters, or one of the other independent international unions.

Some companies with unions also feel that they would rather have an existing weak union than to be union-free, because such unions are certified as the exclusive representative of the employees and ideally will keep a stronger, tougher union out. However, a weak union can elect to merge or affiliate with another union without company input, because the NLRB can consider such a move as strictly an internal union matter. Suddenly, the weak union is now a *local* of a tough, experienced international bent on solidifying its hold on its new dues-paying members. It may also begin organizing the employees of other company units.

Staying Union-Free Through an "Alter Ego" or "Double Breasted" Operation

It may be tempting for management to work a strategy of setting up another corporation to do the same kind of business, but in a non-union environment. Typically, this is not uncommon in the construction field, especially to take advantage of non-union markets that might be unavailable to the unionized firm. While such maneuvering is legal and possible, it is important to understand that the risk associated with such a move may be considerable if challenged by a union.

Typically, a union challenges such an arrangement when learning of it. The heart of the challenge is that a second company should be bound by the union contract in place with the first company. This is because the two companies are so similar that one is really the "alter-ego" for the other for legal purposes. Typically, this challenge will come in the form of a request for information from the union to the unionized company pursuant to the collective bargaining agreement.

In prosecuting these situations, the union will generally send a demand letter asking for information to establish whether or not what the union suspects is true. Failure to answer completely may result in a union charge to the NLRB for "Refusal to Bargain." Of course, in contemplating answering a union questionnaire, many employers feel that because the second corporation may be independent and outside the scope of normal business, they cannot be obligated to know and respond to questions relating to the operations of a separate corporate entity structure.

What kind of information does a union normally try to solicit in this kind of situation? The determination that a corporate entity is an alter ego of another is conditioned upon whether two or more employers share matters governing the essential terms of employment of their respective employees (Capitol EMI Music, 311 NLRB 997 (1993)). Where the union can establish that there is such sharing, then the second corporation is bound to honor the terms and conditions of the contract the union has with the first corporate entity. This includes contributions that should have been made during the life of the contract to the health and welfare funds of the union and back pay if there is any differential in wages between the non-union and union wage scales. This, of course, may amount to a large amount of money, plus interest, where an alter-ego relationship is found.

The chief criteria is the extent of common ownership; the degree of separateness of the labor relations functions; the commonality present or absent relative to employees, supervision, and management; and the extent to which there is an interrelationship of the operations of the two entities.

The kind of information typically requested by a union provides a good measuring stick for evaluating these situations. Here is one example:

Dear Employer,

Please consider this letter a formal grievance pursuant to our Labor Agreement. It has come to our attention that your company may be evading or be in violation of its Labor Agreement with this Union by reason of the operation by your company or its principals of a substandard company called _____, or by the performance of work by _____ which would otherwise be performed by your company.

So that we may properly determine whether you are in violation of your Labor Agreement with the Union, we have attached a questionnaire requesting certain information with regard to your company and _____. We would request you provide us with the information requested in the attached questionnaire within ten days of the date of this letter so that we may meet to attempt to resolve this matter.

Questionnaire

1. Define the geographic area in which your company does business.

    a. Define the geographic area in which _____ does business.

2. State the business address and identify all locations of your company.

    a. State the business addresses and identify all locations of _____.

3. Identify your company's business telephone number and directory listing.

    a. Identify the business telephone number and directory listing of _____.

4. Identify the banking institution, branch location, and the number of your company's payroll accounts.

    a. Identify the banking institution, branch location, and account number of the payroll accounts of _____.

5. Identify where and by whom your company's accounting records, corporate records, and other business records are kept.

    a. Identify where and by whom _____ accounting records, corporate records, and other business records are kept.

6. Identify your company's principal accountant, principal bookkeeper, and principal payroll preparer.

    a. Identify the principal accountant, principal bookkeeper, and principal payroll preparer for _____.

7. Identify your company's license numbers to perform construction work.

    a. Identify the license number of _____ to perform construction work.

8. Identify the carrier and policy numbers for your company's workers' compensation insurance and other health insurance.

    a. Identify the carrier and policy numbers for _____workers' compensation insurance and other health insurance.

9. Identify your company's federal and state taxpayer identification numbers.

    a. Identify the federal and state taxpayer identification numbers for _____.

10. Identify times and amounts of money transferred from your company to _____.

11. Provide the sources and amounts of your company's line of credit.

    a. Provide the sources and amounts of the line of credit for _____.

12. List the occasions when your company has provided _____ with a performance bond in the past for any of its work.

13. Identify the calendar period during which your company provides office space to _____ or when _____ provides office space to your company.

14. Identify from whom your company purchases its office supplies.

    a. From whom does _____ purchase its office supplies?

15. Identify any items purchased by your company for _____.

16. Identify all businesses that use your company's tools or equipment.

    a. Identify any equipment or tools that your company uses which are owned by _____.

17. Identify businesses to which your company sells, rents, or leases operating equipment, office equipment, construction equipment, or tools.

    a. Identify businesses to whom _____ rents or leases operating equipment, office equipment, construction equipment, or tools.

18. Identify any transfers of equipment between your company and _____.

19. Identify the following services that are provided to _____ by or at your company and vice versa:

    a. administrative, bookkeeping, clerical, detailing, drafting, estimating, managerial, pattern making, sketching, or other.

20. Identify your company's customers during the last two years.

21. Identify the customers of _____ during the last two years.

22. Identify customers your company has referred to _____.

23. Identify customers _____ has referred to your company.

24. What customers of _____ are now or were formerly customers of your company?

25. Identify those persons who bid and/or negotiate your company's work.

26. Identify those persons who bid or negotiate for _____.

27. Identify work your company performs or has performed on _____ jobs.

28. Identify work _____ performs or has performed on your company's jobs.

29. Identify by job title or craft position the number of employees employed by your company for the past year, per pay period.

30. Identify by job title or craft position the number of employees employed by _____ per pay period for the last year.

31. Identify by job title or craft position employment date and names of those employees of your company who are or have been employed at _____.

32. Identify by job title or craft position employment dates and names of those employees of ____ who are or have been employed at your company.

33. Identify your company's supervisors, job superintendents, and foreman.

34. Identify the supervisors, job superintendents, and foreman of _____.

35. Identify by project, personnel involved, and the date when your company's personnel performed a supervisory function for _____.

36. Identify by project, personnel involved, and date when _____ personnel performed supervisory functions for your company.

37. Identify the management personnel of your company.

38. Identify the management personnel of _____.

39. Identify any managerial personnel of _____ who have been employed in any capacity by your company.

40. Describe the compensation programs, including wages and fringe benefits, of _____ for persons holding positions such as have been in the collective bargaining unit of your company historically represented by this union.

41. Identify your company's representatives who are involved in labor relations policies.

42. Identify all persons involved in labor relations policies for _____.

43. Identify your company's owners, officers, directors, and shareholders, and the percentage of ownership interest of each.

44. Identify the owners, officers, directors, and shareholders, and the percentage of ownership interest of _____.

The law requires the employer party to a union contract to furnish the union with all information on this questionnaire. A failure to furnish that information is a violation of the National Labor Relations Act and it is remedied through a charge filed with the Board. It is our duty as fair representation to our members that we request this information.

An employer receiving such a questionnaire may at first postpone its answer, or declare it has no duty to reply due to lack of corporate privity. Such was the response of the Walt Disney Company when asked by its union about its relationship with an otherwise independent, yet wholly owned, corporate subsidiary in the October 1999 decision of Walt Disney World Co. and Actors' Equity Association. (329 NLRB No. 77.) However, ultimately the NLRB's order forcing the company to comply with producing the information requested was affirmed despite the distance in the relationship between the two entities.

The point of this is to be sure to keep separate any spin-off company started by identical ownership doing the same kind of work as the "mother" company in the same territory to get away from its contractual obligations. Consider how a company would be responding if it ever received such questionnaire. Would the operations stand up as separate and distinct or as the alter ego of the other company? If the operations are too interrelated, then it is likely not to be an effective way of keeping union-free, if that is part of the strategy of the new business entity.

Typically, even if the new entity may have some common ownership with the already unionized company, where established relations between the companies are done at arm's length, fair market value transactions, backed by invoices and actual payments memorializing them are not fatal to the separate natures of each enterprise. There is nothing improper for an estimator, for example, of the unionized company doing estimating for the other entity as long as he or she accounts and bills for the time and work-product the same as if it for anyone else on the open market.

Likewise, if possible, set up the new entity at a second physical location rather than in an empty office at no rent in the existing enterprise's operational facility. In addition, hire an independent manager to operate the new business. Sometimes, providing incentives such as an equity interest in the new business will help to recruit such an individual to a start-up company. This person then is responsible for the formation of labor relations policy instead of an owner of the existing business doing the same job at each entity.

The idea that mere corporate separation is enough to distinguish two enterprises is false. The two entities, if to be found as not alter-ego corporations, must be consciously operated as independent and separate concerns in fact as well as "on paper."

How Unions Organize a Company

Unions have continued to refine and develop the organizing device of an in-plant committee. Often this is done with full notice to the targeted employer of the committee's activity. Unions take advantage of the best of both worlds due to the decisions of the NLRB that seemingly restrict allowable counter-organizational activities by employers. On the one hand, the union freely advertises which employees are part of the union's in-plant organizing committee. By making itself an easy target, the union invites employer retaliation, which is clearly a part of its program. On the other hand, the organizing union is delighted when it finds employers who do not follow the lure of unfair labor practices and instead do nothing. By keeping a "hands off" attitude for fear of violating the labor laws, these employers give the union free rein to do whatever it wants.

Steps in Union Organizing

Once the union, in its councils, has selected a target or once employees have come to a union for help in organizing their company, the stage is set for the union's organization drive. Generally, there are five principal steps involved.

First, a union will try to gain a foothold by requesting its members who know employees in a non-union plant to put these acquaintances in touch with an organizing agent. The agent will follow through with home interviews, correspondence, and, perhaps later, meetings with a few other interested workers. The union agent will attempt to get the names and addresses of as many employees as possible. In some instances, union organizers may actually attempt to be hired at the company being targeted or have other unemployed union activists apply for employment.

Next, notices about a general organizational meeting for all employees of the targeted plant are mailed out. If such a meeting is well attended, the organizer reviews job classifications, wage rates, and benefit levels that may be expressed in union contracts analogous to the company being organized. Generally, the approach is very soft sell. The organizer tells employees at the meeting that he is not sure what can be achieved for them, and that they must do most of the work of organizing themselves and get as many union authorization cards signed as possible. The drive to get cards signed continues right up to the time of election because, generally, people are honorable. Once someone signs a card, the odds are good that the vote in an election will be the same.

Generally, the organizing agent explains that the emphasis is on signing up employees who are not irrevocably committed to the management side. For example, while there is usually a group of employees who are predisposed to be union supporters because of a variety of reasons, there may be fractionally 25 percent of the employees who would not, for a number of reasons, sign a card for the union. This means that the largest percentage of the remaining employees is undecided. The organizing agent must then direct his campaign to this middle group.

Employee organizers are told to select a target employee, or several targeted employees, who may have a following in the plant or may be considered leaders by their coworkers. These leader employees are then persuasively invited to join, and organizers talk to them at length. These employees will be treated most royally in the union's endeavor to sign them up.

If the standard approach fails, then the *relay system* may be used. This involves a different employee going up to the marked worker every half-hour or so and dunning him to sign a card. The marked worker may sign a card just to get the other employees off his back. Once a card is signed, the organizers will noise about to employees most likely to follow. Remember, sudden interest in a union is no accident.

Once a sufficient number of employees have signed authorization cards for the union, the union may give notice to the employer that it is the employees' representative. Even though the employer may have been aware of organizational activity, the union at this point is giving official notice that it is trying to organize. Apart from the psychological effect, this is often done to arm the employee organizer with protection under the NLRA against retaliatory measures by the employer. Once an employee declares intent to support the union publicly, it is impossible for the employer to disclaim knowledge of that fact. This is a crucial item of proof in any unfair labor practice proceeding in the event the employer finds it must discipline for some reason. Some employees have been seen to set up such a situation intentionally to provoke disciplinary punishment action.

For example, in one situation, an employee of a small company surprised the company's owner when he announced to the owner in a private conversation that he intended to bring a union into the company. The employee then said he needed a raise. According to the owner, when he said that no raises would be granted until the annual review time, the employee threatened physical violence. After the employee was discharged, the employee immediately filed charges with the NLRB, claiming that his discharge was discriminatory because of his statement relative to the union, denying that the allegation of the threat of physical violence was ever made. To the NLRB investigators, it was a question of credibility. Eventually, reasoning that the question was better answered by an NLRB administrative law judge, the local regional director authorized the issuing of an official complaint against the company.

Responding to Letters of Intent

Letters of Intent are usually sent by registered mail, return receipt requested, so that there is no mistake about the employer's receiving it. An employer not knowledgeable in organizing campaigns may decide to:

1. call the union agent (usually the telephone number is clearly indicated on the letter) and invite a discussion;

2. ask the employees if they have joined a union as the letter indicates; or

3. call in the supervisors, read them the letter, and then ask them to find out whether the contents are true.

The best course of action for the employer to follow is none of the above. Under the first option, the employer runs the risk of organizing himself. He invites the union to sign him up rather than having to continue to sign up his employees. Under the law, an employer does not have to insist upon an NLRB election; any employer can voluntarily recognize the union if it so desires. The second option allows the employer more of a chance to commit an unfair labor practice and lays the groundwork for further similar charges. With the third option, the supervisors, in their zeal to reverse the trend of organizing, will probably commit unfair labor practices themselves which, because they are legally regarded as representatives of the employer, would be binding on the employer.

The best thing the employer can do at this point is to first seek experienced legal counsel because, in reality, the organizing campaign may just be starting. The employees may not be angry with the employer. Employees will generally listen to both sides, and the matter might not come to a head for several weeks, or possibly several months.

Another technique of a union organizer is to personally appear at the employer's office, stating that the union represents the employees and that he or she is willing to show proof. Again, the best course of action is to refuse to meet with the union organizer and seek counsel.

Petitioning the NLRB
In the next stage of an organizing drive, the union may petition the NLRB for an election because usually by this time at least 50 percent of the employees have signed union authorization cards. Next the NLRB will schedule a representation hearing to decide what the appropriate bargaining unit is and when and where the vote should be held.

Filing Unfair Labor Practices Charges
Some unions, if they feel they have not organized in depth sufficiently to win an election, will wait and let the employer accumulate unfair labor practices charges. Then, at the first layoff or discharge, even if it is entirely unrelated to union activity, the union will file both interference charges and charges of discriminatory layoff or discharge. The interference charges, if proved, tend to color ordinary business layoffs by making them appear to be directed against union activity. Often, the employer is faced with the choice of considerable litigation and expense or settling the matter, posting notices that he will not "interfere with, restrain, or coerce employees in their right to join the union," and probably setting a snare for its own downfall by reinstatement and back pay to former employees.

Once unfair labor practices (ULP) charges are filed against an employer, the union commonly lambastes the employer. In addition to the persuasive verbal work being done by the union in-plant committee, organizational propaganda in a brochure or letter might be sent to the employees. Even though such charges are not final by any means, the letters will give a one-sided review of the charges, holding the employer as a violator of the law. Of course, nowhere will it be mentioned that the charges are one-sided assertions that must be investigated by the NLRB and either proved or dismissed for lack of credence.

TIPS: Avoiding Unfair Labor Practices Charges
To avoid ULP charges, there are four major actions that an employer cannot take in the midst of a union organizing drive. A simple acronym—

TIPS—makes these easy to remember. The letter T stands for *threaten.* That is, management cannot threaten that benefits will be taken away if the union is allowed to come in. The letter I stands for *interrogate.* This means that employees cannot be asked directly whether they are members or advocates of the union. This has been held by the NLRB to be inherently coercive on the part of the employer. The letter P stands for *promise.* An employer cannot promise its employees that, if they do not vote for the union, benefits will accrue. In addition, in the course of a union organizing drive, generally no raises can be given unless they can be shown to have been previously scheduled. The last letter, S, stands for *surveillance.* It is an unfair labor practice to spy on union meetings.

Positive Management Reactions

It is still possible for supervisors to communicate with employees. They can tell employees that if a majority of them select the union (an outside organization), then the company will have to deal with the union for all their daily problems involving wages, hours, and other conditions of employment. Supervisors can also tell employees that the company would prefer to continue dealing directly with the employees on such matters and that the company and other members of management are always willing to discuss with the employees any subject of interest. Supervisors can remind employees about the benefits they presently enjoy, including how well their wages, benefits, and working conditions compare with other companies in the area, whether unionized or not.

During the course of the campaign, it is important that the employees have the facts upon which they can base an informed vote. These facts include some of the disadvantages of belonging to a union, such as the expense of initiation fees and monthly dues, membership rules which restrict employee freedom, and the loss of the employees' right to make their own decisions on matters involving wages, hours, and working conditions. In addition, there is always the possibility that a union will call a strike or a work stoppage, even though the employees may not want the strike and the employer is willing to bargain or has been bargaining with the union.

Furthermore, the employees can be told that in negotiating with the union, the company does not have to agree to the union's terms and certainly not to any terms that are not in the economic interest of the business. If the union's campaign propaganda to employees contains a promise of obtaining increased wages and the company believes that such wages would impair the profitable operation of the business, then that view should be made clear to employees. Lastly, it is important that employees know that the law permits the company to hire a permanent replacement for anyone who engages in an economic strike. While a company may not want to do this, it still has the right to run its business, strike or no strike. Employees should know this before they vote.

Supervisory Do's and Don'ts

Supervisors should be trained to know that they *can* do the following:

1. Supervisors can tell employees that if a majority of them select the union (an outside organization), the company will have to deal with it concerning all issues related to wages, hours, and working conditions of employment. In essence, this means that employees may have just acquired a second boss—the union steward. The union, through its officials such as the union steward, will have the power to negotiate for the employee instead of the employee negotiating on his or her own behalf with company management. Employees should be reminded that in most circumstances it is not a violation of a union's duty to represent an employee if it chooses not to process an employee's grievance against the company. Accordingly, employees better be "nice" to the union steward; if they are not, the steward can decide whether or not any grievance an employee might have should be handled by the union.

2. Supervisors can tell employees that the supervisor and other members of management are always willing to discuss with them any subject of interest to them. They do not need a union for this to take place.

3. Supervisors can and should advise employees concerning the benefits they presently enjoy. This is true as long as such statements avoid veiled promises or threats.

4. Supervisors can and should tell employees how their current wages, benefits, and working conditions compare with other companies in the area, whether unionized or not. This is true as long as such information comparing conditions is factual.

5. Supervisors can and should tell employees of some of the disadvantages of belonging to a union. In addition to the expenses mentioned above, there also are the restrictions included in union by-laws and constitutions that restrict the freedom of employees. In this regard, supervisors should not mention any reduction in employee paychecks as a consequence of unionization without specifically attributing it to the expensive union dues.

6. Supervisors can and should tell employees that there is always a possibility that whenever a union is involved, there could be a strike

CHAPTER
SIX

or work stoppage, even though employees may not want to strike and the employer may be willing to bargain or has been bargaining with the union. If possible, the most effective references are to strikes or work stoppages that the company has had at one of its plants, or in the nearby geographical area with the same union.

7. Supervisors can and should tell employees about any personal experiences they may have had with unions, especially the union seeking to represent the employees, as long as such information is factual.

8. Supervisors can and should tell employees anything they know about the union or its officers. Again, such statements should be truthful and relevant to the employees' selection or rejection of the union.

9. Supervisors can and should tell employees their own personal opinion about union policies and union leaders even though it may be uncomplimentary. Again, be careful that supervisors are factually correct in referring to such policies and leaders.

10. Supervisors can and should tell employees about untrue or misleading statements made by a union organizer, or in a handbill, or through any other medium of union propaganda. Supervisors may always give the employees the correct facts.

11. Supervisors can and should let employees know that in their own opinion, often international unions try to dominate local unions, or at least try to influence local members.

12. Supervisors can and should tell employees about known racketeering, Communist participation, or other undesirable activities in the union. Again, only established facts should be told.

13. Supervisors can and should distribute reprints of articles containing information about unions or facts revealed through congressional hearings. Such information should refer only to the union seeking to represent the employees and should identify the date and the source of such information or fact.

14. Supervisors can and should tell employees that they are free to join or *not join* any organization, and that doing so will not prejudice their status with the company.

15. Supervisors can and should tell employees that merely signing a union authorization card or application for membership does not mean that they must vote for the union in a secret-ballot election.

16. Supervisors can and should tell employees about NLRB election procedures, the importance of voting, and the secrecy of the ballot. Employees should know that the election will be decided only by those who actually vote in it.

17. Supervisors can and should tell employees that the company favors the principle that union membership should be voluntary and not compulsory. They can inform employees that often a union's first goal in collective bargaining negotiations is to have the company agree that anyone who works for the company must be a member of the union after a certain number of days. Supervisors can and should actually "campaign" against a union seeking representation of the employees. Supervisors can insist that any oral solicitation of membership or discussion of union affairs be conducted outside of working time. (Remember, however, an employee can solicit and discuss unionism on his own time, even on company premises, when it does not interrupt work, such as on break time in the company lunchroom.)

18. Supervisors should know that layoffs, discipline, and discharge for cause are allowed as long as such action follows customary practice and is done without regard to union membership or non-union membership. Assignments of preferred work, overtime, shift preference, and other matters must still be made as long as such are done without reference to any employees' participation or non-participation in union activities.

19. Supervisors can and should enforce plant rules impartially and in accordance with customary action, irrespective of the employee's membership or activity on behalf of a union.

Supervisors *cannot* do the following:

1. Supervisors cannot promise employees a pay increase, promotion, betterment, benefit, or any special favor if they stay out of the union or vote against the union.

2. Supervisors cannot threaten loss of jobs, reduction of income, or discontinuance of privileges or benefits presently enjoyed, or use intimidating language that may be designed to influence an employee in the exercise of his right to belong, or refrain from belonging, to a union.

3. Supervisors cannot threaten or actually discharge, discipline, or lay off an employee because of his or her activities on behalf of the

union.

4. Supervisors cannot threaten, even through a third party, any act of interference with the employee's right to engage in activities or not to engage in activities on behalf of the union.

5. Supervisors cannot threaten to close or move a plant, or to drastically reduce operations if a union is selected as the representative of employees.

6. Supervisors cannot spy on union meetings, such as by parking across the street from the union hall to see which employees are entering the hall or recording license plate numbers of cars parked in front of the hall.

7. Supervisors cannot conduct themselves in a way that indicates to employees that they are watching them to determine whether or not they are participating in union activities.

8. Supervisors cannot discriminate against employees actively supporting the union by intentionally assigning undesirable work to the union employee.

9. Supervisors cannot transfer employees prejudicially because of union affiliation.

10. Supervisors cannot engage in any partiality favoring non-union employees over employees active in behalf of the union.

11. Supervisors cannot discipline or penalize employees actively supporting a union for an infraction that non-union employees are permitted to commit without likewise being disciplined.

12. Supervisors cannot make any work assignment for the purpose of causing an employee who has been active on behalf of the union to quit his or her job.

13. Supervisors cannot take any action intended to impair the status of or adversely affect any employee's job or pay because of his or her activity on behalf of the union.

14. Supervisors cannot intentionally assign work or transfer employees so that those active on behalf of the union are separated from those a supervisor believes are not interested in supporting a union.

15. Supervisors cannot select employees to be laid off with the intention of curbing the union's strength, or to discourage affiliation with it.

16. Supervisors cannot ask employees for an expression of their thoughts about a union or its officers.

17. Supervisors cannot ask employees how they intend to vote. (Supervisors, however, can listen if employees want to tell them.)

18. Supervisors may not ask at the time of hiring whether or not an employee would belong to a union or has signed a union authorization card.

19. Supervisors cannot ask employees about the internal affairs of unions such as what happened at meetings, etc. (However, some employees may, of their own accord, tell of such matters, and it is not an unfair labor practice to listen to what the employee has to say. However, supervisors must be careful not to ask questions to obtain additional information.)

20. Supervisors cannot make a statement that the company will not "deal" with the union.

21. Supervisors cannot make statements to the employees to the effect that they will be discharged or disciplined if they are active on behalf of the union. Supervisors cannot urge employees to persuade others to oppose the union or to stay out of it.

22. Supervisors cannot prevent employees from soliciting union memberships during their free time on company premises so long as it does not interfere with work being performed by others.

23. Supervisors cannot give financial support or assistance to a union, its representatives, or employees.

24. Supervisors cannot visit the homes of employees for the purpose of urging them to reject the union.

25. Supervisors cannot make speeches to massed assemblies of employees on company time within the 24-hour period before the opening of the polls for a representation election vote.

26. Supervisors cannot speak to an employee in their office or the office of some other management official about the union campaign and urge the employee to vote against the union. (The best place to talk to employees about such matters is at their workstations or in work areas or in public areas where other employees are present.)

27. Supervisors cannot help employees withdraw union memberships, although supervisors can give information as to how this is done if asked.

28. Supervisors cannot ask employees about the identity of the instigator or leader of employees favoring the union.

Labor Relations Checklist
Some employers find it helpful to do an audit of their labor relations climate to determine vulnerability to a union organizing drive. Employers can measure their own labor relations climate using the checklist below, which can help to determine compliance with sound employment practice rules. All of the questions should be answered "yes."

A. Employee Job Security
    Is there a complaint or grievance procedure?
        Yes ____ No ____
    Does management listen to gripes?
        Yes ____ No ____
    Does management follow up and investigate gripes?
        Yes ____ No ____
    Are seniority principles generally observed where applicants for promotion are substantially equal in skill and ability?
        Yes ____No ____
    Are warnings given before disciplinary action or discharge?
        Yes ____ No ____
    Do you promote from within where appropriate?
        Yes ____ No ____

B. Employee Expectations
    Are periodic appraisals of performance made by supervisors?
        Yes ____ No ____
    Are the rules and regulations known and communicated in an employee handbook?
        Yes ____ No____
    Do the rules and regulations impose fair standards?
        Yes ____ No____
    Is adequate training given for each job?

Yes _____ No _____

C. Employee Participation
    Are employees' suggestions given consideration?
        Yes _____ No _____
    Are employees given recognition for suggestions that are implemented?
        Yes _____ No _____
    Are job changes made with the employee being informed?
        Yes _____ No _____
    Are job changes made in consultation with the employee?
        Yes _____ No _____
    Are there channels of communication between employees and management?
        Yes _____ No _____
    Are periodic small group meetings held with employees where top management is present?
        Yes _____ No _____
    Are questions answered promptly?
        Yes _____ No _____
    Are promises followed up with action?
        Yes _____ No _____

D. Working Conditions
    Is there proper ventilation?
        Yes _____ No _____
    Are there good rest areas and lunch areas?
        Yes _____ No _____
    Is there adequate parking?
        Yes _____ No _____
    Are the rest rooms clean?
        Yes _____ No _____
    Are there proper lighting, clean work areas, and an absence of safety hazards?
        Yes _____ No _____
    Is proper training given to employees, especially for production safety?
        Yes _____ No _____

E. Employee Information
    Are employees informed about wage scales?
        Yes _____ No _____
    Are employees informed about company benefits and what they mean?
        Yes _____ No _____
    Are employees informed about expansion, new management, new supervisors, and promotions?
        Yes _____ No _____

Are employees informed about new methods and equipment?
Yes ____ No ____
Are employees informed about company plans, profits, sales, etc.?
Yes ____ No ____

F. Advancement
Are promotions made from within where appropriate?
Yes ____ No ____
Are employees informed of advancement opportunities?
Yes ____ No ____
Do employees know how to work for promotion?
Yes ____ No ____
Do employees know why promotions have not been made?
Yes ____ No ____
Are employees informed of promotions made from within?
Yes ____ No ____
Do you have an advancement policy?
Yes ____ No ____

G. Wages
Are wages competitive with like jobs in other companies in the same industry and the same operating area?
Yes ____ No ____
Are employees informed about wage scales and how to make increases?
Yes ____ No ____
Is favoritism nonexistent, i.e., different employees receiving different rates for the same job?
Yes ____ No ____

H. Benefits
Are benefits competitive with other companies in the same industry and the same operating area?
Yes ____ No ____
Do the benefits meet the basic needs of the employees?
Yes ____ No

I. Personnel Policies
Are personnel policies written?
Yes ____ No ____
Are personnel policies published and communicated?
Yes ____ No ____
Are personnel policies understood?
Yes ____ No ____

Do personnel policies meet the needs of both management and employees?
Yes ____ No ____
Are policies explained to new employees during new employee orientation?
Yes ____ No ____

J. Consistent and Fair Administration of Policies, Rules, and Regulations
Are like cases treated alike?
Yes ____ No ____
Are promises kept?
Yes ____ No ____
Is favoritism for reasons unrelated to work nonexistent?
Yes ____ No ____

K. Identification with Company and Management
Do employees have a sense of belonging?
Yes ____ No ____
Are employees treated as individuals?
Yes ____ No ____
Do employees participate in change?
Yes ____ No ____

L. Supervision
Are supervisors concerned about employees, their problems, roles, and advancement?
Yes ____ No ____
Do first-line supervisors appear frequently in the working areas?
Yes ____ No ____
Are supervisors trained in the procedures necessary to maintain good employee relations?
Yes ____ No ____
Are supervisors trained in what to say if they are asked about their opinions of unions?
Yes ____ No ____
Are supervisors in communication with upper management relative to company policy?
Yes ____ No ____
Do supervisors know that what they say to an employee can be legally binding upon the company?
Yes ____ No ____

While there are never any guarantees, following the above guidelines as much as possible will make exceptions a mere aberration and not grounds for distrusting management. As many may recognize, where there is basic human trust between employees and management, unions are unnecessary.

Developing a Legal Employee Involvement Committee

Small group meetings with employees are the great preventative in labor relations for a non-union employer. It is a good practice to meet with employees in small groups from time to time. In almost every union organizing defense campaign, meeting with employees in small groups is an indispensable part of management communication.

These meetings provide the format for a manager or owner to address his or her "jury." It will be the employees who will later vote "yes" or "no" in a secret-ballot NLRB election. Moreover, when held on a regular basis, such small group meetings allow management to observe how employees feel about the workplace and their managers. The meetings are a mechanism for employees to provide real input in their wages, hours, and working conditions, even though management alone will ultimately make the decisions.

This strategy has been recognized by unions and their leadership from the beginning of their experience at organizing employees into collective bargaining units. Indeed, such small group meetings have been called the best single management strategy to help a business ensure harmonious relationships with employees and maintain union-free status.

This point is portrayed by unions and union leadership as unfair. Unions urge in their policy positions and legal arguments that management's freedom to employ two-way communication systems and problem-solving groups should be limited by governmental agency and judicial regulation. This successful union strategy is embodied in an NLRB decision in a case involving a small business in Indiana known as *Electromation*,[3] which is discussed below.

In his book, *The Future of Labor-Management Cooperative Programs* (CCH Incorporated, 1994), author John Phillips used the term *cooperative program* to describe the process for small group meetings. Quoting Susan Gardner from her law review article, "National Labor Relations Act and Worker Participation Plans: Allies or Adversaries?",[4] the term was defined broadly:

A process by which an organization attempts to unlock the creative potential of its people by involving them in decisions affecting their work lives.

John Phillips lists the following kinds of cooperative programs:

1. Self-managed work teams;

2. Employee enrichment, empowerment, or involvement programs;

3. Quality circles; and

4. Participative management or quality of work-life programs.

All of these are organizational devices to engage employees and allow for solicitation of opinions, measurement of progress, planning the future of the business, and determining how it is to be best accomplished by everyone involved. These devices encourage the sense of belonging, community of interests, and tangible cooperation for everyone in a business enterprise.

Some management-employee programs such as the company union and individual yellow dog contracts (employees promised as a condition of employment not to become a member of an independent union) were seen by the unions as devices employed by management to blunt independent union organizing efforts. These tactics were specifically made illegal by the NLRA and other labor laws passed in the mid-1930s during the Great Depression.

The company union was outlawed, and Section 8(a)(2) of the Act made it an unfair labor practice for a private sector employer to "dominate or interfere with the formation or administration of any *labor organization* or contribute financial or other support to it." [Emphasis added.] In this regard, a labor organization is broadly defined as "any organization of any kind, or agency or employee committee or plan in which employees participate and which exist for the purpose, in whole or in part, of dealing with employees concerning grievances, labor disputes, wages, rates of pay, hours of employment, or conditions of work."

The question then becomes, "How can a company have small group meetings with employees from time to time and avoid an unfair labor practice?" The basic answer is to avoid programs that call for dealing with or negotiating with employees directly about mandatory subjects of collective bargaining, such as wages, hours, and the broad category of conditions of work.

The Developing Case Law

The *Electromation*[5] case involved an employer's establishment of action committees composed of employees and management to focus on various aspects of company business and its relationship to its employees. The formation of these action committees coincided with the start of a union organizing campaign by an international union.

A complaint was filed by the Teamsters Union that these action committees were a violation of the Act's Section 8(a)(2) by being dominated by the employer in such a way as to interfere with the employee's right to bring in a union. The NLRB concluded that the committees were dealing with employees and that the employer dominated the relationship in violation of the labor laws. The employer was ordered to disband the committees and post a notice to the employees that it had violated the employees' rights. Ultimately, the Teamsters Union won bargaining rights in a secret-ballot NLRB election subsequently held at the company.

In rejecting the employer's contention that the NLRB can find unlawful domination only where the employer has actually undermined the free and independent choice of its employees, the NLRB found unlawful domination. It cited, in this instance, the findings that the employer actually participated in the internal management of the committees, actively participated in framing the purposes of the committees, and exercised control of the committees' membership, subjects and decisions which could not be fairly characterized as mere cooperation.

However, legal interpretations by courts of appeal maintain that merely because there was a finding of a violation in this case, it does not foreclose the lawful use of legitimate employee participation systems. This is especially true of those that are independent and do not function in a representational capacity, but which instead focus on increasing company productivity.

The key analysis is whether or not any committees established are dealing with an employer relative to wages, hours, and terms and conditions of employment. What will be deemed improper are the kinds of committees conceived as a response to deal with employee dissatisfaction. It is emphasized that "dealing with" includes conduct much broader than collective bargaining. The idea is that where the employer sets up committees to both solicit and resolve issues relating to matters normally includable in collective bargaining with an outside union, it is doing it in a way that interferes with the organizing process improperly.

However, the setting up of small group meetings with employees from time to time is neither illegal nor improper. Indeed, if a company has established a track record when there was no evidence of employee dissatisfaction with non-union status, or an outside union targeting a company for the purpose of organizing the employees, it is evidence of the fact that such communication methods are an ordinary and regular occurrence and not unlawful!

In many business situations, such small group meetings occur on a regular basis as normal supervisory team or departmental group meetings. In this context, the relationship between management and regular employees is clear. Clear also is the understanding that while the purpose of the meeting may be to gain feedback for management on issues related to the workplace, decision-making continues to lie in the hands of management. In other words, management is not going to use the small group meetings to exchange or prioritize potential benefits to employees related to wages, hours, and working conditions for employee commitment and agreement with company policy in other areas that also relate to wages, hours, and working conditions of employees.

How a Lawful Program Can Be Designed and Implemented

As an example, small group meetings with employees from time to time to discuss issues pertinent to the workplace take place at our law firm. Typically, being in charge, in general, of employees/management relations at the firm, it was my decision to implement a system of periodic small group meetings with the support staff. I explained to the individuals on our support team in the very first meeting that I did not believe in the blue-lightning theory of management in employee relations. That is, we would not wait to communicate matters of concern until such time that the clouds are darkening, and the lightning of a management decision is about to strike. I asked them to tell me about concerns with management policy-making that involved employee relations. I also asked them about ways work could be more efficiently coordinated.

In the first few meetings of approximately 30 minutes in length, I found the support staff to be rather unsure of what I was trying to accomplish. They seemed reluctant to tell me what was on their minds as it related to the operation of the firm, both personally and professionally. However, as time went on, the employees seemed to gain more confidence in my ability to treat their concerns confidentially. In the third such meeting, the dam seemed to break and I walked out of my small group meeting with a list of 22 items to discuss with the Board of Directors.

Many of their concerns were immediately understandable, some of the concerns were impossible to fix, and a few were both easy to fix and yet would have gone undetected by management had we not asked questions.

There is an old adage that says in labor relations matters, it is not the elephant that is charging at you that is the thing to worry about. It is the gnats. The elephant can be seen and heard a long way off in the distance and can be dodged on most occasions. The gnats are always with you.

What were the kinds of things I learned by asking the employees and listening to their responses? One legal secretary observed that when she was in the carpeted file room searching for a file that was placed high in the shelving system, she would typically have to stand on an unstable stool to reach the top levels. Would it be possible for the firm to buy a new stool that was larger and more stable? It was not difficult to authorize the expenditure to resolve this workplace safety issue that would never have occurred to me personally.

Another employee mentioned that the mat under her desk chair was worn out. The employee had been reluctant to complain, not because of fear of retribution, but because she considered it a part and parcel of her work space and something to which she just had to adjust. I discovered that the rest of the mats in the secretarial area were also deteriorating and I became a hero authorizing the purchase of higher-grade mats that matched the quality of those used by the attorneys. Was it a small thing? To me, if I were a vindictive sort of person, I might have considered it more than a minor nuisance if as a member of the support staff I got a second grade desk chair mat and was reminded of that fact every time I got in and out of my chair!

Some of the issues could not be resolved to the employees' liking. However, I had the opportunity to explain why. Sometimes understanding something makes it easier to live with if it is impossible to change.

In addition, most of the items we discussed related to how best to organize our working processes for the greatest efficiency. Levels of salary and individual disciplinary matters were not discussed. I find the small group meetings to be most effective when scheduled twice or three times per year. Also, I do not set the schedule of the meetings to be on a predictable basis.

The key is that while I solicit input, I retain the decision-making power. Indeed, employee committees can be set up legally to do the opposite. By this I mean that you can grant total decision-making power to the committee of employees itself. This too would be legal if management wanted to delegate its decision-making authority to the committee. For example, a safety committee comprised of employees and management may have the power given to it by management to resolve safety issues.

The dangerous place is the middle ground where management meets with representatives of various employee interests and then deals with this committee by negotiating with it in a give-and-take process that establishes policy relating to wages, hours, and working conditions. In my opinion, it is possible to set up committees that will do this kind of thing as well if they are set up so that the company is not dominating the process by determining who sits on the committee in a unilateral fashion, determining the committee's agenda, or providing financial support for the committee and its work. However, if the committee and its processes *are* dominated by management (which is tempting to do and difficult to avoid), then the committee that has been formed is in reality a substitute for an independent union.

For example, an owner of a small company told me his employees had a union. I asked if it was affiliated with a larger international union, and the answer was no. It was an independent union. I then asked if there was a contract with it. The answer was yes and that the contract was negotiated every three years. When I asked who negotiated on behalf of the employees with management when it came time to renew the agreement, I was informed that the company would choose three employees from the workforce and then sit down with them to explain what the company was going to do as far as wages for the next three years. Then the company would rewrite the contract unilaterally to reflect the change.

The employees involved were given the job to explain this to the rest of the workers after they signed the agreement. I asked if there had ever been an election at the company sponsored by the NLRB. The answer was no, but that the system had been in place for close to 30 years and always seemed to work out okay for everybody, so no one ever complained about it. Although a small business, the company always prospered and was always able to grant increases to the employees. I was told that from time to time there was some grumbling among some employees, but it would eventually fade away.

I regretfully had to inform the company that, in my opinion, the system they had in place for many years violated the NLRA. I suggested that the contract would never serve as a bar prohibiting a real union from asserting jurisdiction or asking for an NLRB secret-ballot election on whether or not it should be recognized as the exclusive agent for the bargaining unit. The past practice continued at the company and management never saw fit to change it. Likewise, there was never any attempt by a union to organize the employees.

In another case, a company established a grievance procedure to address employee concerns after management received a complaint that employees had nowhere to go to complain about management actions. The grievance system called for a rather typical union process in many respects. The employee was supposed to first report any complaint to his or her immediate supervisor. If the supervisor did not answer the employee's concern to his or her complete satisfaction, the employee would have the right to write a written complaint to the human resources department. The human resources department would then meet with the employee and the supervisor to try and iron things out. If this proved unsuccessful, the employee then could appeal it further to the corporate head of industrial relations. However, the corporate head of industrial relations would serve as the final arbitrator of the complaint, and his decision was final.

The employer designed and promulgated all of the forms in the process, then listed the policy in its employee handbook. The NLRB found that the system was "an unfair labor practice" because it was so dominated by the employer. It was truly not a grievance procedure but instead a simple complaint resolution system in which the employee had no real input. In this case, the system was changed when a union threatened to file a charge with the NLRB.

What kinds of programs are clearly lawful? Brainstorming is used to develop new ideas. Management may or may not adopt ideas from this process. Where there are no group proposals for management to accept or reject or modify, the employer is not dealing with the employees and the committee is not a labor organization. While it may seem little more than a suggestion box, such systems are precisely what most employers should have, and they should know that these are legal. In particular, the sharing of information is clearly a management function, and the sharing of information should be two-way. The element of *dealing with* is missing if the committee does not make proposals to the employer and the employer instead simply gathers the information and does what it wants with it. Suggestion boxes are also legal because when employees make specific proposals to management in this way, these proposals are being made individually and not as a group.

Remember that it is reported that 80 percent of Fortune 1000 firms have employee committees of some form at work—and smaller companies are increasingly adopting the same practice. The idea is to avoid committees whose membership and agenda are dominated by employers and whose agenda typically concerns matters subject to bargaining collectively if a union is on the scene. The point is to allow the committees to have independence, let them choose their representatives and issues to be covered, and make sure they are not financially dependent on the employer.

The worrisome facts of the *Electromation*[6] theories are that a law-abiding company may not know whether or not its committees violate the Act because of the complexity of the above analysis. However, the U.S. Appellate Court in affirming *Electromation* went on to stress that the decision applies only to a specific set of actions taken by a single employer. The loss of legitimate cooperative programs aimed at boosting production, efficiency, safety, and quality would hurt America's global ability to compete.

Audit Checklist: Determining Unlawful Domination According to the NLRB

In deciding a case, the Board looks at the following factors to determine unlawful domination by a company:

- Was the committee created by management?

- Is its continued existence totally dependent on management?

- Does management have ultimate decision-making power?

- Has management determined the structure and function of the committee?

- Has management decided who will serve on the committee and how they are to be selected? (Very important.)

- Has management set time limits for members' terms?

- Has management set election procedures and announced election results?

- Has management dictated meeting days and permitted special meetings only with company approval?

- Has management prepared the committee's constitution and bylaws?

- Does the employer provide space for the committee to meet?

- Is time spent attending meetings during working hours?

- Do members of management attend the meetings? Are they mere observers or facilitators, or do they control the meetings?

- Does management act on the committee's recommendations?

● Are only concerns of management addressed?

While any one of these factors does not necessarily mean that a company is unlawfully dominating the committee, a combination of the factors might do so.

For example, the NLRB has stated that the focus in the analysis would be on whether the organization allows for independent employee action and choice. If the employer does nothing more than tell employees that it wants their participation in decisions concerning working conditions and suggest that they set up a committee for such participation, the Board would find no domination provided the employees controlled the structure and function of the committee and that their participation was voluntary. However, if the employer creates an employee committee in response to a union organization campaign, the Board would draw the inference that the organization was designed to thwart employee independence and free choice.

This is illustrated by Board decisions in the following cases. In *Simmons Industries, Inc.,*[7] safety committees and total quality management committees were unlawfully dominated by the employer. However, "corrective action teams" and ad hoc employee participation corrective action groups were not. In *Webcor Packaging,*[8] a plant-wide council that dealt with management on grievances, pay and work conditions was deemed unlawful. However, in *Vons Grocery Co.,*[9] quality circles devoted to operational matters was not a labor organization in violation of labor law.

The Self-Assessment Union Vulnerability Checklist
Employers who want to remain union-free can self-assess their vulnerability to a union organizing drive by asking themselves the following ten questions.

1. If a union organizer asked an employee to sign a union authorization card, how long would it take for a supervisor to be made aware of it?

2. Would the employee know that it is management's opinion that unions are not necessary for employees to have input into their wages and working conditions? How would an employee know this? Is it communicated in the employee handbook?

3. Is a work rule prohibiting solicitation of employees during working hours and working areas published? Is it enforced for all kinds of solicitations, not just union solicitations?

4. Does management personally communicate face-to-face in small group meetings with employees from time to time to keep them up-to-date on changes in the business?

5. If layoffs or reductions in force are necessary, is there a policy in place and is this policy communicated to employees to handle such events?

6. Does the company ever admit a hiring mistake by allowing employees it would fire to resign instead and provide them with severance pay and/or outplacement services when appropriate?

7. Does the company involve its employees in safety training programs?

8. Does the company promote from within whenever possible? Do employees know what to do to apply for job openings and promotions? Do employees receive training to improve their skills and abilities?

9. Are supervisors trained in union prevention skills? Would they know what to say to an employee who asks them about unions? Would they know what *not* to say?

10. Has management thought about what it would do if it learned a union was trying to organize the company?

In the Event of a Union Campaign

Generally, the following is representative of what happens in an NLRB union election, its attendant processes, and corresponding company campaign strategy.

NLRB Procedures

When a union or group of employees petitions a regional office of the NLRB, the first function of the NLRB is to notify the parties of that fact. Next, the NLRB will seek to verify that the petitioning group actually does account for a "sufficient showing of interest" in the bargaining unit it seeks to represent. Most groups will show the NLRB, as proof of its claim, signed authorization cards or petitions signed by at least the required minimum authorization of 30 percent of the employees in the proposed unit. The employer will then be asked to give the NLRB a list of employees in order to make a finding that a sufficient showing of interest exists.

Once this is accomplished, an NLRB representative will explore the positions concerning the appropriate unit for collective bargaining and voter eligibility once a petition has been filed for an NLRB election. In the interests of economy, the Board seeks to effect an agreement between the parties concerning the details of an election. If an agreement can be reached acknowledging consent of the parties to the details as agreed upon with an NLRB representative, a "Stipulation for Certification upon Consent Election" can be signed. This type of agreement permits appeal of an NLRB regional director's ruling to the NLRB in Washington of any final determination of disputed matters following an election. Absent an agreement between the parties and the NLRB relative to these matters, the NLRB will direct a hearing and unilaterally decide these issues for the parties.

It is sometimes advisable to name all employees who will be included or excluded from the voting unit rather than simply defining the unit in general terms. Such an agreement is called a Norris-Thermador Agreement, which normally minimizes the possibility of challenged ballots and subsequent litigation. This agreement, however, must be approved by the regional director of the NLRB, but approval is usually granted expeditiously.

An important consideration in an election is choosing the optimum election date. Such a date should provide the company with as much time as is required to furnish employees with the essential facts to make an informed decision. Generally, four weeks is the minimum amount of time necessary. Remember, the union has probably been at the task of organizing for some time, and it may take additional argument and explanation of the facts to employees to reverse any union momentum. Often, defection from the union's cause may occur early once the employer takes action. However, in order to be sure of winning a vote, the employer should leave enough time so that it can make at least one presentation to the employees per week to discuss in full the topics the employees need to know. In most circumstances, the NLRB will normally allow an election in three to six weeks, bearing in mind that if the matter went to a hearing, it would be approximately that amount of time before an election could be held anyway.

Another important consideration on the date of the election is which day of the week it should be held. It is beneficial to have the vote late in the week to give the employer more time to campaign during the crucial last week. Indeed, by virtue of the NLRB rule which states that there can be no management speeches to assembled groups of employees within 24 hours of the opening of the election polls (the so-called 24-hour rule), Mondays and Tuesdays should not be considered because they do not give the company time to talk to employees on the heels of a weekend where it can be assumed that union organizers would certainly be telephoning, if not personally visiting, potential voters. The final consideration in choosing the optimum day for the election is the date most employees are likely to be present. Usually, payday is certain to bring employees into the shop. If the company has split shifts and split pay periods, it is important to take these into account. Often, it is possible to have more than one vote if there is more than one shift. It is not uncommon for the polls to be open a half hour before the end of the first shift to a half hour after the beginning of the next shift. The key is to have enough time for balloting to insure that all employees have a chance to vote while at work.

All employees who are paid on an hourly basis in the shop should be included on the list of voters. This would include lead workers in most cases, as long as they are not considered supervisors. The eligibility of individuals hired between the time an election has been agreed upon and the actual vote is determined by who is on the payroll as of the end of the most recent payroll period. If these details were directed after a hearing by the NLRB, the NLRB director's decision would be using the most recent payroll period prior to the issuance of the decision itself. Individuals who were laid off, who quit, or who were discharged before the vote, however, would not be eligible to vote unless the reason for such layoff or discharge was because of the employees' union activities as found by the NLRB. In this regard, the company would still be able to challenge such votes. Lastly, once the election is directed either through the consent agreement or the regional director's decision, no new hires are eligible to vote. If they do vote, such new hires would be subject to challenge by either party.

Relative to the question of lead workers being included in the unit, their status depends upon many factors. The NLRA itself contains the definition of supervisory status. In addition, the authority to exercise or "effectively to recommend" any of the following actions may also establish supervisory status. Inquiries should be made relative to any individuals in question as to whether or not the employee:

- assigns work;

- directs employees;

- grants time off;

- evaluates work;

- schedules work hours;

- recommends or executes discipline;

- hires and fires employees;

- receives a salary;

- receives higher pay than other employees;

- interviews job applicants;

- keeps workers' time records;

- consults with management on production problems;

- exercises independent judgment;

- selects employees for overtime;

- has authority to adjust grievances;

- participates in a profit-sharing benefit plan where other employees do not; and

- attends supervisory meetings.

If employees do the above kinds of tasks or effectively recommend such actions, they are likely to be considered supervisors and should not vote in a union election, despite their lead-worker status.

Also, in determining who should and should not be in the contemplated bargaining unit, employers need not be unnecessarily bound by the list of employees that may be turned in to the NLRB in order to determine whether a sufficient showing of interest exists. Lead workers, if they are included in the unit and the union wins the election, will be covered by the contract. On the other hand, if an employer can be reasonably assured that the votes of such lead workers would be no, or anti-union, it is wise to remember that some elections are lost by only a few votes. Sometimes, with the benefit of hindsight, the employer who has lost an election will regret the day caution influenced the exclusion of such employees from the voting unit.

It is these kinds of issues that an NLRB hearing is designed to resolve, either through agreement among the parties and the signing of a *stipulation for consent election*, or after a hearing on the issues and a decision imposed upon the parties by the NLRB regional director. Election arrangements for the location of balloting should also be agreed upon. The employee lunchroom is often used because it is in all likelihood the spot where the company will hold its employee meetings.

Within seven days after the consent agreement by the regional director, employers must file three copies of a list of the names and addresses of all employees in the bargaining unit with the regional director, pursuant to the NLRB's ruling in *Excelsior Underwear, Inc.* The regional director will then send one copy of this list to the union.

Of course, it seems unfair that the NLRB's rulings prohibit the employer from visiting the homes of employees and yet require them to provide lists that enable union representatives to make such visits. This is a circumstance that must be discussed with employees so that they understand that the company was required by the NLRB to turn over their addresses and that it did not voluntarily do so. Also, many companies advise their employees that they do not have to entertain visits from anyone in their homes unless they desire to do so. Such comments are recognized as proper by the NLRB.

Failure to provide the *Excelsior* list would be grounds for overturning a company election victory. When the list is turned over to the NLRB, employers often consider communicating the following to employees:

> Due to procedures mandated by the National Labor Relations Board, the Company was required to give to the union a list of the names and addresses of all employees eligible to vote in the upcoming secret-ballot union election. We did not want to hand over this information, which we regard as confidential, but we did so only in response to a written instruction from the NLRB. We regret this invasion of your privacy and any annoyance from the union it may cause you as a result.

Continuing along the procedural trail, about 10 days before the election, but no less than five, the regional director will mail a number of copies of a "Notice of Election" to the parties. This poster contains three sections:

1. A sample ballot;

2. A statement of employee rights and examples of improper conduct, identical with the language used in the "Notice to Employees" already posted; and

3. A summary of election rules and procedures.

The employer is required to post copies of the Notice of Election for a period of 72 hours prior to the election. The usual posting places are at the time clock and/or employee bulletin boards, or wherever employees are likely to have the opportunity to read the notices. These notices are not to be defaced in any way. Marking an X in any selection box of the posted notice is a defacement that may void the election. It is the employer's responsibility to police this and, if the need arises, replace the notice where it has been defaced.

Relative to the election campaign itself, there are several basic discussions that must be held with the employees, often best communicated in small group meetings with company management.

First, a short talk informing the employees of the details of the election should be given as soon as possible after the details of the election are confirmed. In all likelihood, this will be immediately following the hearing conference. It is important that employees get the information they need to know from the employer first. The employer wants to be known to the employees as the source of accurate information, because very often in the rhetoric and polarization that often accompany a union election drive, the factors of trust and believability are of paramount importance.

Often, if the company is using labor relations counsel, it is best to introduce such counsel to the employees personally. While such counsel may not engage directly in what is called *persuader* activities unless duly registered with the Department of Labor to do so (most attorneys are not so registered), it will give the employees a chance to meet counsel and get used to the fact that such counsel may be around occasionally to answer questions. Counsel will also want to be present because it is difficult to analyze employee reaction and, therefore, help fashion future presentations in the campaign without actually seeing and meeting the employees who eventually will be voting in the election. Sample presentations to employees are given below.

Speeches to Employees
Details of Agreed-Upon Election

It was about a month ago that we last talked to you in a group to discuss the union situation here at the company. As some of you may know, the union has been using authorization cards, as proof, to file a petition with the National Labor Relations Board to represent you in collective bargaining with the company. The reason we are meeting with you today is to let you know that this morning we have talked with the Board to discuss whether there should be an election concerning this union at the company, and if so, what the details of that election should be.

While the law provides that we could have objected to the election and had a hearing before the NLRB to decide everything, we feel that you should have an opportunity to vote by secret ballot if you want to be represented by an outside union in dealing with the company.

Therefore, we have consented to an election that will be held on Friday, October 30. The voting booth will be set up in this room. The voting will be in two shifts from 4:00 p.m. until 5:00 p.m. in the afternoon and again from 1:30 a.m. to 2:30 a.m. at night. The election will be held under the supervision of the National Labor Relations Board. We mention these details because we think it important that every one of you be here to vote on election day because all of us who work here will be affected by the outcome which is determined only by those who actually vote.

Those people who will be eligible are all regular full-time and regular part-time production, maintenance, laboratory personnel, and working foremen employed as of the current payroll period which ends on September 26.

Naturally, I am disappointed that some of you feel that you need an outsider to represent you. But, I believe, as does the rest of management, that we can better solve whatever problems we may have amongst ourselves, rather than through some outsider who knows little or nothing about our business and who may be more interested in collecting dues from your pay checks than anything else.

Now, I am not going to talk any more about the union today, but we will be meeting together occasionally like this before the election so that when you cast your vote, you will know the facts and that your vote will be based on information and not hollow promises.

It is my hope that, after these few weeks that precede the election, you will come to understand why I believe a union would not be good for either the employees or the company.

Thank you for listening; this is really all I have to say today. If any of you have any questions, I will be glad to answer them as best I can.

The next presentation to the employees generally should follow a week or so later. In structuring a campaign, many feel it is best to start on the positive side of things. Accordingly, a presentation on the good points of the company is appropriate. Sometimes such a presentation helps remind employees of what they already have without having to pay dues to a union and be represented exclusively. In addition, such a talk should include a comparison of wages and benefits of comparable companies in the company's industry as well as comparable companies in the general geographic area. Often these can be reduced to charts and used as visual aids in the presentation. After the meeting is over, the charts can be left up for employees to study. An example of one such presentation follows.

What Is Good About the Company

Welcome. We have called this meeting today to discuss some of the issues surrounding the secret-ballot election to be supervised by the National Labor Relations Board that will be held later this month. In my opinion, I do not feel that we need a union here at the company. As we have done in recent weeks and will continue to do in the coming weeks, we are meeting in order to give you the information you will need to cast your vote and to answer any questions. This is because we feel that it is important that your secret-ballot vote be based on facts and not promises or illusions. Today I would like to talk to you about what's good about the company and also give you a little background information about our history so that you will know how we got to where we are today.

This company started in 1948 as a small block building company. We had four employees, and the company was privately owned by two people. In 1949, my father assumed full ownership and changed the name to XYZ Company, Inc. From 1949, the company struggled to grow. As the economy picked up, the company added what is now called the angle and component phase in 1959. During the period from 1959 to 1970, the company had a great deal of work and averaged about 2,000 tons of fabrication per year. Employees numbered about 10 to 15 people. In 1965, we added a new line, the hollow metal and hardware division, and with it added more employees. By 1970, the company had to make changes to grow and to remain competitive. Additions were made and the original beam line was added. It was among the first in the country. Construction continued almost every year to the present. These moves have allowed us to be more competitive in our markets, and we now average 20 times the amount of fabrication done per year than we did before. Recently, the largest building project we have ever attempted has taken place. The development of equipment to enter the material handling rack market has now been completed and we are ready to claim our share of that market. To the credit of every person in this organization, we have done a lot of rebuilding and retooling in the last five years that have continued to run jobs. The cost has been great, but the price has been more than just money. It has caused constant changes that have disrupted the workplace. However, throughout these years of expansion, we have still been able to maintain and improve upon the number of employees and our share of the work in the market for what we do.

While we realize that not everything may be perfect, we want you to consider what we have already accomplished without any outsider to make this a good place to work. It has been in the past, and will continue to be in the future, our company policy to provide our employees with a total package of wages and benefits that are equal to or better than companies that can be reasonably compared with us. As a family-owned operation, we cannot and should not be compared with everyone. However, it is our feeling that there are other advantages in being the type of growing company we are. Further, we are convinced that we can better solve what problems there may be without the intervention of a union which may know little or nothing about the business from which we all earn our livelihood. Remember, the union can make promises of higher wages and changed working conditions and even say that it won't cost anyone anything (there are no initiation fees or dues until a contract is signed), but promises are only promises. Unions don't invest in processes, they don't purchase steel, they don't fabricate metal, they don't market anything to our customers, and most important of all, they don't pay wages or provide jobs at this company.

In addition to compensation, we discussed other improvements that have been accomplished here. First and foremost, we believe that we have created, through investment back into our business, some of the best working conditions in our industry. Our plants have been designed to be well lit, well ventilated, modern, and safe.

Second, we have provided steady employment and steady growth, even in times of adversity, when the market for our products was low or when machinery was down.

Third, we have tried to create a relaxed and tension-free atmosphere in which to work, unlike other assembly-line operations of our competitors. We also try to be flexible in our personnel policies, such as leaves of absence, breaks, employee assistance programs, and other items.

Other fringe benefits include vacations, night premiums, employee uniforms, and employee assistance in training programs in order to attract, train, and keep good workers such as yourselves.

Importantly, it has been our policy and will continue to be our policy to occasionally review and make improvements in our wages and benefits. This will continue, union or no union. Indeed, all of the good things we have here today we have earned without any interference or intervention from any outsider or without anyone ever having to pay dues or initiation fees, face possible fines or assessments for fear of losing wages, or be permanently replaced from their job because of being taken out on strike. However, we must emphasize that if the union is voted in, all wages and benefits, working hours, and working conditions would then become negotiable with the union. You cannot assume that you will continue to have your present benefits and only negotiate new or additional ones.

I have tried to give you an accurate rundown about what we think is good about our company. I feel that we have made a lot of progress in all of these areas as we have grown through the years, and it is our policy to continue this growth. A majority of these changes have taken place through employee meetings and employee participation, and we have done all of this without anyone ever having had to pay dues to any outsider to do so.

Accordingly, I ask you today to think about the things we already have here at the company. This is part of the reason why I ask that when you vote, you will vote no for "no union."

I will be glad to answer any questions for you.

The next discussion with the employees generally takes on a different tone. It is important that the employer inform employees of the negative aspects of unions. This discussion focuses on what can happen when unions are involved, such as strikes, fees, fines, initiation fees, etc. Avoid statements of prediction such as speech stating "what will happen," or "what is likely to happen." Instead, proclaiming what is "possible to happen" especially because it has happened elsewhere is permissible, persuasive speech. Sometimes this presentation is combined with subject matter relative to the particular union, as well as with unions in general. Any worthwhile union has probably been engaged in job actions in the immediate geographic area at some time in the recent past. Remember, this is an area that a union organizer will not willingly inform the employees about and may prove very persuasive in convincing employees to vote for "no union."

Such a talk may include references to newspaper articles. It is considered relevant to remind employees considering a "yes" vote of the downside of unions, such as corruption. Posting a persuasively credible newspaper clipping is information the people voting should know about before making their decision. For example, in the public sector, it would be important for the voters to read that in a January 21, 2000, article appearing in a major metropolitan newspaper, an internal union report described a picture of extensive corruption in the nation's largest union of governmental employees. "In all the report describes corrupt activities by 35 union officials, ranging from the $2.2 million known to have been misappropriated by a union official to the $96,000 stolen by a local union treasurer to $51,000 taken by a midlevel union official in Washington." In dry language, it describes how union officials forged checks, made unauthorized withdrawals from union accounts, siphoned union dues into their personal accounts, and used union credit cards for personal expenses. The intriguing part is that the report is a comprehensive list detailing the $4.6 million in claims that this very union made to its own insurance company, seeking reimbursement under a policy that covers fraud by union officials involving claims pending since November 1999 only! The voter in this kind of an election has a right to know this information.

For another example, the employees could be shown an article appearing the regular press detailing how the "Mob-Linked Boss of Union Fled Legal Cares with Trips to North Woods." It is legal and relevant to the election to display an article. The particular article referenced here explains how a former national union official liked to fish in the summertime and scoot around on a snowmobile in winter. "If he was a man in disgrace—forced out by corruption allegations after 25 years of leading the Hotel Employees and Restaurant Employees International Union—he didn't show it here . . . [he] was a very generous man, but it was easy to be generous with other people's money." This may be important information for the voter in a representation election to know before the vote is cast, and an employer is not prohibited by the NLRA to say it and publish it.

The employer has a duty to inform employees so that their vote in the election is an informed one. If the employer does not proclaim it, will the union advocates? Some might call providing this type of information "negative," but it is not objectionable conduct on the part of an employer to say what, in its opinion, is the downside of unions, both in general and with the particular local union trying to gain the right to represent the employees. Here is an example of what an employer might say:

What Is Bad About the Union?

During the last several weeks, through the holding of company meetings such as this one and sending you letters to summarize what we have said in the meetings, we have tried to give you as much information as possible about the vote you will be casting.

Because of the importance of this vote to all of us at the company and to our families who depend upon the company, I ask you to vote for "no union" on Wednesday. The problems we may have are problems we have together. It is clear to me, however, that the problems that have been brought up, such as lack of communication, can be solved a lot easier without some outsider who knows nothing about our business.

In my opinion, the discussion and communication we have had in the last weeks proves to me that we can solve our problems without bringing in what eventually would become union rules and union dues.

The union organizer may say he will not promise anything. Why is that? In my opinion, it is because he knows he does not have the power to carry out any promise he might make. What power does this outside union have if the company cannot or is unable to agree to any demand the union might make?

A good example is a demand for a union shop clause that would require employees to be union members and pay dues in order to hold their jobs as a condition of employment. This union has made that demand at other companies. What guarantee do you have that a union shop would never be a demand here if this union were voted in? Also in this regard, has anyone asked the union business agent if he could guarantee that there would never be a strike if the union came in? I believe also that it is important to take a look at the local bylaws and international constitution of this union that wants to represent you. Has anybody taken the time to find out about them? If you did, these are some of the things you might find:

1. All union members must abide by all of the union rules, both the local and international rules. Union members also can be fined by the union and suspended if they do not pay the fine. In addition, most union contracts require a union shop such that the employee must be a member of the union in order to remain employed. If an employee does not follow the union rules or pay the union dues, fines, and assessments that the union has the authority to assess, what effect might it have on one's job security?

2. Did you know that all dues, fines, assessments, etc., must be paid before one can resign from the union, if once a member?

3. Were you aware that the local executive board rules and decisions are final and binding with only limited possibilities for appeal accord-

ing to the union constitution and bylaws? If a decision were ever rendered against you personally, how much clout do you think you would have in changing it on an appeal?

4. Did you know that union members, according to the international constitution, may be assessed whenever the union treasury is low? What would stop the union from saying that their dues are a certain amount now and then raising them later?

5. Relative to strikes, did you know that the rejection of a company offer in collective bargaining negotiations automatically authorizes a strike, and that in some situations, strike votes are not even needed at all? Did you know that the strike benefits pay out $75.00 per week and that they do not even start until after the second week of a strike? Is this enough to offset the loss of wages that happens when we do not work because of a strike? Now, we are not saying that if the union is voted in, a strike will necessarily happen here. However, we think it is important that you know the facts of what can happen whenever a union such as this is here.

6. Relative to the local of this international union, we found it interesting that in reports filed with the Department of Labor, it shows that the local's business agents all earn $68,000 to $87,000 per year. Who do you think pays for these salaries? Do the union business agents lose their salary if the employees go out on strike?

The bylaws show some interesting things, too. Among other things, they show that the representatives of the union do not have to account to the local membership for their expenses. Representatives are provided with automobiles for their private as well as union business use. Initiation fees for membership in the union are $250. Although some unions promise to waive initiation fees for employees of companies they are trying to organize, what would happen if you dropped out, changed jobs, but then wanted to return?

Did you also know that the local union may decline to process any grievant's complaint or dispute if it, in their opinion, lacks merit?

In my opinion, it is important that you know the facts before you cast your secret-ballot vote. This is why we have these meetings. After the vote it will be too late to hold meetings and ask questions. Accordingly, if you favor no union dues, no union rules, no union promises, and no union constitution, please vote *no* for "no union" when you have the opportunity to vote.

Presentations about the union often include charts of quotes from the union constitutions to inform employees about how they might be bound to the union. Also, local bylaws of any particular union should be discussed. These are available through the Department of Labor.

The last talk is generally called the *last chance speech* and is given the day before the election, because it must conclude no later than 24 hours to the minute prior to the first opening of polls the following day (the 24-hour rule). This speech is the most important speech. It should serve as a recap of the entire campaign and also to inform the employees as to what to expect in the future, depending upon the outcome of the vote. The speech represents the last thing an employer may communicate in a mass meeting. Here is an example of one such talk.

Last Chance Speech

This is the last opportunity we will have as a group to meet together before the election tomorrow. If you have any questions left unanswered, ask them now, because after tomorrow it will be too late. To open our meeting today, I want to first ask you whether you have all had a chance to take a look at the Election Poster which we received from the National Labor Relations Board and posted on the wall here last Tuesday. If you have not taken the time to look at it, I urge you to do so before the election takes place tomorrow.

The poster itself, among other useful information for you, contains a sample ballot. As you can see, the ballot asks the question: "Do you wish to be represented for purposes of collective bargaining by the union?" and then it says "to mark an X in the square of your choice—vote *Yes* or vote *No.*"

If you agree with me that we do not need a union at our company and if you are willing to give the company a chance to show you that we do not need some outside third party in order to communicate among ourselves to face the challenges of earning our livelihood together here without union dues, union rules, union shops or the possibility of union strikes, then I ask you to signify that on the ballot tomorrow by voting no for "no union" and putting an X in the box marked *no.*

To describe the election process for you a little bit, let me start by saying that a representative of the National Labor Relations Board will be here to conduct and supervise the election, and to count the ballots immediately after the polls close. The parties involved are permitted to have an observer present during the voting to make sure everything is done fairly and properly. These observers are to act as monitors at the voting place and at the counting of ballots to assist in the identification of voters, challenge voters and ballots, and otherwise assist the regional director or agent from the federal government.

For the company, as we are not permitted to have an employee in the unit or one of your supervisors act as a supervisor, we have decided that Karen will be our observer because she is familiar with most, if not all, of you because of her involvement in administering insurance and other matters with you.

Relative to the union, they can ask any employee to act as an observer. Of course, if you are requested by the union to act as an observer, understand that you have the right to decline, if that is what you want to do.

At any rate, when you come here to vote, and remember you are free to vote at any time the polls are open, the observers will check your name off the list of employees eligible to vote in the election that has been given to the Labor Board. After your name has been checked off by the observers, then the NLRB persons supervising the election will hand you a ballot. You may then go to the voting booth, which has a curtain you can pull behind you to insure your privacy. We ask you to mark your ballot in only one of the squares identified as *yes* or *no*, because otherwise your ballot may become invalid as to your choice. Also, remember if you sign the ballot or deface it or spoil the ballot by crossing out something, your ballot cannot be counted.

Remember, the only time the polls will be open is from 2:00 to 3:00 p.m. tomorrow here in the lunchroom. This will be your only time to vote and you may leave work at anytime during this time to vote. Also, remember that the results will be decided only by those who actually vote. As this is an important moment in the life of this company and in the lives and families of everyone here, I ask everyone to please vote.

Over the last few weeks, we have tried to present you with as much information as we could and to answer as many questions as we could so that when it comes time to vote, you will be casting an informed vote based upon the facts. During this time, we talked about the history of our company. We also talked about the job security we have been able to maintain over the years by meeting the needs of our customers who create work for us by trusting us with their orders. We talked about some of the things we have done together on our own to make this a good place to work. We provide not only a clean, well-lit, and safe place to work, but also many small intangible items that do much to improve the quality of our work life. By this I mean free and adequate parking, fans, lockers, etc. All of these projects were initiated by our company on its own to make this an ever-improving place to work.

However, most important, as I previously stated, is that it has always been and will always continue to be our company policy to pay fair and competitive wages and fringe benefits so that we can attract and keep good workers such as yourselves. This we will do, union or no union. It is our policy to have the best benefits, wages, fringes, and working conditions as we can continue to afford by serving our customers.

Last week, we talked about unions in general and this particular union and its local constitution and bylaws. Remember, if you became a member of the union, you would have agreed to be bound by all of the union's rules. In this case, it means you can be tried, fined, and even expelled from the union for disagreeing with union leadership.

We also talked a little bit about strikes. Now we know that wherever a union is present, there is always the possibility of a strike. Only where there are no unions can there be any guarantee that there will be no strike. In addition, we know that all it takes for the union to call a strike is the mere approval, not a secret-ballot vote, of only those present at any union meeting given with due notice. And, if you were a union member, you would be obligated to go on strike instead of coming to work and earning a living, unless you wished to face crossing a picket line and be subject to a fine assessed by the unions for violating the strike orders. Indeed, these fines would also be enforceable in court if you did not pay them. This is not to mention the harassment of people who choose to come to work that sometimes takes place during strikes.

Remember also, most importantly, that in any economic strike, the company would have the legal right to permanently replace any striking employee. Moreover, when a strike is over, striking employees do not necessarily get their old jobs back, but get placed on a preferential hiring list until the job opens up. Now I am not saying that if this union were voted in tomorrow that there would be a strike here, but as we said before, the only guarantee we know of is that where there are no unions, there are no strikes.

Lastly, let us project a little into the future and consider some of the situations that may exist as a result of the vote. Let's assume just for the sake of argument that the union was voted in. What could possibly happen?

First, I suppose negotiations between the company and the union would begin. Now, such bargaining would take place until either an agreement has been reached or a stalemate or impasse has been reached where neither side can agree with the other's proposal. Remember, and I don't know if you are all aware of this, but there is nothing in the law that can force either side to agree with the other's proposals. Indeed, such bargaining at some companies has lasted a year or even longer. How does that affect you? Normally, no matter how long the negotiations may take, there are no changes in wages or benefits during the period of such negotiations. In addition, there is no guarantee that any agreement, even if one were reached, would necessarily include retroactivity to the contract end.

I think that this fact is so important that I am going to repeat it: Normally, during the time that negotiations continue, there are no changes in wages or benefits, even if negotiations drag on for a year or more.

Again, I am not saying that this is going to happen here, but it has happened at other companies, and I think that it's important that you realize it and understand it before you vote.

Then, of course, if no agreement can be reached, the union can call a strike. Although this is not something we would like to do, I think it's important that you know that we would have the option during a strike of hiring permanent replacements for anyone who went on strike. We would not want to do this, but we must all recognize the fact that we are in business to serve our customers.

It has taken quite a lot of time to give you the facts in the meetings we have had, but when I think of their importance to everyone who owes their livelihood to our company, I believe that it has been time well spent. Accordingly, I hope you will agree with me that we do not need a union here and will vote *no* for "no union" tomorrow.

Are there any questions we can answer? Remember, after tomorrow, it will be too late to ask.

The above is not meant to be a comprehensive review of what needs to be done in an organizing campaign. It is merely an attempt to illuminate the normal happenings in a campaign. No two campaigns are ever alike, because no two companies and its employees are alike. Each campaign should be drafted uniquely for the situation. There is no one way to do this, and there is also no one method that is effective. However, these are general concerns that companies should cover with their employees during this time.

All speeches should be followed up in writing to the employees at their homes. This is to force discussion in the household because, in most cases, the outcome of the vote is very important to the household as well as to the employee personally. The all-important last chance letter should also be mailed in time to ensure its arrival at employees' homes before they vote.

Often, a question arises as to whether or not the employee relations consultant or attorney should appear at any of these employee meetings. In many cases, at the beginning of the campaign, it is not necessary because the speeches are simple and the questions are generally easy to answer. However, deeper into the campaign as new issues may arise, certain legal questions are better answered by the professional consultant than by the company, and this is appropriate and legal. For example, sometimes labor relations counsel can answer questions about the legal meaning of a union's constitution or the legal rights of the parties in collective bargaining. Also, just before the vote, employees may have procedural questions on the mechanics of voting itself and other miscellaneous concerns. However, legal counsel must weigh the possibility that if performing what may be deemed to be *persuader* activities, it may have ramifications under other labor laws requiring disclosure of amounts of time and fees generated in performing such persuader activities.

The best results are usually achieved when, as in most things, companies "plan the work, and follow the plan." Often, employers are tempted to deviate from the plan because of the roller-coaster emotions that often take place in the weeks prior to the election. However, while certain discussions can be added to the presentation or excluded, the information is important for the employees to know and not only serves to help companies win the election, but also to lay the groundwork for either avoiding future elections or preparing for negotiations if the company does not prevail.

In conclusion, while NLRB elections may be extremely time-consuming and destructive to operations, they often also serve, once and for all, to clear the air about challenges to the company and its employees. In fact, the end result can be a morale-boosting experience, but until that result is reached, it can be draining on both the company and its employees.

What Supervisors Should Say

Supervisors can and should reinforce the opinion that a union is not necessary at their company. Supervisors should be trained to properly respond to employees' questions about unions as they arise. The response of the supervisor—the person that most employees look to for wage increases, promotions, leadership, and direction—can be the crucial factor in labor relations. How should supervisors respond to questions such as:

- Would I make more money if we had a union?

- Isn't it true that workers at union jobs make more money than workers at non-union jobs?

- Would the union be good for us here?

- Why is the company so anti-union?

- Doesn't signing a union card only give one a chance to vote on whether employees want a union?

- Even if a union came into our company, would I have the right not to join it if I didn't want to?

An untrained supervisor's response could land the employer in much legal contention because, according to the agency principles adopted by the NLRB, anything a supervisor says is legally binding on the company. Most importantly, it is probably more persuasive than what higher management might say. Here are some suggestions as to what a trained supervisor might answer to these questions.

- Would I make more money if we had a union?

  Answer: Union or non-union, our company pays fair wages. Our wages are competitive within our industry and our area of the country so that we can attract and retain good employees such as you.

  The union cannot force us to pay any more than we want to pay. The union does not own and operate our business. It invests no capital and assumes no risk. While it has the power to ask for wage increases, it has no power to grant them. Nothing in the law can force a company to agree to a union demand. However, a union can attempt to make companies meet their demands by ordering its members to strike, and, in my opinion, during strikes, no one wins.

- Isn't it true that workers at union jobs make more money than workers at non-union jobs?

  Answer: First of all, whatever happens at some other company is not necessarily what would happen here. If a union came in, wages and benefits under the law are negotiated through collective bargaining. A union can only promise to ask the company for an increase. No wage increases are granted unless the company agrees. Recent statistics show that wage increases on average are greater at non-union companies than at union companies. In addition, at non-union companies, no one can be forced to pay dues, follow union rules, or be taken out on strike. Some unionized operations do pay more, but ultimately it is the customer who pays our salaries. If, because of excessive union demands, we lose our customers, there may be no business here for any of us. Also, if there ever were a strike because of a union, no one makes money during strikes.

- Would the union be good for us here?

Answer: In my opinion, no. Union or no union, our work is to produce quality products delivered on time so that we have repeat business placed in our shop instead of our competitor's shop. This is job security.

A union can promise, but only the company can deliver. A union can only represent people; it can't guarantee anything. It is the company that signs our paychecks.

Furthermore, in return for being your exclusive representative with your employer, the union demands a certain price. By belonging to a union, you will be obligated to abide by a union's bylaws and constitution, the first such obligation being the commitment to pay dues, initiation fees, and possibly fines and assessments as the union sees fit to assign. Moreover, once you have agreed to be obligated to the union, sometimes by oath, this agreement becomes legally binding. The union then can enforce the collection of its dues, fees, fines, and assessments in court and maybe even garnish your wages until such debt is paid off.

Just as important is the loss of personal freedom. Employees may still be able to come to a supervisor with problems. However, most contracts spell out a formal grievance procedure. One may have to file a formal grievance with another employee, a union steward, instead of dealing with the supervisor, and only if the union steward agrees with the grievance does a question proceed. Such decisions may also have to be approved by an international union business representative. Accordingly, unions just add another obstacle to getting dissatisfactions heard, instead of getting them resolved.

Lastly, added to the costs of union dues and union rules, there are the costs of possible strikes. Only where there are no unions can there be the guarantee that there will be no strikes. What is the cost of a strike? Not only do employees lose wages that they might have otherwise earned, but those who strike may also lose their health insurance and other fringe benefits. In addition, in most states, strikers cannot collect unemployment compensation benefits during a strike. Worst of all, being pulled out on strike by a union can cause an employee to be permanently replaced, legally, by the company. Unions don't produce anything, sell anything, or develop any new customers or new products; they won't improve our company's competitive position, and they can't create jobs or job security. Would a union be good for us? I don't think so.

● Why is the company so anti-union?

Answer: Personally, I do not believe a union is necessary or beneficial to the best interests of either the company or the employees. I am not necessarily anti-union; I am pro-employee. In my opinion, many normal union demands, if fulfilled, might result in our company being noncompetitive with the rest of our industry in the market we service. This may result in fewer jobs and fewer opportunities for growth and advancement. Moreover, where a company refuses union demands, some unions may strike. I am not saying that if a union were brought in there would be a strike, but strikes have happened before in union companies around here. Strikes benefit no one, neither the employee who may lose wages and fringe benefits, nor the company who may lose customers because we can't service our orders. All too often, in my opinion, strike situations serve union policy to the detriment of both the company and its employees.

● Doesn't signing a union card only give one a chance to vote on whether employees want a union?

Answer: The purposes of union cards can be more than just to have a vote on the issue. It is true that such cards can be used to substantiate the union's claim to the National Labor Relations Board that there is a sufficient showing of interest (30 percent of the employees in an appropriate unit) to hold an election. However, what most organizers do not say is that the real purpose may be to support a request that the company bargain with the union without an election. Also, these cards can be used to obtain an order from the NLRB or the courts that the company must bargain with the union even though the vote turned out to be against the union.

Moreover, these authorization cards may be used as evidence that the employee who signed one agreed to be legally bound to honor the union's bylaws and international constitution, unless later revoked by the employee. Under the law, employees have the right to sign such cards, and an equal right not to sign. No one can legally be threatened or coerced into signing up with the union. Also, if employees sign cards but change their minds, they have the right and the power to write to the union and ask to have the cards back.

● Even if a union came in to our company, would I have the right not to join it if I didn't want to?

Answer: Not if the company and the union reach agreement in collective bargaining on a contract that includes a *union shop clause*. Such clauses have the effect of requiring that, after a short time period, often after just 30 days on the job, all employees, as a condition of employment, must be members of the union in good standing (i.e., all dues, initiation fees, and fines paid up) in order to be employed at the company. With good reason, these clauses are called *union security clauses*. Although such clauses are illegal in many right-to-work states, in many other states, they are valid. As can be imagined, the negotiation of such a union security arrangement is at the top of many union demand lists. Also, the refusal of companies to agree to such arrangements has been a factor in many strikes.

● Suppose the union is voted in and then the employees don't like it— what can be done then?

Answer: If a union is voted in, employees cannot get rid of it for at least one year, like it or not. If the union negotiates a contract, employees are then locked in for the term of that contract up to a maximum of three years. And the union will fight every step of the way if employees try to decertify it.

Issues in Merger and Acquisition Transactions

The presence of a union should not necessarily scare off potential buyers of a business. In fact, in many cases unionized operations may be exactly where the "bargains" might be found in an acquisition or merger. Part of the reason for this is that the usual tight grip of the labor relations laws loosen a bit if handled correctly, and afford the opportunity for those willing to invest the time, energy, and thought to discovering situations that may be susceptible to the positive effects of good management.

Not every labor organization is automatically a negative. On the contrary, most are anxious to work with management cooperatively because "what is good for the company can be good for the employees, too." This may be especially true in distressed situations. A "new broom" can sweep away prior entanglements with new management in some cases after adversarial-based management-labor relations have failed.

The flip side is the situation where employees are disenchanted with the union after years of representation. This situation may arise where employees were forced to become union members in order to hold their jobs because of a union security clause negotiated by the union with former ownership. Many times such employees, if given the opportunity, would prefer not to be members of the union. In an acquisition or merger, it is possible to give such employees the opportunity to act on the desire not to be represented by a union.

One recent example involves a business of about $20 million in sales with approximately 35 employees that was closed by its creditors and put into receivership. An international union local had been the exclusive representative of the employees for the purposes of collective bargaining for about 20 years. The union contract contained a "union shop" clause that required every individual employed more than 30 days to belong to the union and have dues automatically deducted from his or her paychecks.

The business was acquired in an asset purchase, and reopened for business approximately one month after having been closed down. All of the former employees were contacted and offered employment as new employees of the new business. In this case, of the 35 former employees contacted, 33 were rehired.

Under the rules and case law of the NLRB and the U.S. Supreme Court, it is presumed that all employees of the old company still desired to be union members. Of course, in the actual world this may or may not be the reality. However, the law is that if the new workforce is comprised of a majority of employees who worked at the old company, the old union retains its status as the exclusive representative for all the employees. Accordingly, while the new company under such circumstances should recognize the union's status, as long as it makes it perfectly clear to the union that the new company is not adopting the old contract, then the new company can set the initial terms and conditions of employment. The new company would have a duty to meet at reasonable times and reasonable places with the intent to reach an agreement with the union on a new contract, but until such time as a new collective bargaining agreement was reached between the parties, there would be no union contract in effect.

This distinction is important under labor law principles because there are two time periods when a union can be decertified by the employees of a company. This first window is 90 to 60 days before the expiration of a contract term, or where there is no contract in effect.

In this case, on the morning of the first day of employment when the new company reopened the doors for business, the employees received a copy of a new employee handbook explaining the new terms and conditions of employment. In most respects, these terms were substantially the same as under the old contract relative to wages and fringe benefits. For example, although there was a new carrier for health insurance, the benefits were approximately the same. Relative to vacations, the company stated it would honor length of service at the former company so that employees would pick up exactly where they left off for their vacation entitlements.

In one area of benefits there was a subtle but, to many of the employees, important change from the way things used to be at the old company. At one point former company management had established an attendance bonus program, only to later decide that paying employees for something that they should ordinarily do anyway was not good business. However, as in the old adage "it is easier to get a fish hook in than it is to get it out," subsequent attempts to remove the attendance bonus from the collective bargaining agreement were only partially successful. The result was that the local union president, the local union officers, and the local union bargaining committee were "grandfathered" to receive the attendance bonus, to the exclusion of every other employee. A part of the new terms and conditions of employment established on the first day in the new employee handbook was that there would be an attendance bonus, and that although not as large as it had formerly been, it would be one that applied to everyone who qualified for it, not just a select few.

Most importantly, the employees were also informed about the new company's relationship with the old union. In other words, the new company was recognizing the old union as the representative of the employees for the purposes of collective bargaining; however, the old contract was not in effect. The employees were informed that because of this fact, the old union shop clause and old dues check-off clause were not being adopted by the new company as a part of its initial terms and conditions of employment. This meant that those employees who wished to remain union members were free to do so and should contact the old union relative to the payment of monthly dues, but if an employee chose not to remain a union member, the company would not require it. The choice was up to each employee.

This was welcome news to approximately 45 percent of the workforce who chose not to be union members, despite the urging of the local union president, officers, and bargaining committee.

Within about a month after the company reopened, a petition was filed with the local office of the NLRB, asking for a secret-ballot vote supervised by the NLRB to determine whether or not the union still represented a majority of those employed at the company. NLRB rules required that such a vote be a minimum of 30 percent of the employees working at the company. As the number of signatures apparently exceeded this number, the company and the union were notified of the petition. Within three and a half weeks of notification of the petition, a secret-ballot election was held, which resulted in the employees' votes demonstrating that the union did not represent a majority of the employees (13 "yes" votes for the union and 18 votes for "no" union. Two employees had quit by the time of election and did not vote.). The union was decertified at the company.

It was up to the new owner to continue its modern management techniques to improve employee relations. There was a one-year period in which there could be no new election to determine whether or not the old union, or any new union for that matter, could demonstrate that it represented a majority of the employees. During that first year, new management, through employee involvement, increased plant efficiencies, allowing the company to reduce its prices, and thereby increasing sales in a highly competitive and price-sensitive market.

Ultimately, about three years after buying the company, the new owner sold it as a thriving, efficiently run union-free enterprise to a competitor when the owner changed the nature of his overall business direction. The company grew larger with the additional business lines, and operates with full employment in a generally depressed and highly competitive industry. Moreover, the original local general manager who also earned the trust of the employees is now an equity partner in the company.

Important Recent Decisions

It is not uncommon for an employer to desire to "poll" employees to determine union support. Under limited circumstances this is not an unfair labor practice. However, an employer should be very careful when deciding to use this strategy, in my opinion, unless it can demonstrate clearly the "objective considerations" it has which form the basis of a "reasonable doubt" that the union has lost its former support among the employees.

In the case of *Allentown Mack Sales and Service, Inc. v. NLRB*,[10] the U.S. Supreme Court found that the NLRB's "good-faith reasonable doubt" test for employer polling of employees is facially rational and consistent with the National Labor Relations Act.

On December 29, 1990, the company purchased the assets of a business formerly known as Mack Trucks, Inc. From December 21, 1990, to January 1, 1991, Allentown hired 32 of the original 45 Mack employees. Previously, Local Lodge 724 of the International Association of Machinists and Aerospace Workers, AFL-CIO (Local Lodge 724) represented the employees. Before and after the sale, several employees suggested to Allentown that the incumbent union had lost support among the employees in the bargaining unit. Eight employees said they did not want the union, and two employees indicated others did not want the union.

On January 2, 1991, Local Lodge 724 asked Allentown to recognize it as the employees' collective bargaining representative and to begin negotiations for a new contract. Allentown rejected that request claiming a "good-faith doubt as to support of the Union among the employees." Allentown arranged for an independent poll. It was conducted on February 8, 1991, and the union lost, nineteen to thirteen.

The union then filed an unfair labor practice charge with the NLRB. The NLRB ordered Allentown to recognize and bargain with Local Lodge 724. The District of Columbia Circuit Court of Appeals enforced the order.

In writing for a unanimous court, Justice Scalia stated that the Board's rule stands if it is rational, consistent with the NLRA, and adequately explained. The Board's requirement that an employer have a reasonable doubt based on objective considerations, before polling employees (which is the same requirement as for representation elections and withdrawal of recognitions) is rational. The Board properly may deem polling disruptive and unsettling. Compared to a more lax standard, this approach may reduce the utility of polling as a way of avoiding unfair labor practice charges, "but there is more to life (and even to business) than escaping unfair-labor-practice charges."

The Court found that based on the evidence presented to the NLRB, a reasonable jury could not have found that Allentown lacked a genuine, reasonable uncertainty about whether Local Lodge 724 had the support of the majority of unit employees. Allentown received reliable information that seven of the employees did not support the union, two employees had stated that the union had lost support, and there was little evidence to the contrary.

The Administrative Procedure Act, which governs the proceedings of administrative agencies, establishes a scheme of "reasoned decision making." The agency's decreed result must be within the scope of its lawful authority, and the process by which it reaches that result must be logical and rational; otherwise, courts are required to set aside the agency action. If the agency states one rule, yet adopts another, it acts improperly. In this case, the administrative law judge and the NLRB acted in error by discounting reports of employee dissatisfaction with the Union according to legal standards that do not align with the articulated rule. The reports were substantial enough to be prohibitive to some degree of the employer's good-faith reasonable doubt.

In another case, *San Diego Gas and Electric* (1997-98 CCH NLRB ¶ 16,655), the Labor Board in a 3-2 decision ruled that the provisions of the NLRB Casehandling Manual that restricted mail balloting to particular situations were no longer controlling.

> Although parties should continue to adhere to the NLRB's longstanding policy that due to "the value of having a Board agent present at [an] election. . .elections should. . .be conducted manually," the strict "infeasability standard" was abandoned, and is replaced by "guidelines" clarifying the circumstances that warrant a mail ballot election.

According to the majority, a mail ballot election or a mixed manual-mail ballot election would normally be appropriate in three situations: (1) where eligible voters' job duties "scattered" them over a wide geographic area; (2) where eligible voters were "scattered" not so much in the geographic sense but in the sense that they were not present at a common location at common times; and (3) where there was a strike, lockout, or picketing in progress. In these situations, regional directors should also take into account such secondary factors as the parties' preferences, the ability of voters to read and understand ballots, access to eligible employee's addresses, and the method that makes the most efficient use of Board resources.

Decertifying Existing Unions

One of the goals of the National Labor Relations Act is to ensure the right of workers to be represented in collective bargaining by a representative of their own choosing, or to refrain from being represented in collective bargaining.

For those employees already represented by a labor organization, the NLRA provides for a mechanism by which workers can refrain from being so represented. This process, called *decertification*, is in many respects the mirror process through which labor unions organize existing union-free employees.

Following are the legal concepts involved in the decertification process. They may be used as a guideline for understanding the protections afforded by the NLRA to those wishing to decertify a union.

First of all, it must be understood that the NLRB does not act on its own initiative in any given case. The NLRB only responds to the charges of unfair labor practice and requests for secret-ballot elections that are brought to it.

For the NLRB to consider a petition for decertification from employees (what the NLRB would call an RD *petition*), in general, the following conditions must be met:

1. At least 30 percent of the workers in a bargaining unit must sign a decertification petition requesting an election. This petition need say nothing more complicated than: "We, the undersigned, do not want to be represented by a union."

2. The petition cannot be filed until at least one year after the existing union has been certified.

3. The petition must be filed during the *window period*, the 30-day period that is no less than 60 days nor more than 90 days prior to the expiration of the existing collective bargaining agreement, or at a time when there is no contract, such as after the expiration of a contract where no new contract has replaced it. This is often only during a strike situation.

If a union fails to renegotiate a contract after the 60-day insulation period that precedes the expiration of the existing contract, employees can file an RD petition at any time.

In the event that an economic strike takes place upon the expiration of a contract, both strikers and replacement workers can vote in a decertification election for up to 12 months after the strike's beginning. After 12 months, economic strikers may not participate in the election, and only replacement workers and workers who refused to strike may vote.

Management can also file a petition for a representation election (what the NLRB labels an RM *petition*). However, before the NLRB will hold such an election, management must establish to the NLRB's satisfaction that management has good faith proof through *objective considerations* that the union either has abandoned the employees or that its status as the employee representative is in question.

In order to prove the latter, management must establish that at least 30 percent of the workers no longer wish to have the union as their bargaining agent. As in the RD decertification petition, the filing of both the evidence and the RM petition must fall within the window, the 30-day period that is no less than 60 days nor more than 90 days prior to the expiration of the collective bargaining agreement. The only exception to this is in the event of an economic strike, in which case such RM petition may be filed at any time.

In the secret-ballot election administered by the NLRB, the ballot will simply read: "Do you wish to be represented in collective bargaining by _____ union? yes ☐ no ☐." A union is decertified if the final vote tally shows a tie or a simple majority in favor of "no union," and there are no objections to the conduct of the election sustained by the NLRB that might nullify the election or force a repeat vote.

Endnotes

[1] *Epilepsy Foundation of Northeast Ohio,* 2000-01 CCH NLRB ¶15,508.

[2] *NLRB v. Weingarten, Inc.,* USSct, 76 LC ¶10,662.

[3] 309 NLRB No. 163, 1992-93 CCH NLRB ¶17,609.

[4] 16 PEPPERDINE LAW REVIEW 1, 5 (1988-89).

[5] 309 NLRB No. 163, 1992-93 CCH NLRB ¶17,609.

[6] *Id.*

[7] 1995-96 CCH NLRB ¶16,023.

[8] 1995-96 CCH NLRB ¶15,932.

[9] 1995-96 CCH NLRB ¶15,944.

[10] 118 S. Ct. 818 (1998).

Answers to Chapter Six Test Your Knowledge

All true except number 7. When unions send their agents into a bargaining unit it is called, "Salting the workforce," a legitimate union tactic or strategy recognized and approved by the U. S. Supreme Court.

CHAPTER SEVEN

Terminating Employees

Incident Investigation Protocol Checklist

Discharge for Just Cause

Discipline and Discharge Decision-Making

Employee Separation Agreements

Test Your Knowledge

of Employee Termination Issues

1. True or False? Although there are limited exceptions, the general common law rule in the United States is that an employee-at-will may be discharged from employment at any time for any cause, any reason, no reason, a bad reason, or even an immoral reason, and the employee has the same right to quit.

2. Which of the following are important to consider when a manager decides to terminate an employee from employment?
   a. How long the employee has been employed.
   b. If the employee's overall record includes prior incidents of counseling or corrective discipline.
   c. If the employee was aware that his or her conduct violated the business interests of the employer.
   d. All of the above.

3. True or False? It is never necessary to discharge an employee "on the spot." It is better to suspend employment first, investigate, review the employee's record, and then decide if discharge is the best option.

4. True or False? An important method to establish "due process" in a termination from employment decision is to ask the employee for his or her side of the story in the investigation.

5. Which of the following questions is important to ask when evaluating whether an act of carelessness justifies a decision to discharge an employee?
   a. Was the employee properly trained to perform the task?
   b. Was the employee's conduct part of a pattern of carelessness?
   c. What was the actual or potential damage that resulted from the careless act?
   d. Did the employee seem willing to learn from the mistake?
   e. All of the above.

6. In complying with the Older Workers Benefit Protection Act in obtaining a knowing and voluntary release of liability from an employee age forty or over in return for consideration over and above what the employee would otherwise receive, which of the following conditions must be met?
   a. The employee must be given at least three weeks to sign the release agreement.

      b.   The employee must be informed that after signing the agreement, he or she has another seven calendar days in which to revoke it.

      c.   The employee must be informed of the right to see an attorney concerning the agreement.

      d.   The employee must be informed that the release includes any rights pursuant to the Age Discrimination in Employment Act (ADEA).

      e.   The employee must be informed that the release does not apply to any action that might arise after the agreement is signed.

      f.   All of the above.

7.   True or False? It is legal for an employer to include in the draft of an employee separation agreement language stipulating arrangements concerning non-competition covenants, non-disparagement clauses, and confidentiality of the terms of the agreement.

8.   True or False? When giving a reference concerning a former employee an employer is precluded by law from saying or writing anything other than verifying dates of employment, positions held, and final salary or wage.

9.   In order to prove defamation by an employer, which of the following elements must be established in a claim by a former employee?

      a.   A false statement has been made by management concerning the employee.

      b.   The statement was expressed to a third party not privileged to learn it.

      c.   The statement caused harm or damage to the employee or to his or her reputation in the community at large.

      d.   All of the above.

10. True or False? An employer may lose the privilege to communicate an unfavorable reference if it can be established that there was an excessive publication of the statements made or there was a reckless disregard for whether or not the contents of the reference are true or false.

The answers to these questions are at the end of this chapter.

Terminating employees is one of the least favorite, but most important, tasks a responsible manager has to perform. Its importance is underscored by multimillion-dollar verdicts against companies and businesses for mishandling this delicate task.

Of course, no discharge should come as a surprise to an employee being terminated from employment. If the performance issues are long-term, then the employee should have received warnings, poor evaluations, or even coaching and training from the manager to help him or her overcome obstacles that impede or prevent success in the job. Also, the work rules and policies of the employer should have been well known to the employee so that he or she understood the standards of behavior and performance expected at the workplace. However, when an employee is aware of what the company's expectations are and either cannot or will not abide by them, then a discharge is best for both parties.

Not all discharges are for misconduct connected with employment. However, where reasonable rules have been established, the employee has been made aware of these rules, and the employee has been warned concerning the violations, the decision to discharge should not be too difficult to make. Such violations harm the employer's business. In this case, the employee can be told in a termination interview, with a follow-up letter confirming, in no uncertain terms, the reasons for management's decision.

If the discharge is based on a single culminating incident, it is commonly advised that the employer establish fairness and due process. The initial step is taking the time to investigate the employee's side of the story. This way the employer can discover immediately if there are any contradictory views or reports between supervisors, witnesses, and the person being discharged that relate to the incident. Because of the need for due process investigation, it is never advisable to discharge anyone on the spot. The employer should always indefinitely suspend (with or without pay), investigate, and then make a decision based on the facts of the last incident. Simultaneously examine the employee's prior record, particularly in the last year or so of employment. Include the employee's side of the story in the investigation. Inform the employee that, before a certain date, a written response concerning the action being considered in the decision-making process would be a tremendous aid. Upon receiving such a response, it may be decided that it is not appropriate to discharge the employee after all. Other factors may come to light from the employee's point of view that will change the decision. Moreover, asking shows that any investigation and decision-making was fairly considered under the circumstances. It puts the burden of responding squarely on the individual under investigation, and it is important to listen to a response if forthcoming.

Incident Investigation Protocol Checklist

To ensure consistency in any investigation, it is important to follow certain steps. The following protocol checklist may be helpful in making sure all the proper steps have been taken before making a decision to terminate an employee.

1. Ask the employee for a written statement.

Obtaining the employee's written testimony is crucial. Memory may be dulled from the date of the incident that led to the discharge to the time a request for unemployment compensation benefits is filed or, even worse, to a time usually much later in front of an administrative agency, such as the National Labor Relations Board (NLRB) or the Equal Employment Opportunity Commission (EEOC). A signed statement, written at or about the time of the event that describes what led to the discharge, is invaluable. This is important because the employee's testimony may later vary from what was said at the time of discharge.

2. Review company rules or policies that relate to the incident.

In making a decision to discharge, all the facts, including any remarks the employee in question wants to make, should be on file. Once it has been determined that there are rules or policies that call for the discharge of an employee and that the employee was aware of these rules and policies (often proved through the receipt of an employee handbook that details these rules and policies), precedent is established. If there have ever been any exceptions made to these policies, the reasons for them should be part of the file.

3. Check that the rule or policy identified in step 2 is still applicable.

Especially where the incident in question is the first time that discharge is being considered based upon a certain rule or policy, be sure that the original purpose and intent of the rule or policy is still applicable.

4. Check the steps of any progressive corrective disciplinary system.

The personnel file should also be checked to see whether the discharge is being made as the last step in the progressive corrective disciplinary system (such as after a first warning, second warning, and last warning, for example). If it is, make sure that the discipline at all of the prior steps was appropriate.

5. Are the standards for termination being applied consistently?

If the employee is a member of a "protected class" for purposes of equal rights law or the employee was engaged with another employee in the final incident protesting a working condition, the facts should be closely examined before making the decision to discharge. If the decision is challenged in an equal rights proceeding, the employer may have to establish that it has not been applying its standards differently for other employees. In this example, the activity may be in violation of the National Labor Relations Act (NLRA), and the discharged employee may have rights to reinstatement and back pay through the auspices of the NLRB. Accordingly, reasons for discharge should be examined very closely.

6. Is the documentation complete?

Lastly, the employee's personnel file, which in many states the employee has a right to examine, should contain the necessary documentation and evidence that witnesses are prepared to support the discharge decision.

Discharge for Just Cause

In a union setting, an employee has the right to contest a discharge on the basis that it was not for just cause. Just cause has been interpreted individually by each and every arbitrator in each and every case in over 75 years of labor/management discharge arbitration cases. However, a sort of "common law" has been developed over the years by arbitrators in discharge decision-making. The criteria are interesting to review.

First of all, there is the question of whether the company gave the employee forewarning or foreknowledge of the possible or probable consequences of engaging in certain conduct. This knowledge can be given to the employee orally or in writing. This most commonly takes the form of shop rules and the penalties for violating such rules. These rules can best be disseminated to employees in an employee handbook that lets them know what the company expects of their behavior on the job.

However, a lack of such rules does not necessarily mean that any discharge will not be for just cause. Also, given the variety of human behavior, sometimes it is impossible to codify all possible violations. Common sense must play a part. Remember, Moses came down from the mountain with ten rules that have stood the test of time pretty well. The true test for proper discharge is whether a reasonable person in like circumstances *would have known* that the act, or failure to act, that led to the decision of discharge by the employer was damaging or potentially damaging to the business or property of the company.

The second issue is if the company has a rule or policy, is it reasonably related to the orderly, efficient, and safe operation of the company's business and the performance that the company might reasonably expect of employees? Some courts have stated that a rule is reasonable if its violation harms the employer's business.

Next, before discipline is administered to an employee, did the company make an effort to discover whether the employee in fact violated a rule or engaged in conduct in substantial disregard of the obligation that employees owe to their employer? It has been held that employees have the right to know with reasonable precision the offense with which they are being charged and be given the opportunity to organize a defense. In addition, the company's investigation should be made during the period of indefinite suspension pending a decision and not afterwards to justify it. It is during this decision-making period that the company should not only record the employee's statement, preferably in writing, but also take statements from other possible witnesses to the action.

An arbitrator may next ascertain whether the company conducted its own investigation fairly and objectively. In this regard, arbitrators may overturn a discharge for lack of just cause if the decision had already been reached before the investigation took place or if the investigation itself denied a common sense due process procedure to the employee.

After the above questions are answered, the arbitrator will examine whether there was substantial evidence or proof that the employee was guilty as charged. It is not required that the evidence be absolutely conclusive or meet criminal legal standards. However, such evidence should truly be substantial and not merely based on hearsay or rumor. If there were eyewitnesses to the conduct, their statements should be on file. Often at a hearing, there can be great conflicts in the testimony, even when such testimony is given under oath.

The company will next be asked if it has applied its rules, orders, and penalties without discrimination; if the employee had sufficient notice that the conduct was objectionable to the company; and what precedents exist. Of course, in such an event, the employer should be sure to discipline when it is necessary because its failure to do so raises the benchmark for future actions. This applies to equal rights cases as well as to union just cause discharge situations.

The last consideration is whether or not the punishment fits the crime. In this regard, arbitrators not only look at the seriousness of the employee's conduct and its harm or potential harm to the employer, but also at the record of the employee. Was this a long-term employee whose behavior, although improper, was merely an isolated instance of poor judgment? A long-term employee's unblemished record may make a discharge inappropriate and less than for just cause. In such case, a discharge decision may be overturned with resulting back pay and other "make whole" liability on the part of the company.

Discipline and Discharge Decision-Making
Incompetence and Failure to Perform
Many argue that in certain cases, an employee's incompetence or failure to perform essential job duties should be handled, at least initially, through counseling instead of through discipline. They reason that usual progressive disciplinary measures are inappropriate if the problem is that the employee is unable to live up to the company's performance requirements.

However, it is important that employees know where their performance is lacking. In fact, good employees want to know if they are not performing adequately so that they can improve. Accordingly, in most cases, disciplinary action for improper performance, even if due to incompetence, should be progressive and the employee counseled.

Key questions to ask in determining when discipline is not working and whether discharge is appropriate:

● Has the company documented or otherwise substantiated the alleged instances of incompetence?

● Has the company provided the employee with the proper training and supervision needed to do the job correctly?

● Has the company warned the employee that a continuation of the performance problems will result in discipline and may ultimately result in discharge?

In one case, in the context of a union discharge grievance, an arbitrator decided that an employee was improperly discharged for incompetence after the employee was charged with two avoidable accidents while driving a company vehicle. Although acknowledging that the employee's negligence clearly caused the accidents, which resulted in financial losses to the employer, the arbitrator maintained that the employee's temporary lapses in judgment while driving fell far short of the lack of care tradition- ally needed to support a finding that the employee was incompetent.

While disciplinary action may have been justified, according to the arbitra- tor, the company had an obligation to make sure that there was a reason- able and close correlation between the offense committed and its re- sponse to the problem. The arbitrator questioned whether the employee had proper job training. In this case, the application of discipline, with retraining measures, would have been the appropriate company response.

In another case, a meat market employee had been discharged for incompetence because management was concerned about the unsani- tary condition of the store. Here, however, the arbitrator noted that the employee had never been warned that his continued poor job perfor- mance might lead to discipline or discharge. When the company failed to inform the employee of the poor performance, the company, by its silence, condoned it.

Carelessness

Generally, a single act of carelessness is not enough to justify discharge. Before discharging an employee for carelessness, the employer should ask itself the following questions:

- Was the employee properly trained to perform the task?

- Was the employee's conduct a part of a pattern of carelessness?

- Did the employee seem willing to learn from the mistake?

- What was the actual or potential damage that resulted from the employee's carelessness?

- How would the company's decision on discipline influence other workers?

- Would the employee's act of carelessness have any negative effects on the company's public image?

When discharging for acts of carelessness, employers should show either a continuing pattern of conduct or that the single incident of carelessness was caused by willful or intentional action on the part of the employee.

Investigating and Interviewing

Sometimes an incident connected with employment occurs that is either too public to handle confidentially or too serious to leave alone. Where discipline is necessary and cannot be avoided, an employment decision with its attendant emotional overtones and ramifications must be made. People look to the manager for leadership in making a decision. Indeed, making such decisions is what justifies the manager's salary. Some kind of action must be taken.

The first step is to investigate the incident and gather the information necessary to make a fair decision. It is obvious that the manager is eventually going to have to talk to the person involved to learn the employee's side of the story. In handling these kinds of interviews, it is generally best not to meet with the employee alone because there should be a witness to corroborate the testimony. Having a witness shows the employee that the manager's interest in the matter is not personal, but professional and on behalf of the company.

The interview should be conducted in a reasonably quiet place where interruptions are unlikely and where there is no possibility of being overheard. Try to put the employee at ease, and do not jump into a cross-examination. Describe to the employee in general terms how the incident is understood and express a desire to learn the employee's side of the story. In a union environment, the employee may ask to have the steward present for this investigatory interview. This request should be granted. However, if the employee desires other representation such as an attorney or a family member, advise the employee that such a meeting may be held at some later date, but that for purposes of a fair investigation, usually the most accurate information is obtained as close in time to the actual incident as possible. If the employee still refuses to participate in the investigation, the employee should be informed that a manager may be more convinced by what is said now. Also, the employment decision may then have to be based on the only information available, which will not include the employee's testimony.

At the start of the interview, it is important to make a statement of positive intent to investigate the incident thoroughly before making any decisions. The employee can be told that what he or she has to say is the most important part of that investigation.

The agenda to be followed at the meeting should be outlined so that the employee understands that the procedure is for the interviewer to briefly explain the existing knowledge of the incident and for the employee to then give an honest reaction. The employee should be informed that what he or she says may be written in a memo for the employee to approve for inclusion in the investigation file. Finally, the employee should be told that the discussion will be kept as confidential as practicable.

The brief explanation of the circumstances should use the facts, if the facts are known. The best results are achieved when the manager is nonjudgmental about the facts. Opinions, especially about who is and isn't believed and what the ramifications of the facts are, should not be discussed.

The employee should then make a statement without interruption, except to answer clarifying questions, and this statement should be condensed and repeated to the employee in order to correct any misunderstandings.

After the interview, the employee should be thanked for participating and informed as to what will happen next. If the employee is on indefinite suspension until a decision is reached, the employee should be reminded that if there is anything else that should be added for consideration, he or she must call or write the company immediately. It is often very helpful to set a definite deadline after which no more information will be received, for example, after "the close of the business day on Thursday." Indicate that the decision-making will be finished shortly thereafter, and the employee will be notified of the final decision.

The Termination Interview

Once the decision is made to discharge, it is often best to present the employee a discharge letter containing the reasons for the discharge. Following such a procedure will keep the company from being accused of inventing new reasons for the discharge after it occurred. All the company need do in any subsequent litigation will be to establish proof of the events described in the discharge letter. Often a management decision to discharge an employee is based upon the employee's overall record as well as some triggering incident as being the culmination of conduct that led to the discharge decision. The decision may further include other events of counseling and corrective discipline. If so, a recitation of the event dates and reasons for such action should be included.

From a personnel perspective, a discharge letter is also a good method of informing the employee of rights for continuing health insurance benefits. Under most circumstances, an employee who is separated from employment may continue to be part of a group medical plan for up to 18 months by paying the premiums pursuant to provisions of the Consolidated Omnibus Budget Reconciliation Act (COBRA). This notice is most often handled separately through an employer's insurer upon notification, but can also be alluded to in the employer's letter.

In the COBRA law a separate provision states that an employer need not offer such an opportunity if the employee was discharged for "misconduct connected with employment." Some managers feel that this is a right discharged employees forfeit when they are fired for cause. However, before denying COBRA benefits, a careful check with labor relations counsel is advised because the penalty for being wrong could be very stiff under COBRA law. If an employee who has been fired for cause later prevails in an unemployment compensation hearing or arbitration, what was originally thought to be an open-and-shut matter may be further complicated.

For the final interview, the manager should be firm in the decision to discharge. There is no longer room for argument as long as the employee has been given ample opportunity to state his or her case before this time. Of course, occasionally the discharge may come as a complete shock to the employee. Examples of situations of a surprise discharge interview include when there is discovery of misconduct, when a manager decides it is time for a change in management of a unit, or in an economic business reorganization. Usually, however, discharge interview situations are anticipated by the employee. In either situation, managers conducting the interview should retain a courteous demeanor in this final encounter. The decision, having been made, need not be justified by the manager who is merely informing the employee of a decision that has already been reached.

A good way to begin the interview is by simply thanking the employee for coming. Then quickly and quietly tell the employee that the reason for the meeting is that the company has decided it would be best if the employee "parted company" as an employee with the company. Next, hand to the employee the termination letter, keeping a copy of it in front of you. Then ask the employee to read along silently with you as you read the letter aloud. My personal experience in numerous contexts and varied situations is that no matter what the employee may do next, in using this method the overall message delivered is that the "decision" to discharge the employee has been made and it is irrevocable and irreversible. The time for the employee to negotiate for his or her job is past, and the employee should be told this, if need be. Whatever the employee does, the manager should respond as humanely as possible. However, in many circumstances, the presence of private security can facilitate the transfer of company property such as cell phones, laptops, keys, computer passwords, and the like. Security can also assist the employee as the personal workspace is cleared. Having a cardboard box handy for personal items is a good idea. Ultimately, if the employee refuses to leave or fails to cooperate, call police. In fact, in cases where an employer may have reason to anticipate improper behavior, notifying local police of the interview in advance is helpful.

Employee Separation Agreements

In some discharge situations, employers know in advance that a discharge decision may bring with it expensive litigation costs. In these cases, employers should recognize a hiring mistake and "buy out" the employment relationship. Of course, this is a very bitter pill for many managers to swallow, but it is often the best course of action. This can be accomplished by offering an employee separation agreement to sever the employment relationship.

The employer can inform the employee that it has decided to terminate the employee's services and that this can be done by mutual agreement. Then the employer offers to resolve the situation by giving the employee an agreement to consider. The key point here is that the employer is not negotiating the fact of the discharge, but rather that the company is willing to negotiate the manner in which the separation will be made.

The terms of the agreement depend entirely upon the circumstances. Sometimes the mere promise of the employer to allow the employee to resign is enough to effectuate an agreement. Often the most important negotiating point is extended health insurance benefits or even outplacement counseling until the ex-employee finds another job, which then cuts off unemployment compensation benefits.

Considering outplacement or job search assistance counseling as a part of a settlement package can be extremely beneficial in avoiding future problems. In fact, it may be surprising to learn that the Association of Outplacement Consulting Firms reported that, in one year, outplacement services were provided to 1.1 million Americans!

While not every discharge situation calls for such measures, outplacement assistance should be considered as an amicable way to prevent future problems and maintain a company's goodwill in the community. It may be most appropriate in situations involving personality conflicts and disagreements between an owner or manager and a subordinate.

It is advantageous for the employer to settle cases beforehand, when they are usually easiest to resolve. If an employer generally provides severance pay and other unemployment benefits, especially to former long-term employees, the employer can take steps to protect itself from vindictive, ex-employee backlash. In one instance, a small business owner fired a 15-year veteran office manager and provided her with two months' severance and unemployment benefits, only to receive a lawsuit as soon as the severance pay and unemployment compensation expired.

This backlash can be avoided. It is legal and binding to get employee consideration, in the form of an enforceable waiver from filing legal actions against an employer, at a later time as long as such an agreement is voluntarily signed by the employee.

An employer may wish to consider using such agreements in a litigation-preventive labor relations program. What follows is a blank employee separation agreement form that is used in many cases.

Employee Separation Agreement

This Agreement, made and entered into between _____, employee of _____, (hereinafter referred to as "Employee"), and _____, (hereinafter referred to as "Company");

Witnesseth:

A. Employee is employed at Company.

B. Employee is willing to tender his voluntary resignation from employment with Company and to waive all rights with respect to any matter connected with his employment with Company.

C. Company is willing to accept such resignation, and will give additional compensation to Employee as set forth below.

Now, Therefore, in consideration of the mutual covenants of the parties hereto,

It Is Agreed:

1. Employee herewith voluntarily resigns from employment at Company effective _____, 20____.

2. Employee expressly waives any and all rights with respect to all matters relating to or connected with his employment at Company which he now has or hereafter may acquire and agrees not to initiate any action, legal or otherwise, against Company or any successor or assign or any other employee, agent or representative of Company.

3. Company agrees not to contest or object to any claim for unemployment compensation benefits by Employee based on his employment with Company so long as Employee is

out of work and otherwise eligible for such unemployment compensation benefits within the meaning of the _____ Statutes.

4. Company agrees to pay to Employee _____, and Employee hereby acknowledges receipt of same.

5. Relative to any reference for future employment, Company agrees to respond that Employee's reason for leaving employment with Company was due to his voluntary resignation.

Signed in duplicate this ____ day of _____, 20____, at

_____, _____.

Employee:_____ Company by:_____

An alternate method is to draft a Release of Liability for signature by the former employee only, such as follows:

Release of Liability

IN RETURN FOR CONSIDERATION of the payment to me of [the amount of $], receipt of which I hereby acknowledge, and the provision to me of outplacement counseling services, and the payment of premiums for health insurance coverage through _____, I, [name of employee] of [address of employee] hereby knowingly and voluntarily waive any and all rights related to all matters connected with my employment at [name of company.]

I AGREE not to initiate any claim, demand, or cause of action, legal or otherwise, against [name of company], or any successor, or any assign, or any other employee, officer, board director, agent, or representative of [company]—none of whom admit any liability to me but expressly deny any liability from any such claim, demand, or cause of action.

[Name of employee, address, date]

I personally prefer as short and non-threatening a form as possible. However, it should be clear to everyone what is happening when the transaction is made. The true goal is 100-percent "psychological" agreement to the deal from the employee being terminated. In almost every case, if this is accomplished, it will end the matter for all time. This is especially so once the employee goes about the earnest endeavor of finding his or her next employment situation with the help of the outplacement counselor. As of this writing and for the foreseeable future, it is a good time to look for employment. The primary challenge for employers in the United States today is finding people to fill the jobs needed to be done. Once the former employee is working at his or her next job, the employee separation becomes old history and buried in the depths of the past. Moving on is the ultimate desire of all concerned parties in most every case. The idea is to minimize, as much as possible, the natural feeling of unpleasantness for an employee when he or she is not the one calling the timing of the termination of employment. This may take some time and distance. By being perhaps even overly generous in some circumstances, the employer can accomplish practically and legally what it wants from the situation—removing the employee from the payroll. This is the price one pays as an employer, and it is an inherent risk of entering into an employment relationship. Buying out the relationship can be a bitter pill for the employer to swallow, particularly after an investment in wages and training turns sour for whatever reasons. This is true even when the employee's own poor performance, negligence, or even malfeasance was cause of the termination from employment. However, the termination can save time, trouble, and expense in the long run.

For larger employers or more potentially complicated employment termination situations, there may be other "recitals" appropriate to draft in the agreement. Such recitals may also be true in reduction in force (RIF) situations where several employees or even whole departments are affected by the "downsizing" or "business reorganization decisions." Although such job loss situations may not be the particular fault of the employees involved, an employee may have rights of legal action through age discrimination or other means. Therefore, the Release of Liability documents should be drafted specifically identifying these considerations.

What follows is what might be called the long form for a Settlement Agreement and Release document.

Settlement Agreement And Release

This Settlement Agreement and Release ("Agreement") is made by and between _____, a wholly owned subsidiary of _____ Corporation (the "Company"), and _____ ("Employee").

WHEREAS, Employee was employed by the Company;

WHEREAS, the Company and Employee have entered into a Confidential Information and Invention Assignment Agreement (the "Confidentiality Agreement") on [date].

WHEREAS, the Company and Employee have terminated the employment relationship;

NOW THEREFORE, in consideration of the mutual promises made herein, The Company and Employee (collectively referred to as "the Parties") hereby agree as follows:

1. TERMINATION. Employee has been terminated from his position on [date].

2. CONSIDERATION. The Company agrees to pay Employee an additional ___ weeks of base salary, less applicable withholding. He will continue to receive regular semimonthly paychecks through this ___ week period, ending on [date].

3. VESTING OF STOCK. The Parties agree that for the purposes of determining the number of shares vesting of the Company's common stock which employee is entitled to purchase from the Company, Employee will be entitled to continue vesting stock until [date]. The exercise of any stock options shall continue to be subject to the terms and conditions of the Company's Stock Option Plan and the applicable Stock Option Agreement between Employee and the Company.

4. BENEFITS. The Company agrees to pay for Employee's COBRA through [date] or until he is covered under another group medical plan.

5. CONFIDENTIAL INFORMATION. Employee shall continue to maintain the confidentiality of all confidential and proprietary information of the Company and shall continue to comply with the terms and conditions of the Confidentiality Agreement between Employee and the Company. Employee shall return all the Company property and confidential and proprietary information in his possession to the Company on the effective date of this Agreement.

6. PAYMENT OF SALARY. Employee acknowledges and represents that the Company has paid all salary, wages, accrued vacation, and any and all other benefits due to Employee. Any bonus due for quarter ending [date] will be paid no later than [date].

7. RELEASE OF CLAIMS. Employee agrees that the foregoing consideration represents settlement in full of all outstanding obligations owed to Employee by the Company. Employee, on behalf of himself, and his respective heirs, family members, executors and assigns, hereby fully and forever releases the Company and its respective officers, directors, employees, investors, shareholders, administrators, affiliates, divisions,

subsidiaries, predecessor and successor corporations, and assigns from, and agrees not to sue concerning any claim, duty, obligation or cause of action relating to any matters of any kind, whether presently known or unknown, suspected or unsuspected, that he may possess arising from any omissions, acts or facts that have occurred up until and including the Effective Date of this Agreement including, without limitation,

(a) any and all claims relating to or arising from Employee's employment relationship with the Company and the termination of that relationship;

(b) any and all claims relating to, or arising from, Employee's right to purchase, or actual purchase of shares of stock of the Company, including, without limitation, any claims for fraud, misrepresentation, breach of fiduciary duty, breach of duty under applicable state corporate law, and securities fraud under any state or federal law;

(c) any and all claims for wrongful discharge of employment; termination in violation of public policy; discrimination, breach of contract, both express and implied; promissory estoppel; negligent or intentional infliction of emotional distress; negligent or intentional interference with contract or prospective economic advantage; unfair business practices; defamation; libel; slander; negligence; personal injury; assault; battery; invasion of privacy; false imprisonment; and conversion;

(d) any and all claims for violation of any federal, state or municipal statute, including, but not limited to, Title VII of the Civil Rights Act of 1964, the Civil Rights Act of 1991, the Age Discrimination in Employment Act of 1967, the Fair Labor Standards Act, the Employment Retirement Income Security Act of 1974, the Worker Adjustment and Retraining Notification Act, Older Workers Benefit Protection Act; any claims for violation of statutes or laws of the states of _____;

(e) any and all claims for violation of the federal, or any state, constitution;

(f) any and all claims arising out of any other laws and regulations relating to employment or employment discrimination; and

(g) any and all claims for attorney's fees and costs.

Employee agrees that the release set forth in this section shall be and remain in effect in all respects as a complete general release as to the matters released. This release does not extend to any obligations in-curred under this Agreement

8. ACKNOWLEDGMENT OF WAIVER OF CLAIMS UNDER ADEA. Employee acknowledges that he is waiving and releasing any rights he may have under the Age Discrimination in Employment Act of 1967 (ADEA) and that this waiver and release is knowing and voluntary. Employee and Company agree that this waiver and release does not apply to any rights or claims that may arise under ADEA after the Effective Date of this Agreement. Employee acknowledges that the consideration given for this waiver and release Agreement is in addition to anything of value to which Employee was already entitled. Employee further acknowledges that he has been advised by this writing that (a) he should consult with any attorney prior to executing this Agreement; (b) he has at least twenty-one days within which to consider this Agreement; (c) he has at least seven (7) days following the execution of this Agreement by the parties to revoke the Agreement; and (d) this Agreement shall not be effective until the revocation period has expired.

9. CALIFORNIA CIVIL CODE SECTION 1542. Employee represents that he is not aware of any claims against the Company other than the claims that are released by this Agreement. Employee acknowledges that he has been advised by legal counsel and is familiar with the provisions of California Civil Code Section 1542, which provides as follows:

A GENERAL RELEASE DOES NOT EXTEND TO CLAIMS WHICH THE CREDITOR DOES NOT KNOW OR SUSPECT TO EXIST IN HIS FAVOR AT THE TIME OF EXECUTING THE RELEASE, WHICH IF KNOWN BY HIM MUST HAVE MATERIALLY AFFECTED HIS SETTLEMENT WITH THE DEBTOR.

Employee, being aware of said code section, agrees to expressly waive any rights he may have thereunder, as well as under any other statute or common law principles of similar effect in any other state.

10. NO PENDING OR FUTURE LAWSUITS. Employee represents that he has no lawsuits, claims, or actions pending in his name, or on behalf of any other person or entity, against the Company or any other person or entity referred to herein. Employee also represents that he does not intend to bring any claims on his own behalf or on behalf of any other person or entity against the Company or any other person or entity referred to herein.

11. APPLICATION FOR EMPLOYMENT. Employee understands and agrees that, as a condition of this Agreement, he shall not be entitled

to any employment with the Company, its subsidiaries, or any successor, and he hereby waives any right, or alleged right, of employment or re-employment with the Company, its subsidiaries or related companies, or any successor.

12. CONFIDENTIALITY. Employee agrees to use his best efforts to maintain in confidence the existence of this Agreement (hereinafter collectively referred to as "Settlement Information"). Employee agrees to take every reasonable precaution to prevent disclosure of any Settlement Information to third parties, and agrees that there will be no publicity, directly or indirectly, concerning any Settlement Information. Employee agrees to take every precaution to disclose Settlement Information only to those attorneys, accountants, governmental entities, and family members who have a reasonable need to know of such Settlement Information.

13. NO COOPERATION. Employee agrees he will not act in any manner that might damage the business of the Company. Employee agrees that he will not counsel or assist any attorneys or their clients in the presentation or prosecution of any disputes, differences, grievances, claims charges or complaints by any third party against the Company and/or any officer, director, employee, agent, representative, shareholder or attorney of the Company, unless under a subpoena or other court order to do so.

14. NON-DISPARAGEMENT. Employee agrees to refrain from any defamation, libel or slander of the Company and its respective officers, directors, employees, investors, shareholders, administrators, affiliates, divisions, subsidiaries, predecessor and successor corporations, and assigns or tortious interference with the contracts and relationships of the Company and its respective officers, directors, employees, investors, shareholders administrators, affiliates, divisions, subsidiaries, predecessor or successor corporations, and assigns. All inquiries by potential future employers of Employee will be directed to the Company's Vice President of Human Resources. Upon inquiry, the Company shall only state the following: Employee's last position and dates of employment.

15. NO ADMISSION OF LIABILITY. The Parties understand and acknowledge that this Agreement constitutes a compromise and settlement of disputed claims. No action taken by the Parties hereto, or either of them, either previously or in connection with this Agreement shall be deemed or construed to be (a) an admission of the truth or falsity of any claims heretofore made or (b) an acknowledgment or admission by either Party of any fault or liability whatsoever to the other Party or to any third party.

16. COSTS. The Parties shall each bear their own costs, expert fees, attorney's fees and other fees incurred in connection with this Agreement.

17. ARBITRATION. The Parties agree that any and all disputes arising out of the terms of this Agreement, their interpretation, any of the matters herein released, shall be the subject to binding arbitration in (state employee lives/works) before the American Arbitration Association under its rules. Employee agrees to hereby waive his right to a jury trial as to matters arising out of the terms of this Agreement and any matters herein released. The Parties agree that the prevailing party in any arbitration shall be entitled to injunctive relief in any court of competent jurisdiction to enforce the arbitration award.

18. AUTHORITY. The Company represents and warrants that the undersigned has the authority to act on behalf of the Company and to bind the Company and all who may claim through it to the terms and conditions of the Agreement. Employee represents and warrants that he has the capacity to act on his own behalf and on behalf of all who might claim through him to bind them to the terms and conditions of this Agreement. Employee warrants and represents that there are no liens or claims of lien or assignments in law or equity or otherwise of or against any of the claims or causes of action released herein.

19. NO REPRESENTATIONS. Employee represents that he has had the opportunity to consult with any attorney, and has carefully read and understands the scope and effect of the provisions of this Agreement. Neither party has relied upon any representations or statements made by the other party hereto which are not specifically set forth in this Agreement.

20. A FULL AND COMPLETE DEFENSE. It is specifically agreed that in the event of any legal proceeding against the Company of the nature of that addressed by this Agreement, this Agreement shall serve as a full and complete defense to any such proceeding. It also further agreed that should Employee breach any of the terms of this Agreement, the Company shall be entitled to recover all sums paid pursuant to this Agreement and take any and all legal action should Employee fail to reimburse the Company, which action shall include the cost of recovery, including attorneys' fees.

21. SEVERABILITY. In the event that any provision hereof becomes or is declared by a court of competent jurisdiction to be illegal, unenforceable or void, this Agreement shall continue in full force and effect without said provision.

22. ENTIRE AGREEMENT. This Agreement represents the entire agreement and understanding between the Company and Employee concerning Employee's separation from the Company, and supercedes and replaces any and all prior agreements and understandings concerning Employee's relationship with the Company and his compensation by the Company.

23. NO ORAL MODIFICATION. This Agreement may only be amended in writing signed by Employee and the President of the Company.

24. GOVERNING LAW. This Agreement shall be governed by the laws of the State of _____.

25. EFFECTIVE DATE. This Agreement is effective seven days after it has been signed by both Parties.

26. COUNTERPARTS. This Agreement may be executed in counterparts, and each counterpart shall have the same force and effect as an original and shall constitute an effective, binding agreement on the part of each of the undersigned.

27. VOLUNTARY EXECUTION OF AGREEMENT. This Agreement is executed voluntarily and without any duress or undue influence on the part or behalf of the parties hereto, with the full intent of releasing all claims. The Parties acknowledge that:

(a) They have read this Agreement;

(b) They have been represented in the preparation, negotiation, and execution of this Agreement by legal counsel of their own choice or that they have voluntarily declined to seek such counsel;

(c) They understand the terms and consequences of this Agreement and of the releases it contains;

(d) They are fully aware of the legal and binding effect of this Agreement.

IN WITNESS WHEREOF, the Parties have executed this Agreement on the respective dates set forth below.

Dated: _____
By: _____
for [Corporation Name]

SEVEN CHAPTER

Dated: _____

_____, an individual.

Other documentation sometimes attached as an appendix to the agreement might include a negotiated reference statement.

Complying with the Older Workers Benefit Protection Act

Terminating older employees involves some additional legal concerns. Employees 40 years of age or older are a protected class as proscribed by the Age Discrimination in Employment Act (ADEA). Under the Older Workers Benefit Protection Act, when dealing with these older employees, certain procedures must be complied with by employers in order for a release of liability and waiver of rights to sue the company to be valid and enforceable. This is to insure that such waivers are indeed knowing and voluntary on the part of the employee. The six basic requirements for a valid waiver are as follows.

1. The release of liability must be part of an agreement in writing between the employee and the employer and written in plain, understandable, and ordinary English. This means no legalese. The employee must understand what rights he or she is relinquishing and do so in a *knowing and voluntary manner*.

2. The employee must receive compensation in consideration for the waiver of rights that is *above and beyond* what he or she is otherwise entitled to receive from the company. For example, if the employee handbook stipulates that all employees will receive a certain amount of severance pay upon separation from employment, then the agreement must stipulate an amount of money exceeding what is stated in the employee handbook. In this regard, it is often a good idea to pay the employee some hard cash as part of the consideration underlying the agreement on the part of the employee not to sue the company. Keep in mind that pay for the provision of outplacement counseling services also constitutes valid consideration as long as it is something that the employee would otherwise not be entitled to receive by virtue of his or her employment.

3. The agreement must specifically refer to, and waive, any rights arising under the ADEA. Otherwise, the agreement will not constitute a waiver of any possible age discrimination claim the employee may have and later decide to file against an employer.

4. The agreement and cover letter should provide that the employee understands that he or she is *not* waiving any rights or claims that might arise *after* the agreement is signed. For example, say that the

employer provides a false or inaccurate reference. The employer still could be sued by the employee for such defamation. Enforceable waivers cannot cover rights or claims that might arise after the date the agreement is executed.

5. The employee must be advised in the body of the agreement that he or she has the right to consult with an attorney before signing the waiver agreement. To borrow a phrase from criminal law, this can be called the Miranda Rights of employment termination law. The employee must be given sufficient time to decide whether or not to sign the employee separation agreement. In order for the agreement to effectively waive rights under the ADEA, the employee must be given at least 21 days to consider the agreement. However, if the employer is seeking the waiver of rights in connection with a program being offered to a group or class of employees, this period must be at least 45 days. The employee need not take 21 days or 45 days to sign the agreement, but the employee must be *offered* that much time to do so.

6. The employee must be allowed seven calendar days after signing the agreement to revoke it. Typically, the employer provides the employee with a form to signify that the revocation period has run before tendering the agreed-upon consideration to the employee. This cannot be waived by the employee. However, in many cases, the employee will realize that the sooner he or she signs the agreement, the sooner the seven days begin to run, and the sooner, therefore, he or she will receive the agreed-upon consideration which underlies the promise not to take legal action against the employer.

Questions often arise relative to structuring the payment of monies to employees for the consideration underlying the agreement from the employee not to sue the employer. Some companies prefer to pay the employee on a regular basis as if the employee were retained on the payroll through a certain date. This has the advantage of being easier on an employer's cash flow in most cases. There may also be benefits to the employee relative to eligibility for certain fringe benefits such as pension and profit-sharing bonuses. In such cases the employee's actual ending date for employment purposes can be extended, even though the employee's last day of work may be the date of the termination interview itself.

However, in some situations, a lump-sum payment to the employee is more advantageous to both the employee and the employer. In this regard, lump-sum payments can be treated as non-wage compensation to the employee. This means the employee will receive a 1099-MISC income statement for the amount of money tendered at the end of the applicable tax year. The advantage to the employer is that it need not pay matching FICA payments to the employee as if they were wages and the employee need not have wage deductions that reduce the payment. The additional advantage to the employee is that such payment then would not be considered wages paid for unemployment compensation purposes and the employee could begin collecting unemployment compensation immediately. The expense to the employer is still fully deductible as a business expense in the same way the payment to a vendor is considered a business expense because it is payment of consideration underlying the contract for services rendered.

In some situations in the past, for tax purposes such monetary consideration has been dealt with by the parties to the agreement as nontaxable income to the terminated employee in the same manner as payments in the settlement of a personal injury are usually treated. However, the U.S. Supreme Court has decided that the IRS has the legal right to treat such payments in age discrimination cases as taxable income. While the Court took great pains to express that its decision was limited to the facts of the case before it, the ruling is certainly subject to extension to other kinds of employment law cases such as Title VII discrimination cases.

The following are samples of forms that can be used for these kinds of situations:

[COMPANY LETTERHEAD]

[Date]

HAND DELIVERED

NAME AND ADDRESS OF EMPLOYEE

Re: Employee Separation Agreement

Offer by [Name of Company]

Dear _____:

After consideration and deliberation, it has been decided by the partners of the _____ Company that the position of office manager be eliminated.

It is, therefore, our duty to inform you that effective [Date], your position has been terminated with the Company.

However, in light of your years of service, it is our intention to offer you the enclosed Employee Separation Agreement as the means by which to terminate the employment relationship you have with the Company.

The terms of the offer to you are essentially as follows:

1. Your employment relationship ends with the Company effective [Date].

2. In agreeing to the Employee Separation Agreement, please understand that this Agreement includes the fact that you will be expressly waiving any and all rights with respect to all matters related to or connected with your employment at the Company which you now may have, and that you agree not to initiate any claim, demand, or cause of action, legal or otherwise, against the Company or any successor or assign or any other employee, officer, Board Director, Partner, agent or representative of the Company.

3. In return for this release of liability, the Company agrees to do the following for you:

    a. The Company will not object to any claim you may wish to make for unemployment compensation if you are out of work and otherwise eligible for it within the meaning of the State of Wisconsin Statutes.

    b. The Company agrees to provide you with outplacement counseling services through _____.

    c. The Company will pay the premium for your existing health insurance coverage for coverage through [Date].

    d. The Company will pay you the gross amount of _____ Dollars ($_____).

Please be advised that you will have until the end of the business day on Wednesday, [Date], three weeks from today's date, to accept this offer by the Company of the enclosed Employee Separation Agreement. After the close of the business day on Wednesday, [Date], the Company reserves the right to withdraw this offer.

Please be advised that in the event you choose not to sign this offer, you will be paid through [Date], but no additional consideration will be tendered to you by the Company.

In making this Employee Separation Agreement offer, the Company wants you to know that this Agreement must be voluntarily accepted by you for the purpose of making a full and final compromise adjustment and settlement of any and all claims, disputed or otherwise, on account of the employment relationship you have with it. This offer is made for the expressed purpose of precluding any further or additional claims arising out of the aforesaid relationship. In accordance with federal law, you have three weeks to accept this offer by the Company and, if you choose to accept it, another seven calendar days to revoke that acceptance should you change your mind.

In addition, please know that you have the right to consult an attorney of your own choosing prior to executing this Agreement.

Lastly, as expressly stated in the Agreement itself, please understand this waiver of any and all claims includes the waiving of potential claims which might arise under the Age Discrimination in Employment Act (ADEA). However, by signing this Agreement you are not waiving any right, claim, or cause of action which might arise after the Employee Separation Agreement is executed.

Please understand that any of the consideration provided for in the Employee Separation Agreement by the Company to you in return for your waiver of any and all rights against the Company is in addition to and does not affect in any manner other compensation you may have coming to you by virtue of your employment at the Company, such as your retirement plan payout, which will be accomplished pursuant to the terms of the Plan's procedures independent of the Employee Separation Agreement being offered to you.

Should you have any questions relative to the above or the enclosed, please feel free to contact the undersigned concerning them. We will be happy to answer any questions you or any representative you may choose to employ may have concerning the above or the enclosed.

In closing, we would like to extend our sincere gratitude for your many years of service and wish you the best of success in your future endeavors.

Sincerely,

[Company name]

By:_____

cc: Company Attorney

Employee Separation Agreement

THIS AGREEMENT, Made and entered into between [NAME AND AD-DRESS OF EMPLOYEE], employee of [Company], (hereinafter referred to as "Employee"), and [NAME AND ADDRESS OF COMPANY], (hereinafter referred to as "_____");

WITNESSETH:

A. Employee will be separated from employment at Company effective [Date].

B. Employee is willing to waive all rights with respect to any matter connected with her employment with Company.

C. In consideration for Employee's willingness to waive all rights connected with employment, Company is willing to give additional compensation to Employee as set forth below.

NOW, THEREFORE, IN CONSIDERATION OF THE MUTUAL COVENANTS of the parties hereto,

IT IS AGREED:

1. It is contemplated between Company and Employee that Employee's last day of work will be [Date], and her employment relationship will end effective [Date].

2. Employee expressly waives any and all rights with respect to all matters relating to or connected with her employment at Company which she now has and agrees not to initiate any claim, demand, or cause of action, legal or otherwise, against Company or any successor or assign or any other employee, officer, Board Director, agent or representative of Company, none of whom admit any liability to employee, but all expressly deny any liability from any such claim, demand, or cause of action.

3. Company agrees not to contest or object to any claim for unemployment compensation benefits by Employee based on her employment with Company so long as Employee is out of work and otherwise eligible for such unemployment compensation benefits within the meaning of the State Statutes.

4. Company agrees to pay to Employee upon signature of this Agreement and Seven-Day right to revocation Acknowledgment Form the gross amount of _____ Dollars ($_____) in release and forbearance of any and all claims, causes of action, and legal rights Employee may have based upon employment at Company.

5. Company will provide and pay for outplacement counseling through [Name and Address of Outplacement Agency].

6. Company agrees to pay Employee's COBRA continuation premium for health insurance coverage through [Date].

7. Employee and Company hereby declare that the terms of this Agreement have been completely read and are fully understood and are voluntarily accepted for the purpose of making a full and final compromise adjustment and settlement of any and all claims, disputed or otherwise, on account of the employment relationship above mentioned, and for the expressed purpose of precluding forever any further or additional claims arising out of the aforesaid relationship. Employee hereby acknowledges that in compliance with the Older Workers Benefit Protection Act that Employee has been notified that she has until [insert date 21 days later] to accept this offer by Company of the Employee Separation Agreement; that the above referenced consideration is above and beyond that to which she is already entitled by virtue of her employment relationship; that the above referenced waiver specifically also includes the waiving of potential claims which might arise under the Age Discrimination in Employment Act (ADEA); that the individual does not waive any rights or claims which might arise after this Employee Separation Agreement is executed; that Employee has been advised that after signing of this Agreement she will have seven (7) calendar days within which to revoke this Employee Separation Agreement; and that the Employee has been advised in writing of her right to consult with an attorney prior to executing this Agreement.

Signed in duplicate this ___ day of _____, 20___, at _____.

EMPLOYEE_____

COMPANY_____
By:_____

(Executed in Duplicate)

SEVEN-DAY RIGHT TO REVOCATION ACKNOWLEDGMENT FORM

I, [NAME OF EMPLOYEE], hereby acknowledge that [NAME OF COM-PANY] has tendered an Employee Separation Agreement offer which I voluntarily agreed to accept on [Date].

By this writing, I hereby certify that seven calendar days have elapsed since my voluntary acceptance of the above referenced offer and that I have voluntarily chosen not to revoke my acceptance of the above referenced Employee Separation Agreement.

Signed this _____ day of _____, 20___, at

_____

[Name of Employee]

A common question is: How much consideration should be paid to an employee? A rough rule of thumb is one week's pay per year of service. This seems to hold up generally well until there is a situation where the employee has been employed in excess of 20 years. Then this may amount to too much compensation.

Smaller businesses might consider using as a rule of thumb the average of 20 years of wages, not just the employee's wage as of the last day of work. However, if this sounds a little high to some employers, keep in mind that the European standard is actually one month's pay per year of service. Additionally, this was the amount recommended for a valid and enforceable waiver under the Model Termination of Employment Act as proposed by University of Michigan law professor, Theodore St. Antoine. In reality, this is a question that must be dealt with on a case-by-case basis by each employer.

In my opinion, these agreements can be the best way to deal with a difficult situation. In some situations, the employer knows that a discharge will bring with it a corresponding complaint of discrimination or other lawsuit. These situations can unnecessarily tangle the employer up in litigation and resulting attorneys' fees even if the complaint is defended successfully. Typically, what both the employer and the employee want most is to move ahead without being bound by the past. In fact, it is said that a poor manager can give an employee a raise and be hated for it, and a good manager can fire an employee and be thanked for it. Though the latter is rare, it is typically where, with the help of an outplacement counselor and time that heals all wounds, the former employee has been successful at obtaining new work in more favorable circumstances that pays more money than the previous job. All too often an individual is simply a bad fit for the company and not a bad person. Fitting the right person to the right job requires work and skill, but is almost always the result if this delicate matter is handled correctly by both parties.

Dealing with the Aftermath

When an employee is fired, his or her coworkers naturally want to know why. The trick is to alleviate their concerns while protecting the former employee's rights and avoiding a defamation lawsuit. Here's how you can do so:

Limit the number of people you inform. Start with management and supervisory staff. Call a small group meeting with the former employee's department as quickly as possible following the discharge. In a smaller shop a simple notice by the time clock might be appropriate to inform those outside the immediate department. If anyone has questions, they can be directed to supervisors who are alert and know what to say.

Don't give out too much information. Simply tell the employee's immediate coworkers that he or she has been discharged, so that the information remains in the circle of privileged communication. If they press for more information, tell them that the reasons will be kept confidential to protect the former employee's privacy. Everyone should appreciate the sensitivity of the matter.

Answer employees' questions. It is best to give out information on a need-to-know basis, explaining that certain information will remain confidential. But always address questions about how the situation will affect current employees. Most workers will want to know, for example, how work will be redistributed and if their own jobs are secure.

Sometimes the employee being discharged may ask to be the one to inform others in the department or throughout the company of the termination. Generally, this is not appropriate to allow because management has no control over what the discharged employee might say. However, in one case where a long-term manager had amicably agreed to an employee separation agreement, and it was emotionally important to the manager to say his good-byes, the company agreed to it under the following procedure. The manager was allowed to talk to certain individuals on a one-to-one basis for a short (no more than five-minute) conversation. What the discharged manager said was generally agreed upon upfront. The manager was informed that company management would be talking to each individual he spoke with immediately after the manager's conversation.

In this particular case, the arrangement worked smoothly because all parties to it were in harmony about the situation. However, this is an exception to the rule. But, as the discharged manager pointed out, his intentions were merely to affirm to his immediate subordinates that his termination was an amicable one and that he had enjoyed his working relationship with each of them over the years. In this particular case, the discharged manager had hired many of the subordinates. In the end, this approach worked to calm the fears of the people the manager had hired.

The idea is to handle the entire matter in a way which is as "face-saving" for the employee as possible, yet clearly notifies him that he no longer is employed at the company.

Giving Job References
Many employers dread the day they will be asked to give a reference for a less-than-satisfactory former employee. But if the situation is handled properly, providing a negative reference doesn't have to mean legal trouble.

The facts in one case are typical. An employee resigned her five-year post at an airline following a dispute over working conditions. She set about finding a new job and gave prospective employers the names of two of her supervisors for references.

Some time later, however, she still hadn't landed a job and became suspicious about the references she was receiving. She asked her boyfriend to call the firm and represent himself as an interested employer. One of her supervisors, who should have directed the inquiry to the personnel department, instead told the caller that she "does not work good with other people," "is a troublemaker," and "would not be a good person to rehire." The former employee then sued for defamation of character.

While this particular case ended favorably for the employer, it brings to light the concerns of many small-business owners who are asked to give job references. Certainly, when an employer provides a false reference that damages a former employee's reputation, that worker has every right to sue for defamation. But employers can be legally protected when giving a reference to another employer, and knowing the circumstances that can lead to a defamation suit will help you to avoid one.

Defining Defamation
Employees who claim defamation by an employer generally must show the following: that a false, defamatory statement has been made up; that the statement was expressed—either spoken or written—to a third party (known as publication); and that the statement caused harm or damage

to the employee or to his or her reputation and standing in the community at large.

Obviously, then, the first line of defense is to provide truthful references. If you make false statements, former employees could very well claim that your reference deterred others from hiring them and harmed their reputation. But even when you give a truthful reference, you must be particularly careful with your phrasing. Objective measures of job performance ("the individual was consistently late for work") are less susceptible to legal action than opinions of character ("she was lazy"). The same holds for subjective comments phrased as your opinion rather than as fact.

Once an employee shows that a statement is false and defamatory, he or she must prove that it was communicated to others. Clearly, if an employer makes a statement that might be considered defamatory directly to an employee, and nobody else hears it, there is no basis for a defamation suit. In addition, internal company communications, such as performance evaluations, are not considered public and therefore will not affect an employee's reputation in the community. These documents are considered to be privileged, and the employer is protected as long as the information remains internal.

By their very nature, of course, references are external. But communications between former and prospective employers also are privileged when they are made in good faith and for a legitimate purpose. In the aforementioned case, for example, this reasoning led the court to rule in the employer's favor. It found that the company's reference was "clothed with the mantle of a qualified privilege" because a former employer has an interest in open communications regarding an employee's work characteristics. The court pointed out that "without the protection of the privilege, employers might be reluctant to give sincere yet critical responses to requests for an appraisal of a prospective employee's qualifications."

This doesn't mean, however, that all unfavorable references will be protected by privilege. You could lose this privilege if a former employee shows that a negative reference was given with an intent to injure without just cause or excuse, or with wanton disregard for his or her rights. You'll also defeat the privilege if there appears to be *excessive publication* of the statements or a reckless disregard for whether the contents of a reference are true or false.

Preventive Measures

Unfortunately, no matter how objective and honest your reference, there's no guarantee that a former employee won't file a lawsuit. But there are some steps you can take to avoid, or at least prepare yourself for, this type of litigation.

Keep accurate files. Save all documentation, investigation reports, and proof of employee misconduct or poor work habits. This will help you defend yourself on the basis that there was substantial truth in the reference and that, therefore, it was not defamatory.

Take the time for exit interviews. When an employee resigns or is dismissed, discuss the type of information you'll provide in a written reference so that he or she is not surprised in the future.

Ensure that supervisors are properly trained. They should refer requests for references to human resources personnel who can handle the matter within the bounds of the law. Had the supervisors in the Chambers case followed this procedure, there would have been no case.

Determine whether the caller has a legitimate interest in the information. If you have any doubt about releasing information, ask the inquirer to submit a written release, signed by the former employee, authorizing your reference. This may help prove that you acted carefully and without malice.

Avoid answering requests for references over the phone. Instead, put your answers in writing. This way, there can be no misunderstanding about the tone of your voice or any pauses you make in your response to a question.

Choose your words objectively. You might say, for instance, that an individual was unproductive as opposed to lazy. And be particularly cautious when discussing crime. Instead of saying that the employee was a thief, consider saying he or she violated your policy concerning the private and personal use of company property. A more benign statement is less likely to have a long-term impact on the employee's ability to get a new job.

Obtain a written release of liability from the former employee before responding to reference requests. There should be a company policy for all such inquiries. The person asking for the reference should be told that this is your policy on *all* reference requests and that you would be happy to respond in writing once you receive the release.

Of course, to be completely safe, a company may adopt a policy of not providing references at all. Although this approach will indeed limit liability, it does a disservice to prospective employers and to former employees who deserve a favorable reference. With a little preparation and discretion, there really is no need for avoidance; you should feel free to give references, good and bad. Moreover, adopting a "no reference" policy removes a strong motivating tool from a manager's "toolbox." When working under a no reference policy, employees have no fear of ever receiving a negative reference so there are no ramifications for poor performance beyond an existing position.

As part of a trend to encourage the practice of giving references, many states have taken the step of codifying by statute the employer's right to provide another employer a reference, good or bad, as long as this privilege is not abused. Follow the guidelines provided above, and it can be a powerful tool for proper hiring that will benefit all concerned.

Answers to Chapter Seven Test Your Knowledge

1. True, 2. d, 3. True, 4. True, 5. e, 6. f, 7. True, 8. False, 9. d, 10. True.

CHAPTER EIGHT

Winning Denials of Unemployment Compensation Benefit Claims

Unemployment Compensation in a Nutshell

The Employer's Obligations

General Rules for Benefit Eligibility

Types of Employee Misconduct

Winning Benefit Denial at Appeal Hearings

Test Your Knowledge
of Unemployment Compensation Issues

1. True or False? An employee out of work is presumed eligible for unemployment insurance benefits if he or she worked a sufficient amount of time in four of the last five calendar quarters to qualify.

2. True or False? An employee who is fired for cause from employment is automatically disqualified for unemployment insurance benefits.

3. Which of the following conduct connected with employment, if proved, would result in a finding of "misconduct" such that an employee would be determined to be ineligible for unemployment insurance benefits?
    a. Insubordination.
    b. Neglect of duty.
    c. Absence without notice after warnings.
    d. Violation of employer policy prohibiting sexual harassment.
    e. Falsification of work record such as an employment application.
    f   All of the above.

4. True or False? Employer conduct such as a significant reduction in salary or failure to stop sexual harassment after a complaint may result in an award of unemployment insurance benefits even though the employee voluntarily quit employment.

5. True or False? Employer policies and work rules are considered reasonable if violations of them harm the employer's business interests or property.

6. True or False? An employee's continued pattern of indifference toward the rules and policies of an employer, especially after warnings, may result in a finding of misconduct even if any of the incidents taken alone may not have been serious enough to lead to a decision to discharge from employment.

7. True or False? An employer must prove that employee misconduct connected with employment violated a specific published work rule before a claim for unemployment insurance benefits against the employer will be denied.

8. True or False? Employee conduct outside the workplace can result in a finding of misconduct connected with employment if a rea-

sonable employee in like circumstances would have known that such conduct was or would be harmful to the employer's business or property, such as striking a supervisor while off-duty away from the plant.

9. True or False? A single, isolated incident in itself may be serious enough to justify a denial of a claim for unemployment insurance benefits if it is conduct of a serious nature and likely to cause damage to the business or property of the employer, such as insubordination or dishonesty.

10. True of False? On average, unemployment insurance claim statistics reveal that approximately 25 percent of the time an employee's appeal of a denial of a benefit claim will be successful and approximately 20 percent of the time an employer's appeal of an initial determination of benefit eligibility will be successful. After the Appeal hearing approximately 3 percent of the appeals of either party succeed.

The answers to these questions are at the end of this chapter.

Unemployment Compensation—Background

In 1935, as part of the Social Security Act signed by President Roosevelt, a federal-state unemployment insurance system was established. This system was designed to provide weekly cash benefits to unemployed workers who lost their jobs through cyclical or structural changes in the economy. In other words, an insurance-type fund was created to pay people who were generally unemployed through no fault of their own. These benefit payments were designed for those workers who had at least moderate work experience in the year prior to losing their jobs and were otherwise able and available for work on the general labor market. Thus, the intended function of the system was to provide a type of insurance to workers who are subject to cyclical swings in income as a budgeting aid, to provide jobless workers with the income to search for new jobs, and to stabilize the overall level of economic activity as a counter-cyclical program which would serve to decrease the extent of depressionary swings in the economy.

Unlike social welfare programs, such as Aid to Families with Dependent Children (AFDC), which are assessed on a needs basis, unemployment compensation is an insurance program and is provided without regard to the economic condition of the unemployed claimant. While there is a joint federal-state administrative responsibility to provide for the program, each state remains responsible for funding its own regular unemployment compensation benefit costs, regardless of how severe unemployment may become or how such unemployment has been caused. State unemployment tax contributions that are not immediately paid out in benefits are used to build up a state's unemployment insurance reserves. Accordingly, states generally build up their funds during economic upswings and run them down during hard times. Regardless of what any existing state philosophy may be relative to employer contribution taxes, recent history has shown us that long periods of higher-than-expected unemployment can "break" a state fund and force borrowing from the federal government. Indeed, at one time, Wisconsin's state fund, reputed to be one of the best-administered state systems, was losing $1 million a day in benefits and was nearly $650 million in the red. Employers in those states that were forced to borrow in the early 1980s have only recently finished paying off the interest due to the federal government through special assessments and contribution tax increases.

Unemployment Compensation in a Nutshell

Unemployment compensation is a program administered by the individual states, within mandated federal guidelines, that provides for the payment of benefits in specified amounts to legally covered workers

Winning Denials of Unemployment Compensation Benefit Claims

when they are out of work and otherwise eligible. These benefits are financed by a payroll tax assessed against an employer's defined payroll. The level of such benefits and tax contribution rates varies from state to state, being generally influenced by the employer's benefit claim experience. For employers who have stable employment and who win their contested cases, the unemployment compensation tax rates will be lower.

A claimant's potential benefit rights are determined by his or her work in a "base period." This is usually determined by a claimant's work experience in the year preceding the filing of the first benefit claim. Those benefit rights are then available to the claimant during the "benefit year." This is normally the next year after the commencement of a "valid new claim."

The eligibility requirements vary, but generally, to be eligible for benefits, a claimant must have a specified amount of work experience in the base period preceding the claim. The amount of work and level of earnings necessary varies from state to state. However, it is important to note that the work does not have to be with one employer, but can include work with several employers combined.

The number of weeks of eligibility for benefits will be determined as a function of the duration of employment and the amount of earnings in the base period, for up to a specified maximum number of weeks. There is also a cap on the highest weekly benefit rate. As a rule of thumb, it can be estimated that claimants will be entitled to one-half their average weekly earnings for six months, with maximum payout at approximately between $250 to $350 per week, the total maximum payout being approximately $7,500 in any one-year period. However, once a claimant's benefit rights have been established, they will remain in effect until exhausted or until the benefit year expires, whichever comes first.

The Employer's Obligations

Several obligations are imposed upon employers by the unemployment compensation laws. In addition to being obligated to pay the payroll tax, certain notices and reports are required from covered businesses.

First, the state unemployment compensation departments will furnish posters that notify workers that they might be eligible for benefits should they become unemployed. The posters also indicate the location of the office where an employee may file a claim and the type of information required. These posters must be placed where they will most likely be seen by employees; for example, on a bulletin board near the time clock, if the employer uses one.

The importance of posting this information is that the employer is relieved of the obligation to individually notify each worker of possible eligibility for benefits when a worker is laid off or terminated. Displaying the poster in a proper location will protect the employer against claims that may be filed long after an employee's termination. This can happen where the claimant asserts that the reason for delayed filing was that the employee was unaware of possible benefits and eligibility.

In the early years of unemployment compensation, laid-off workers were given a slip of paper in their last paycheck with information as to where and when to file for unemployment compensation benefits. The color of this form was pink, hence the origin of the term "pink slip." Today this information is conveyed by the poster.

A second obligation imposed upon employers is that of completing and returning to the unemployment compensation departments certain benefit-related reports. When an employee files for unemployment compensation, a report form is generally sent to the employer. This report will ask how many weeks the employee worked and what earnings were made during these weeks. These facts are then used to determine if the claimant has the necessary qualifying employment and what may be the potential benefit rights. The report also usually includes a box or space that may be checked or filled out to indicate whether the employer believes there may be some legal reason why the employee is ineligible or disqualified for benefits. It is here that an employer first begins to contest benefits.

A report filed without an entry indicating a reason for disqualification will be treated as conceding the payment of benefits to the employee. Unless the payment of unemployment compensation benefits is contested by the employer, any and all claims will be treated as if conceded by the employer and will be paid if the claimant is unemployed and otherwise eligible.

Typically, this preliminary notice will also ask if the employer desires to be present when the former employee is interviewed about the employer's objection to the benefits claim. A personal appearance at this interview is the single most important action an employer can take to help it win objections to contested claims. There is no substitute for a personal presentation in persuading an official to deny a claim. Moreover, when a company responds by mail or telephone, there simply is no way to counteract false statements made by a claimant to win eligibility for benefits. Often personal appearances will be discouraged. However, if an employee holds firm, in many cases it will be allowed.

Modern communications technology makes it possible for an ex-employee to file a claim for benefits over the telephone in contrast to the traditional method of facing the dreaded "unemployment insurance line." Indeed, given the mobility of our society, even telephone hearings are common. At the same time, employers can still make their objections to claims in person, if one is willing to take the time and trouble to do so. In practice most correspondence is handled by fax and telephone.

Other forms are typically required by a state unemployment agency when during a claim period the employer learns that the claimant earned some wages in a week for which benefits are also claimed. Inform the Agency if there is any possible disqualification for benefits by reason of employment (or re-employment) or separation from work under disqualifying circumstances. Again, a late or incompletely filed report will be treated as a concession of benefit eligibility. If this concession results in an erroneous payment of benefits to the claimant, the employer's account will be nonetheless charged for all of these. In some states this can happen even though such payments might not be based on work for that employer; for instance, where the claimant held several jobs during the year before layoff. This may result in an increased tax contribution rate, depending upon the experience of the employer in the future.

A failure to pay attention to these reports and notices can cost businesses money.

General Rules for Benefit Eligibility

The key to most eligibility determinations is ascertaining the cause of the separation from employment. Was it the result of an action on the part of the employer, such as a layoff for lack of work, or was it the result of an action by the employee, such as a voluntary quitting of employment or job-related misconduct that prompted a discharge?

In the first example, a layoff for lack of work is certainly not the fault of the employee. An individual so laid off would be eligible for benefits if enough weeks had been worked and sufficient wages earned to qualify during the base period year prior to first claiming benefits.

In the second example, it is the employee's own conduct that occasioned the separation from employment. Where the employee is the cause of the unemployment, ineligibility for benefits is based on events that occurred at the time of separation from the last employer. In theory, but for the individual's own actions, he or she would still be working.

The "Quit" Exceptions

Normally, a voluntary termination of employment by the employee, commonly referred to as a "quit," will result in disqualification for unemployment compensation benefits. As stated above, employees are in control of their destiny in this regard and, in theory, would otherwise be working but for their own decision not to. In such cases, employees should not be eligible for benefits. However, there are exceptions to this general rule.

Employees lose substantial rights when they quit. For example, in most states, they will be ineligible for benefits until they find new work and remain employed for a certain period of time. In some states this period can be up to two months long, and the workers must be earning at least their former salary or average weekly wage at such work before they can requalify for further unemployment compensation benefits. Typically, in most states, any benefits received by the claimant will not be charged against the original employer's account for the determination of unemployment compensation tax rates.

Accordingly, the nature of the separation from employment is often an important issue in these situations. The circumstances under which the separation from employment occurred can often be ambiguous or disputed and may be interpreted in a variety of ways by an adjudicator. For example, they may be treated as a discharge, a layoff, a suspension, or even a job refusal in addition to being a quit. Under each situation, the rules for eligibility for unemployment benefits are different, and the burden of proof may change. Normally, the party objecting to the payment of benefits, the employer, has the burden of proving the reason for the disqualification. However, after the fact of a quit has been established, the burden of persuasion shifts to the employee to prove that eligibility may be established under one of the exceptions to the statute.

Any particular quit situation often presents the following issues to be decided in the administration of a claim for benefits:

- Did the employee quit or was the employee discharged?

- If the employee quit, does one of the exceptions apply so that eligibility is nevertheless retained?

- If the employee was discharged, did the reason for discharge amount to misconduct so that the employee is otherwise disqualified for benefits?

- Was the employee suspended for disciplinary reasons before quitting? If so, what was the major force causing the separation from employment, the discipline or the quit?

- In lieu of a layoff, was the employee offered other work which he or she refused? Was such a refusal a quit in reality?

Obviously, this issue is not as clear-cut as it may appear at first glance. The advocacy of a particular interpretation flowing from the nature of the facts can be very important in determining benefit eligibility.

Distinguishing a Quit from a Discharge

The most common question where the facts are uncertain is whether an employee quit or was discharged. However, when an employee shows that he intends to leave his employment and he indicates such intention by word or matter of action, or by conduct inconsistent with the continuation of the employee-employer relationship, it will be held that the employee intended and did leave his employment voluntarily.

How is this applied? Where an employee was told by the manager in a conference to "get the hell out," the leaving of work was reasonably based on the conclusion that he was discharged. Similarly, where the employer sent an employee home accompanied by statements of the nature that the employee "better clean up his act," it could also be construed as a discharge. However, in most situations, it will be held that the employee has an affirmative obligation to confirm the fact of the discharge, and failing to do so may be considered a quit. For example, an employee may object to a reprimand and tell the supervisor that he doesn't have to take this kind of treatment, to which the supervisor responds that if the employee cannot take the treatment of being corrected, he might as well go home. The employee who goes home can be construed to have quit if he does not come back to work and, should he file a claim, he will therefore be ineligible for unemployment compensation benefits.

As always, the best preventive practice for employers to take is to avoid ambiguous situations by sending a letter confirming the status of employment based on the employer's understanding of events. This can also arise in the context of an employer's work rule stating, for example, that three days' absence without notice will be construed a quit on the part of the employee. In such cases, it is suggested that the best method of winning the case is not to argue the quit, but to immediately say that the employee had been discharged pursuant to company policy, of which the employee was well aware.

In such situations, the employer must be ready to establish that it does indeed have such a policy. For example, in one case an employer, without putting into evidence the work rules listed in the employee handbook, said that an employee had been absent for three days without notice and therefore had quit. The employee countered by saying that he had not quit and, in fact, had been absent without notice on a prior occasion for two days without sustaining any penalty and therefore felt that three days would make no difference. The Administrative Law Judge (ALJ), in awarding benefits, ruled that because the employer did not introduce evidence of its work rule in the employee handbook to sustain its burden of proof, the ALJ believed, rightly or wrongly, that the employee was not engaging in misconduct when he failed to contact the employer and that therefore the employee should not be denied benefits under the circumstances.

Quitting Without Formal Notice

In many cases, the employee's intention to quit may be inferred from situations where the employee's actions are inconsistent with continuing the employment. Examples of such situations include employee absence without notice, refusal of a transfer, or refusing to meet job requirements without proper justification.

If an employee takes an unauthorized leave or is absent for a prolonged period of time without proper notice or justification, this in and of itself may constitute misconduct. Sometimes these situations arise when employees are absent on personal or medical leave and do not contact the employer after such leaves have expired. For example, many leave provisions, embodied as policies in employee handbooks, give a specific length of time that employees may take. If this period expires without notification from the employee, and the employer can prove that the employee was or should have been fully aware of the end of such leave of absence, it may be deemed a quit on the part of the employee. In this regard, employers should be careful to document by letter to the employee the employer's understanding of the situation at the beginning of such leave of absence. This is particularly the case for medical leaves where certification by a physician of physical inability to work is for an indefinite period.

It has also been held by the courts that an employee's refusal to accept reasonable transfer when work is being cut back is a "constructive quit" that disqualifies the employee from receiving benefits. This is true even when the transfer perhaps could have been properly refused by the employee within the parameters of a union contract but nevertheless results in the employee being out of work. In such situations, it is held that the employee could be working but for the employee's own decision not to accept suitable work and therefore is ineligible for unemployment compensation benefits.

An interesting situation occurs where an employee acts reasonably in refusing to abide by company work rules or contractual requirements.

Winning Denials of Unemployment Compensation Benefit Claims

Such employees often are held not to have demonstrated an intent to sever the employment relationship and, therefore, not to have quit if the refusal or failure to follow rules has "meritorious justification." This might be found in cases where employees refuse to pay union dues on religious grounds and are subsequently discharged, or where liquor store employees refuse to be bonded because of the additional personal liability that would be imposed.

Employer-Induced Discharges

In certain cases, a quit that appears to be a voluntary termination of employment on its face may be found to be a discharge because the employer provoked or induced the resignation. Again, the focus of the hearing officer or ALJ is often related to which party initiated the separation action.

For example, in one case, a high school teacher was informed that if her performance did not improve, the high school principal would recommend nonrenewal of her contract. The principal then went one step further and advised the teacher to quit before such action happened. The teacher followed the advice and quit because she feared that her future employment would be jeopardized if her appeal of a nonrenewal decision was unsuccessful. It was held that the teacher's action was not a quit, but rather a discharge.

In another case, a school employee having a romantic affair with a school board member was given full wages through the end of his contract on the condition that he waive his right to a hearing and submit his resignation immediately. It was held that since the employer initiated the separation and induced the employee to resign, it was not a quit, but rather a discharge, even though the employee signed a statement that he voluntarily terminated his employment.

Discharge Before Resignation Date

Another issue that often arises is the effective date of a quit and its implications. For example, an employee who gives a definite date of termination may be held to that date by the employer, even if the employee later changes his or her mind and attempts to rescind the decision to quit. However, if an employee indicates an intention to quit but does not specify a date and the employer thereafter discharges the employee, it has been held not to be a quit. In one situation, a maintenance worker informed the employer that he would be looking for new work. When the employer replaced him, it was held to be a discharge. The employer then had the burden of proof to show the discharge was for misconduct connected with employment if it was to contest the former employee's claim for benefits.

What happens when the employee announces an intended date to quit, but the employer accelerates the process? Such claimants are found to have been discharged on the earlier date and are initially eligible for benefits unless discharged for misconduct, in which case they would later become ineligible after the intended date of the quitting.

Quitting for Good Cause

From the employer's point of view, the largest loophole in these discharge/quit situations is where the employee admits quitting but claims that the action was for good cause attributable to the employer. In this regard, it has been held that "good cause attributable to the employing unit" means some act or omission by the employer that justifies the employee's quitting. It must involve some fault on the part of the employer that is real and substantial. In addition, the cause of the quit must be attributable to the employer, and not just any good cause such as compelling personal reasons.

Ordinarily, to hold the employer responsible for real and substantial harm to the employee which justifies a quit, the employee must have made timely and adequate complaints to the employer and must have given the employer adequate time to rectify the situation. However, these efforts are not required if they would be unreasonable or futile, considering the circumstances. As such, these situations are decided on a case-by-case basis, but some common situations can be identified.

Where the employee quits because of a unilateral, material change in the terms of employment by the employer, such as a reduction from full-time to part-time status, it can be held to be good cause for quitting. This also includes cases where an employer may change the terms or basis of compensation to the detriment of the employee. For example, if a salesperson's compensation is changed from a weekly salary to a low base pay plus commission, that may justify an employee's quitting with good cause attributable to the employing unit. Therefore, the employee may be eligible for benefits. However, this does not mean that all "concessionary" readjustments (such as lowering an employee's pay) will justify quitting. If the cuts apply uniformly to all workers, the hearing officer or ALJ may hold that although it may be a reduction in pay, the employee would otherwise be working and earning but for his or her own decision to quit. In some states, in order to be a substantial pay cut that would justify a quit, the cut must be more than one-third of the employee's wages. Uniform cuts in wages, necessitated by an employer's financial problems and not designed to induce the employee to quit, have been held not to be good cause for a quit.

However, an employer's failure to comply with the terms of a union contract or issuance of paychecks that are returned for insufficient funds may be good cause. Additionally, failure to sell a business to a manager who was promised the opportunity to buy it as an inducement to accept employment has been held good cause to quit.

Another category of good cause is where the employer engages in illegal acts and the employee quits because of them. For example, an employee may have good cause to quit if the employer makes unlawful wage deductions or requires an employee to work excessive hours in violation of state law, or attempts to implicate an employee in criminal fraud.

In addition, employees are not expected to suffer abuse or mistreatment from an employer and its supervisors. This might include continuous harassment and undue criticism, or improper investigation of employee actions, such as the invasion of an employee's locker and unreasonable interrogation in front of other employees during the course of an investigation for theft. Of course, reasonable criticism and the denial of greater compensation are prerogatives of management and do not constitute good cause. However, if an employer's discipline can be found to be improper or abusive, the employee may have good cause to quit. For example, in one case, a disciplinary layoff imposed for excusable medical absence constituted such improper discipline that gave the employee good cause to quit. In another case, a four-week disciplinary suspension imposed on an employee for an error in bookkeeping that had resulted in part from poor training was held to be improper or abusive and justified a quit.

An employee may quit with good cause if working conditions are dangerous, unhealthy, or unsatisfactory due to lack of proper equipment. In one case, it was held that a production worker had quit for good cause when he refused to clean the employees' restroom because proper cleaning equipment was not available. An employee quit because his request for investigation and protection by the employer when his ribs were broken at work by a coworker was not satisfied, and such quitting was held to be with good cause. For a truck driver on an inner-city route where the company refused to protect him from harassment and potential robbery, such working conditions were found to be too dangerous and his quitting was with good cause, so that he was awarded unemployment compensation benefits.

Lastly, in some states, a compelling reason for quitting would by statute include sexual harassment of an employee.

One of the most complicated areas in this regard is where an employee quits for personal or family health reasons. Often, an employee who quits because of being physically unable to do his or her customary work may nevertheless be eligible for benefits, if the worker had no reasonable alternative to quitting, but is still physically able to do work in the general labor market. Here, an example would be an employee who develops a disabling allergy to materials he is required to work with and is, therefore, forced to quit. However, if there is other work available in the general labor market that would not affect such an allergy, the employee would not be eligible for benefits. The important criterion here is that the employee is still available for other work in the general labor market. In addition, the employee must explore every "reasonable alternative to quitting" and must ordinarily give the employer notice of the health problem and an opportunity to accommodate the employee, if possible.

Benefits Denied Because of Misconduct Connected with Employment
Misconduct in General

The most frequently cited employer frustration with unemployment compensation is when an employee is fired for misconduct and yet is found eligible for benefits. In this regard, an employer's objection to a claim for unemployment compensation benefits can be likened to the prosecution of a criminal matter by a district attorney. The burden of proof is upon the employer to establish the misconduct connected with the employee's employment. Remember that the presumption is that a claimant is deemed eligible for benefits unless the employer properly establishes timely objections to the contrary. However, through a blend of normal management practices, diligent preparation, and the establishment of the employer's case through correct testimony at the investigations and hearings, most objections to unemployment compensation claims can be won and, if appealed, later affirmed through the agency review procedures and reviewing courts.

It's important to understand that discharge decisions should not be made on the basis of the employer's desire to avoid unemployment compensation liability. A counterproductive employee can cost a business enterprise much more in the long run than any increase in the employer's experience rating for unemployment compensation taxing purposes. However, many discharges can be shown to be for what would be called "misconduct connected with employment" so that the discharged employee is ineligible for benefits and the employer's tax rate is unaffected.

The following pages discuss disqualifications from unemployment compensation benefit eligibility for misconduct connected with employment.

The standard definition for misconduct is reviewed with a brief analysis of its application in several areas of employee conduct. An explanation of the proper application of corrective progressive discipline and documentation thereof is followed by a review of the evidence necessary to establish misconduct. Lastly, a checklist of sample basic interrogatories to use for the employer's witness in an unemployment compensation proceeding is provided.

The Standard Definition of "Misconduct"

The Wisconsin Supreme Court, in the case of *Boynton Cab Company v. Neubeck and Ind. Comm.* (237 Wis. 249 (1941)), set the standard meaning of the term "misconduct connected with employment" in the United States as applied to unemployment compensation. The court stated in part, as follows:

> . . . the intended meaning of the term "misconduct" . . . is limited to conduct evincing such willful or wanton disregard of standards of behavior which the employer has a right to expect of his employee or in carelessness or negligence of such degree or recurrence as to manifest equal culpability, wrongful intent or evil design, or to show an intentional and substantial disregard of the employer's interests or of the employee's duties and obligations to his employer.

In other words, almost as in a criminal matter, did the employee intend to harm the employer's interests by the action or omission to act that brought about the employee's discharge? Was the employee trying to do a good job but just did not perform up to expectations, or was the employee purposely involved with something more important than doing the job he or she was being paid to perform?

Under the statutes governing unemployment compensation as interpreted by the courts, the mere fact that the employee has been fired is not in and of itself sufficient grounds for that employee to be automatically disqualified from benefits. The burden of proof is on the employer to establish the reason for discharge and also that the employee's conduct that prompted the discharge was a willful or wanton disregard of the employer's interests and the standard of behavior the employer had a right to expect.

In explanation of the judgment of employee intent, the Wisconsin Supreme Court, in *Boynton Cab, supra,* drew from coherent explanations in prior English law:

> [However, while a single isolated instance of impropriety generally does not amount to misconduct so as to result in a

denial of unemployment compensation benefits,] a continued course of indifference toward work, particularly after repeated warnings, may be tantamount to an intentional disregard of the employer's interest so that they constitute misconduct. In such cases, it can be assumed that, although the worker may not have intentionally disregarded rules and instructions, his past behavior indicates in a general way that he is indifferent toward his obligations and his duties.

The seemingly overlooked question that often arises is whether a single isolated incident can be construed as misconduct. The *Boynton Cab* court again cited from English interpretation, which stated as follows:

As a general rule, it may be said that a single instance of negligence or mistake is not sufficient evidence of misconduct . . . but to this rule there are exceptions . . . and when the direct consequences of an act or omission are fairly obvious to an applicant, and are such as to be likely to cause serious loss to the employer, his business or his property, a finding of misconduct is not unreasonable . . . .

From another English source, the court also stated:

Gross and serious carelessness in even a single instance . . . may be tantamount to an intentional disregard of the employer's interests so that they constitute misconduct.

The courts have affirmed recognition of this principle. In one such case, an employee was discharged for bringing a six-pack of beer onto the employer's premises in violation of the employer's work rule prohibiting "the possession or use on the company premises of intoxicating beverages, narcotics, or other dangerous drugs." In reversing the agency ruling allowing unemployment compensation benefits, the court stated as follows:

The mention of it being an isolated incident and of the employee's prior good work record in the findings indicates that the department considered the penalty of discharge for a first offense . . . too severe a form of discipline. However, so long as a violation of the rule was intentional . . . the discharge was for misconduct connected with the employment within the meaning of the statutes. The statute does not require that the employer first resort to some lesser degree of discipline than discharge merely because it is a first violation of a shop rule.

Types of Employee Misconduct

General examples of employee conduct that have been found to consti-tute misconduct include excessive absenteeism and excessive tardiness; dishonesty, such as theft or falsification of work records; insubordination, such as direct disobedience of valid work orders, refusal to perform assigned work, and disregard or ridicule of those in authority; and neglect of duty such as sleeping on the job, horseplay, or extreme carelessness in the performance of work duties.

Regarding absenteeism and tardiness, the element of intent is not estab-lished unless it can be shown that the employee's absences were without valid reason and insufficient notice was given to the employer. However, repeated absence and tardiness, especially after warnings, for reasons such as transportation problems or personal errands can amount to misconduct. The courts' and agency's position on this issue was made clear recently in a decision that stated: "It is the employee's responsibility to arrange his personal life in such a manner which will allow him to arrive at work on time."

Regarding negligence or carelessness on the job, it is quite evident, as pointed out in *Boynton Cab, supra,* that "failure in good performance as a result of inability or incapacity, inadvertencies or ordinary negligence and isolated instances, or good faith errors in judgment or discretion are not to be deemed 'misconduct' within the meaning of the statute." The key elements, then, in establishing misconduct for negligent actions are that the conduct is part of a continuing pattern of behavior, that the employee has the ability to do the work, and that he or she has been given the proper training to perform the work. In one case dealing with this issue, a court stated:

> The four incidents referred to were more than inefficiency and unsatisfactory conduct; the employee did have the ability and capacity to do the work as demonstrated by almost three years of satisfactory performance; her negligence was not an isolated incident; she was not required to use judgment or discretion, but merely follow simple orders clearly given.

While self-defense would generally be a valid defense to an employee's involvement in an altercation in the workplace, an employee who pro-vokes an assault by use of threatening words or gestures, or by directing profane and obscene language at a coworker, may be found to have been discharged for misconduct. In addition, a worker who responds to such language by assaulting another worker also may be discharged for mis-conduct, even if provoked

Regarding insubordination, work assignments are generally within the prerogative of the employer and cannot be refused unless shown to be totally unreasonable. Furthermore, in a case where a worker was discharged for refusing to perform an assignment that he alleged violated the collective bargaining agreement, the court stated that "it is an elementary principle of labor law that an employee must accept the work assignment and then file a grievance to correct the situation if he believes the assignment violated the contract."

An important part of the definition of misconduct is that it is "connected with employment." However, merely because an incident may have taken place outside of work hours does not necessarily mean that it was not connected with employment. In one case, an employee was discharged after he engaged his supervisor in a fight over the weekend on a Saturday night. It was shown that the employee was disgruntled for the imposition of disciplinary action during the preceding week. Although the incident itself took place outside work hours and outside of the workplace, the court, in reversing the agency's decision, held that the battery was precipitated by a three-day disciplinary suspension for tardiness and insubordination given to the employee by the supervisor approximately a week before the incident. The court stated that an "objective test" of intent should be implied, i.e., would a reasonable person in like circumstances know that he was harming the employer's interests? The court found that a reasonable man would conclude that striking a supervisor is a willful interference with an employer's authority and "would likely undermine the ability of the supervisor to effectively supervise."

Proper Management of Corrective Progressive Discipline

The best way to establish disqualification for benefits because of a continued course of indifference toward work is through the mechanism of issuing progressive-step discipline to employees for violations of the standards of conduct an employer expects. While the courts have made it clear that "the unemployment compensation statute is not a single, 'little' labor relations law," progressive corrective discipline, as has been developed through the course of union/management labor relations history, is a guide for management to follow. When an employee's overall employment record shows prior warnings before the employee was discharged because of a culminating incident of employee misconduct, decisions have held that while perhaps each of the incidents in the employee's record standing alone would not amount to misconduct, the employee's overall record shows a continued pattern of indifference so as to amount to misconduct within the meaning of the statutes. Once an employee has received warnings for improper conduct, continuing that conduct not only establishes that the employee has been put on notice that such conduct will not be condoned by the employer, but also proves an intentional pattern of disregard for the employer's interest.

Proper documentation of progressive discipline steps would be to include notes in the employee's personnel file concerning the specific instances of misconduct. While the initial step in the process is often called a "verbal" warning, it is really a misnomer. Merely because a warning is verbal does not mean that it is not documented. A better term would be to call it a "first warning."

In addition, for subsequent evidentiary purposes, warning notices should be signed by the employee's supervisor at or about the time of the event that is described in the writing, with a copy provided to the employee. The form of the writing is immaterial and need not be on any specified company grievance forms. The notice should include a description of the conduct, the manner in which this conduct harmed the employer's interests, the extent to which future conduct of this type would jeopardize the employee's record, and the dated signature of the supervisor who observed the conduct and imposed the disciplinary action.

The question often arises as to the value of a warning notice that is not signed by the employee. While an employee's signature on the warning notice itself removes any possible claim that the disciplinary action was not received, it is not necessary to have the employee's signature on that document. When confronted with a situation where the employee disagrees with the given warning and then refuses to sign the warning notice, the supervisor should make a notation on the warning notice that the employee refused to sign it and then initial and date that notation.

Establishing Misconduct

After an employer objects to an unemployment compensation claim by an employee, an initial determination interview is held by an unemployment agency hearing officer or adjudicator. The adjudicator receives any information, both written and oral (either in person or over the telephone), that the employer chooses to provide and also takes a written statement from the employee. From this information, the adjudicator will make an initial determination regarding the eligibility of the claimant for benefits, from which the losing party has a right to appeal. Upon receipt of a timely appeal, an appeal hearing is held with an Administrative Law Judge presiding. This hearing is a trial *de novo*, meaning any evidence given earlier is wiped off the slate and the ALJ starts fresh with new evidence and testimony. With rare exceptions, it is the record from the ALJ that forms the basis of any further review by the unemployment agency or the state courts.

In establishing that the employee's conduct that led to the discharge was an intentional disregard of the standards of behavior that an employer has a right to expect, a four-part analysis has proven useful. It must be established that:

- here is a rule prohibiting the conduct that the employee engaged in;

- this rule is a reasonable rule;

- the employee was or reasonably should have been aware of the rule; and

- the employee violated this rule of conduct.

It must be understood that while it is recommended that the employer have rules of conduct, it is not necessary that employee misconduct be in violation of a specific written rule. There are many forms of conduct that violate the interest of the employer and do not need to be written down, because they are intuitively harmful to the employer's interests. However, the employer is best advised to have a set of written rules of conduct that it expects employees to follow. These can be placed in the employee handbook.

At the appeal hearings, the best results are obtained when a copy of the employee manual or handbook, which contains written work rules, is put into evidence. It is best when these rules are compiled in an easy-to-understand list, a copy is given to the employee when hired, and the rules are discussed with the employee in the new employee orientation program.

The work rules should always be submitted for admission into evidence at the appeal hearing. When doing so, it is best to elicit testimony that these work rules cover all employees in the shop, and that the rules were in effect during the time of the claimant's employment.

In order to establish that the rules are reasonable, the courts have looked more to the conduct of the employee rather than to the rule itself. However, in one case, a court gave a succinct definition: "A rule is reasonable if a violation of it is likely to harm the employer's interests."

It is important to establish in what way the employee's conduct was harmful to the interest of the employer. For example, if the employee's negligence caused a dollar amount of loss to the employer, that dollar amount should be put into evidence. If the employee's tardiness without notice rendered an assembly line inoperable, the dollar amount of product that was lost because the assembly line was not running should be put into evidence. The harm also could be intangible, such as that the employee was not on time to receive instructions from the employees leaving the preceding shift. In any event, it is important to establish the reasonableness of the rule by showing how a violation of the rule was harmful to the employer's interests in the particular circumstances involving the employee.

The third prong of the analysis is to establish that the employee was aware of the rule. The best method to establish this is to have the employee sign a statement acknowledging receipt of a copy of the rule or employee handbook. This signed and dated receipt can then be put into evidence. Such an exhibit makes it difficult to find credible an employee's defense that the existence of the rule was not known, or that the employer did not exercise due diligence in informing the employee of the rules.

It is only after establishing the foundation of the first three steps that direct testimony should be taken concerning the actual conduct of the employee that led to the discharge. It is vitally important to have the supervisor who actually witnessed the employee's conduct present at the hearing to describe what happened. Although the rules of evidence are somewhat lax in their application in an administrative hearing, the courts have made clear that no denial of benefits can be based upon hearsay testimony. A signed affidavit will not be enough to establish misconduct for a denial of benefits. A recommendation is to have the personnel manager or corporation official testify as to the employee's record and the reasons for the discharge, and to have the supervisor who witnessed the culminating incident also testify. In this manner, direct testimony becomes corroborated and therefore more credible to the administrative law judge.

It is important to remember that the legal files on all hearings, being public records, are available for inspection before the day of the hearing. These files should be reviewed prior to the hearing, as they normally contain statements taken from the employer, a signed statement given by the employee that may be used for impeachment purposes (i.e., to show that the employee changed his or her story or is otherwise unreliable as a witness), a copy of the initial determination, a copy of the losing party's appeal, and any additional information submitted, such as doctors' reports and statements of witnesses.

At the beginning of a hearing, it is the Administrative Law Judge's duty to focus the issue for the hearing. This important part of the hearing must not be overlooked, because the employer may inadvertently limit the areas of proof if the position is misstated. It is usually best to state at this stage of the hearing that the discharge was for "misconduct connected with employment based upon a review of the employee's overall record and the culminating incident on his or her last day of work." Do not dwell upon past incidents, but for purposes of the record bring them all to the attention of the examiner to show a continuing pattern of behavior.

At this stage of the hearing, if it is feasible to state that the employee quit employment, the employer should do so by pleading that "the employee quit" or, in the alternative, "was discharged for misconduct." In this manner, if the examiner decides that the employee did not quit, the employer's position will not be limited. If the examiner decides that the employee quit, the burden of proof will have shifted to the employee to prove that he or she quit within one of the exceptions to the statute in order to be eligible for benefits.

Sample Basic Interrogatories for the Employer-Witness

The testimony here is for the personnel manager or company officer in charge of the personnel files of the employee and who made the decision to discharge the employee. Corroborating evidence regarding the actual event or conduct that precipitated the discharge should be given by the company supervisor who actually witnessed the event. However, as this inquiry will change on a case-by-case basis and will, in all probability, be more narrative in form, no basic interrogatories have been listed.

Foundation Testimony
- State your name, spelling your last name for the record.

- Where do you live?

- Where do you work?

- What is your position there?

- How long have you held that position?

- What are your job duties?

- Describe the nature of the business of the employer.

- Approximately how many employees work there?

Foundation Testimony for Admission of Business Records

- Does the company keep business records?

- Who is the custodian of those records?

- As custodian, do you have access to those records?

- Are similar records maintained for all employees?

- Are entries on these records made at or about the time of the events that they describe?

- Was any record you might testify from prepared especially for this hearing? (This answer should be no.)

Background Information

- Do you know when the claimant-employee began employment with the employer?

- What was the employee's job?

- Did the employee work full-time?

- What shift did the employee work?

- What was the employee's rate of pay?

Work Rules

- Does the employer have work rules?

- How would the employee have been given notice of these work rules?

- Were the rules explained to the employee?

- Was the employee given the opportunity to ask questions if he or she did not understand what these rules meant?

- Do these rules cover all employees?

- Were these rules in effect on the day of the employee's termination from employment? (Introduce the work rules.)

The Discharge Itself

- What was the date of the employee's discharge?

- What was the date of the employee's last day of work?

- Did you personally discharge the employee?

- What was the reason for the employee's termination? (Introduce the employee's overall work record.)

- Does the employee's work record disclose any events of counseling or corrective discipline?

- Would you please explain what these events were and give the dates they occurred? (Introduce the employee's disciplinary notices.)

- Were these events considered in the decision to discharge?

- Describe the culminating incident that led to your decision to discharge the employee.

- What work rule(s) did the employee's conduct violate?

- How did the violation of this rule harm your employer's interest?

By using the above system, relevant information concerning the discharge can be adduced at the hearing. It is recommended that the discharge be based upon the employee's overall record, but with the evidentiary emphasis placed upon the culminating incident that led to the termination from employment. As the burden of proof is upon the employer, the employer's testimony will normally be taken first. By presenting a complete case, many of the possible employee defenses can be credibly eliminated.

It is important for these cases to be won to minimize the ever-increasing taxes being levied upon employers for the upkeep of the unemployment insurance funds as well as for the effect on collateral litigation in certain cases. Moreover, a determination that a terminated employee was discharged for misconduct connected with employment can be important in defending against other actions, such as NLRB unfair labor practice, employment discrimination, workers' compensation, unreasonable refusal to rehire, and wrongful discharge cases. In some cases, a favorable unemployment compensation decision is admissible and persuasive evidence that the employer's reason for discharging an employee was not a pretext masking some other, perhaps actionable, motive

Lastly, the unemployment compensation decision is usually, in contested situations, the first confrontation that takes place. Winning an objection to an unemployment compensation claim often takes the momentum away from a former employee who could consider filing other claims as well. Accordingly, a winning decision often paves the way to early settlement of the entire situation.

Answers to Chapter Eight Test Your Knowledge

1. True, 2. False, 3. f, 4. True, 5. True, 6. True, 7. False, 8. True, 9. True, 10. True

CHAPTER NINE

Handling Equal Employment Opportunity Law Challenges

The Equal Employment Opportunity Complaint Process

Pregnancy and Maternity Issues

Sexual Harassment

The Americans with Disabilities Act

Test Your Knowledge

of Equal Employment Opportunity Issues

1. True or False? The standard burden of proof for a plaintiff in an equal rights case to establish liability on the part of an employer is the same as in a civil case. The plaintiff needs to prove its case by a "preponderance of the evidence," or in other words, only that what the plaintiff contends happened is more likely than not to have happened and for the reasons claimed. To accomplish this the plaintiff need not have any direct evidence of unlawful discrimination, but can prove the case by circumstantial evidence. Moreover, such unlawful discrimination does not necessarily have to be shown as intentional.

2. Which of the following elements must be proved by a plaintiff in an equal right case to establish a *prima facie* case requiring the employer to articulate a nondiscriminatory reason for its actions?
   a. The plaintiff is a member of a class protected by the equal rights laws such as race, sex, national origin, religion, or age (age 40 or older).
   b. The plaintiff was connected with employment as an employee or applicant for employment.
   c. The plaintiff suffered some adverse employment action.
   d. The employer treated other employees more favorably.
   e. All of the above.

3. True or False? Unless a "continuing violation" can be shown, an EEOC complaint must be filed within 300 days of the alleged discriminatory act.

4. True or False? If successful in litigation, a plaintiff can be awarded his job back (if he has been fired), his attorney's fees for prosecuting the case, any back pay he may have lost because of the discrimination, and punitive damages of up to an additional $300,000 if the employer has more than 500 employees.

5. Which of the following factors may be relevant in determining whether the employer has allowed the creation of a hostile sexual environment such that it amounts to sexual discrimination?
   a. Whether conduct of a sexual nature was verbal or physical.
   b. The frequency, severity, and pervasiveness of the conduct.
   c. Whether the conduct was physically threatening or humiliating.
   d. Whether the conduct was unwelcome.
   e All of the above

6. True or False? A defense available to employers in sexual harassment cases is that a policy prohibiting sexual harassment existed and the employee unreasonably never used the policy to complain about the conduct.

7. True or False? Pursuant to the Americans with Disabilities Act (ADA), an employer is permitted to have all applicants take a physical exam as part of the pre-hiring interview process.

8. True or False? A "qualified individual with a disability" is defined to mean an individual with a disability who, with or without reasonable accommodation, can perform the essential functions of a job.

9. In determining whether there is undue hardship on an employer in accommodating an employee, which of the following factors may be relevant?
   a. The financial resources of a facility.
   b. The number of employees.
   c. How much the accommodation would cost.
   d. All of the above.

10. True or False? When an employee asks for an accommodation to perform a job, employers are best advised to ask the employee in an interactive process what the employee suggests be done.

The answers to these questions are at the end of this chapter.

No other statutory law has impacted the employment relationship to the extent that equal employment opportunity laws have. My personal experience is that the typical businessperson has too much competition and too little precious time and energy to *intentionally* discriminate in the workplace and still fulfill all the responsibilities necessary for success. However, without doubt, these laws have served to raise the level of consciousness concerning the evil effects of discrimination in the working world, and the availability of remedies to those who feel their rights have been illegally violated.

Using an individual employee's membership in a selected class of people as the basis for employment related decision-making is rare. However, the number of complaints being filed is rising at an astronomical rate as people become savvier about their legal rights. In fact, as reported in the January 17, 2000, issue of the *Chicago Tribune*, job bias lawsuits have more than tripled in the last decade, according to a report issued by the Justice Department. It cites an increase from 6,696 job bias lawsuits filed in U.S. District Courts in 1990 to 21,540 in 1998. The Bureau's statistician said the increase was not due to government action, but, rather, "the growth in civil rights cases has been due largely to the increase in employment cases between private parties." Civil rights complaints of all varieties have more than doubled each year, from 18,793 to 42,354 from 1990 to 1998, accounting for 16.5 percent of all the civil cases filed in federal court.

For managers who want to limit liability in their business activities, the logical result of the laws designed to protect people from discriminatory employment actions could be a disincentive to employ anyone other than the classic "straight, white, single male under 40 years of age." Such an employee may be the only individual unable to file a lawsuit alleging discrimination in the event the employment relationship turned sour for one reason or another, unless it be for "reverse discrimination."

Of course, for businesses today, the trend is to find the right person for the job regardless of race, sex, national origin, or creed. The resulting diversity in the workforce is a major strength for these companies because, in the customer-oriented perspective of the working world, it is clear that the all-important customers are a diverse mix of people, too.

Nevertheless, despite the best of intentions at the start of an employment relationship, when the relationship is threatened or severed, it is only human to look to the law for a remedy for perceived injustices.

What makes these laws so contentious, in my opinion, stems from the *proof* problems inherent in establishing an unjust act of a discriminatory nature. Only rarely in today's sophisticated business setting will direct evidence of discriminatory intent be found. Therefore, the laws have been fashioned by federal, state, and local legislative bodies and interpreted by the administrative agencies and courts in a way that relaxes the normal judicial requirements of establishing a cause of action and liability. In other words, discrimination need not be blatant, but is allowed to be inferred from the overall circumstances presented by the evidence in a case.

Day-to-day decision-making may blur the typical manager's memory of the details of certain acts or series of acts involving personnel at any level of an organization. However, a manager is still required to remember in court or an administrative proceeding everything that took place with every employee every working hour of every working day. This is especially difficult when the actual legal proceeding takes place years after the actual events.

In contrast, what does the individual employee alleging a violation of the equal employment opportunity laws have to testify about and remember? He or she has to remember only one thing—his or her own story. It is surprising with what crystal clarity complainants remember individual incidents when they have the luxury of time to think about them. Some litigants' memories are enhanced by astute note-taking on the job, which they often claim to have done at or about the time the event took place. It is amazing what these often one-sided documents can contain if introduced as contemporaneous expressions corroborating witness recollections of events and conversations. Sometimes even conversations with friends and relatives can be probative to establish the credibility of what a witness may say on the stand at trial years after the events. Many managers are dumbfounded as to how this testimony reflects a different worldview from the manager's or supervisor's memory of the events and conversations.

More problematic is what happens in the jury process when cases go that far. One need only look at the recommended jury instructions for discrimination cases that a judge is obliged to give the jury. For example, think about the following recommendations and imagine yourself in the jury room debating the merits of a case. The following instructions are similar those that a judge might give to a jury to help it evaluate evidence.

> This is a civil case. The plaintiffs have the burden to prove their claims by a preponderance of the evidence. There is a different standard in criminal cases of proof beyond a reasonable doubt which many of you probably have heard of before. In a civil case such as this to prove a claim by a preponderance of the evidence simply means to prove that something is more likely so than not so. Or to look at it another way, the

plaintiff has the obligation to prove to you that it is more likely than not that what he says happened did in fact happen and for the reasons that he claims.

Under Title VII of the Civil Rights Act it is a violation of the law for an employer to treat an employee differently on account of his race, nationality, religion, or sex. The plaintiff charges that he was subjected to harsher discipline than were white employees and that his race contributed to the decision to discharge him. There is no dispute about the fact of the discharge from employment. The dispute relates to what factors determined the imposition of discharge and whether or not the discharge was imposed in a discriminatory manner based on race. The plaintiff, an African American individual, claims he received different treatment than white individuals who were similarly situated to him, and that his race was a factor in that treatment contributing to the decision to discharge him.

It is not easy to prove race is a motive or factor. There is no way to look at the human mind. Direct evidence of discriminatory intent may be difficult to find. And so, the law allows you, the fact finder, to infer intent from surrounding circumstances. Intentional discrimination does not mean that a plaintiff must prove that there was racial hatred or dislike, it means only that he must prove that there was a difference in treatment that was the result of purposeful actions and not accidental, and that race was a determinative factor in the treatment; that is, that race made a difference. The law does not require that the plaintiff prove that race was the sole reason for the way he was treated. Several reasons may have contributed to the decision to terminate the plaintiff. The law was violated, however, if race made a difference in the decision to discharge.

The plaintiff has presented a variety of different types of evidence in his effort to persuade you that race was a factor in the decision to discharge him. There was some direct evidence—testimony of statements made and actions taken by individuals. There was also indirect or what the law calls circumstantial evidence. Circumstantial evidence does not have any less weight than does direct evidence. What is most important to keep in mind is you should not give any evidence lesser or greater weight because it is direct or indirect. Rather, give consideration to all of the evidence, direct and indirect, and decide whether or not the plaintiff's evidence has persuaded you by a preponderance of the evidence.

CHAPTER NINE

What follows in this chapter is a brief review of the legal analysis being applied today in equal employment opportunity law: a short description of the various protected classes; an explanation of the procedures that take place when a discrimination complaint is filed; examples of management systems that will help defend against such discrimination charges, and a discussion of some of the emerging hot spots such as sexual or racial harassment; claims of retaliation for filing a complaint; and the concept of constructive discharge. The chapter will then discuss other laws impacting the employment relationship, including the Americans with Disabilities Act.

Background

In 1964, the federal government found that a pattern of restriction, exclusion, discrimination, segregation, and inferior treatment of minorities and women existed in many employment areas in the United States. Evidence produced in congressional hearings established that the denial of equal rights in employment had led to higher exclusion, lesser occupational status, and the consequent lower income levels of minorities and women. Accordingly, the rationale for the passage of Title VII of the Civil Rights Act was to promote an individual's ability to pursue the work of his or her own choice and to advance in that work, subject only to consideration of the individual's qualifications, talents, and energies. In the law itself, unlawful employment discrimination is defined to be:

1. To fail or refuse to hire or to discharge any individual, or to discriminate against any individual with respect to compensation, terms, conditions, or privileges of employment because of such individual's race, color, religion, sex, or national origin; or

2. To limit, segregate, or classify employees or applicants for employment in any way which would deprive or tend to deprive any individual of employment opportunities or otherwise adversely affect his or her status as an employee, because of such individual's race, color, religion, sex, or national origin.

To administer this anti-discrimination law, Congress created the Equal Employment Opportunity Commission (EEOC). The Civil Rights Act covers any employer engaged in an industry affecting commerce that employs 15 or more employees each working day in each of 20 or more calendar weeks in the current or preceding year. The Act was later amended to also include federal, state, and local public employees, and educational institutions as well. Additional protected classes of employment were added to include age, pregnancy, and disabilities.

Intentional discrimination may occur in many different ways. Sometimes intentional discrimination may be referred to as *conventional* or *overt* discrimination. This results when an employer consciously bases an employment decision on a person's protected status. For example, hiring a less-qualified non-minority individual after more-qualified minority individuals were rejected would amount to proof of intentional discrimination. This is also referred to as *disparate treatment*. The idea is that individuals in the protected classes are being treated differently in some aspect of the employment relationship than others not in the protected class.

However, in order to prove a violation of the law, discrimination need not be intentional. Any employment practice that impacts members of a protected group by screening them out at a disproportionately higher rate than persons not belonging to the group may be a violation, even though it may be unbiased on its face. When an individual complainant can establish that an employer uses a particular employment practice that causes a disparate impact and that practice is not job-related for the position in question nor consistent with business necessity, a finding of a violation of the law will take place even though no intent to discriminate has been shown. The reasoning is that such an employment practice may perpetuate past discrimination. An example is employee ability testing that cannot be shown to be related to the actual job to be performed if the results operate in practice to screen out members of a protected class from getting the job or a promotion. This is called disparate impact.

Moreover, a neutral policy that has a disparate impact but is job-related for the position in question and consistent with business necessity may nonetheless still be unlawful. If the complaining party can show that a less discriminatory alternative employment practice would serve the employer's business needs and that the employer refused to adopt it, that can be enough to establish a violation.

It is also possible for a plaintiff to establish discrimination by demonstrating that race, color, religion, sex, or national origin was a motivating factor for an employment practice, even if other factors affected the employment decision being challenged as well. In other words, if a plaintiff can show to the satisfaction of the administrative law judge or court that unlawful discrimination was one of the reasons motivating a discharge, then the action becomes discriminatory as a matter of law.

An example of this situation might be where a member of a protected class is discharged from employment. The employer defends by saying the reason for the discharge was the employee's continuing tardiness and absenteeism. However, based upon a review of the employer's own records, even though the employee may have been late or absent without excuse

from time to time more than the employer liked, there were past incidences with other employees not in the protected class who had as bad
or worse records but were not discharged. This is described as a *mixed
motive decision* on the part of the employer, which is unlawful. In other
words, because of the difference in treatment the inference can be made
that the legitimate, non-discriminatory reasons were not the only true
reasons for the different treatment, but that the individual's membership
in a protected class was also a determining factor in the decision that
harmed the individual's employment relationship with the employer.

Analysis

An employee may establish what is called a *prima facie* equal employment
opportunity case by showing four basic elements:

1. he or she belongs to some protected class,

2. he or she performed his or her work satisfactorily,

3. he or she suffered an adverse employment action, and

4. his or her employer treated similarly situated employees outside the
    classification more favorably.

When an employee satisfies these elements, there is the inference of
discrimination. Typically, discrimination is not a difficult thing for a plaintiff to establish. To satisfy the first element, one is either a member of a
protected class or one is not. It may surprise some to learn that whites
are in the protected class for race discrimination. Some call this *reverse
discrimination*, but every individual is a member of some race. The second
element is whether there is some connection to employment with the
employer. This takes in individuals who apply for work, whether or not
they actually obtain the work, and extends through every term, condition,
or privilege of employment. For the third element, the individual must
have been harmed in some way in that employment relationship. This
could be the loss of some privilege, or even the assignment of work that
may be perceived as less desirable than other assignments of work,
whether or not there is any change in the wage rate for doing it. The last
element speaks for itself and, in my opinion, is all too often an unfair
comparison. This is because many seemingly similar events may have
been treated differently by the employer for a variety of reasons including, but not limited to, a difference in the people involved at the time
decisions were made. For example, a change in supervision often brings
with it a change in the level of acceptance of performance required for
the position; by that I mean a higher level of performance. Accordingly, it

is not uncommon for an individual to never have received any criticism of his or her performance for years, and yet a new supervisor may suddenly state that the employee is no longer able to meet the higher standards of performance.

Once a *prima facie* case is established, the employer must account for its allegedly discriminatory actions. An employer may rebut a *prima facie* case by articulating some legitimate, nondiscriminatory reason for its allegedly biased employment decision.

The employee may then challenge the employer's stated reasons as being merely pretextual. In proving its argument, the employee may establish pretext by proving the employer's explanation had no basis in fact or the explanation was not the real reason, or at least that the reason stated was insufficient to warrant the discharge. In this regard, the employee tries to establish that an employer's explanation is pretextual and in so doing can focus on the specific reasons advanced by the employer.

Another avenue of attack against an employer is now developing at an increasing frequency. This is the claim that an employer is violating the rights of an employee in retaliation against the employee for exercising his or her rights under the Civil Rights Acts. The most disconcerting aspect of these kinds of allegations is that the courts have held that even though the underlying charge of discrimination may have no merit, this fact is immaterial to whether or not there may have been retaliation because of voicing the complaint. This kind of complaint is the fastest growing category of discrimination complaints.

The Equal Employment Opportunity Complaint Process
Filing the Complaint
The complaint must be filed within 300 days of the date of the alleged discrimination. This time begins to run when facts that would support a charge of discrimination are apparent or should be apparent to a person with a reasonably prudent regard for his or her rights.

This time limit may be extended if an employer misleads an employee, for example, by not posting the appropriate EEO poster, and the employee did not know of his or her rights because of it. The time period for filing a complaint might also be extended if the facts that would support the charge of discrimination were not apparent at the time of the discriminatory action. To extend the time period, the burden of proof rests with the complainant. The time period might also be extended if it can be shown that there is a continuing violation. This is defined as either a continuing course of conduct or series of acts, or the maintenance of a system or policy which discriminates continuing into the charge-filing period. Such a series of acts must be sufficiently related in nature, such as in the case where numerous decisions were all based on the same objective policy.

A complaint must identify the full name and address of each complainant and each respondent. It must state clearly and concisely the facts that constitute the alleged unlawful discrimination, including the dates of each occurrence. While both state and federal agencies have forms for a complaint, it is not necessary that such forms be utilized. However, the complaint must be signed, notarized, and verified. Complaints can be filed either in person or by mail. They may be filed by the complainant or the complainant's duly authorized representative.

The Complaint Process

After a complaint is filed, the receiving agency will review it to determine if the complainant is protected by the equal employment opportunity statutes, if the respondent is subject to the statutes, if the complaint states a claim for relief, and if the complaint has been filed on a timely basis within the 300-day time limit. Complaints failing to meet these criteria are dismissed.

Complaints can be withdrawn at any time and also can be amended no later than 10 days before a hearing unless good cause is shown for such failure to amend the complaint prior to that deadline.

Notice will then be given to the respondents named in the complaint. The notice requests a response to the complaint, typically within 10 days after the date of the notice. In practice, the 10-day time period within which to respond is easily extended upon request.

Investigations

Equal employment opportunity agencies, both state and federal, must investigate all complaints that satisfy the minimal review requirements mentioned above. As part of this investigation, the agencies may subpoena necessary persons and documents. If during the investigation it appears that the respondent has engaged in some type of discrimination against the complainant other than what was alleged, the agencies typically advise the complainant that the complaint should be amended to allege the additional basis of discrimination.

The purpose of the initial investigation is to determine whether or not there is probable cause to believe that the alleged discrimination has occurred. At the conclusion of the investigation, which will include a review of all information provided to the compliance officer by both parties, a written Initial Determination will be issued stating that there is probable cause or there is no probable cause to believe unlawful discrimination occurred. *Probable cause* means a reasonable ground for the belief, supported by facts and circumstances strong enough in themselves to warrant a prudent person to believe that discrimination probably has been or is being committed. In most states, included in the probable cause determination will be an analysis of the credibility of the witnesses and the information presented.

Typically, to make this determination, agencies will request information from the respondent. The employer/respondent may be asked to respond item-by-item to each allegation in the written complaint and to provide supporting affidavits where appropriate. The respondent may be asked to provide a list of all individuals who have been separated from employment, the reason for their separation, and their membership or nonmembership in the protected class of the complainant over the last two years (assuming the complaint of discrimination alleges discriminatory discharge from employment). Discrimination due to discharge accounted for almost 50 percent of the cases filed in the last reported fiscal year with the EEOC.

In most states, all discrimination complaints filed with the state agency are cross-filed with the federal EEOC agency and vice versa. Typically, whichever agency first receives the complaint will be the agency that takes the laboring oar to do the initial probable-cause investigation. While both state and federal agencies have concurrent jurisdiction, unless there are exceptional circumstances, usually one agency will affirm the other's findings once they are made.

The federal agency, upon reaching its decision, may issue the complainant a right to sue letter in which the employee may take the case to federal court. In many state agency proceedings, if probable cause is found, the matter will proceed to a hearing "on the merits," at which both sides will present witness testimony before an Administrative Law Judge. In many state proceedings, if the Initial Determination finds no probable cause to believe that discrimination occurred, the complainant will then have a right to have a hearing on that issue alone. If the Initial Determination is reversed at this probable cause hearing, a second hearing will then be held on the merits.

State Agency Hearings

At Administrative Law Judge hearings, the matter is handled in a similar fashion to a regular lawsuit. Pre-hearing motions for summary judgment can be requested, subpoenas may be issued, and pre-hearing disclosure and discovery depositions may be taken of either party. At the hearing itself, a record will be made of the proceedings either on tape or by court reporter, and post-hearing briefs typically are allowed to be filed. A written decision will be issued as to whether or not discrimination in violation of the fair employment statutes took place. These decisions can be appealed by either party for further review, and ultimately to the court system itself for judicial review.

Remedies

If successful, the remedy for a complainant may include hiring, promotion, accommodation, back pay (mitigated by interim earnings or other compensation), or other action that will make the victim of discrimination whole. In this regard, a valid offer of reinstatement of employment will automatically terminate the accrual of back pay liability in a discharge case. A remedy may also include reinstatement to the former position; if reinstatement is not appropriate, the potential exists for "front pay." Successful complainants will typically receive attorneys' fees, expert witness fees, and court costs as well. As one Administrative Law Judge put it to me quite succinctly, "Whenever I find liability against an employer, I always award attorneys' fees and costs."

In federal proceedings, under the Equal Rights Act of 1991, punitive damages may be available up to a maximum of $300,000 against employers of 500 or more employees. Employers of 201 to 499 employees are potentially liable for up to $200,000, employers of 101 to 200 employees up to $200,000, and 15 to 100 up to $50,000.

The U.S. Supreme Court decided in *Kolstad v. American Dental Association*[1] that an employee need not establish that conduct was "egregious" in order to recover punitive damages. It rejected the "egregious conduct" standard and instead decided that an employer will be liable for punitive damages when the alleged offender acted "with malice or with reckless indifference to the federally protected rights of an aggrieved individual." The Court also found that even if there is a finding of "malice" or "reckless indifference," punitive damages can be awarded against an employer for the acts of its employees only if: (a) the employer authorized the doing and the manner of the act; (b) the employee was unfit and the employer was reckless in employing him/her; (c) the employee was employed in a managerial capacity and was acting within the scope of his/her employment; *or* (d) the employer ratifies or approves the act. The Court also recognized that there may be a reverse incentive to not implement important anti-discrimination programs or provide anti-discrimination training under these tough-to-meet standards. Therefore, the Court further held that an employer could not be held for punitive damages based on the acts of an employee where the employer has made good-faith efforts (e.g. training, policies, programs) to comply with the requirements of federal employment discrimination laws.

In cases involving reasonable accommodation of an individual with a disability, compensatory and punitive damages may not be awarded if an employer can show that good-faith efforts were made to provide reasonable accommodation. The meaning of "reasonable accommodation" will be discussed later in this chapter.

Pregnancy and Maternity Issues

At many levels of governmental jurisdiction, from the municipal level to the federal level, there exist, by ordinance, administrative code, or statutory legislative authority, regulations relating how an employer must deal with pregnancy and maternity issues.

The basic principle or foundation upon which the law relating to equal rights in employment stands is that applicants for employment or current employees shall be treated equally without regard to the various protected classifications such as age, race, creed, and so on. Likewise, pregnant employees must be treated equally because pregnancy is unique to the female sex. Put more simply, an employer must treat both sexes equally in its employment policies, no matter what the cause of the temporary medical disability.

Any policies or procedures that treat pregnant females less favorably than other employees with temporary medical disabilities become sex discrimination on the part of the employer. Accordingly, it is against the law for an employer to use the pregnancy of an employee as an opportunity to take any adverse personnel action that would not have been taken otherwise.

Since the art of law is to apply basic legal principles to specific situations, what follows are commonly faced situations in this area.

A woman is not required to tell an employer when she applies for a job that she is pregnant. An employer may not ask a woman if she is pregnant or is planning on having children in the near future, unless the question is relevant to a bona fide occupational qualification in performing the specific job in question. Since only women may become pregnant and bear children, if the answer is unrelated to the work, questioning prospective applicants for employment or current employees can be evidence of discriminatory intent by the employer.

In regard to an employee who is temporarily unable to perform her job functions because of pregnancy, the employer is required to treat such an employee in the same manner as it treats other temporarily medically disabled employees. If modified tasks, alternative assignments, available "light" work, or disability leaves with pay are provided, these all must be provided to the pregnant employee as well.

The law does not require an employer to "make work" for a pregnant employee if lighter duty work is not available, unless it is normal practice to do so for other medical disabilities.

An employer may legally discipline or terminate a pregnant employee for reasons relating to work performance. But, in so doing, the wise employer follows the preventive labor relations strategies as outlined in Chapter Five of this book. If an employer imposed the same discipline on a pregnant employee as it does on all other employees, and discipline would have been imposed regardless of the employee's pregnant status, any such equal rights complaints should be dismissed.

An employer may not force an employee to take a maternity leave at some arbitrary point in her pregnancy, unless she is unable to perform the functions of her job. The length of temporary disability should be determined by the employee and her doctor or the company's doctor, as are all other medical absences. However, a company can and should directly contact the physician involved to clarify any possible safety fears. For example, an employee's job may include heavy lifting, stair climbing, or excessive standing that may be detrimental to the employee's physical condition. Some physicians will even take the time to view plant conditions to see the working conditions for themselves, if asked. However, the medical decision is one for the doctor, and not the company, to make.

With regard to the payment of maternity benefits, employers are required to provide disability coverage for pregnancy on the same basis as they provide it for any other medical condition. This means that both disability income protection and medical expense insurance must cover maternity-related disabilities and maternity-related health care expenses if such are covered for other medically related conditions. Moreover, any health insurance plan offered in connection with employment must cover the maternity on the same basis as other conditions, whether or not the employer makes contributions to the plan. An employer that does not have any disability coverage for employees is not obligated to provide such coverage for maternity, but must still treat the pregnant employee equally to other employees who are temporarily disabled. Additionally, employees can employ the same waiting period before maternity coverage takes effect as there is for other health conditions covered by the insurance policy.

The employer is not required to pay part of a woman's salary while she is on a pregnancy disability leave. The employer is required to pay only such benefits as are paid to employees who are on disability leaves due to reasons other than pregnancy.

Where an employer provides no health insurance coverage for dependents, it is not required to institute coverage for the medical expenses of pregnancy-related conditions of male employees' spouses or of the dependents of all employees. However, if an employer's insurance program covers the medical expenses of spouses of female employees, then it must equally cover the medical expenses of spouses of male employees, therefore including pregnancy. For example, in Wisconsin, the Wisconsin Insurance Commission has ruled that the complications of pregnancy must be covered in all health insurance plans.

An employee who is unable to work because of pregnancy-related temporary disability is not eligible for workers' compensation. Workers' compensation is available only to those who have a job-related illness or injury.

If a pregnant employee, who is physically able to work, was laid off during her pregnancy and unable to obtain other work, though available for such work, she would be eligible for unemployment compensation until she is medically determined to be physically unable to work. In addition, the pregnant employee of an employer covered under state and federal acts will have additional statutory rights for leaves of absences. See the Family and Medical Leave Act discussion in Chapter Two.

Sexual Harassment

The United States Supreme Court has held that the creation of a hostile sexual atmosphere or the allowance of such an atmosphere to exist after complaints have been made is sex discrimination in violation of the Civil Rights laws of Title VII. Accordingly, complaints may be filed with state and federal agencies, and may be investigated and/or prosecuted by such agencies and/or by private attorneys in the agency forums.

Employers can be held responsible for the acts of their agents and supervisory employees with respect to sexual harassment, regardless of whether the specific acts complained of were authorized or even forbidden by the employer, and regardless of whether the employer knew or should have known of their occurrence.

With respect to conduct between fellow employees, employers can be held responsible for acts of sexual harassment in the workplace where the employer, or its agents or supervisory employees, knew or should have known of the conduct, unless it can be shown that the employer took immediate and corrective action. Moreover, this principle has been extended to potential employer liability for the acts of outside third parties such as vendor representatives or delivery agents if an employee complains and nothing is done about it such that the unwanted conduct continues in the employment environment.

Violations will be determined based upon "the totality of the circumstances from the point of view of a reasonable person." In this regard, the conduct must be objectively severe or persuasive to offend a reasonable person and must also be subjectively perceived as abusive by the charging party. Of course, to satisfy the latter point, the charging party need only testify that he or she found the conduct to be hostile or abusive at the time it occurred.

Relevant factors that will be examined include:

● whether the nature of the conduct was verbal or physical;

● the context in which the conduct occurred;

● the frequency, severity, and pervasiveness of the conduct;

● whether the conduct was physically threatening or humiliating;

● whether the conduct was unwelcome; and

● whether the conduct unreasonably interfered with the employee's work performance.

Defining sexual harassment or the creation of a sexually hostile environment is difficult. However, unwelcome sexual advances, requests for sexual favors, and other verbal or physical conduct of a sexual nature may be considered harassment when:

● submission to such conduct is made either explicitly or implicitly a term or condition of the individual's employment (*quid pro quo*—"this for that" in Latin—kind of conduct);

● submission to or rejection of such conduct by an individual is used as a basis for employment decisions affecting such individual; or

● such conduct has the purpose or effect of unreasonably interfering with an individual's work performance or creates an intimidating, hostile, or offensive working environment.

It is absolutely imperative that all companies have a policy prohibiting sexual harassment in the workplace. (A sample of such a policy is included in Chapter Two.)

The policy is best distributed to employees in the employee handbook, but it can also be communicated in other ways. In fact, many companies not only provide training to supervisors relative to the policies, but also provide employees with information in small group meetings. There should be no mistaking a company's intent on this matter, and a company should be readily able to prove the existence and communication of a specific policy that allows the offended employee to complain to *any* management official concerning conduct prohibited by the policy. A company should also be in a position to prove that once a complaint was received, the company followed its policy by investigating and, if appropriate, disciplining the offending employees or supervisors appropriately. Some federal appellate courts have held that for an employer to be found liable for sex discrimination in violation of Title VII, the plaintiff must establish both that the sexual harassment took place *and* that the company did not follow its policy because it failed to investigate and properly act on the results of that investigation to relieve the circumstances that caused the complaint.

Remember, the company's potential liability is not limited to action solely by a management employee; employers also can be subjected to claims if one employee sexually harasses another. In fact, there can be liability when an outside third party, such as a vendor or delivery driver, is the party doing the harassment if an employee files a complaint and management does nothing about it. Moreover, same-sex harassment is culpable conduct as well in certain situations.

It is important to have a procedure in place to deal with these situations, because merely having a general policy may not be enough to satisfy the courts. In one case, an employer had an established grievance procedure, but the plaintiff testified she was afraid she would lose her job if she used it. The court, therefore, found that the policy was ineffective. The fatal flaw identified by the court was the fact that the plaintiff would have had to take her complaint to the manager who was harassing her. In addition, several courts have commented that the lack of a sexual harassment policy in and of itself may be evidence of employer liability.

In investigating an internal complaint, it is important to know that once a charge has been filed, the company is obligated to act. Failure to do so is evidence against the company. It is obvious that doing nothing about a complaint will not make the complaint go away. In fact, common sense dictates that the matter will only get worse, not better, without attention.

In most cases, complaints can be settled internally. For a better understanding of conducting an investigation of a sexual harassment complaint, see Chapter Five.

In 1998, the U.S. Supreme Court issued several decisions defining the duties and obligations of employers and employees in dealing with claims of sexual harassment. In *Burlington Industries, Inc. v. Ellerth*,[2] the Court held that under Title VII, an employee who refuses the unwelcome and threatening sexual advances of a supervisor, yet suffers no adverse, tangible job consequences, may still recover against the employer. This is true even without a showing that the employer was negligent or otherwise at fault for the supervisor's actions. That is, an employer can be liable where its own negligence is the cause of the harassment. In addition, a supervisor may bring liability upon a company when the official power of the company is brought to bear on an employee in a tangible employment action, such as failing to promote or firing an individual. An employer is negligent if it knew or should have known about the conduct and failed to stop it.

However, if no tangible employment action is taken by the supervisor against the employee being harassed, the employer may interpose an affirmative defense. The defense comprises two elements: (1) that the employer exercised reasonable care to prevent and correct promptly any sexually harassing behavior, and (2) that the plaintiff employee unreasonably failed to take advantage of any preventive or corrective opportunities provided by the employer. In this regard the Court recognized that promulgation of an anti-harassment policy is pertinent to the first, and proof that the employee unreasonably failed to use a complaint procedure generally suffices to satisfy the second.

In the second decision, *Faragher v. City of Boca Raton*,[3] issued by the U.S. Supreme Court the same day, the Court held "An employer is vicariously liable for actionable discrimination caused by a supervisor, but subject to an affirmative defense looking to the reasonableness of the employer's conduct as well as that of the plaintiff victim." The defense in part was that the supervisor's actions were outside the scope of their employment, and therefore not actionable against the employer. However, in the opinion of the Court, the standard determining the scope of employment is

> whether or not it is just that the loss resulting from the servant's act should be considered as one of the normal risks to be borne by the business in which the servant is employed. It is well recognized that sexually hostile environments are a common problem in many work places, therefore an employer can

reasonably anticipate the possibility of such conduct occurring, and bearing its cost might be thought of as one the costs of doing business.

The third case dealing with sexual harassment involved *Oncale v. Sundowner Offshore Services, Inc.*[4] In this case the Court held that, "sex discrimination consisting of same sex harassment is actionable under Title VII." The prohibition of discrimination "because of . . . sex" protects men as well as women if the behavior is so objectively offensive as to alter the "conditions" of the victim's employment, although "male-on-male horseplay" and intersexual flirtation are not actionable.

In the aftermath of these decisions, the EEOC issued guidelines stating its view that the employer's defense applies to all forms of harassment based on membership in a class protected by the Acts. However, the EEOC made it clear that the defense would be construed narrowly. An employer will only be shielded from liability when it establishes that it exercised reasonable care and that the employee acted unreasonably. If both parties act reasonably, the defense fails. However, if an employer cannot use the defense to avoid liability entirely, it may assert it to limit damages in cases where the employee could have avoided some, but not all, of the harm from harassment. For example, this might occur when a more prompt complaint would have reduced harm, even if not entirely eliminated it.

For the first part of the defense—to exercise reasonable care—it is generally required that a policy prohibiting the conduct of sexual or other harassment be established, disseminated, and enforced with a complaint procedure made clear to all employees. Such a policy should have the following elements: (1) clearly defined prohibited conduct; (2) protection from retaliation for complaining employees; (3) accessible avenues for employee complaints; (4) a call for prompt and thorough investigation; and (5) a call for immediate and appropriate employer corrective action when warranted.

The EEOC further suggests that such a policy be written in a manner to be understood by all employees, distributed and periodically redistributed to every employee, posted, and accompanied by training. The agency also promulgated sample questions for an employer's investigator to ask the complainant, alleged harasser, and third parties, as well as factors for evaluating witness credibility and reaching a determination.

If an employer determines that unlawful harassment has occurred, the EEOC suggests the employer must stop the harassment and prevent its reoccurrence through actions directed at the harasser, such as discipline, demotion, training, and future monitoring, and should attempt to correct the effects of the harassment through actions including: (1) restoration of leave taken by the victim because of the harassment; (2) expungement of negative evaluations in the victim's personnel file that arose as a result of the harassment; (3) reinstatement; (4) apology by the harasser; (5) monitoring the victim to prevent retaliation by the harasser or coworkers; and (6) correction of any other harm, such as compensation for losses.

The second prong of the defense—the employee's duty to exercise reasonable care—places the burden on the employee to prevent or mitigate the harm from harassment. A complaining employee must give truthful information and cooperate in an investigation. Yet, an employee may be excused from failing to report harassment if he or she reasonably feared retaliation, was blocked by obstacles to complaining, or perceived that the complaint process was ineffective. Finally, the EEOC confirmed that when harassment is perpetrated by an "alter ego" or "proxy" of the employer, such as the president or owner of the company, the affirmative defense is not available.

There can be no underestimation of the power of the sexual harassment issue in the workplace today. What once may have been seen as normal day-to-day conduct in the workplace, with no intention or idea to harass anyone, is no longer acceptable behavior in the workplace. While there will always be a certain percentage of individuals who attempt to take advantage of situations either for protection or profit, there are far too many sincere situations that have led to unfortunate results for everyone involved. This area of human behavior, and of the law that regulates it, is certainly all too susceptible to fabricated or exaggerated complaints, but also to fabricated or exaggerated denials. However, when the abusive behavior does take place, it is harmful to all concerned.

One particular case followed an all too familiar destructive pattern in which everybody lost. A female medical technologist worked in a health-care laboratory supervised by two male physicians. It was the habit of the physicians to tell dirty jokes and make innuendoes of a sexually related nature. On one occasion, the doctors went so far as to inquire of the medical technologist, "Did you get any last night?" Of course, the physicians thought it was all good-natured fun and convivial personal relations. To the female under their supervision, it was a nightmare. In the investigation after she complained to the personnel department, coworkers not only confirmed her allegations, but echoed her distaste and frustration at the behavior. The confidential report was taken by the hospital president to the hospital board of trustees for action. The board decided to admonish the physicians, which was done in a private session.

The next day in the laboratory, the atmosphere was very cold, and it remained that way thereafter. This was more stressful to the medical technologist than before. She was the first to admit that it affected her work performance, which steadily declined. Mistakes began cropping up on laboratory reports. Her performance evaluations from the doctors reflected her poor performance. Eventually they recommended her termination from employment.

After her discharge for poor performance, the medical technologist filed a lawsuit with the state Equal Employment Opportunity Agency. Eventually her claim was settled in a monetary settlement.

The fact that a settlement was needed to resolve her complaint angered the board of trustees against the doctors involved. At year-end bonus time, the amount of the settlement was removed from their discretionary bonus, which angered the doctors. In a very short time they left their residency at the health care institution and went to a competing provider, taking their patients with them.

The best response for an employer in this brave new world is training, training, and more training concerning the legal exposure for this kind of conduct; the issuance of strongly worded, clear policies prohibiting the conduct; and immediate response to all complaints.

Successful Equal Employment Opportunity Practice Tips

- Have an equal employment opportunity policy and publish it in the employee handbook.

- In all public advertisements, state that you are an Equal Employment Opportunity Employer.

- Monitor the hiring process to insure that in every new hiring situation, the proper procedures have been followed. In particular, always have at least two final candidates for each position and choose one or the other based upon the information gathered in the hiring process. Do not use the pass–fail method of accepting or rejecting one applicant at a time. Instead, form a pool of candidates and choose one. Following this procedure, if the selection process were challenged by an employee who was not chosen for the job, such an individual would have the proof problem of having to establish he or she was better qualified than the applicant chosen for the position. This is a much more difficult task than only being required to prove that the employee was qualified for the position, in order to win a big legal judgment.

- In the hiring process, ask questions from a prepared list, and keep the list of questions and the notes made by the interviewer in the file. Only allow supervisors who have been adequately trained in the proper procedures for interviewing to take part in the process. Keep the hiring process standardized so that it can be easily established that the company did not vary its routine from candidate to candidate in the selection process.

- Be sure to investigate employees' complaints and properly document disciplinary actions. Follow the proper investigative and procedural steps. *Always* get the employee's side of the story. Before disciplining or discharging employees, check the discipline of other employees in the past. Unfortunately, if you discover prior leniency in similar situations, at least you have discovered a past practice standard that needs to be changed. Past practice can always be changed by simple notification of the new standard to the employees. It is not uncommon that managers new to an employment situation will set their own standards, which are sometimes higher than the standards for performance in the past. There is nothing discriminatory about this new standard because it applied to all employees. The message here is that a company is not bound by past practice to continue past mistakes. Just advise the employees when the standards change; indeed, involve them in the change itself.

- Provide pro-active training to your supervisors about equal employment law policies. Involve employees, too, in small group meetings to discuss the standards of behavior you expect from them. Include outside training consultants from time to time to present programs to educate employees. This is especially true for newer concepts such as sexual or racial harassment. For example, it may come as a surprise to an employee that engaging in sexual harassment may be a reason for discharge. Employees might wrongly assume that only a supervisor has to worry about it.

- Involve specialty assistance when necessary. Do not be afraid to contact your consultants or legal counselors for advice before acting. View such help as the enabling process for your legitimate business decisions, and not just as another layer of expense. Maintain this view even if the advice you receive is that you are doing everything correctly. The law is rapidly changing in this area, the stakes for making a mistake are increasing, and they are likely to continue to do so in the future. Most cases are won or lost by the events and decisions that take place at the time an incident takes place, and not by how eloquently your legal representative may later argue or how well researched the legal briefs may be.

The Americans with Disabilities Act

Employers who have 15 or more employees for each working day in each of 20 or more calendar weeks in the current or proceeding calendar year must pay close attention to *The Americans with Disabilities Act of* 1990 (ADA). Since its enactment, more than 108,000 complaints have been filed against employers, resulting in employers paying out more than $211 million according to one source, and that figure does not include privately filed suits. It is estimated that as many as 43 million Americans have conditions that may qualify as disabilities under the Act.

In general, the Act states:

> no covered entity shall discriminate against a qualified individual with a disability because of the disability of such individual in regard to job application procedures, the hiring, advancement, or discharge of employees, employee compensation, job training, and other terms, conditions, and privileges of employment.

Discrimination includes by definition:

- Limiting, segregating, or classifying a job applicant or employee in a way that adversely affects the opportunities or status of such applicant or employee because of the disability of such applicant or employee;

- Participating in a contractual or other arrangement or relationship that has the effect of subjecting a covered entity's qualified applicant or employee with a disability to the discrimination prohibited by this title;

- Utilizing standards, criteria, or methods of administration that have the effect of such discrimination on the basis of disability or that perpetuate the discrimination of others who are subject to common administrative control;

- Excluding or otherwise denying equal jobs or benefits to a qualified individual because of the known disability of an individual;

- Not making reasonable accommodations to the known physical or mental limitations of an otherwise qualified individual with a disability who is an applicant or employee, unless such covered entity can demonstrate that the accommodation would impose an undue hardship on the operation of the business of such covered entity, or denying employment opportunities to a job applicant or employee who is an otherwise qualified individual with a disability, if such denial is based on the need of such covered entity to make reasonable accommodation to the physical or mental impairments of the employee or applicant;

- Using qualification standards, employment tests, or other selection criteria that screen out or tend to screen out an individual with a disability or a class of individuals with disabilities unless the standard, test, or other selection criteria, as used by the covered entity, is shown to be job-related for the position in question and is consistent with business necessity; and

- Failing to select and administer tests concerning employment in the most effective manner to ensure that, when such test is administered to a job applicant or employee who has a disability that impairs sensory, manual, or speaking skills, such test results accurately reflect the skills, aptitude, or whatever other factor of such applicant or employee that such test purports to measure, rather than reflecting the impaired sensory, manual, or speaking skills of such employee or applicant (except where such skills are the factors that the test purports to measure).

It is important to remember that pre-employment medical examinations and inquiries are prohibited by this Act. A covered entity may not make pre-employment inquiries into the ability of an applicant to perform job-related functions. However, the Act specifically states that an employer may make post-employment offer inquiries, including medical exams, to determine the ability of an applicant to perform job-related functions and may disqualify someone if this inquiry reveals an inability to perform those essential functions.

Definitions

The term "qualified individual with a disability" is defined to mean an individual with a disability who, with or without reasonable accommodation, can perform the essential functions of the employment position that such individual holds or desires. The phrase "essential functions" means job tasks that are fundamental and not marginal. This is meant to ensure that employers can continue to require that all applicants and employees, including those with disabilities, are able to perform the essential, i.e., non-marginal, functions of the job in question. However, in determining what constitutes the essential functions of the job, it is important to note that consideration must be given to the employer's judgment regarding what functions are essential. Indeed, the law states that an employer may require that every employee be qualified to perform every essential function, not just most of them.

The committee report and legislative history specifically state that the legislation does not undermine an employer's ability to choose and maintain the most qualified employees. This legislation simply provides that employment decisions must not have the purpose or effect of subjecting otherwise qualified individuals with a disability to discrimination on the basis of their disability.

Thus, an employer is still free to select applicants for reasons unrelated to the existence or consequence of a disability. For example, the committee reports describe one situation where an employer has an opening for a typist and two persons apply for the job—an individual with a disability who types 50 words per minute and an individual without a disability who types 75 words per minute. The employer is permitted to choose the applicant with the higher typing speed if typing speed is necessary for the successful performance of the job.

On the other hand, these reports also point out that if the two applicants included one individual with a hearing impairment requiring a telephone headset and amplifier and a second individual without a disability, both of whom have the same typing speed, the employer is not permitted to choose the individual without a disability because of the need to provide reasonable accommodations. In other words, the employer's obligation is to consider applicants and make decisions without regard to an individual's disability or need for reasonable accommodation. It is emphasized that the employer has no obligation to prefer applicants with disabilities to other applicants on the basis of disability.

An employer may still devise physical and other criteria for a job as long as the criteria are job-related and consistent with business necessity. For example, an employer can adopt a physical criterion that an applicant be able to lift 50 pounds, if that ability is necessary to an individual's ability to perform the essential functions of the job. For example, security concerns may constitute valid job criteria. If jewelry stores choose to employ security officers because of the frequency of snatch-and-run thefts, mobility and dexterity may be essential job criteria for the performance of such jobs. Where the criteria are legitimate, it is acceptable to deny employment to an applicant, or to fire an employee with a disability who does not meet, with reasonable accommodation, performance requirements.

In addition, it is acceptable to deny employment to an applicant or to fire an employee with a disability if the individual poses a direct threat to the health or safety of others. If this is so, the employer must identify the specific risks that the individual with the disability would pose. The standard to be used in determining whether there is a direct threat is whether the person poses a significant risk to the safety of others or to property and not a speculative or remote risk. It must be established that no reasonable accommodation is available to remove that risk.

When determining coverage under the ADA, employers must first determine whether or not the individual has a "disability" as defined by the ADA. Under the Act, a disability means (1) a physical or mental impairment that substantially limits one or more major life activities of an individual; (2) a record of such impairment; or (3) being regarded as having such an impairment. The U.S. Supreme Court stated a three-step process for determining whether a plaintiff has a disability limiting a major life activity in *Bragdon v. Abbott*.[5] First, a court must determine whether the plaintiff suffers from a physical or mental impairment. Second, it must determine whether the life activity cited by the plaintiff as impaired "constitutes a major life activity" as defined by the ADA. Third, it must determine whether the plaintiff's impairment "substantially limits" the major life activity. Accordingly, the next question becomes, "Just what constitutes a physical or mental impairment?"

The Act defines a physical impairment at 29 C.F.R. Sec. 1630.2(h)(1) as follows:

> A physical impairment includes "any physiological disorder, or condition, cosmetic disfigurement, or anatomical loss affecting one or more of the following body systems: neurological, musculoskeletal, special sense organs, respiratory (including speech organs), cardiovascular, reproductive, digestive, genito-urinary, hemic and lymphatic, skin and endocrine."

> A mental impairment includes "any mental or psychological disorder, such as mental retardation, organic brain syndrome, emotional or mental illness and specific learning disabilities." 29 C.F.R. Sec. 1630.2(6)(2). Examples of emotional or mental illness include major depression, bipolar disorder, anxiety disorders (which include panic disorder, obsessive compulsive disorder, and post-traumatic stress disorder), schizophrenia, and personality disorders.

Important is what is not recognized. Traits or behaviors are not, in and of themselves, impairments even though they might be linked to impairments. Traits such as irritability or grouchiness, chronic lateness, poor judgment, and advanced age are not impairments. For example, in *Palmer v. Circuit Court of Cook County*,[6] the court found that evidence that plaintiff had a personality conflict with her supervisor which caused her to suffer anxiety and depression was not an ADA disability. The inability to tolerate stressful situations is also not an impairment.[7] In *Greenberg v. New York State*

Dept of Correctional Service,[8] a federal court ruled that a chronically late employee was not disabled despite her claim that her depression prevented her from getting to work on time.

In addition, in *Sutton v. United Airlines, Inc.*,[9] the Supreme Court held that whether an individual is disabled under ADA should include a consideration of any measures that might mitigate the individual's impairment or its effects. In the *Sutton* case the plaintiffs were very nearsighted but had 20/20 vision with use of corrective lenses. The airline refused to hire them because of their uncorrected vision, but the Court held that the plaintiffs were not "disabled" as defined by the Act because the ADA requires that a person be "presently—not potentially or hypothetically—substantially limited" in a major life activity.

What constitutes a major life activity? The EEOC lists life functions such as caring for oneself, performing manual tasks, walking, seeing, hearing, speaking, breathing, learning, and working.[10] Additional mental major life activities include thinking, concentrating, interacting with others, and sleeping. However, in *Solieau v. Guilford of Maine*,[11] the First Circuit threw out a claim that the plaintiff's mental illness (dysthmia) substantially limited his ability to get along with others by stating although the "ability to get along with others is a skill to be prized, it is different in kind from breathing or walking."

What is a substantial limitation? In determining this question courts have looked at the severity and nature of the disability, the duration (or expected duration) of the impairment, and the permanent or long-term impact. For example, numerous people are unable to lift 50 pounds on a regular basis. Therefore, an individual who cannot lift 50 pounds is not substantially limited.[12] By contrast, most individuals can lift ten pounds. Therefore, an individual with a physical impairment who cannot do so may be considered substantially limited. Relative to "duration," the EEOC states that temporary, non-chronic limitations of a short period, with little or no long-term or permanent impact, are usually not disabilities. While the boundaries and definitions used in determining what is a disability under the Act are not tightly constructed, there are some generally recognized exclusions, such as conditions including stress, irritability, poor judgment, and pregnancy.

However, according to the EEOC, the top ten most common disabilities claimed to trigger an employer duty to accommodate are, in order: (1) back problems, (2) mental illness, (3) neurological disorders, (4) blood disease/HIV, (5) heart conditions, (6) diabetes, (7) drug and alcohol abuse (recovered or recovering addicts and alcoholics–not current users), (8) vision impairments, (9) hearing impairments, and (10) cancer.

The Employer Duty to Accommodate

The definition of "reasonable accommodation" sets forth examples of types of accommodations that could insure that a person with a disability will be able to perform the essential functions of a job. These include:

- Making existing facilities used by an employee or applicant readily accessible to and useable by the individual with the disability;

- Job restructuring;

- Part-time or modified work schedules;

- Reassignment to a vacant position;

- Acquisition or modification of equipment or devices or appropriate adjustment or modifications of examinations, training materials, or policies;

- The provision of qualified readers or interpreters where this does not create an undue hardship on the employer.

These are legal obligations that only depend upon whether the accommodation would impose an undue hardship on the employing entity. Thus, covered entities are required to make employment decisions based on facts applicable to individual applicants or employees, and not on the basis of presumptions as to what a class of individuals with disabilities can or cannot do. This is the heart of the Act.

Perhaps the most important action an employer can take if an applicant or employee voluntarily reveals a disability is to ask the individual what he or she thinks the employer could do to accommodate the challenge. This is what is called engaging in the "interactive process." It is reasoned that the individual with a disability should be in the best position to know what to do about it. However, be sure to remember that this only applies when the applicant or employee gives the employer knowledge of the potential challenge. Under the Act, the employer is prohibited from asking questions that might reveal this problem. But if the applicant or employee mentions it, then the employer is supposed to ask what to do about it. Once the employer learns what the employee wants, it can make the decision as to whether or not it can make the accommodation without causing undue hardship to itself. Also, the employer can propose alternatives it believes will work. As a part of this process, the physician for the employee can be asked what to do as well. The biggest failure is the failure to ask.

While the term "reasonable accommodation" may mean many things, the decision as to what reasonable accommodation is appropriate must be determined by the particular facts of an individual case. This may include job restructuring or modifying a job so that a person with a disability can perform the essential functions of the position. Such barriers to performance may be removed by eliminating nonessential elements of the job, delegating assignments, exchanging assignments with another employee, or redesigning procedures for the task accomplishment.

According to the legislative history, the Act does not require an employer to make any modification, adjustment, or change in a job description or policy that an employer can demonstrate would fundamentally alter the essential functions of the job in question. Again, this is an issue dealt with on a case-by-case basis to determine whether an undue hardship is created for the employer by making such accommodations. The key ingredient in determining the essential functions, however, is still left up to the employer. In this regard, existing job descriptions will be given the greatest weight. Accordingly, employers who wish to prevent problems in this area should review existing job descriptions before a complaint is filed because job descriptions already in existence may provide the basis of an employer's refusal to hire an individual with a disability. Also, as discussed in Chapter Four, an excellent time to review the job description is when the job needs to be filled with either a promotion or a new hire. Prior to any new posting or advertising, review the job description to see if it still applies to the job or needs to be updated or modified.

The courts have not agreed upon a single standard for determining what "reasonable" means. However, it is clear that in determining whether an accommodation is reasonable, the employee is not entitled by law to the accommodation of its choice.[13] Therefore, if an employee requests one accommodation, but the employer offers another reasonable accommodation, the employer remains in compliance with the Act. For example, in *Webster v. Methodist Occupational Health Center, Inc.,*[14] a nurse who had been placed by her employer as a contract industrial nurse had a stroke, which left her unable to perform her job. Her employer offered to explore the possibility of assigning her to a non-nursing situation, which she refused. The court found that the employer had satisfied its duty to reasonably accommodate the nurse. It is important to note that an employer cannot force an employee to take medications or seek treatment. However, an employer may be allowed to require an employee to take medications, submit to monitoring, or seek treatment as a condition of retaining his or her employment in some circumstances.[15] In one case it was found that the employer could require that the employee not take certain medications and could require drug testing.

Undue Hardship

The term *undue hardship* means an action requiring difficulty or expense, i.e., an action that is unduly costly, extensive, substantial, and disruptive and that may fundamentally alter the nature of the entity's business. Remember that the employer has the burden to prove in any contested case that providing a specific accommodation would be an undue hardship. Usually, the proof turns on the size of the employer, the cost of the accommodation, the effect of the accommodation on other employees, and the impact on operations.

In this regard, the following factors can be considered:

● the nature and cost of the accommodation;

● the overall financial resources of the entity;

● the overall size, structure, and function of the entity's workforce;

● the number, type, and location of facilities; and

● the geographic separateness and the administrative and fiscal relationship of the facility in question to the entity in question.

This will all be determined on a case-by-case basis. For large employers with different facilities in various locations throughout the country, the degree of accommodation necessary will vary from plant to plant and city to city. The factors to be considered in evaluating undue hardship to a specific facility include:

● the overall financial resources of the facility;

● the number of persons employed at the facility;

● the effect on expenses and resources of the facility; and

● the other impacts of the accommodation on the facility; for example, whether it would violate a collective bargaining agreement or bump an innocent employee.

Accordingly, the employer need not make an accommodation if it can show that to accommodate the individual with a disability would pose an undue hardship on the employer. This is true even if the employer cannot show that standards, policies, or decisions with discriminatory effect are job-related, are a business necessity, or that no reasonable accommodation is possible.

The ADA adopts a framework for employment selection procedures that is designed to assure that persons with disabilities are not excluded from job opportunities unless they are actually unable to do the job. The three most important provisions to assure that there is a fit between job criteria and an applicant's actual ability to do the job are defined as:

1. The requirement that individuals with disabilities not be disqualified because of their inability to perform non-essential or marginal functions of the job;

2. The requirement that any selection criteria that screen out or tend to screen out individuals with disabilities be job-related or consistent with business necessity; and

3. The requirement to provide reasonable accommodation to assist individuals with disabilities to meet legitimate criteria. In this regard, the legislation prohibits an employer from making any inquiries as to the existence or nature of an applicant's disability prior to an offer of employment. However, an employer may make pre-employment inquiries into the ability of an applicant to perform job-related functions.

Employers wishing to avoid lawsuits in dealing with individuals with disabilities should do the following.

1. Have clearly defined job descriptions that are current and up-to-date, clarifying the "essential" job functions. These will be used as *prima facie* evidence on behalf of the employer relative to what the real job requirements are. If an employer's job descriptions are out-of-date, they should be reviewed immediately.

2. Employers should make any offer of employment contingent upon the successful passing of a physical examination where a qualified medical person will be making the assessment of whether the applicant's disabilities are going to affect his or her ability to perform the essential job elements established in the job description. As long as the opinion is founded upon actual job abilities and actual job functions, the medical assessment protects an employer in making an employment decision. This decision should also include an opinion as to whether the employer could reasonably accommodate without undue hardship to it. There are many vocational physicians qualified to make these determinations. If there is a question, such a physician should be consulted before the decision is made to hire or not to hire an individual who may be covered by the ADA

3. Engage interactively with an employee who feels he or she needs an accommodation to do the work. While an employer is not obligated to adopt whatever is suggested by the employee, it is best to approach such situations with the idea that something could help to allow the employee to do the job, or continue to do the job.

Endnotes

1   USCt 1998 73 EPD ¶45,401.

2   118 S. Ct. 2257 (1998).

3   118 S.Ct. 2275 (1998).

4   118 S. Ct. 998 (1998).

5   118 S. Ct. 2196 (1998).

6   905 F. Supp. 499 (N.D. Ill. 1995).

7   *Manudo v. Sanus Health Plan of Greater New York,* 966 F. Supp. 171 (E. D. N.Y. 1997).

8   919 F. Supp 637 (E.D.N.Y., 1996).

9   119 S.Ct. 2139 (1999).

10   29 C.F.R. Sec. 1630.2(i).

11   105 F. 3d (1st Cir. 1997).

12   See *Kirkendall v. UPS,* 964 F.Supp. 106 (W.D.N.Y. 1997), *Aucutt v. Six Flags Over Mid-America, Inc.,* 85 F. 3d 1311 (8th Cir. 1996).

13   See *Stewart v. Happy Herman's Cheshire Bridge, Inc.,* 117 F. 3d 1278 (11th Cir. 1997).

14   141 F. 3d 1236 (7th Cir. 1998).

15   *Sadler v. Southwest Alabama Medical Mental Health/Mental Retardation Board, Inc.,* 1997 West Law 607475 (S.D. Ala 1997).

Answers to Chapter Nine Test Your Knowledge

1. True, 2. e, 3. True, 4. True, 5. e, 6. True, 7. False, 8. True, 9. d, 10. True

Miscellaneous Employment Law Issues

AIDS

Telecommuting

Violence in the Workplace

Workplace Privacy

Employment Practices Liability Insurance

Test Your Knowledge

# of Miscellaneous Employment Law Issues

1. True or False? The United States Supreme Court has ruled that from the moment of infection an individual with the HIV virus is considered to be "disabled" as that term is defined pursuant to the Americans with Disabilities Act (ADA).

2. True or False? Employers should engage in an "interactive process" with an individual who has been infected with the HIV virus to determine what, if any, accommodation the employer could reasonably make that would allow the individual to keep working.

3. True or False? To manage an individual who works via computer at his or home it is best to reduce to writing an understanding as to what the employer expects from the employee, and what the employee can expect from the employer.

4. True or False? Employers are subject to the OSHA "general duty" violations if they fail to take steps necessary to reduce or eliminate hazards for even criminal acts of violence that can be recognized as part of the nature of doing business.

5. True or False? For a private sector employer, forcing an employee under penalty of discharge to take a lie detector test in an investigation of unintentional loss to the employer, such as a traffic or workplace accident, is a permitted exception for an employer under the Employee Polygraph Protection Act (EPPA).

6. True or False? Under a 1999 federal appeals court ruling, a private sector employer insisting under penalty of discharge that an employee's interview be tape-recorded can violate the EPPA if the resulting tape might be analyzed by a "voice stress analyzer" to determine the employee's honesty.

7. True or False? Employers in the private or public sector are best advised if monitoring computer, e-mail, or voice-mail systems to communicate this so employees will have no reasonable expectation of privacy in such communications.

8. True or False? Investigatory searches by private sector employers are not covered by the U.S. Constitution, and are only subject to the limitation of common law restrictions of invasion of privacy, unlike investigatory searches by public sector employers.

9. True or False? Employers can purchase special insurance to help manage the risk of exposure to being found guilty of violations of employment practices, except for intentional acts and punitive damage awards by federal juries and courts.

10. True or False? It is recommended that all payroll records be retained a minimum of six years, some records longer.

The answers to these questions are at the end of this chapter.

There are many important additional topics to understand in today's complicated legal and regulatory employment environment that do not fit the functional progression of the preceding sequence of chapters for successful employment practices. Accordingly, these topics are covered here. Issues discussed in this chapter include the ramifications of AIDS, telecommuting, dealing with the tragedy of workplace violence, understanding the legal restrictions on polygraph testing, the changing attitudes toward smoking at work, knowing the legal boundaries of workplace privacy, and managing the inherent risks of employment errors and omissions through employment practices liability insurance. Lastly, a helpful list of employment laws and recommended record-keeping requirements are provided.

AIDS
The Importance of an AIDS Policy
Although many questions about the legal and medical implications of AIDS remain unanswered, employers often face policy decisions about employees who have the disease. How should an employer treat employees who are HIV-positive but are not ill? Are high health care costs considered just cause for terminating an employee with AIDS? Can employees and applicants be tested for evidence of AIDS? Are persons with AIDS protected against discrimination in employment?

Despite the fact that executives have ranked AIDS among the biggest problems facing the United States, most companies do not have an AIDS policy. However, according to the manager of personnel for a major insurance company quoted in the *Milwaukee Journal*, "It is vital for companies to act before they have an AIDS case to deal with. If you wait until you have a case to develop a policy, you will have turmoil and chaos because emotional reactions will take over."

General Information
The virus that causes AIDS has been given the acronym HIV. The scientific/medical community has said that if an individual is infected with HIV, this does not mean that he or she necessarily has AIDS. Instead, medical terminology categorizes someone infected with HIV as HIV-*positive*. An HIV-positive individual cannot always fight infections that someone with a healthy immune system might be able to resist. This infection progresses in stages and, over time, makes the body more vulnerable to severe illness such as pneumonia, cancer, nervous system damage, weight loss, and blindness. AIDS is the last and most serious stage of an HIV infection. According to the medical community, for an individual to have AIDS, the person must both be HIV-positive *and* have certain specific medical symptoms.

Employment Law

For federal contractors and subcontractors, AIDS has been included in the definition of handicap discrimination protection provided by the Rehabilitation Act of 1973. In one case, a California teacher was removed from his duties as an instructor of hearing-impaired students after he was diagnosed as having AIDS. He was given, instead, a desk job writing grant applications. When he filed suit in federal court, the teacher claimed that he had suffered discrimination in violation of the Rehabilitation Act. The lower court said the risk to the students outweighed the harm to the teacher. However, that decision was reversed on appeal, and the appeal court wrote:

> Evidence before the District Court overwhelmingly indicates that casual contact incident to the performance of his teaching duties in the classroom presents no significant risk of harm to others, and although handicapped, because of AIDS, appellant is otherwise qualified to perform his job within the meaning of Section 504 of the Rehabilitation Act of 1973.

The court further stated that to prevent the teacher from "assuming his classroom occupation subjects him to irreparable injury."

Relative to the Americans with Disabilities Act, Section 1630.2(j) of the Interpretive Guidelines for Title I expressly provides that HIV infection is "inherently substantially limiting," and thus covered by the Act. In fact, even an individual who is HIV-negative might be covered by the Act if such individual were perceived or regarded by others as having AIDS. This might even include, according to the Interpretive Guidelines, an employee doing volunteer work with people who have AIDS and whom the employer feels might, therefore, contract the disease.

Medical Screening and Testing

Medical screening or testing of applicants or employees for the AIDS virus also raises serious legal issues. Some states, such as California, Florida, Massachusetts, and Wisconsin, have already passed laws that specifically prohibit the use of a blood test by employers to detect the presence of AIDS.

Because current tests can only reveal that someone has been exposed to the AIDS virus and do not prove that someone has AIDS, those who test positive may include individuals who will never contract the disease and will still be physically able to perform their jobs. Thus, the use of tests as a basis for employment is questionable under the equal employment laws. It is not advisable for an employer to ask directly whether a job applicant has a particular illness or disability, including AIDS.

Procedure for Employers

In the view of the courts and the agencies administering the Americans with Disabilities Act (ADA), AIDS is a "disability." This view was most recently confirmed by the U.S. Supreme Court in the case of *Bragdon v. Abbot*, 118 S. Ct. 2196 (1998). Although not directly an "employment discrimination" case because it concerned the Public Accommodations portions of the ADA, the Court held "Even though respondent [patient's] HIV infection had not progressed to the so-called symptomatic phase, it was a 'disability' under the ADA, that is, 'a physical . . . impairment that substantially limits one or more of an individual's major life activities.' "

The facts in *Abbot* were that Sydney Abbot had been infected with the HIV virus since 1986. On September 16, 1994, Abbot went to the office of Dr. Randon Bragdon, a dentist. Abbot revealed that she was infected with HIV, and Bragdon refused to treat Abbot's cavity at the office. Bragdon indicated he would fill the cavity at a hospital at no extra dental charge, but that Abbot would have to pay for the extra cost of the hospital facilities. Abbot refused this offer and later brought suit for discrimination in public accommodation on the basis of her disability.

In the opinion of the Court, HIV infection is a "physical impairment" even though it is not listed in the list of specific disorders identified as physical impairments in the Code of Federal Regulations (CFR). The Court explained that once a person is infected with HIV, the virus invades different cells in the blood and the body. The virus passes through stages in which different symptoms appear, with the onset as soon as six days after infection. In light of the immediacy with which the virus begins to damage the infected person's white blood cells and the severity of the disease, it is considered impairment *from the moment of infection.*

While HIV affects many life activities, the Court focused on the major life activity of reproduction, the activity raised by *Abbot*. It found that reproduction is a major life activity because it is essential to the life process itself. Also, major life activities are not limited to those that fall only within the categories of public, economic, or daily activities. Reproduction is no less major than working and learning, which are mentioned in the federal regulations. One might argue that the failure to specifically mention AIDS was intentional given the knowledge of the condition at the time the ADA was passed and the regulations were written, indicative to me of the requisite intent of specifically excluding it, but the Court held otherwise. Instead it said that Abbot's HIV infection substantially limited her major life activity of reproduction for two reasons: (1) a woman with HIV who tries to conceive a child imposes on the man a significant risk of becoming infected, and (2) an infected woman risks infecting her child. Reproduction in the face of

HIV entails public health dangers as well as economic and legal consequences. When significant limitations result from impairment, the definition is met even if the difficulties are not insurmountable.

Interestingly, the Court went on to find that by statute Bragdon could have refused to treat Abbot if her infectious condition imposed "a significant risk to the health or safety of others." The ADA defines a direct threat as a "significant risk to the health or safety of others that cannot be eliminated by a modification of policies, practices or procedures or by the provision of auxiliary aids or services."[1] The existence or non-existence of a significant risk must be determined from the standpoint of the person who refuses to provide the treatment or accommodation, as of the time of that refusal; and the risk assessment must be based on medical or other objective evidence. The views of public health authorities are of substantial weight, but are not conclusive. The issue, said the Court, is one of statistical likelihood of risk, not "professional responsibility." Accordingly, the Court remanded the case back to the trial court for further inquiry into whether Bragdon had presented adequate evidence under this standard. Shortly thereafter the case was settled out of court without a ruling on that issue.

Therefore, it is imperative that employers respond to persons with AIDS in the same manner as those with other disabilities.

One of the most challenging aspects of this issue is dealing with and implementing reasonable accommodations for infected individuals. The appropriate reasonable accommodation must be established on a case-by-case basis and is best determined through a flexible, interactive process that involves both the employer and a qualified individual with a disability. In cases where there are two possible accommodations, the employer may choose the one that is the less expensive or easier to implement so long as it gives the individual a meaningful employment opportunity. Typical accommodations for individuals with AIDS fall into four basic categories. To minimize contact with others, some employers purchase computer equipment that enables individuals to telecommute and live at home, although this accommodation is not necessarily required. Individuals can be allowed to work flexible hours that enable them to perform the essential functions of their jobs. It may be possible to transfer persons with AIDS to positions that are either less physically demanding or provide better hours of work. Lastly, co-workers may be able to assist employees with AIDS in performing certain functions of their jobs. Looking for ways to include, rather than exclude, an employee is the key, so employers should explore as many of the possible accommodations for individuals with AIDS as possible to maximize their strengths. Consider and document those considerations of how an accommodation could be made. Being able to establish an adequate attempt to employ the individual with AIDS should be the employer's focus.

OSHA Blood Borne Pathogen Regulations

The OSHA Blood Borne Pathogen Regulations protect workers against exposure to microorganisms such as Hepatitis B virus (HBV) and HIV where employees *might* have exposure to blood and risk infection with such pathogens. It is estimated that these regulations affect more than 500,000 business establishments.

These regulations require employers to perform six essential tasks:

1. Design an exposure control plan that identifies and documents potential risks and provides a procedure for evaluating circumstances surrounding exposure incidents. All employees should have access to a copy of the Exposure Control Plan. This Plan must be updated at least annually or whenever necessary to reflect new or modified tasks and procedures that affect exposure.

2. Certain universal precautions provisions must be implemented that contain the presumption that any blood and certain human body fluids are potentially infectious. Such provisions must provide specific guidelines for engineering and work practice controls, personal protective equipment, and recommended housekeeping procedures. Such housekeeping procedures should include descriptions for the provision of hand-washing facilities; instructions on the use and disposal of needles and other *sharps*; instructions on the handling of specimens; the provision of protective equipment including gloves, gowns, lab coats, masks, etc.; developing and maintaining housekeeping systems to keep the working environment clean and sanitary; and the provision for contaminated laundry to be placed in color-coded bags that prevent soak-through and/or leakage.

3. Employers are required to make available, free of charge and at a reasonable place and time, the Hepatitis B vaccination program to all employees who have occupational exposure. If an employee initially declines a vaccination but at a later date wishes to accept it, the employer must still make it available.

4. A post-exposure evaluation and follow-up program must be implemented where employers provide a confidential medical evaluation and follow-up to the employee.

5. Employees must establish a *communication of hazards* program such that designated contaminated or hazardous materials are put in color-

coded containers that bear a warning label. Employers must also provide a training program that is repeated at least on an annual basis.

6. New record-keeping procedures must be established that maintain accurate medical records for each employee with occupational exposure. These records must be kept confidential and maintained for 30 years after the termination of an individual's employment.

Failure to comply with these regulations may result in the assessment of civil penalties up to $7,000 for each alleged violation. The penalties for willful violations shall not be less than $5,000.

Other Workers' Rights

Confidentiality is an important issue. The diagnosis of an AIDS infection in an employee may evoke unwarranted fear and suspicion in coworkers. This medical information should be considered confidential and should not be disclosed to other individuals without the infected employee's consent. In addition, if it is necessary to keep such information, it should be kept in a confidential separate file to avoid negligent disclosure of the medical information to unauthorized individuals.

Another important issue is employee right-to-know laws. Employees have certain rights to be informed about the presence of hazardous substances in the workplace. Employers must follow the statutory procedures in notifying employees when the employer introduces toxic substances to the workplace. However, most statutes indicate that the term "infectious agent" does not include an agent in or on the body of a person who is present in the workplace for diagnosis or treatment. Therefore, other employees do not, in most cases, have the right to know if a coworker has AIDS, and it is a violation of the right to privacy to distribute such information.

Developing an AIDS Policy

A written AIDS policy should contain several elements, including but not limited to the following:

● There will be no discrimination or harassment of individuals affected with HIV or who have AIDS.

● All infected employees will be reasonably accommodated by the company where possible.

● All policies will be applied uniformly and all medical information will remain confidential.

- Infected individuals will be allowed to continue working if they can effectively perform the essential functions of their jobs and do so in a safe manner in regard to others. Because it has been found that HIV is not transmitted in normal working circumstances, there will be no allowance for other employees to refuse to work with fellow employees or customers who are HIV-positive.

Wise employers should also examine their policies in certain areas. For example, attendance policies should be drafted carefully. All employees should understand that violations of the attendance policy will be cause for discipline even for an employee with AIDS, as long as the employer has made attempts at reasonable accommodation.

Another sensitive policy is leave of absence. Employees with disabilities are not necessarily entitled to more paid leave time than nondisabled employees. However, a person with AIDS should not be disciplined, involuntarily reassigned, or forced to go on mandatory leave unless performance has declined to an unsatisfactory level and it cannot be improved with reasonable accommodation.

Moreover, it is good to develop an AIDS policy that addresses the treatment of AIDS under various employee benefit plans, reasonable accommodation of persons with AIDS (such as whether part-time employment or transfers will be made available), and employee assistance programs' coverage for AIDS patients. Such a policy should also provide guidance to supervisors and managers dealing with reactions by coworkers fearful of working with an individual infected with the AIDS virus.

Lastly, the development and implementation of a company policy regarding AIDS can be coupled with an educational program. Rather than wait for coworkers to refuse to work with an HIV-infected employee, employers should make an AIDS education program part of ongoing training programs. As an educational program aimed at employees, some employers use medical experts and printed materials to help minimize employee fears and reassure them that casual workplace contact does not transmit the disease.

In conclusion, AIDS implications in the workplace cannot be ignored.

Telecommuting

What an age we live in! In many jobs, it is not even necessary to leave home to do our work. However, in that gray territory where jobs and lifestyles intertwine, what are some of the hazards and pitfalls? How do the employment laws impact this new world?

CHAPTER TEN

While the high-tech workplace may reduce the need for onsite labor, there are still concerns about the safety of radiation from video display terminals, managing distant employees, and the lack of belonging and identification with an organization when one seldom visits company headquarters. However, in many situations today, the benefits of telecommuting outweigh the disadvantages and risks. Every reader can relate to the stories of individual commodity traders working thousands of miles from the trading pits or editors of magazines working via computer networks on publications produced in other cities.

It is ironic that work at home via telephone, fax, and computer actually takes the working world back to where it was before the industrial revolution. In many ways it finds our practical ways of living and our existing employment laws and regulatory systems outdated because of their fixation on the factory or office paradigm. The new technologies are changing, and for some of us the types of jobs, the performance criteria of these jobs, relationships between employee and supervisor, and the work being done are greatly changed. After all, have you ever tried raising your voice in an e-mail message by typing it in all capital letters?

Clearly, not every employee or employer is a good candidate for telecommuting. Some employees do not respond well to the absence of direct supervision. Some employers are also wary of the inherent lack of immediate control that seems to be present only in a face-to-face working environment. However, many employers are reporting that the right employee with the proper training can increase productivity and improve quality by telecommuting. Additional benefits are exemplified by few sick days, reduced turnover, and increased job satisfaction.

Self-motivated, independent, responsible, and trustworthy employees make the best telecommuters. Of course, they need to respond well to written commands and other communications from their direct supervisors.

The Dark Side of Telecommuting

A decentralization of the workforce can lead to isolation from coworkers, supervisors, and the organization as a whole. There are many benefits to accidental staff interaction. Much knowledge is distributed through simple observation of others and in informal channels of communication at the coffee machine, photocopy machine, or water cooler. Of course, telecommuting also means that management is no longer able to directly monitor employees. Therefore, changes in communication style are important to avoid more difficult and time-consuming corrections. It is no longer possible to simply walk down the hall or pick up the interoffice intercom to resolve an issue, personally clarify an assignment, or defuse an argument. Lastly, some say the greater use of technology will increase the risk of theft, forgery, and untimely disclosures of information.

The Benefits of Telecommuting

Many surveys show that employees who are well trained and receptive to working at home are more productive. They report fewer interruptions and less time away from actual work. There is obviously also less energy spent on getting to work and returning home from work. With greater job satisfaction there should be less turnover. This is not to mention the benefit of the decreased cost of real estate because of the need for less office space at company headquarters.

Employers who use telecommuters also report improvement in recruiting and retaining high-quality employees. This is because there are fewer lifestyle issues, lower employee costs, greater flexibility for employees, and the ability to adopt more casual and functional dress. Accordingly, in most situations there should be less stress and more opportunity for self-actualization. There are also individual tax benefits of having a home office.

Managing the Telecommuter

Companies that successfully use telecommuting have adopted policies that identify certain principles and ground rules. They stress that telecommuting does not change the basic terms and conditions of employment. That means that telecommuting should be viewed as an assignment and not as an option. It is based on the needs of the job and the work group, and is not an entitlement. It is contingent upon an employee's past and present levels of performance. The most successful telecommuting jobs are those with clearly defined tasks and deliverables. In addition, the telecommuting arrangement must be understood to be one that is mutually beneficial because it is cost-justified. Telecommuters must know that they will have regularly scheduled work hours and that they must deliver their assigned work on time. While their work performance may be measured more by results, telecommuters must still be as accessible as on-site employees during the agreed-upon business hours.

Management strategies to address the challenges of telecommuting often include regular meetings with supervisors both at the company headquarters and at the employee's in-home office. The more clearly defined the roles, goals, and timetables, the better likelihood that the telecommuting employee and supervisor will be able to establish the proper reporting and exchange of information necessary for success.

In addition, an emphasis will be placed on proper time recording and reporting commitments on the part of the employee. Telecommuters are subject to the equal rights laws, workers' compensation, and other employment law regulations that govern the workplace. These include the wage and hours laws, Clean Air Act requirements, OSHA regulations on safe equipment in the home, and the reporting of injuries pursuant to workers' compensation law. However, because of intermix of individual personal privacy rights guaranteed by the U.S. Constitution and other considerations in this potentially highly charged area, the OSHA regulations regarding home office safety issued in early 2000 were withdrawn after one day and remain unresolved as of this writing.

The best management results generally occur when an agreement stating the policies, ground rules, and respective responsibilities is memorialized in writing and signed by both the employee and the manager.

Some telecommuters fear that the potential isolation from coworkers and the inevitable invisibility with their immediate supervisors will lead to less opportunity for advancement. However, these challenges can be managed. After all, the idea of working outside a central office is not new. Outside sales and customer representatives have been on the road for decades. Now, because of the explosion in new communications and computer technologies, there are many other kinds of jobs that can be organized to function more productively using telecommuting. One of my publisher's editors functions easily from her home in a major city in preparing a specialty publication issued on a monthly basis. Many jobs can easily be performed via e-mail, fax, and telephone.

It has been said that if just five percent of the commuters in Los Angeles County stopped driving and starting telecommuting, it would save more than 200 million miles of travel per year and eliminate 50,000 tons of smog. If the main challenge for business is attracting and retaining key competent people, perhaps it is time to give telecommuting a try.

Violence in the Workplace

In a tragic incident, a former client of a San Francisco law office armed with a handgun opened fire in the law firm's offices, killing eight people and wounding six more before killing himself. He was reported to have held a deep-seated resentment for the firm after it represented him in a financial transaction that went poorly for him. This case, and many others like it, have sent shock waves through the media and the employer community. In fact, in the United States there are approximately 18,000 to 23,000 incidents of workplace violence per year. In one year, of the women who died in the workplace, 42 percent were victims of homicide. The number of employees who killed their boss has doubled in the last ten years.

According to an American Management Association survey:

- Almost half of the reported instances of workplace violence involve threats.

- The attacker was either a current or former employee in more than one-third of the cases.

- The attacker was a customer or client in 12 percent of the cases.

- The victim was a coworker of the attacker in 28 percent of the cases.

- The victim was a direct supervisor of the attacker in 15 percent of the cases.

- Almost half of the instances reported multiple victims.

- Warning signs of threats and odd, secretive, strange, or compulsive/obsessive behavior were ignored by coworkers or company officials in 25 percent of the reported cases.

According to the Department of Labor, in its "Census of Fatal Occupational Injuries," violence was the second leading cause of death in the workplace and accounted for 17 percent of all workplace fatalities. The primary motive of homicides at work was robbery. About half of all homicide victims were employers or employees of retail establishments such as grocery stores, restaurants, and taverns. Retail sales was the deadliest profession, accounting for 33 percent of the workplace fatalities. Fourteen percent of the workplace homicides involved a personal acquaintance or a work associate of the victim, and in 82 percent of the workplace homicides a gun was the weapon of choice.

Employer Liability

Many security experts believe that most workplace homicides are preventable. Also, because most perpetrators kill themselves and few leave behind any assets attractive enough to draw a lawsuit, many victims' lawyers have only the employer to look to for recovery of any remedy.

In addition to the doctrine in many states that employers have an implied obligation to employees and customers to provide a safe environment, other actions are being heard by courts as well, including:

- *Negligent hiring lawsuits.* Employers can be liable if they fail to check references or do any kind of background checks where it could be shown that the employer would have known an employee had a propensity to violence when hired. Additionally, hiring someone when such a background search has uncovered past violent episodes is a ticket for trouble.

- *Negligent training lawsuits.* The theory in this emerging area has been applied mostly to cases where the employees are armed, such as security guards. Can the employer show that such employees have received adequate training in communication skills as well as in weaponry?

- *Negligent supervision lawsuits.* Has the employer failed to discipline or recognize problem employees by their behavior on the job?

- *Negligent retention lawsuits.* Has the company retained or, worse, rehired someone who has had instances of violence?

The OSHA General Duty Clause states that employers are required to keep the workplace free of recognized hazards. A violation of the general duty clause can occur when:

- A condition or activity in the employer's workplace presents a hazard to employees;

- The condition or activity is recognized as a hazard by the employer or industry;

- The condition is one that is likely to cause death or serious physical harm; and

- Feasible means exist to eliminate or materially reduce the condition.

A memorandum from the Associate Solicitor of OSHA regarding the employers' duty to protect employees of acts of criminal violence stated:

> The general duty clause require(s) employers to take steps necessary to reduce or eliminate the recognized hazards present which are likely to cause death or serious physical harm to employees. There is no reason to exclude from the list of hazards criminal acts of violence which are recognized as part of the nature of doing business.

Safeguards Against Liability

There are many steps employers can take to reduce the risk of violence and thereby reduce potential liability in the unfortunate case where violence takes place. For employers in high-risk establishments and occupations, the following measures are recommended by the National Institute for Occupational Safety and Health (NIOSH):

- Install bright external lighting, silent alarms, and surveillance cameras.

- Make high-risk areas more visible to more people.

- Use drop-safes to minimize cash or carry only small amounts of cash.

- Post signs stating that limited cash is on hand.

- Increase the number of staff on duty.

- Train employees in conflict resolution and nonviolent responses.

- Instruct employees not to resist during a robbery.

- Provide bullet-proof barriers or enclosures.

- Have police check workers routinely.

- Close establishments during the high-risk late night and early-morning hours.

- Have employees work in teams rather than alone.

- Equip every reception area desk with a silent alarm button that will notify building security of any problem.

It is important to have a clear company policy concerning violence and violent behavior. Many times this can be expressed in the employee handbook. Included in this policy should be the importance of letting employees know they *must* report to management whenever court orders have been obtained for protection against threatening friends or even a spouse or ex-spouse. The policy should stress that it is required, not optional, that employees report any employee who threatens a coworker. Employers should provide training so employees will recognize a threat. Any threat should be taken seriously, and employees must be told that shielding a potentially violent coworker can have tragic consequences.

Employers should control the manner in which stress-inducing events are handled on the premises. These include notifications of temporary or permanent layoffs, negative discipline, evaluations, and discharge situations.

Companies should have a plan of action in place before violence occurs. Such a plan might include the following:

- Have a plan for building lock-down. Amazingly, sightseers, looters, and potential copycats may visit your premises after a violent event. When the police arrive, they will want to know which entrances are secured and which are not. Although a security force may be present, they are not a law enforcement body. Therefore, do not seal off a killer's escape route. Let him or her go. The employers' primary responsibility is to maximize the safety of others and to minimize the length and severity of an incident—not to catch the assailant. That's a police matter.

- Know who will be notified and in what order. When lawsuits follow such incidents, attorneys are often extremely interested in knowing whether the employer called for medical and police help promptly.

- Have your plan prepared for the media. While you may not be able to avoid a wounded worker's conversation with the press, an employer should have a designated representative ready to share information with the media as candidly and quickly as possible.

- Have a trauma consultant on call that you can notify immediately. This can be arranged through an Employee Assistance Program.

- Discuss in advance with legal counsel how violent incidents should be handled.

- Plan for how the company will control operations in a crisis. Someone must be designated to take calls from customers and report to them. Be sure to assign someone at senior management level to be ready to talk to family members of coworkers. A quick offer of concern or regret and the comfort of knowing help is available will be important to the victims' survivors.

Experts disagree about the exact behavior pattern or psychological profile of a potentially dangerous employee, but potentially violent people are generally said to:

- Often identify unfairness or malice in the intentions of others and find it easy to do so.

- Seem disgruntled most of the time with job and/or life situation; have an unstable domestic situation.

- Not take responsibility for compromising circumstances but instead blame others consistently.

- Challenge and complain constantly about authority and decision-making by superiors.

- Remember and record others who break company rules to use in defense of personal actions.

- Be obstinate thinkers who refuse to accept or understand opposing arguments, but reject them quickly without thinking.

- Be unable to handle or withstand criticism in even small, obvious matters.

- Trigger reports of threats and/or repeated conflicts with coworkers.

In conclusion, while violence is never expected, if it does take place, a prepared employer will limit its liability and be less likely to be exposed to threatening situations, and its trained employees will be better able to escape harm's way. At the very least, an employer should assure that the receptionist is equipped with a hidden button to silently summon security assistance and train all staff on how to respond if it is used.

The Employee Polygraph Protection Act of 1988

The Employee Polygraph Protection Act (EPPA) is designed to prohibit most private employers from using any polygraph examinations, either for pre-employment screening or, more importantly, after an applicant is hired. Limited testing is permitted only by federal contractors engaged in national security intelligence or counter-intelligence functions. However, the law does contain several limited exemptions that authorize private employers to conduct polygraph exams under certain conditions. These conditions are described below.

This Act is enforced by the Secretary of Labor. Employers who have been found to violate its provisions may be assessed civil penalties of up to $10,000 for each violation. In addition, employers may be liable for violations to employees or prospective employees who have been affected by improper conduct. In these cases, appropriate relief includes employment, reinstatement, promotion, payment of lost wages and benefits, reasonable costs, and attorneys' fees.

Requirements

Each employer subject to the Act is required to post the EPPA poster in a prominent and conspicuous place where other employment law notices are normally displayed. The Act precludes employers from doing the following:

- Requiring, requesting, suggesting, or causing any employee or prospective employee to take or submit to a polygraph exam;

- Using, accepting, or inquiring about the results of a polygraph exam of any employee or applicant for employment; and

- Discharging, disciplining, discriminating against, denying employment or promotion to, or threatening any employee or prospective employee on the basis of the results of the exam, for refusal or failure to take or submit to such exam, for the filing of complaint against an employer relative to the Act, or for testifying in any proceeding or exercising any rights that may be afforded by the Act.

Exemptions

The Employee Polygraph Protection Act provides for five exemptions.

The first exemption is for public sector employers. Excluded from coverage under the Act are the United States government and any state or local government, or any political subdivision of a state or local government that may act in the capacity of an employer. This exclusion also extends to any interstate governmental agency. However, it does not extend to contractors or nongovernmental agents of a governmental entity.

The second exemption is for the federal government in the performance of any counter-intelligence function. This would mean that the federal government can apply polygraph exams to any expert, consultant, or employee of any contractor of the Department of Defense or the Department of Energy. In addition, under this umbrella exemption are also included any function of the National Security Agency, the Defense Intelligence Agency, or the Central Intelligence Agency. However, the national defense and security exemption does not allow private employers or contractors with such agencies to administer a polygraph exam.

The third and most significant exemption is for employers conducting investigations of economic loss or injury, which includes such actions as theft, embezzlement, misappropriation, industrial espionage, sabotage, check kiting, money laundering, or the misappropriation of confidential or trade secret information. In instances such as theft from property managed by the employer or property held by the employer as a fiduciary or custodian, polygraph exams may be administered.

In this regard, however, one has to keep in mind that such economic loss must result from intentional wrongdoing. Unintentional losses, such as those stemming from truck, car, workplace, or other accidents, will not serve as a basis for the administration of a polygraph exam.

In addition, an economic loss incident to a lawful union or employee activity will also not satisfy the economic loss or injury exemption from the Act. It is the business of the employer that must suffer the economic loss or injury. Accordingly, a theft committed by one employee against another will not satisfy the requirement.

In order for this ongoing investigation to be an exempted activity, there must be an investigation of a specific incident. An employer may not request an employee to submit to a polygraph exam in an effort to determine whether thefts have occurred. Moreover, random testing is specifically prohibited by the Act, and an employer may not use the exemption of the so-called "ongoing investigation" to do so. If items in inventory are frequently missing, this is not a sufficient basis for administering polygraph exams.

Further, an employer may request that an employee submit to a polygraph exam only if, in the course of an ongoing investigation, the employee had access to the property subject to the investigation; the employer has a reasonable suspicion that the employee was involved in the incident or activity under investigation; and the employer provides the examinee with a statement before the test explaining what is being investigated and the reason the examinee is being tested.

"Additional supporting evidence" to the action includes evidence indicating that the employee had access to the missing or damaged property that is the subject of the investigation, evidence that led to the reasonable suspicion that the employee was involved in the incident or activity under investigation, or admissions or statements made by the employee before, during, or following such polygraph examination.

Remember, the employer has the burden of establishing that the specific individual or individuals to be tested are reasonably suspected of involvement in the specific economic loss or injury in the event of a complaint.

Lastly, there are exemptions from the Act for prospective employees of manufacturers, distributors, or dispensers of controlled substances, and an exemption for employers who provide security services as the primary business purpose of the enterprise.

If an employer is going to give a polygraph examination and feels that it meets the exceptions, the Act also requires that the following records be kept for a minimum period of three (3) years from the day of the polygraph examination. For each employer who requests an employee to submit to a polygraph exam, a copy of the statement setting forth the specific incident or activity under investigation and the basis for testing that particular employee must be kept.

For any employer who administers a polygraph examination under the controlled substances exemption, which could include many health care employers, the records specifically identifying the loss or injury in question and the nature of the employee's access to the property that is the subject of the investigation must be held for three years.

Also, federal law does not preempt any provision of state or local law. Many states have a polygraph law as well. Lastly, if a collective bargaining agreement provides greater protection to an employee, the greater protection is applicable and is not preempted by the Act.

The best advice to a company intending to use polygraph examinations is to seek legal advice before doing so, to obtain an EPPA poster from the nearest federal Department of Labor, Wage-Hour office, and to display it prominently.

In an interesting 1999 decision from the Seventh Circuit Federal Court of Appeals,[2] the definition of the term "lie detector" was expanded to include a tape recorder in certain circumstances.

In the case, the employee was terminated from employment for refusing to allow the employer to tape record an investigative interview. The court found that in the facts of this case, where the tape recording of the voice could later be analyzed with the use of a "voice stress analyzer" or one of the other devices enumerated, and therefore fit the definition of being a "lie detector," the plaintiff made out an actionable claim that the employer violated the EPPA.

While the dissenting opinion argued that until a voice stress analyzer is actually used there is no violation, the majority disagreed. Accordingly, a wise employer should make it clear in documentation to the employee prior to commencing a tape interview that the purpose of the recording is simply to preserve statements, and that it will not be used in conjunction with devices prohibited under the Act for purpose contrary to the

Act. This is primarily to memorialize all parties' knowledge of the situation at the time of the proposed interview. This is especially so if a refusal to proceed will be considered insubordination subjecting an employee to discipline up to and including termination from employment. Of course, in my opinion, these potential challenges are avoided if employers refrain from tape recording meetings. It is far better to take notes of the conference and, if one must, have all parties to the meeting agree to and sign the meeting notes as constituting the "minutes" of the meeting. Part of this opinion is based on the belief that such a procedure better preserves the record of all parties' "intent," avoids surprises, and is less threatening and far more manageable.

Smoking at the Workplace

In Milwaukee, Wisconsin, the Hospital Council of the Greater Milwaukee Area announced that area hospitals were to be smoke-free. Their prominently placed newspaper ads declared:

> Scientific evidence leaves no doubt that tobacco smoke is the number one avoidable cause of death in our society. Evidence further indicates that nonsmokers should avoid exposure to second-hand tobacco smoke to the fullest extent possible. All individuals who either provide or use hospital services must be assured of a healthy environment.

At one time, smoking was accepted as an inevitable part of the workplace landscape and was regarded by smokers as a right, absent an established fire hazard. However, since the U.S. Surgeon General's landmark reports on the health hazards of smoking and the subsequent public warnings on cigarette packaging and advertising, smoking has been a controversy, culminating in the recent explosion of workplace laws, policies, and lawsuits.

In one case a state supreme court held that the state workers' compensation law does not bar a claim directly against the employer if the claim asserts that the employer breached a duty to provide a safe workplace for an employee. In this case, the employee alleged that she contracted chronic obstructive pulmonary disease because of a smoke-filled office environment in which she was negligently required to work. Although the court reserved its decision on the question of whether an employer has such a duty, three members of the court joined in the opinion that they would recognize such a legal duty on the part of an employer based on its "general duty to provide a safe workplace and the well-documented health hazards of passive smoke inhalation."

CHAPTER TEN

In another case, an employee was permitted to argue constructive discharge when she proved discrimination after complaining about secondhand cigarette smoke. Although the problem was eventually addressed, the employee maintained that after she complained, her work environment became so terrible that she was forced to quit. A state court in Illinois approved the employee's cause of action because the Illinois Clean-Indoor Air Act expressly prohibited discrimination for any individual who exercised her statutory rights, and the employee was not barred from bringing common-law claims of negligence and willful and wanton misconduct. However, the court dismissed her claim of battery, concluding that smoking was a lawful activity and that since smokers generally do not intend to touch other employees with their smoke, the elements for a battery claim did not exist.

Additionally, rules have been proposed by the federal Department of Labor that would require employers to have a policy on smoking with the option of either banning it entirely or allowing it only in ventilated lounges.

Under OSHA proposals, companies could face a maximum $70,000 fine for a willful violation of indoor air quality regulations if they do not adopt a policy to limit worker exposure to secondhand smoke. The basis for much of this activity is an Environmental Protection Agency report that said environmental tobacco smoke causes lung cancer and is the underlying cause of about 3,000 deaths among nonsmokers each year.

These proposals are especially cause for concern for many smaller businesses because accommodating smokers by having a separate smoking lounge separately ventilated to the outside can be very expensive. There is no question that the general trend is to ban smoking entirely in the workplace.

Reasons to Ban Smoking
Many employers that prohibit smoking assert that they do so for the health of their employees and to prevent the aggravation of other health-related conditions such as asthma and allergic reactions to smoke. Employers often justify such actions by citing the 1985 U.S. Surgeon General's report which states that cigarette smoking is clearly the major cause of lung cancer and chronic lung disease in the United States. Moreover, nonsmokers now far outnumber smokers. While there is some disagreement over the threat of smoking to nonsmokers, nonsmokers are likely to grow more militant and litigious if the evidence keeps mounting that they face real danger. Also, many experts feel that nonsmokers are healthier in general and thus save employers' costs for ever-rising group health insurance claims and rates.

Another reason often cited in the debate is the potential for damage to sophisticated computer equipment. Over time, a buildup of the film residue of smoke damages such equipment, and it is difficult to design adequate methods of cleaning parts and machinery.

Law

For the most part, on the federal level in the United States, the private smoking habits of individuals and companies are not regulated. It is not a violation of federal equal employment opportunity law to have a policy prohibiting smoking or even of not hiring smokers. Smokers are not designated a "protected class" of individuals.

However, some courts have protected the privacy rights of job applicants who are smokers. For example, a Florida city violated the privacy rights of a job applicant when it denied her application for a clerk-typist position due to her noncompliance with a city regulation requiring all job applicants to sign an affidavit stating that they have not used tobacco or tobacco products for at least one year immediately preceding the application. The court reasoned that the city's legitimate interests in saving money for the taxpayers by reduced health insurance costs and increased productivity did not override the applicant's privacy interest in being free from regulation of her personal life as a condition of government employment, especially because that condition was lawful and unrelated to job functions. The court held that the off-duty use of tobacco has no relevance to a clerk-typist's ability to perform the duties required by that job.

Additionally, before developing a policy of excluding smokers it is important to check state statutes. For example, in Wisconsin, as is true in several states, an employee cannot be discriminated against for the use of a lawful product outside of work. This does not mean that employers are limited from having a policy of nonsmoking at work; it simply means they cannot have a policy of only hiring nonsmokers.

While federal action as of this writing is mostly in the form of statutory proposals and proposed regulatory reform, many states have regulated the issue in the absence of federal legislation. For example, the State of Wisconsin has had a statute on the books for several years that "protects people who don't smoke tobacco from the smoke generated by those who do," as stated in a Wisconsin Department of Industry, Labor and Human Relations pamphlet. In essence, this law takes a reverse posture: Smoking is restricted unless posted signs indicate otherwise in areas covered by the law.

Workplace Policy

Increasingly, businesses are establishing their own policies, ranging from a policy of not hiring smokers and forcing existing employees to quit or be terminated (in those states that allow smoking in the workplace), to having no policy whatsoever. Many manufacturing companies prohibit smoking during working hours in working areas of the company. Some specifically prohibit smoking in the washrooms as well. Some companies give nonsmokers a bonus reward and give double bonus rewards to smokers who quit. It is up to an owner or manager to establish a policy that fits the business.

One issue today comes from nonsmokers who complain that smokers have more benefits because they get to take a break for smoking and nonsmokers do not. Some managers fear to face this issue due to its inherent challenge to overall morale in an organization, but whatever policy is ultimately adopted in each workplace should clearly discussed and communicated to all concerned. For many, the issue is no problem, but for many others, the issue is a great challenge due to past practice concerns. However, managers should remember that "past practice" that is no longer relevant to current conditions is always subject to change.

Workplace Privacy

The right to privacy has been generally defined as the right to be free from unreasonable searches and seizures, the right to be left alone, and the right to keep private facts private. The right to privacy emanates from the United States Constitution and various state law constitutions and statutes. It is also embodied in the common law. Many issues arise in the workplace concerning whether an individual's right of privacy is being violated. Examples include employment-related testing such as drug tests, polygraph tests, AIDS tests, personality tests, physical examinations, and employment questionnaires. Other areas of concern include the enforcement of work rules and employer searches of lockers, desks, purses, and so on. Questions often arise concerning surveillance of employees at work and off-premises, medical records relative to fitness for duty, claims for workers' compensation and disability benefits, and the extent of corporate communications in statements to employees, third parties, and personnel files relative to privacy rights of an employee.

Workplace searches and seizures by public sector employers are "state actions" and therefore are governed by the Fourth Amendment to the United States Constitution, which states that "the right of people to be secure in their persons, houses, papers, and effects against unreasonable searches and seizures, shall not be violated...." Therefore, search and seizure actions are very limited in the public sector.

However, the same does not apply to private sector employers. Such action in the private workplace is not governmental action and therefore need not be violative of the Fourth Amendment. The Fourth Amendment is not intended to be a limitation upon any private sector employer.

For example, although it has been held by the National Labor Relations Board to be a collective selective bargaining issue, drug testing is not prohibited, and failure to take a drug test can be cited as insubordination that could result in discipline up to and including discharge. However, many states do recognize a right of privacy and that intrusion upon the privacy of another of a highly offensive nature to a reasonable person, in a place that a reasonable person would consider private or in a manner that is actionable for trespass, may be improper. Indeed, the remedies for plaintiffs include not only equitable relief to prevent and restrain such invasions, but also compensatory damages and attorneys' fees. Accordingly then, if the intrusions are done in a reasonable manner, such search and seizure operations are not improper.

It has been held to be lawful for an employer to use a powerful camera lens to observe an employee through the window of his home where such surveillance involved matters that the employer had a right to investigate and about which the employee had no legitimate expectation of privacy, such as a work-related disability claim against the employer. In another case, an action for invasion of privacy due to a drug test, the employee's case was dismissed because a reasonable person would not find the test objectionable and the employer had a significant interest in insuring that employees in the workplace were drug-free.

Many state statutes prohibit the interception and disclosure of wire, electronic, or oral communications through the use of electronic, mechanical, or other devices. However, in many jurisdictions it is not unlawful for a person to intercept a wire, electronic, or oral communication where the person is a party to the communication or where one of the parties to the communication has given prior consent to the interception. This is true as long as the communication is not intercepted for the purpose of committing an unlawful act. Occasionally, an employer may wish to place private investigators in the workplace to investigate employee wrongdoing. It is important for private sector employers to know that such a policy is not prohibited. This is particularly true in retail sales establishments, where internal employee theft can be a concern. In such situations, notifying employees upfront about this condition of employment in the employee handbook will help to avoid misunderstandings concerning the employer's practices.

Relative to the subject of confidentiality of medical records, many state statutes require that patient health care records be kept confidential. This applies especially to mental health records, drug and alcohol treatment records, and other records that may be generated in the course of an employee's use of an employee assistance program. However, patient/ physician privileges are waived when an employee reports a work-related injury and, in the context of a workers' compensation claim, all medical records become public.

In the private sector, the employer has wide discretion and may more often expose itself to liability for not acting out of fear of damaging an individual's privacy rights than it does when acting as it should to protect its own interests. However, especially in these days of computer workstations and high-tech telecommunications, if a company makes the decision to monitor e-mail and computer work product and/or telephone communications for supervisory or quality control, this fact should be made clearly known to the affected employees in policy and training. Failure to do so may result in more serious employee morale and other problems.

The public sector employer may have an even higher duty to notify its employees of its monitoring activities. Consider the April 1999 incident involving a State of Colorado manager who without notice to his employees reviewed their computer work product and e-mail. He was so appalled by what he found in the misuse of the computer system for personal matters that to dramatize his criticism and justify his disgruntlement, he reprinted a pre-nuptial agreement he found on the system from one of the employees without her authorization or knowledge. However, upon the release of this information the rest of the department, instead of taking to heart the warning, filed grievances against him for what they considered an invasion of their privacy. They had received no notice that their computer entries might be monitored and possibly publicly disclosed. This they felt was in violation of past agency practice. It almost cost the manager his job in the uproar over the privacy invasion and publication of personal information, which became more important an issue than the original complaint about poor work performance!

The rule of "privacy" in these situations is similar to when, in a factory environment, an employee is issued a lock for a locker. The individual employee should not be allowed to place his own lock on the locker because this gives rise to an inference of a reasonable expectation of privacy. Instead, it should be made clear that lock and locker are company property, subject to the company master key and possible inspection of contents. The same is true for keys to file drawers and desk drawers, and the contents thereof, in an employee's office. They are company property subject to inspection without notice and without cause. An employer should not give an expectation of privacy in the private or public sector but instead retain its rights to inspect and examine its own property. For employers, it is mostly a matter of confirming one's own natural rights so that there is no surprise among the employees.

Some states protect privacy in their state constitutions. These are Alaska, Arizona, California, Florida, Hawaii, Illinois, Massachusetts, Montana, and Rhode Island. The key is correctly balancing the employer's interest in having a safe and efficient workplace with an individual employee's right to be free from unreasonable invasions of his or her privacy.

A government employee generally has a reasonable expectation of privacy, especially where the individual employee has taken action to secure or keep private their materials without objection by the employer. Searches of a governmental employee's office or where the individual can establish a right to privacy are unreasonable if the search can be proven to have been motivated by other than work-related need or was a mere "fishing expedition" seeking to recover evidence to use against an employee. For example, a search of a state psychiatrist's office was held to be "highly intrusive," and it resulted in a damage award for the plaintiff against the hospital of over $400,000. The court held that absent a clear practice or regulation to the contrary, employees such as the psychiatrist had a reasonable expectation of privacy. It further found that a public sector employer must establish reasonable grounds for suspecting that a search of an office would turn up evidence supporting the suspicion of sexual harassment charges.

Relative to medical testing, privacy rights manifest themselves in several ways. For example, the privacy right includes the right to keep certain personal information from distribution to the public. Accordingly, publication of private information, such as infection with the HIV virus or the development of AIDS, may give rise to liability for an employer. Part of the inquiry is whether the disclosure of the information would be offensive to a reasonable person and is of legitimate concern to the general public. In this regard, remember the "statistical basis" of proof required by the U.S. Supreme Court to defend a refusal to accommodate a disability, and that the Centers for Disease Control in Atlanta has stated officially that the transmission of the HIV virus is unlikely in the workplace. If an investigating manager publishes false attributes or associations about an employee, such as being a Communist or homosexual, this may be enough create liability even if there is no monetary damage or injury to the mislabeled employee's reputation. Always consider whether the communication places the individual in a wrong light to the public. Lastly, unless there is some legitimate business purpose in the medical disclosure by the employer, an employer's intrusion into an individual employee's physical or psychological liberty may expose an employer to legal risk for violation of the basic right to be left alone.

Relative to e-mail and telephone use, the employer's best practice is to have an employee sign an acknowledgment that the e-mail and telephone systems and all e-mail and voice mail messages on it are the employer's property and subject to being monitored. This is an employer right verified by the 1986 Electronic Communications Privacy Act.

To best control the risk in protecting employee privacy, employers should be sure to have systems in place to control access to personnel files because of the confidential (medical or otherwise) information that they may contain. Generally this is accomplished by making such files available only on a "need to know basis." Typically an employee's supervisor would have little reason to review an employee's medical records, for example, so they should be kept in a separate file. Employers are also advised to regularly review files to see if the information in them remains relevant. In addition, exactly what is and what is not a "personnel file" should be defined. Lastly, procedures for how information is disclosed should be reviewed. Employers should have a "disclosure" policy.

Employment Practices Liability Insurance

The very question of whether or not to purchase insurance for coverage of employment practices risk exposure is indicative of how important it is to manage this area of one's business. The decision to self-insure the risk depends upon the controls a company already has in place to manage the risk and the importance to the company of the human resources function in managing the employment relationship. Is there an experienced HR professional on hand, or is there access (typically through corporate or general counsel) to specialized management labor relations and employment law counsel for guidance in decision or strategy making? Sometimes the question is expressed by asking how big a company needs to be before hiring a human resources professional. A rule of thumb is that a company of about 100 employees needs a full-time HR professional for privately or closely held concerns. The risk of a problem is greater for smaller businesses, however one chooses to define "smaller," due to the expense for EPLI. The premiums generally seem to be too high to general business owners, especially if there have been no past problems. Of course, if a company has at least 15 employees or more for a 20-week period in any rolling calendar year, it must be as compliant with the myriad of EEOC and other regulations and other laws as larger companies. Firms with less than 15 employees are more self-monitoring and are typically sensitive to changes in attitudes. Accordingly, managers are more accessible to receive complaints and have true power to affect immediate, correcting change in the employment environment. This is especially true of smaller family-owned and managed businesses. The risk is more a function of a lack of experience in how to deal with severe, puzzling, or antisocial behavior. Some employees, or their trusted, significant others, are "street-smart" relative to the administrative and judicial systems. They know what to say, when to say it, and have a tendency to remember incidents and conversations differently from the smaller business owner or manager, and to their own advantage. Therefore, smaller businesses can be an easier target for someone to set up for a lawsuit.

When considering EPLI coverage, the first question employers usually ask is "Isn't this coverage already included under the general liability policy?" General liability policies, according to the carriers of such insurance, were not specifically designed to cover today's employment discrimination, breach of employment contract, or wrongful discharge claims. Numerous courts have held that such employer conduct does not constitute an "accident" or "occurrence," but rather constitutes "intentional acts" that fall outside the coverage provided by the standard general liability policy. Other exclusions might also apply. For example, most general policies specifically exclude wrongful discharge type claims and discrimination claims brought by past, present, or prospective employees. In addition, many general liability carriers exclude bodily injury claims by employees and may consider employment-related emotional injuries to be bodily injury and therefore uncovered. Likewise, so-called "umbrella" policies may further contain exclusions relating to termination from employment and failure to promote or failure to hire a prospective employee. A manager should be sure to understand what limitations there may be with existing policies for any coverage issues.

Another common question is whether a "directors and officers" (D & O) liability or fiduciary liability policy provides coverage in this area. D & O liability coverage may be triggered only if and only for as long as a director or officer is named in the suit. Generally, the defense provisions under a fiduciary liability policy may be triggered only if the claim alleges a breach of fiduciary duty or error or omission in the administration of a covered plan. Thus, other forms of insurance may not provide adequate protection for employers facing today's employment claims. This void in the insurance marketplace has led to the development of EPLI policies.

Generally, insured under EPLI policies are the organization and its directors, officers, and employees on a claims-made basis. This is an important expansion because in employment law cases often the culpability of the corporation and the resulting allocation of costs assigned to the corporate employer make the D & O policy an incomplete source of protection. In contrast, the corporation is also insured under an EPLI policy.

An advantage to separate EPLI coverage is the broad range of employment-related actions specifically covered, including wrongful termination, breach of contract, discrimination, workplace harassment, failure to employ or promote, deprivation of career opportunity, negligent evaluation and employment-related misrepresentation, defamation, or wrongful infliction of emotional distress. Such policy should cover written demands for monetary damages as well as civil and arbitration proceedings brought by or on behalf of past, present, or prospective employees. Regulatory and administrative proceedings may also be covered.

EPLI policies should include coverage for judgments, settlements, and defense costs. Most policies will not cover fines or penalties imposed by law, the multiple portions of any multiplied damage award, or matters uninsurable by law. Punitive damages are not generally covered because they may be awarded as a matter of public policy to punish the defendant for egregious behavior. Punitive awards are considered fines or penalties and in many jurisdictions are uninsurable. Acts committed against public policy are likewise uninsurable.

Some policies contain an exclusion for intentional acts. However, many will not because carriers reason that an employer that follows the appropriate human resources policies and practices can still be sued by plaintiffs who perceive that an actual or alleged injustice (intentional act) has been done to them. Most policies will differentiate between intentional acts done in good faith as opposed to purposeful violations of the law or deliberately fraudulent acts.

Most policies include a "duty-to-defend" policy, and defense costs are included in the limit of liability. EPLI is generally available for companies of all sizes with good human resource policies and practices, capable management, and strong financial results. Most carriers look for companies that utilize a standard of fairness in the employer-employee relationship, that care about their employees, and that promote employee welfare. Generally, limits of up to $10 million or more are available based upon the specifics of a particular company. Underwriting factors include the nature of the business, number of employees, financial condition, stability of the industry, quality of human resources functioning, and litigation history. Deductibles are determined on a case-by-case basis as well. Most carriers will require review of the latest audited annual report, a copy of the employee handbook (see Chapter Two), and the most recent EEO-1 Report, if applicable. Most applications will ask for a listing of recent employment lawsuits as well as administrative proceedings.

One recent article suggests that for a company with 50 employees a typical policy might have a $6,000 premium, a $5,000 deductible, and five percent copayment. Average premiums may range from $2,000 to $2,500 for very small employers to $20,000 per year for a company of around

500 employees. Whether or not EPLI is worthwhile is up to the employer, its risk manager or consultant, and its agent.

List of Employment Laws, Required Record-Keeping
Employment Laws

There are numerous state and federal employment law regulations that apply to businesses, depending upon the number of employees at a particular business establishment. While these may vary from state to state, in general, employers can expect to be subject to the following list of laws.

One or More Employees

1. Child labor laws (state and federal)

2. Clean Indoor Air Act (state and federal)

3. Consumer Credit Protection Act

4. Contract Compliance Laws (state)

5   Davis-Bacon Act

6. Drug-Free Workplace Act of 1988

7. Employee Polygraph Protection Act

8. Employee Retirement Income Security Act (ERISA)

9. Equal Pay Act (Amendment to FSLA)

10. Fair Credit Reporting Act

11. Fair Employment Acts (state)

12. Fair Labor Standards Act (FLSA)

13. Federal Immigration Reform and Control Act (I-9 Form)

14. Health Insurance Portability and Accountability Act of 1996 (HIPAA)

15. Federal Unemployment Tax Act (FUTA)

16. Labor Management Reporting Act (Landrum-Griffin Act)

17. National Labor Relations Act, as amended

18. Mental Health Parity Act

19. OSHA's Hazard Communication Standard

20. Occupational Safety and Health Act

21. Portal-to-Portal Act

22. Reconstruction Era Statutes

23. Rehabilitation Act of 1973

24. Right-to-Know Laws (state Hazard Communication Statutes)

25. Social Security Act

26. Unemployment Compensation Acts (state)

27. Walsh-Healey Act

28. Workers' Compensation Acts (state)

15 Employees
1. Americans With Disabilities Act

2. Civil Rights Act of 1991

3. Pregnancy Discrimination Act

4. Title VII of Civil Rights Act of 1964

20 Employees
1. Age Discrimination in Employment Act

2. Consolidated Omnibus Reconciliation Act (COBRA)

    a. Omnibus Reconciliation Act of 1986 (Bankruptcy Proceedings)

    b. Omnibus Reconciliation Act of 1989 (Disabled & Medicare)

    c. Omnibus Reconciliation Act of 1993 ($150,000 Limit Retirement Plans)

3. Older Worker's Benefit Protection Act of 1990

50 Employees
1. EEO-1 Report (Federal Contractors)

2. Executive Order 11246 (Affirmative Action)

3. Family & Medical Leave Act (and most state Acts)

4. Plant Closing Laws (state)

5. Vietnam Era Veteran's Readjustment Assistance Act

6. Vocational Rehabilitation Act (Federal Contractors)

75 Employees
Omnibus Reconciliation Act of 1990

100 Employees
1. EEO-1 Report

2. Employee Commute Options

3. VETS 100

4. Worker Adjustment Retraining Notification Act (WARN)

Required Record-Keeping
Keeping business records can have a big impact in the event of a lawsuit. Not only can a company be fined by governmental agencies for not keeping required records, what a company does keep, if not required, can cause them trouble too.

For example, in one situation a summer employee is assigned to write a memo on company safety issues. To make the report, he noted as many safety concerns as he could find, such as greasy floors, blocked emergency exists, etc. He also included quotes from shop employees. He was very proud of his report and showed it to other employees. Fortunately for the company, all the safety hazards noted were corrected. However, had that not taken place, and had an accident occurred, any of the problems cited in the report could have been used against the company as testimony that it was aware of violations of federal and state safety laws. Smart employers pay attention to the record-keeping requirements to make sure they are complied with, but also understand that many sensitive topics should not be handled in a way that might provide disclosure on discovery requests in any contested case, either involving employment law violations, safety violations, or accident and injury liability matters.

CHAPTER TEN

The following simple rules outline what *not* to do.

- Never write on file folders or jackets. These can be subject to subpoena, and sharp personal injury lawyers or governmental attorneys would be sure to do so in a broad discovery request. Also, never make notes on resumes or job applications in the interview process.

- Be sure to read all correspondence before it goes out. This may sound simple, but can save a company much grief later.

- Remember that computer files are documents and can be subpoenaed as well. Therefore, know that any e-mail messages are just as much company documents as any other written record.

Relative to personnel files, keep in mind that in any employment-related litigation, the first thing that will be requested by an employee's attorney is to see the personnel file. The best protocol to follow is to never put anything into the file that has not also been viewed by the employee, so that there are no surprises when the file is opened and reviewed by some third party. Attorney/client work product concerning individual employees can be held confidential and should not be placed in an employee personnel file, even though that work product may describe questions relating to the individual employee. Any document to be kept confidential should be marked "confidential." It is a good practice to open the personnel file contents to the employee periodically, such as during annual performance appraisal evaluation interviews. If miscellaneous documents have found their way into a personnel file and should not be there, they should be purged. Keep in mind also that many state statutes require review and photocopying of personnel files upon request of an employee or former employee.

Relative to general business records, the following records and record retention schedule are recommended.

Record Retention Schedule
It is recommended that businesses follow the record retention schedule outlined below:

The following records should be kept for at least one (1) year:

Bank reconciliations

Correspondence (routine) with customers or vendors

Duplicate deposit slips

Purchase orders (except purchasing department copy)

Receiving sheets

Requisitions

Stenographer's notebooks

Stockroom withdrawal forms

The following records should be kept for at least three (3) years:

Correspondence (general)

Insurance policies (expired)

Internal audit reports (in some situations, longer retention periods may be desirable)

Internal reports (miscellaneous)

Petty cash vouchers

Physical inventory tags

Savings bond registration records of employees

The following records should be kept for at least seven (7) years:

Accident reports and claims (settled cases)

Accounts payable ledgers and schedules

Accounts receivable ledgers and schedules

Checks (canceled, but see exception below)

Contracts and leases (expired)

Expense analyses and expense distribution schedules

Inventories of products, materials, and supplies

Invoices to customers

Invoices from vendors

Notes receivable ledgers and schedules

Option records (expired)

Payroll records and summaries, including payments to pensioners

Plant cost ledgers

Purchase orders (purchasing department copy)

Sales records

Scrap and salvage records (inventories, sales, etc.)

Stock and bond certificates (canceled)

Subsidiary ledgers

Time books

Voucher register and schedules

Vouchers for payments to vendors, employees, etc. (includes allowances and reimbursement of employees, officers, etc., for travel and entertainment expenses)

The following records should be kept permanently:

Audit reports of accountants

Capital stock and bond records; ledgers, transfer registers, stubs showing issues, record of interest coupons, options, etc.

Cash books

Charts of accounts

Checks (canceled, for important payments, i.e., taxes, purchases of property, special contracts, etc.; checks should be filed with the papers pertaining to the underlying transaction)

Contracts and leases still in effect

Correspondence (legal and important matters only)

Deeds, mortgages, and bills of sale

Depreciation schedules

Financial statements (end-of-year, other months optional)

General and private ledgers (and end-of-year trial balances)

Insurance records, current accident reports, claims, policies, etc.

Journals

Minute books of directors and stockholders meetings, including by-laws and charter

Property appraisals by outside appraisers

Property records, including costs, depreciation reserves, end-of-year trial balances, depreciation schedules, blueprints, and plans

Tax returns and worksheets, revenue agents' reports, and other documents relating to determination of income tax liability

Trademark registrations

Requirements for Retention of Personnel Records

Again, this is not an exhaustive list of every record possible, and you will note in some areas there is no definite period of retention specified by statutes, only a recommendation based upon experience. Please note that in some cases the recommendation exceeds the actual statutory requirement. Lastly, regardless of any retention period, if a lawsuit or other legal proceeding is involved, any records that relate to the case should be retained until the matter is finally resolved.

Type of Record	Records to Be Retained	Period of Record Retention
Payroll Records	Name, address, Social Security number, date of hire and termination, time each workday began and ended, time each meal period was started and concluded, total hours worked	3 years from termination of employment is statutory requirement, but 6 years is recommended; the longest statute of limitations is 6 years

Type of Record	Records to Be Retained	Period of Record Retention
	in each day and each week, rate of pay and wages paid during each pay period, amount of and reason for each deduction from wages, and daily output of an employee not paid on an elapsed time basis.	for the filing of a personnel-related legal action
Jobs Evaluations, Seniority System Records, and Documents Relating to Disciplinary Action	Job and/or merit evaluations; other data that explains any pay differential between the sexes; records relating to promotion, demotion, transfer, discipline, termination; copies of tests given to employees; and the results of physical examinations considered in connection with any personnel action.	2 years from making the record or related personnel action
Employment Taxes	Income tax withholding, Social Security, unemployment compensation, and advanced date earned income credit payments.	4 years from date of filing
Employment Applications	Applications for positions known by the applicant to be of a temporary nature.	90 days from date of filing
	All other applications including related records, job orders to employment agencies or labor organizations, and advertisements.	1 year from date of filing (If federal contractor or subcontractor, then retain for current year and prior affirmative action year.)
Employment Eligibility and Verification	I-9 Form	3 years from date of filing or 1 year from termination of employment, whichever is later.

Type of Record	Records to Be Retained	Period of Record Retention
Apprenticeship	All employment records of apprentice in a program for skilled trades certified by the Federal Department of Labor.	5 years from the date an employee completes the program
	All employment records of apprentices in a program for skilled trades under which the employer pays a subminimum wage.	3 years from the termination date of the program
	A chronological listing of the names, addresses, sex, and minority group identification of all applicants for an apprentice-ship program; any test papers and notes of interviews.	The greater of 2 years or program length
Family and Medical Leave	Medical certifications and related medical information; type of leave taken; dates or hours of leave taken; name, position, and pay rate of individual on leave; copies of all notices given to or received from employee; documents describing employee benefits and status; records of any dispute between employer and employee.	3 years
Affirmative Action Records	Written affirmative action plans; supporting documentation, analyses, and related records or raw data; tests given to employees; documents on their use and validation studies.	Duration of federal contract
	Internal complaints and related documents from handicapped workers, termination of disabled veterans and veterans of the Vietnam era; all records concerning the action(s) taken in response to such complaints.	1 year from employment
	EEO-1 Reports	Retain a copy of the most recent report filed for each reporting unit
Handicapped Workers Paid at a Subminimum Wage	Certificates authorizing payment at less than minimum wage.	3 years from termination of employment

Miscellaneous Employment Law Issues

Type of Record	Records to Be Retained	Period of Record Retention
Pensions, Profit Sharing, and Other Employee Benefit Plans	Plan documents, reports, and all recorded information used in compiling required reports.	6 years from date of filing
	Listing of years of services and vesting percentage of each employee.	No definite period specified
	Records required to determine eligibility and employee benefits, including age, service, marital status, and pay records; documents relating to discipline and promotion, demotion, or transfer.	No definite period specified
	Records indicating the amount of separation and/or sickness and accident benefits paid out of a Supplemental Unemployment Benefit trust to each employee as well as records of employee contributions, if any.	6 years from the date of making the record or the related personnel action
Employee Benefit Plans and Seniority or Merit Rating Systems	Plan descriptions, insurance contracts, labor agreements after termination.	Full period that plan is in effect plus 1 year
Employment of Minors and Student Learners	**Student Learners:** Copies of employment applications; certificates authorizing the employment of student learners; payroll records; and a notation of occupation.	3 years from termination of employment
	Minors: Name, address, and date of birth; certificate of age; dates of hire and termination; times each work day began and ended; times of daily meal period(s); total hours worked in each day and week; output of minor employee if paid other than on an elapsed time basis; and any written training agreements.	3 years from termination of employment

Type of Record	Records to Be Retained	Period of Record Retention
Occupational Injury and Illness	Documents concerning work-related injuries or illnesses for worker's compensation purposes.	The later of 12 years from date of injury, death, or last payment of compensation
	As to minors, employees in the armed services or suffering from insanity; for worker's compensation purposes.	12 years from the date the limitation on a claim would expire
	General OSHA employee medical records (which may include documents concerning work-related injuries or illnesses kept for workers' compensation purposes but does not include first aid and medical records of short-term employees, i.e., individuals employed for less than one year).	30 years from termination of employment
	OSHA Forms 100, 101, 102, and 200, including supporting records.	5 years after year reported
	Noise exposure measurement.	2 years
	Audiometric exams.	Duration of employment
	OSHA employers subject to special standards:	
	Asbestos - Personal and environmental monitoring records and employee medical examinations for asbestos.	30 years from termination of employment
	Carcinogen - Roster of personnel and medical records.	30 years from termination of employment
	Bloodborne Diseases - Personnel and medical records.	30 years from termination of employment
	Radiation - Records of exposed employees.	30 years from termination of employment
Toxic Substances	MSDS regarding toxic substance of written lists identifying toxic substances	30 years from date substance was last received in the workplace and 30 years from date of last complaint for records of significant adverse reaction to employee's health

Federal Posting Requirements

The following chart indicates federal requirements for posting notices. All required posters should be displayed in a prominent location on the employer's premises where employees are likely to see them. Employers should check for what other notices are required, such as those ordered by fire, factory, and safety inspectors concerning floor capacity, no smoking, and so on, as well as the duplicative state and municipal regulatory posters.

Why is it important to post the posters? In one federal case, an employer was sued by a former employee who alleged his termination was a result of age discrimination. The employer defended by showing that the employee's action was filed untimely and was, therefore, barred by the applicable statute of limitations.

However, what otherwise would have been a winning defense by the employer failed. The court found that since the employer had never posted the required notice to the employee in the form of the poster regarding the employee's rights regarding age discrimination, there could be no presumption that the employee was aware of the time requirements for bringing his action. According to the court, the only way the employer could win absent having posted the proper notice was to produce evidence that the employee had general knowledge of his rights through some other source. Of course, no direct evidence of this knowledge could be produced.

Subject: Safety
Statute: Occupational Safety and Health Act
Federal Posting Requirements: "Job Safety and Health Protection" OSHA 2203-1989 (revised) for employers engaged in interstate commerce; effective 1/1/83, the following industries are exempt: retail trade, finance, insurance, and real estate services.
Order from: Local or regional OSHA office
Jurisdiction: Required of all employers with 11 or more employees
Federal Posting Requirements: Annual summary of the previous year's occupational injuries and illnesses is to be posted by February 1. Use OSHA Form 200.

Subject: Equal Employment Opportunity
Statute: Civil Rights Act of 1964, Title VII
Federal Posting Requirements: One poster "Equal Employment Opportunity is the Law" is issued jointly by the EEOC and OFCCP. This poster satisfies posting requirements for handicapped veterans, age, and non-discrimination in employment under Title VII and E.O. 11246.

Subject: Federal Contractors
Statute: E.O. 11246, as amended

Subject: Handicapped Workers
Statute: Rehabilitation Act of 1973, Section 503
Order from: Local EEOC or OFCCP office

Subject: Persons over 40 years of Age
Statute: Required of most employers with 20 or more employees
Federal Posting Requirements: ADEA of 1967, as amended

Subject: Veterans
Statute: Vietnam Era Veterans' Readjustment Assistance Act of 1974

Subject: Disabled Workers
Statute: The Americans with Disabilities Act of 1990

Subject: Family Leave
Statute: Family & Medical Leave Act of 1993
Federal Posting Requirements: Wage Hour Publication 1420 (June 1993)

Subject: Minimum Wage
Statute: Fair Labor Standards Act
Federal Posting Requirements: Wage-Hour Publication 1088 (rev. August 1982)
Order from: Local or regional Wage & Hour office

Subject: Government Contractors
Statute: Walsh-Healey Public Contracts Act or Service Contract Act
Federal Posting Requirements: "Notice to Employees Working on Government Contracts" WH 1313 (rev. January 1986)
Order from: Local or regional Wage & Hour office

Subject: Government Contractors
Statute: Davis-Bacon Act
Federal Posting Requirements: "Notice to all Employees Working on Federal or Federally Financed Construction Projects" WH 1321 (rev. January 1986)

Subject: Polygraphs
Federal Posting Requirements: "Employee Polygraph Protection Act" WH 1462 (September 1988)
Order from: Local or regional Wage & Hour office

Endnotes

1   42 U.S.C. 12182 (b)(3).

2   *Veazey v. Communications & Cable of Chicago, Inc.*, 139 CCH Labor Cases ¶10,556.

Answers to Chapter Ten Test Your Knowledge

1. True, 2. True, 3. True, 4. True, 5. False [there is no exception to the EPPA for unintentional loss investigations for covered employers], 6. True, 7. True, 8. True, 9. True, 10. True

Epilogue

Looking Backward and Forward

In 1990 I was asked the following intriguing question by the executive director of an international manufacturing association: "What were the two most significant developments in the decade of the 1980s for business, and what are the two most significant things to look for in the decade of the 1990s?"

I answered that I believed that one of the most significant events of the 1980s was the recession of 1982-83, because it forced a rethinking of management philosophy in the way we must compete to survive. No longer was it viable to merely pass cost increases onto a customer who was also struggling to compete, or even to buy labor peace by capitulating to ever-increasing wage demands with no accompanying increase in productivity. The new way of management re-recognized the traditional values of the importance of the customer by just-in-time delivery of competitively priced quality products.

At the same time, management was forced to get tough, not only with the representatives of labor, but also internally with its own management personnel. Getting by was no longer enough. Being on the cutting edge meant improvement upon, not maintenance of, the status quo. Business responded by improving its technology as well as its management practices. Now we see as the norm not only computer-programmed production methods, but also better personnel management, including the implementation of innovations such as "quality circles," "gain-sharing," and "team-building" techniques.

The second major development of the 1980s was the explosion of information technology brought about by the realization of the computer revolution. Information systems, such as statistical data control, reduced the need for middle management personnel. We all run leaner and faster than ever before, unencumbered by middle managers interpreting local conditions to top management. Now production information can be readily accessible to top management so that necessary decision-making can be easily based on current, accurate read-outs of the crucial information. This is a concept that, before the computer revolution of the 1980s, had never been thought possible.

Looking at the 1990s, because of the obvious census information about the aging of the baby boom generation, the trends we saw predicted that the mass training of the past in our public and vocational schools may be replaced by a more individualized training on the job and at the direction and control of the employer. Accordingly, managers, because of the shortage of qualified, competent personnel, became as much training agents as directors and coordinators of the workflow. Because of the labor shortage projected by the certain census downturn in an expanding economy, we looked within our operations more and more in the 1990s in training existing competent personnel rather than hiring new, scarcer, untested, and untrained individuals to perform in an increasingly complex and complicated work environment. Management and training of our personnel were more important than ever before to the successful operation of our business in the 1990s.

The second significant development of the 1990s was a continuation of what some call the "politics of envy." The deepening abyss separating the haves and the have-nots drove our free society to move backward to a more socialized way of life. It is important, therefore, to be wary about the encroachment of the socialist-styled "do-gooders" into the regulation of industry and commerce. I saw their activity manifested in such congressional mandates as the infamous IRS Section 89 (which was ultimately repealed), vaguely worded disabilities discrimination laws, increasingly impossible environmental waste regulations, OSHA safety standards and increased penalties for violation, the debate about mandated health insurance, and the taxation increases to pay off our massive federal debt without apparent decreases in the size of the federal budget.

In thinking about these issues, I felt it was important to keep in mind some interesting facts released by the United States government. According to statistics prepared by the United States Labor Department, in dealing with wage and hour law violations, in one fiscal year, the federal government handled over 74,000 complaint actions which resulted in more than $25 million in minimum-wage back payments due to 133,000 employees and $135 million in overtime underpayment due to 331,000 employees.

In one fiscal year, the Equal Employment Opportunity Commission (EEOC) reported it received the most charges of discrimination ever. The Agency received 87,942 new charges, a 21.6 percent increase in filings. The most common issue was discriminatory discharges from employment, accounting for 49.6 percentage of the cases. The EEOC itself also filed more lawsuits than ever before against employers, recovering a record monetary benefit of $126.8 million through its effort. In addition, resolution of its legal actions added $34.2 million, mostly in the form of back pay. In figures released by the EEOC concerning the Americans with Disabilities Act (ADA), the EEOC said that in one fiscal year, 11,215 charges were filed under the ADA and an additional 4,149 ADA charges were filed concurrently with other statutes as well. This accounted for 17.4 percent of all the charges filed with the EEOC in 1993. Of these, 22.8 percent were related to allegations that the employer failed to provide reasonable accommodation.

The NLRB reported employers in a fiscal year paid over $44 million in back-pay orders. At first blush it may not appear that the NLRB has the monetary impact of the other agencies. However, when one considers that employees covered by the NLRA may be only as little as 12 percent of the workforce, by comparison the impact of the NLRB is actually much greater. Also, think about the impact of the decision by the NLRB to seek an injunction against the major league baseball owners to remedy allegations of refusal to bargain charges. Due to the fact that if the major league baseball owners refused to accept the offer to return to work by the players, they would have risked back pay assessments of millions of dollars if the NLRB could establish that the owners' actions had changed the character of the work stoppage to an unfair labor practice strike. This risk was so great that although the owners had suffered the loss of one-third of the baseball season, its Play-offs and the World Series in 1994, they opened the 1995 season even though there was no settlement of the issues with the union that brought about the situation in the first place. The fiscal impact is that player contracts for certain stars are negotiated for over $100 million!

Finally, added to that were the numerous awards of money damages awarded by courts and juries to disgruntled employees in wrongful discharge actions. It has been reported that as of 1985, two million of the sixty million at-will employees in the United States are fired annually, of whom it is estimated 150,000 to 200,000 would have causes of action if there existed just cause requirements for termination under the law (Stieber, "Recent Developments in Employment-At-Will", 36 Labor Law Journal 557, 558 (1985)). Consider the famous California study that found jury verdicts in favor of the employee in approximately three-fourths of the cases, with an average verdict amount of over $500,000. Of course, many cases are settled out of court and never reach a jury. Clearly, the structure of the laws in the United States seemed to have a direct bearing on the cost of doing business, and therefore a major impact on our global competitiveness.

However, our global competitiveness did not diminish even though all of these statistics are greater than ever imagined—in fact, even though punitive damages were awarded in more employment disputes and employer negligence cases than in any other kind of lawsuit. Indeed, punitive damages were awarded in 34 percent of discrimination cases and 38 percent of sexual harassment cases, with plaintiffs prevailing in 58 percent of such cases in 1997, up from 51 percent the year before. Yet our economy has been humming against the background of a sluggish European Community economy and until recently a depressed Asian one. Accordingly, one can only draw the conclusion that some inner strength overrides these statistics in the aggregate, and it is only individual businesses, not business as a whole, that seems to suffer. In the United States, one must then feel like the prosperous farmer, hoping it only rains on his field while crop-damaging hail falls on his neighbor's. This danger becomes one of greater significance to the smaller business that lacks the resources and talent to arm itself against the larger risk of liability for employment practices exposure. Moreover, this process of change toward increased risk has not been abated by such insecurity in the 1990s. While some of the following has gone unnoticed, the trend toward greater liability and risk exposure has been all too unmistakable.

Changes Already Made

President Clinton was inaugurated January 20, 1993. On February 1, 1993, he signed Executive Order 12836, revoking Executive Order 12818 signed by former President Bush prohibiting any agency, contractor, or construction manager from imposing a union-only requirement on any other contractor or subcontractor seeking to perform federal construction work. Now such union-only project agreements between federal contractors and labor organizations, which have the effect of eliminating competition from non-union organizations in the name of securing freedom from labor strife, are permitted. The elimination of potential competitive bidders for federal work by executive fiat and the impact on the cost to the taxpayer for the work to be performed did not seem to enter into the equation of the deficit-reducing budget Chief Executive. However, this appears to be part of the price for labor peace.

Interestingly, Executive Order 12836 reversed another policy of the Bush Administration, Executive Order 12800. This order required unionized federal contractors to post workplace notices informing employees of their right to refrain from joining a union and of nonmembers' right to object to the use of mandatory union dues for activities unrelated to collective bargaining, contract administration, and grievance adjustment. It was reported that President Clinton characterized the effect of the notification to employees of their rights under federal law as "distinctly antiunion."

After the devastating hurricane in Florida in the fall of 1992, President Bush suspended the Davis-Bacon regulations which mandate prevailing wages (i.e., union wages) on federal clean-up projects. President Clinton rescinded that suspension.

On February 5, 1993, the Family and Medical Leave Act of 1993 (FMLA) was enacted, guaranteeing eligible employees the right to take unpaid leave from a job for family or medical reasons. Of course, in some states, employees have had similar rights for some time. However, the law providing employees with the more liberal benefits is the controlling law.

In general, the FMLA requires employers with 50 or more employees to provide, upon request, up to 12 weeks of unpaid leave upon the birth, adoption, or serious illness of a child; the serious illness of a parent or spouse; or the employee's own illness. The employer must continue health benefits during leave time. If an employee exercises these rights but fails to return to work after the expiration of the leave, the employer may recoup the cost of continuing the health insurance benefits. All covered employers are required to notify employees of their rights by posting the appropriate poster and publishing the employer's policy for exercising rights pursuant to the FMLA. This is normally done in the company employee manual or handbook.

Finally, making good on Vice President Al Gore's promise to the AFL-CIO, on March 8, 1995, President Clinton signed Executive Order 12954, "Ensuring The Economical And Efficient Administration And Completion Of Federal Government Contracts." Pursuant to this order, if the Secretary of Labor finds that a federal contractor (of which there are more than 28,000 doing business of the government in excess of $100,000 that meet the minimum threshold of coverage under the Executive Order's terms) is violating labor law in the use of hiring permanent replacement employees, the Agency involved will be directed to terminate any contract in existence and prospectively debar such employer from future contracts. To provide a frame of reference to understand the significance of this order, in 1994 about 30 of the recorded 454 strikes involved the use of replacement workers.

According to a House of Representatives Committee Report on legislation introduced to nullify Executive Order 12954, the majority found:

- There is no connection between the Executive Order and the goal of economy and efficiency in federal procurement.

- The Executive Order is inconsistent with the National Labor Relations Act.

- The Executive Order is an exercise of regulatory authority that can not be justified as a legitimate condition of doing business with the federal government.

- The Executive Order revises 55 years of labor management law that recognizes the right of employers to maintain operations during an economic strike by hiring replacement workers.

Which view will prevail? As of this writing, Republicans make up the majority in both Houses of the U.S. Congress. For now, it is doubtful that any of the legislative initiatives proposed to further regulate the employment relationship during the first two years of the Clinton Administration's term will be acted upon because of the change in leadership. However, this may create a pent-up demand to do so in the future. Undoubtedly, the following proposals would likely become part of a new agenda in the future if political conditions changed again. Therefore, I think it is important to take note of some of these proposals.

These include the following:

1. The Chavez Workplace Fairness Bills. These companion pieces of legislation were introduced almost simultaneously in the first few weeks of January 1993 in the House of Representatives and the Senate by Representative Clay, D-MO., and Senator Metzenbaum, D-OH. This legislation would have overturned existing U.S. Supreme Court precedent of more than 55 years by making it an unfair labor practice for employers to continue operating during an economic strike by hiring permanent replacements. Other elements in the proposed law would have allowed recognitional picketing for the purpose of union organizing. This also would have been a tremendous change in existing law, and is especially feared by small and mid-sized businesses because such small enterprises might not have the economic strength to legally resist such picketing.

2. The National Labor Relations Fair Elections Act was also introduced in the first month of the legislative term of the first two years of the Clinton Administration in January 1993. This bill's purpose would have changed the procedures by which a union becomes certified as the exclusive representative of a bargaining unit of employees at any previously non-union operation. Currently, in order for the national Labor Relations Board to hold a secret-ballot election, a union must establish a sufficient showing of interest from employees in the unit by signing up a minimum of 30 percent to union authorization cards or other genuine evidence signifying such interest. Once a petition is filed with the NLRB, generally, an election is conducted within four to eight weeks. If the union receives a majority of those that vote, it will be certified as a persuasive representative of the employees in that unit.

This bill would change existing procedures. First, the NLRB could certify the union *without an election* if the union collected authorization cards from 75 percent of the employees and if no union had existed at that company. If the union could show it had signed authorization cards from 50 percent of the employees in the unit, the NLRB would be required to hold the election within 15 days of the filing of the petition. Because the union would control the timing of the filing of the petition, it would drastically reduce the time an employer would have to present its reasons to employees as to why it would be legally opposed to the union. Another change would be that if the employer chose to present such reasons to employees on its own premises during working hours, an equal opportunity for representatives of the labor organization to address the employees for an equal amount of time on company premises during company-paid time would also be required.

These changes would have made it much easier for unions to organize businesses, in my opinion. President Clinton stated that he favored the concept of making it easier for unions to organize businesses and would have signed such legislation had it reached his desk.

3. Increases in the minimum wage were introduced that would have indexed the minimum wage in the same manner as Social Security benefit increases and raised the minimum wage to $6.75 per hour beginning in September 1995. A stated goal of the Clinton Administration has always been to "make work pay." In fact, one of its proposals included mandating double pay for all hours worked over 40 in a workweek. While it has been some time since the minimum wage was raised to its current $5.15 per hour, since the start of the Fair Labor Standards Act (FSLA) in Franklin Roosevelt's Presidency, the minimum wage has never been indexed to any variable economic indicator.

4. The Equal Remedies Act of 1993, also introduced in January 1993 in the House of Representatives by Representative Kennelly, D-CT, and in the Senate by Senator Kennedy, D-MA, would have lifted the caps on punitive and compensatory damages contained in the Civil Rights Act of 1991 and the Americans with Disabilities Act of 1990. Current law limits compensation and punitive damages to $300,000 for companies with more than 500 employees. Many commentators remember that Senator Kennedy's first words to the press after emerging from the all-night negotiating session with the Bush Administration on the heels of the Clarence Thomas–Anita Hill hearings were to vow to remove the damage caps he had just agreed to in order to have the bill passed and signed into law by President Bush.

5. The Comprehensive Occupational Safety and Health Act would have mandated employers to establish joint labor-management safety committees and greatly increase monetary and even criminal penalties available under the law for violations. Many employer organizations pointed to the fact during the debate that the filing of OSHA complaints is often a tactic utilized by labor organizations in union organizing drives. Some commentators opposing this legislation pointed out that OSHA did not need more power. While safety is a laudable goal—and since the agency's creation in 1970 it has produced numerous detailed rules, and American industry has spent over several hundred billion dollars to comply with those rules—the rate of work days missed due to injury is about the same as it was in 1973. Indeed, one expert estimated that it takes businesses 54 million hours per year just to fill out the OSHA forms, and OSHA still issued 19,233 citations in 1994 for not keeping its forms correctly.

6. Privacy for Consumers and Workers Act would have prohibited an employer from engaging in electronic monitoring of employees who have been employed for five or more years and severely limit the monitoring of other employees in the workplace as well. With the advent of telecommuting, the issues surrounding the supervision of employees working at distant places from company headquarters would become much more difficult under this legislation.

7. The Worker Adjustment and Retraining Notification Act would have amended the existing WARN Act by extending the notification time to employees for plant closings from 60 to 180 days. Moreover, the proposed Act would mandate employers to pay up to $10,000 in training and other benefits to U.S. employees who lost their jobs because of a "transfer of work" to certain foreign countries. In addition, because of the fact that very few lawsuits were filed to enforce the provisions of the original WARN law, considerations in the proposal would have changed its enforcement by private lawsuit to enforcement by the U.S. Labor Department itself and increase dramatically the penalty damages for violations.

8. The Protection From Coercive Employment Agreements Act was introduced by U.S. Senator Russell Feingold, D-WI, to amend the Age Discrimination in Employment Act, the Americans with Disabilities Act, the Civil Rights Act of 1964, and several other civil rights laws by prohibiting employers from requiring employees to submit discrimination claims to mandatory arbitration.

    This legislation is intended to counter a 1991 U.S. Supreme Court decision that upheld the validity of private agreements to arbitrate disputes related to employment. While a system of impartial arbitrators has successfully resolved many employment disputes in the unionized work environment, it appears that the idea of a *privatized* system of conflict resolution for non-union employers and employees desiring to use it is not acceptable to some civil rights activists and litigators.

9. In the "Reinventing Government" legislation, many commentators were appalled at the substantial and in some cases astronomical increase in fines. For example, the fine for not displaying an Equal Employment Opportunity Commission poster would have risen 400 percent. The overall result would have been increases in more than 250 civil penalties and automatic increases indexed to the level of inflation.

10. No list such as this would be complete without mentioning the findings and recommendations of "The Commission of the Future of Worker-Management Relations." The Secretary of the Department of Labor and the Secretary of the Department of Commerce established this Commission, staffed it with a majority of academics, and charged it to focus on three issues: (1) what, if any, new methods or institutions should be encouraged, or *required*, to enhance workplace productivity through labor-management cooperation and employee participation?; (2) what, if any, changes should be made in the present federal labor law?; and (3) what, if anything, should be done to increase the extent to which workplace problems are directly resolved by the parties themselves rather than through recourse to state and federal courts and governmental regulatory bodies?

After almost two years of hearings and fact-finding, the Commission formulated the following ten goals that it felt would position the American workplace and the economy for the twenty-first century:

1. Expand coverage of employee participation and labor-management partnerships to more workers, more workplaces, and more issues and decisions.

2. Provide workers with a readily accessible opportunity to choose, or not to choose, a bargaining representative and to engage in collective bargaining.

3. Improve resolution of disputes about workplace rights.

4. Decentralize and internalize responsibility for workplace regulations.

5. Improve workplace health and safety.

6. Enhance the growth of productivity in the economy as a whole.

7. Increase training and learning at the workplace and in related institutions.

8. Reduce inequality, which has increased in the American labor market over the past 10 to 15 years, by raising the earnings and benefits of workers in the lower part of the wage distribution.

9. Upgrade the economic position of contingent workers.

10. Increase dialogue at the national level and local level.

This all may sound very high-minded in concept. However, the specific recommendations proposed to implement these goals, although perhaps not as radical as they could have been, would still result in dramatic changes from existing law, in my opinion. For example, the Commission recommended changing current labor law as follows:

1. Representation elections within two weeks of the filing of a representation petition;

2. Hold hearings on any contested issues after the election;

3. Encourage authorization card check agreements that allow recognition of unions *without a secret ballot election;*

4. Establish a First Contract Advisory Board with powers to resolve disputes in first contract situations not settled by negotiations or mediation, with the power to mandate arbitration;

5. Expand the availability of injunctive relief to remedy unfair labor practices;

6. Restrict the exclusion of managers and supervisors by adopting a single, simplified definition of *managerial employee* that includes statutory supervisors and manager but excludes (1) members of work teams and joint committees to whom managerial and/or personnel decision-making authority is delegated, or (2) professionals and paraprofessionals who direct their less skilled coworkers;

7. Expand the use of pre-hire agreements that will allow the employer to negotiate a contract with the union with which it already has a bargaining relationship to cover employees at a new plant and allow the union to demonstrate majority support after one year;

8. Relative to contingent employment relationships, the Commission recommends proposals that it says would "remove the incentives to use those arrangements in ways that under-cut national employment standards . . ."

Oddly enough, many of these recommendations were included in legislation already introduced during the first two years of the Clinton Administration, such as: the Labor Relations Representative Amendment Act of 1993, which would have required the NLRB to order expedited elections; the Labor Organizations Equal Presentation Time Act of 1993, which would have granted unions access to the employers' facilities for union meetings on the employers' premises during work hours if the employer talked to employees about union representation; and the Labor Relations Remedies Act of 1993, which would have authorized the NLRB to award workers determined to have been wrongfully discharged for union activities back pay equal to *three times the employee's wage rate and to allow the employee to sue for punitive and compensatory damages as well.*

Has the legislator's appetite for more restrictions, liability, and laws governing on the employment relationship abated in the so-called "good-times" of low unemployment and economic prosperity?

The answer would seem to be no, despite the inability to pass much of the proposed legislation in the teeth of an opposition congress set against apparent executive will. For example, U.S. Senator Tom Harkin, (D-IA) introduced the Fair Pay Act of 1999 (S. 702), which would have required equal pay for "equivalent" jobs requiring comparable skills. This was intended to fill gaps in the Equal Pay Act prohibiting sex-based discrimination in compensation for doing the same job. Additionally, The Paycheck Fairness Act (S. 74, H.R. 541) was introduced in the Senate by Senator Daschle and in the House by Representative De Lauro (D-CT) to "toughen" remedies for gender-based wage discrimination under the Equal Pay Act. In his 1998 State of the Union Address, President Clinton proposed extending the FMLA to cover parent-teacher conferences and doctor's visits, and to lower the threshold for cover under the Act to employers with 25 or more employees. In 1999 President Clinton proposed using unemployment insurance funds to finance paid leave under FMLA. Senator Paul Wellstone (D-MN) introduced legislation that would increase the fines and penalties the NLRB could award against employers found guilty of discharging employees for attempting to organize a union, plus triple back for wrongfully discharged employees and punitive damages recoverable in federal court. This is not to mention new OSHA ergonomic standards that threaten to bring a brave new world of government-imposed change on the workplace in the name of safety, or proposals to expand discrimination-protected classes to include "parents," or extending Medicaid to the working disabled, and increasing the minimum wage.

Merely because such self-imposed regulations do not seem to stifle our economy for now, can anyone expect the pressure to micro-manage our employment relationships through government regulation to decrease in the decade to come?

Conclusion

In my opinion, despite the country's obvious economic recovery and success during the years of the Reagan presidency, the pent-up demand of the liberal left continues to push those who create wealth to redistribute it to those who do not. Participation in the government of our country and in the system that makes the laws that govern us will have to remain a significant priority in the future in order for business to continue to prosper.

Roman Catholic Pontiff Pope Pius XI wisely said just after World War II, "If you want peace, work for justice." In applying this maxim to labor relations and employment law matters, the years ahead will determine how much those in political power will view existing law as a detriment to labor and employment law justice.

All of the above measures should be scrutinized closely by the public to see whether they truly introduce more justice, or merely introduce more costs to doing business. Are these measures going to "level the playing field," or merely "change the ground rules?" Are these measures being proposed to increase fairness, or to accumulate political capital from those who benefit from such "rifle-shot" measures to regulate the employment relationship? The final result will be up to the voters to decide.

Index